Japanese Approaches to International Law

International Law in Japanese Perspective

Series Editor

Yuji Iwasawa

VOLUME 17

The titles published in this series are listed at *brill.com/iljp*

Japanese Approaches to International Law

Theory and Practice

Edited by

Chie Kojima and Masatoshi Takeuchi

BRILL | NIJHOFF

LEIDEN | BOSTON

Library of Congress Cataloging-in-Publication Data

Names: Kojima, Chie editor | Takeuchi, Masatoshi editor
Title: Japanese approaches to international law : theory and practice / edited by Chie Kojima and Masatoshi Takeuchi.
Description: Leiden ; Boston : Brill Academic Publishers, Inc, 2026. | Series: International law in Japanese perspective, 0929-7111 ; volume 17 | Includes bibliographical references and index.
Identifiers: LCCN 2025041474 | ISBN 9789004545212 hardback | ISBN 9789004548824 pdf
Subjects: LCSH: International law--Japan | International and municipal law--Japan
Classification: LCC KNX2325 .J375 2026 | DDC 341.0952--dc23/eng/20250908
LC record available at https://lccn.loc.gov/2025041474

Typeface for the Latin, Greek, and Cyrillic scripts: "Brill". See and download: brill.com/brill-typeface.

ISSN 0929-7111
ISBN 978-90-04-54521-2 (hardback)
ISBN 978-90-04-54882-4 (e-book)
DOI 10.1163/9789004548824

This book is printed on acid-free paper and produced in a sustainable manner.

Contents

Preface

The purpose of this book is to demonstrate, from a Japanese perspective, how Japan contributed to the making and implementation of international law. As early as 1853, Japan had to open the country to the outside world when the "Black Ships", led by Commodore Perry of the United States Fleet, arrived at Edo Bay. Japan and the United States then concluded their very first treaty, a Treaty of Peace and Amity with the United States on Perry's second visit in 1854. Japan concluded similar treaties with the UK (1854), Russia (1855), and the Netherlands (1855), followed by a series of treaties of amity and commerce with the United States, the United Kingdom, France, Russia, and the Netherlands, all concluded in 1858. Concluding these treaties with Western States urged Japan to study what the Western powers called "international law."[1] More than 170 years have passed since the opening of the country. The Japanese government promotes the rule of law as a fundamental value of the international community and places its policies within the framework of international law.

What States understand as the rule of law based on international law varies. Inter-State disputes concerning the application and interpretation of international law always occur. Moreover, non-compliance with international judgments by some States leads to disappointment and frustration for the rest of the international community. From such a perspective, this book offers valuable insights on what Japan considers as the rule of law in the international community for non-Japanese scholars and practitioners of international law and related disciplines. It is essential for the readers to understand not only how Japanese law and policy are formulated in implementing different branches of international law, but also how the Japanese authors approach the making and implementation processes of international law, vividly expressed in each chapter.

We humbly place our work in a larger international trend; namely, a trend toward understanding international law as comparative international laws. As Anthea Roberts and others have noted, contrary to the ideal of an invisible college of international law,[2] "[m]any scholars and practitioners

---

1 Hamamoto S., "International Law, Regional Developments: East Asia" (updated September 2017), in *Max Planck Encyclopedia of Public International Law (online edition)*, paras. 46–47.

2 Schachter O., "Invisible College of International Lawyers" *Northwestern University Law Review*, 72.2(1977), 217–26.

have noted that international law is often understood, interpreted, applied, and approached differently in different settings".[3] Other works related to this project include a Russian approach,[4] Chinese approach,[5] Italian approach,[6] and Korean approach,[7] among others. With these intentions, each chapter introduces specific Japanese laws, leading judgments rendered by Japanese courts and academic discourses in Japan, along with relevant treaties and international judgments. The editors would like to draw the readers' attention to the Japanese names in this volume. These are indicated by the author's first name followed by their last name, as in Western names. In the footnotes, however, only the family names are spelled out in full, followed by the initial of their first name.

Chapter 1 sets the scene by describing how Japan encountered modern international law. Today, European internationalists are interested in the European character of modern international law and the manner by which late 19th century internationalists regarded the process of colonization. Asian historians and lawyers are interested, in their turn, in the process of reception and application of modern international law by Asian countries. Nishiumi clarifies Japan's attitude towards modern international law, from the second half of the 19th century to the Second World War. He demonstrates that this attitude towards modern international law was far from coherent, but evolutional and ambivalent and that it resembles the mentality of a Japanese person situating themselves in face of European culture.

In Chapter 2, Sasaki analyzes how international law including treaties and customary international norms, is incorporated into and applied in Japan's domestic legal system today. While international law primarily regulates relationships between sovereign States, domestic law regulates the relationship between citizens or a State and its citizens. Popular discussions on how international law is applied in domestic legal systems often begin with two different approaches: monism and dualism. Japanese law is understood as belonging to the latter, wherein international and domestic laws operate separately and independently. Following the dualistic approach,

3 Roberts A., Stephan P., Verdier P-H. and Versteeg M. (eds.), *Comparative International Law*, (Oxford University Press, 2018), 3.

4 Mälksoo L., *Russian Approaches to International Law* (Oxford University Press, 2015).

5 Xue H., *Chinese Contemporary Perspectives on International Law: History, Culture and International Law* (Brill Nijhoff, 2012).

6 Messineo F., "Is There an Italian Conception of International Law," *Cambridge Journal of International & Comparative Law*, 2.4 (2013), 879–905.

7 Lee S. and Lee H. E., *The Making of International Law in Korea: From Colony to Asian Power*, (Brill Nijhoff, 2016).

international law is required to be translated into the national legal system through mechanisms such as the adoption of national legislation and application in domestic courts.

Chapter 3 introduces Japan's practice on State recognition. Kato discusses the current status of State recognitions granted by Japan, and covers the country's practice relating to the review process, criteria, policy factors, timing as well as types of State recognition. This chapter is based on a report the author compiled while serving as an officer at the International Legal Affairs Division of the International Legal Affairs Bureau of the Ministry of Foreign Affairs in charge of State recognition from late 2011 until early 2015. It aims to partially fill the information gap on Japan's practice on State recognition more than 30 years after the publication of the volume "State Recognition" in the *Kokusaiho Jirei Kenkyu* [Case Studies in Japanese International Law] series by discussing, albeit briefly, cases of State recognition since 1990.

Chapter 4 discusses a major and multifaceted representation of sovereignty: State jurisdiction. Like other States Japan has taken a long journey from absolute immunity to a more restrictive approach. Focusing on State immunity, it discusses well-known cases such as the *Pakistan Loan Claim* case to highlight how the Japanese adapted to the changing environment of the international community and enacted the 2009 Act on the Civil Jurisdiction of Japan with respect to Foreign States. Takeuchi M. further analyzes the recent conflict between Japan and South Korea regarding the 2021 "comfort women" case by the Seoul Central District Court. By making comparisons with the *Jurisdictional Immunities of the State* (*Germany v. Italy: Greece intervening*) case before the ICJ, it analyzes how each State sought to examine the limits of State jurisdiction.

Chapters 5 and 6 discuss Japan's State practice related to ocean law and policy and how Japan balances its traditional interests in the freedoms of navigation and fishing as well as present-day interests shared by the international community, including maritime security and the protection and preservation of the marine environment. Chapter 5 analyzes a series of Japanese legislation related to the establishment of maritime zones in Japan as well as those related to maritime security, such as the 2008 Act on Navigation on Foreign Ships through the Territorial Sea and Internal Waters and the 2009 Law on Punishment of and Measures against Piracy. In Chapter 6, Kojima analyzes developments of the Japanese laws related to the protection of the marine environment by focusing on salient issues such as marine protected areas, illegal, unreported and unregulated fishing, whaling, and the discharge of ALPS treated water into the sea.

In Chapter 7, Nishiumi examines the international legal aspects of three territorial disputes that Japan is involved in – the Northern Territories dispute with Russia, the Takeshima dispute with the Republic of Korea (ROK), and the Senkaku Islands dispute with People's Republic of China (PRC) – with references to historical background, claims by the parties, and legal assessment. Nishiumi emphasizes that Japan's territorial disputes are multifaceted and have a combination of legal, historical, political, economic and cultural dimensions, and that understanding these dimensions is a key for international law to fulfill its role in resolving the disputes.

Chapter 8 discusses maritime disputes with neighboring States, which are closely connected with the territorial disputes discussed in Chapter 7. Japan has a vast exclusive economic zone and continental shelf based on its territories consisting of four main islands – Hokkaido, Honshu, Shikoku, and Kyushu – and numerous small islands. The exclusive economic zone is approximately 4.05 million km^2, ten times larger than the land territory. Although some of Japan's maritime claims overlap with its neighbors', only a small part of the disputed areas is delimited by an agreement. Takeuchi A. gives an overview of the maritime boundary situations and discusses, in particular, the issues of the East China Sea, including the boundary claims, the joint development agreements, and the unilateral development of natural resources by the PRC, in light of existing rules and principles of international law.

Chapter 9 sheds light on the protection of vulnerable individuals and minority groups, focusing on refugees and an Indigenous people of Japan, the Ainu. In February 2021 and March 2023, the Immigration Services Agency of the Ministry of Justice submitted Bills to the Diet to partially amend the Immigration Control and Refugee Recognition Act (ICRRA). These bills included various problematic proposals regarding the protection of asylum-seekers and refugees, which were criticized by the United Nations High Commissioner for Refugees and United Nations Special Rapporteurs. Osakada analyzes these criticisms and clarifies the problems of Japan's immigration administration regarding refugees. Moreover, Osakada examines the 2019 Ainu Policy Promotion Act of Japan which legally recognized the Ainu as an Indigenous people and clarifies the problems of Japan's Indigenous policy.

In Chapter 10, Taniguchi critically examines the Japanese laws and policies on LGBTQ issues in light of current international human rights standards. While UN human rights bodies gave recommendations to the Japanese government on how to improve equal protection for same-sex relationships with a *de facto* marriage of different-sex couples, Japan failed to take effective legislative action in legally recognizing same-sex relationships. Taniguchi also analyzes the inadequacy of the current Japanese law and policy in relation to legal gender alteration and anti-discrimination.

Chapter 11 analyzes the Japanese government's approach to security issues revolving around Article 9 of the Constitution of Japan. Takeuchi M. provides an overview of the background and domestic legal/moral restraints, which forms the basis of Japan's approach regarding the UN collective security system and security issues in general. Takeuchi further explores the expanded approach provided by the Legislation for Peace and Security but finds that Japan is still restrained within the boundaries of domestic law and the Constitution.

Chapter 12 covers a wide range of Japanese practice in the field of international criminal law, ranging from general issues such as criminal jurisdiction, extradition, and mutual legal assistance to specific issues such as Japanese involvement in the negotiation of multilateral criminal law conventions and domestic legislation implementing them in the area of drug offences, transnational organized crime, money laundering, terrorism, and cybercrime. Ozaki further analyzes Japanese approaches to so-called "core crimes" and transitional justice, namely the Tokyo Tribunal and related Asia-Pacific Military Commission jurisprudence, as well as Japanese legislation related to humanitarian law and human rights conventions applicable to conflicts situation, negotiation, and the ratification of the Statute of the International Criminal Court by Japan.

Chapter 13 introduces the debate in Japan regarding the concept of international economic law and examines how the WTO agreements are implemented within Japan's domestic legal system. Kodera focuses on the domestic application of the WTO agreements, Japan's implementation of the trade remedy system, and its relationship with the WTO dispute settlement mechanism. Kodera also addresses a recent Japanese practice related to international economic security with emphasis on the export control system of Japan and the recent conflict with the Republic of Korea in regards to economic security.

In Chapter 14, Kaneto critically discusses Japan's responses to Multilateral Environmental Agreements (MEAS), including Japan's decisions to ratify, not to ratify, or withdraw from MEAS. Kaneto then analyzes several different methods to incorporate international environmental norms into domestic law and identifies two counteractive facets of Japan's commitment to MEAS: one being a reliable performer, while remaining a minimalist in its implementation.

Chapter 15 discusses how Japan participated in and has built its confidence towards the peaceful settlement of international disputes in accordance with international law after World War II. Kojima examines Japan's policy choices regarding relevant procedures such as the optional clause declaration under Article 36(2) of the Statute of the International Court of Justice, as well as cases to which it became a Party. Kojima assesses Japan's compliance with international decisions and its signs of commitment to the rule of law from its participation in proceedings before the international courts and tribunals.

The chapters are written by our dear colleagues, with whom we have worked together and gathered to discuss various issues of international law at the research seminars organized by the Association of International Relations Law at Chuo University in Japan, since its establishment in 1995. We would like to sincerely thank the authors for collaborating with us for this book project. The editors also would like to thank Marie Sheldon and Ingeborg van der Laan from Brill for providing this opportunity. The editors received assistance in reviewing the text from our colleagues and student assistants to whom we are very grateful. They include Stéphane Boeuf, Sarah Birchley, Andy Boon, Jeffrey Durand, José Escalante, Mizuki Endo, Kodai Fukazawa, Angelina Maleska, Kohei Mochizuki, Henri Nemitz, Duyen Nguyen and Jennifer Zhang. Finally, needless to say, all responsibilities of any possible errors rest on the editors.

Chie Kojima
Masatoshi Takeuchi
Tokyo, June 16, 2025

Treaties

Year	Treaties and agreements (in chronological order)
1855	Russo-Japanese Treaty of Friendship, *signed on* February 7, 1855, *entered into force on* August 7, 1855
1858	Treaty between France and Japan, *signed on* October 9, 1858, *entered into force on* September 22, 1858
1875	Treaty of Exchange of Sakhalin and Kuril Islands, *signed on* May 7, 1875, *entered into force on* August 22, 1875
1905	Russo-Japanese Peace Treaty (Treaty of Portsmouth), *signed on* September 5, 1905, *entered into force on* November 25, 1905
1905	Treaty of Portsmouth, *signed on* September 5, 1905
1910	Treaty regarding Annexation of Korea to the Empire of Japan, *signed on* August 22, 1910, *entered into force on* August 29, 1910
1933	Montevideo Convention on the Rights and Duties of States, Article 1, *signed on* Dec. 26, 1933, *entered into force on* Dec. 26, 1934, 165 LNTS 19
1941	Atlantic Charter, released *on* August 14, 1941
1943	Cairo Declaration, released *on* December 1, 1943
1945	Statute of the International Court of Justice, *signed on* June 26, 1945, *entered into force on* October 24, 1945
1945	Potsdam Declaration, *issued on* July 26, 1945
1945	Yalta Agreement, *signed on* February 11, 1945
1946	International Convention for the Regulation of Whaling, *signed on* December 2, 1946, *entered into force on* November 10, 1948, 161 UNTS 72
1947	General Agreement on Tariffs and Trade 1947, *signed on* October 30, 1947, *entered into force on* January 1 1948, 55 UNTS 194
1948	Convention on the Prevention and Punishment of the Crime of Genocide, *adopted on* December 9, 1948, *entered into force on* January 12, 1951, 78 UNTS 277
1948	Universal Declaration of Human Rights, GA Res 217 (III) A, UN Doc A/810 (December 10, 1948)
1949	Geneva Convention I for the Amelioration of the Condition of the Wounded and Sick in Armed Forces in the Field, *adopted on* August 11, 1949, *entered into force on* October 21, 1950, 75 UNTS 31
1949	Geneva Convention II for the Amelioration of the Condition of the Wounded, Sick and Shipwrecked Members of Armed Forces at Sea,

adopted on August 11, 1949, *entered into force on* October 21, 1950, 75 UNTS 85

1949 Geneva Convention III Relative to the Treatment of Prisoners of War, *adopted on* August 11, 1949, *entered into force on* October 21, 1950, 75 UNTS 135

1949 Geneva Convention IV Relative to the Protection of Civilian Population in Time of War, *adopted on* August 11, 1949, *entered into force on* October 21, 1950, 75 UNTS 287

1951 Convention relating to the Status of Refugee, *adopted on* July 28, 1951, *entered into force on* April 22, 1954, 189 UNTS 137

1951 Treaty of Peace with Japan, *signed on* September 8, 1951, *entered into force on* April 28, 1952, 136 UNTS 45

1954 International Convention for the Prevention of Pollution of the Sea by Oil, *signed on* May 12, 1954, *entered into force on* July 26, 1958, 327 UNTS 3

1956 Joint Declaration of the Soviet Union and Japan, *signed on* October 19, 1956

1960 Treaty of Mutual Cooperation and Security between the United States and Japan, *signed on* January 19, 1960, *entered into force on* July 23, 1960, 11 UST 1632

1965 Agreement between Japan and the Republic of Korea on Fisheries, *signed on* 22 June 1965, 583 UNTS 51

1965 Agreement on the Settlement of Problems concerning Property and Claims and on Economic Cooperation, *signed on* June 22, 1965, *entered into force on* December 18, 1965, 583 UNTS 173

1966 International Convention on the Elimination of All Forms of Racial Discrimination, *signed on* March 7, 1966, *entered into force on* March 12, 1969, 660 UNTS 195

1966 International Covenant on Civil and Political Rights, *signed on* December 16, 1966, *entered into force on* March 23, 1976, 999 UNTS 171

1966 International Covenant on Economic, Social and Cultural Rights, *signed on* December 16, 1966, *entered into force on* January 3, 1976, 993 UNTS 3

1967 Protocol relating to the Status of Refugees, *signed on* January 31, 1967, *entered into force on* October 4, 1967, 606 UNTS 267

1969 International Convention relating to Intervention on the High Seas in Cases of Oil Pollution Casualties, *signed on* November 29, 1969, *entered into force on* May 6, 1975, 970 UNTS 211

1969 Vienna Convention on the Law of Treaties, *signed on* May 23, 1969, *entered into force on* January 27, 1980, 1155 UNTS 331

1971 Ramsar Convention on Wetlands of International Importance especially as Waterfowl Habitat, *signed on* February 2, 1971, *entered into force on* December 21, 1975, 996 UNTS 245

1972 Convention concerning the Protection of the World Cultural and Natural Heritage, *signed on* November 16, 1972, *entered into force on* December 17, 1975, 1037 UNTS 151

1972 Convention on the Prevention of Marine Pollution by Dumping of Wastes and Other Matter, *signed on* December 29, 1972, *entered into force on* August 30, 1975, 1046 UNTS 120

1973 Convention on International Trade in Endangered Species of Wild Fauna and Flora, *signed on* March 3, 1973, *entered into force on* July 1, 1975, 993 UNTS 243

1973 Protocol relating to Intervention on the High Seas in Cases of Pollution by Substances other than Oil, *adopted on* November 2, 1973, *entered into force on* March 30, 1983, 1313 UNTS 3

1974 Agreement between Japan and the Republic of Korea concerning establishing a boundary in the northern part of the continental shelf adjacent to the two countries, *signed on* January 30, 1974, *entered into force on* June 22, 1978, 1225 UNTS 103

1974 Agreement concerning joint development of the southern part of the continental shelf adjacent to the two countries, *signed on* January 30, 1974, *entered into force on* June 22, 1978, 1225 UNTS 113

1977 Protocol I Additional to the Geneva Conventions of 12 August 1949 and Relating to the Protection of Victims in International Armed Conflict, *adopted on* June 8, 1977, *entered into force on* December 7, 1978, 1125 UNTS 3

1977 Protocol II Additional to the Geneva Conventions of 12 August 1949 and Relating to the Protection of Victims in Non-International Armed Conflicts, *adopted on* June 8, 1977, *entered into force on* December 7, 1978, 1125 UNTS 609

1978 International Convention for the Prevention of Pollution from Ships of 1973 as modified by the Protocol of 1978, *signed on* November 2, 1973, *not in force*, 12 ILM 1319; the Protocol, *signed on* February 17, 1978, *entered into force on* October 2, 1983, 1340 UNTS 61

1978 Treaty of Peace and Friendship between Japan and the People's Republic of China, *signed on* August 12, 1978, *entered into force on* October 23, 1978, 1225 UNTS 257

1979 Convention on the Conservation of Migratory Species of Wild Animals, *signed on* June 23, 1979, *entered into force on* November 1, 1983, 1651 UNTS 333

1979 Convention on the Elimination of All Forms of Discrimination Against Women, *signed on* December 18, 1979, *entered into force on* September 3, 1981, 1249 UNTS 13

1979 International Convention Against the Taking of Hostages, *adopted on* December 17, 1979, *entered into force on* June 3, 1983, 1316 UNTS 205

1982 United Nations Convention on the Law of the Sea, *adopted on* April 30, 1982, *entered into force on* November 16, 1994, 1833 UNTS 3

1983 Gaborone Amendment to the Convention on International Trade in Endangered Species of Wild Fauna and Flora, *adopted on* April 30, 1983, *entered into force on* November 29, 2013, 2993 UNTS 85

1984 Convention against Torture and Other Cruel, Inhuman or Degrading Treatment or Punishment, *adopted on* December 10, 1984, *entered into force on* June 26, 1987, 1465 UNTS 85

1987 Montreal Protocol on Substances that Deplete the Ozone Layer, *signed on* September 16, 1987, *entered into force on* January 1, 1989, 1522 UNTS 3

1988 United Nations Convention against Illicit Traffic in Narcotic Drugs and Psychotropic Substances, *adopted on* December 20, 1988, *entered into force on* November 11, 1990, 1582 UNTS 95

1989 Basel Convention on the Control of Transboundary Movements of Hazardous Wastes and their Disposal, *signed on* March 22, 1989, *entered into force on* May 5, 1992, 1673 UNTS 57

1989 Convention on the Rights of the Child, *signed on* November 20, 1989, *entered into force on* September 2, 1990, 1577 UNTS 3

1991 Convention on Environmental Impact Assessment in a Transboundary Context, *signed on* February 25, 1991, *entered into force on* September 10, 1997, 1989 UNTS 309

1992 Convention on Biological Diversity, *adopted on* June 5, 1992, *entered into force on* December 29, 1993, 1760 UNTS 79

1992 United Nations Framework Convention on Climate Change, *adopted on* May 9, 1992, *entered into force on* March 24, 1994, 1771 UNTS 107

1994 Agreement on Agriculture, *adopted on* April 15, 1994, *entered into force on* January 1, 1995, 1867 UNTS 410

1994 Agreement on Implementation of Article VI of the General Agreement on Tariffs and Trade 1994, *adopted on* April 15, 1994, *entered into force on* January 1, 1995, 1868 UNTS 201

1994 Agreement on Safeguards, *adopted on* April 15, 1994, *entered into force on* January 1, 1995, 1869 UNTS 154

1994 Agreement on Subsidies and Countervailing Measures, *adopted on* April 15, 1994, *entered into force on* January 1, 1995, 1869 UNTS 14

1994 Understanding on Rules and Procedures Governing the Settlement of Disputes, *adopted on* April 15, 1994, *entered into force on* January 1, 1995, 1869 UNTS 401

1994 United Nations Convention to Combat Desertification in Those Countries Experiencing Serious Drought and/or Desertification, Particularly in Africa, *signed on* June 17, 1994, *entered into force on* December 26, 1996, 1954 UNTS 3

1995 Ban Amendment to the Convention on the Control of Transboundary Movements of Hazardous Wastes and their Disposal, *adopted on* September 22, 1995, *entered into force on* December 5, 2019, UNTS A-28911

1996 London Protocol, *signed on* November 7, 1996, *entered into force on* March 24, 2006

1997 Agreement between Japan and the People's Republic of China concerning Fisheries, *signed on* November 11, 1997, *entered into force on* June 1, 2000, 2731 UNTS 181

1997 Convention on the Law of Non-Navigational Uses of International Watercourses, *adopted on* May 21, 1997, *entered into force on* August 17, 2014, 2999 UNTS 77

1997 International Convention for the Suppression of Terrorist Bombings, *adopted on* December 15, 1997, *entered into force on* May 23, 2001, 2149 UNTS 256

1997 Kyoto Protocol, *signed on* December 11, 1997, *entered into force on* February 16, 2005, 2303 UNTS 162

1998 Agreement between Japan and the Republic of Korea concerning Fisheries, *signed on* November 28, 1998, *entered into force* on January 22, 1999, 2731 UNTS 305

1998 Convention on Access to Information, Public Participation in Decision-making and Access to Justice in Environmental Matters, *signed on* June 25, 1998, *entered into force on* October 30, 2001, 2161 UNTS 447

1998 Rome Statute of the International Criminal Court, *signed on* July 17, 1998, *entered into force on* July 1, 2002, 2187 UNTS 3

1998 Rotterdam Convention on the Prior Informed Consent Procedure for Certain Hazardous Chemicals and Pesticides in International Trade, *signed on* September 11, 1998, *entered into force on* February 24, 2004, 2244 UNTS 337

1999 Protocol on Liability and Compensation for Damage Resulting from Transboundary Movements of Hazardous Wastes and Their Disposal, *adopted on* December 10, 1999, not yet in force, Doc. UNEP/CHW.5/29, Annex III

2000 Cartagena Protocol on Biosafety, *signed on* January 29, 2000, *entered into force on* September 11, 2003, 2226 UNTS 208

2000 Protocol against the Smuggling of Migrants by Land, Sea and Air, *adopted on* November 15, 2000, *entered into force on* January 28, 2004, 2241 UNTS 507

2000 Protocol to Prevent, Suppress and Punish Trafficking in Persons, especially Women and Children, *adopted on* November 15, 2000, *entered into force on* 25 December 2003, 2237 UNTS 319

2000 Protocol to the OPRC Convention on Preparedness, Response and Cooperation to pollution Incidents by Hazardous and Noxious Substances, *adopted on* March 15, 2000, *entered into force on* June 14, 2007, UNTS I-56797

2000 United Nations Convention against Transnational Organized Crime, *adopted on* November 15, 2000, *entered into force on* September 29, 2003, 2225 UNTS 209

2001 Stockholm Convention on Persistent Organic Pollutants, *signed on* May 22, 2001, *entered into force on* May 17, 2004, 2256 UNTS 119

2001 International Convention on the Control of Harmful Anti-Fouling Systems on Ships, *adopted on* October 5, 2001, *entered into force on* September 17, 2008, UNTS I-56215

2001 Protocol against the Illicit Manufacturing of and Trafficking in Firearms, their Parts and Components and Ammunition, *signed on* July 11, 2001, *entered into force on* July 3, 2005, 2326 UNTS 208

2004 International Convention for the Control and Management of Ships' Ballast Water and Sediments, *adopted on* February 13, 2004, *entered into force on* September 8, 2017, UNTS I-55544

2006 International Convention for the Protection of All Persons from Enforced Disappearance, *adopted on* December 20, 2006, *entered into force on* December 23, 2010, 2716 UNTS 3

2007 United Nations Declaration on the Rights of Indigenous Peoples, UNGA Res 61/295 (September 13, 2007)

2009 Hong Kong International Convention for the Safe and Environmentally Sound Recycling of Ships, *adopted on* May 15, 2009, *entered into force on* June 26, 2025

2009 Agreement on Port State Measures to Prevent, Deter and Eliminate Illegal, Unreported and Unregulated Fishing, *adopted on* Nov. 11, 2009 and *entered into force on* June 5, 2016, 3161 UNTS 377

2010 Nagoya Protocol on Access to Genetic Resources and the Fair and Equitable Sharing of Benefits Arising from their Utilization to the Convention on Biological Diversity, *signed on* October 29, 2010, *entered into force on* October 12, 2014, 3008 UNTS 3

2010 Nagoya-Kuala Lumpur Supplementary Protocol on Liability and Redress to the Cartagena Protocol on Biosafety, *signed on* October 15, 2010, *entered into force on* March 5, 2018, 3239 UNTS A-30619

2013 Minamata Convention on Mercury, *signed on* October 10, 2013, *entered into force on* August 16, 2017, 3201 UNTS 3

2015 Paris Agreement, *signed on* December 12, 2015, *entered into force on* November 4, 2016, 3156 UNTS 79

Cases

Domestic Cases

Japanese Courts

Breaching Cannabis Control Act and Customs Act Case, Case no. 1992 (U) 1138, Judgment of 3 February 1993, Tokyo High Court, *Tokyō Kōtō Saibansho Keiji Hanketsu Jihō* [Tokyo High Court Criminal Casebook] 44 (1–12) (1993)

Crime Victims Case, Case no. 2018 (Gyo-U) 76, Judgment of 4 June 2020, Nagoya District Court, *Hanrei Taimuzu* [The Law Times Report] 1482 (2021)

Crime Victims Case, Case no. 2022 (Gyo-Tsu) 318, Judgment of 26 March 2024, Supreme Court of Japan, *Saikō Saibansho Minji Hanreishū* [Supreme Court Reports (civil cases)] 78 (1) (2024)

CRT Cartel Case, Case no. 2016 (Gyo-Hi) 233, Judgment of December 12, 2017, Supreme Court of Japan (Third Petty Bench), *Saikō Saibansho Minji Hanreishū* [Supreme Court Reports (civil cases)] 71 (10) (2017)

Daedong-ho No. 909 Case, Case no. 1997 (Wa) 35, Judgment of 15 August 1997, Supreme Court of Japan, *Saikō Saibansho Keiji Hanreishū* [Supreme Court Reports (criminal cases)] 53 (8) (1997)

Daedong-ho No. 909 Case, Case no. 1998 (A) 1137, Judgment of 30 November 1999, Supreme Court of Japan, *Saikō Saibansho Keiji Hanreishū* [Supreme Court Reports (criminal cases)] 53 (8) (1999)

Daedong-ho No. 909 Case, Case no. 1998 (U) 32, Judgment of 11 September 1998, Supreme Court of Japan, *Saikō Saibansho Keiji Hanreishū* [Supreme Court Reports (criminal cases)] 53 (8) (1998)

Demands for no-night-flight hours at Yokota Air Base Case, Case no. 1999 (O) 887, Judgment of 12 April 2002, Supreme Court of Japan (Second Petty Bench), *Saikō Saibansho Minji Hanreishū* [Supreme Court Reports (civil cases)] 56 (4) (2002)

Fuchu Youth Hostel Case, Case no. 1991 (Wa) 1557, Judgment of 30 March 1994, Tokyo District Court, *Hanrei Tamuzu* [The Law Times Report] 859 (1994)

Fuchu Youth Hostel Case, Case no.1994 (Ne) 1580, Judgment of 16 September 1997, Tokyo High Court, *Hanrei Taimuzu* [The Law Times Report] 986 (1997)

Kyoto Korean Elementary School Case, Case no. 2010 (Wa) 2655, Judgment of 7 October 2013, Kyoto District Court, *Hanrei Jihō* [The Hanrei Jiho] 2208 (2014)

Legal Gender Recognition Case, Case no. 2018 (Ku) 269, Decision of 23 January 2019, Supreme Court of Japan, *Saikō Saibansho Saibanshū Minji Hanreishū* [Supreme Court Reports (civil cases)] 261 (2019)

Legal Gender Recognition Case, Case no. 2019 (Ku) 791, Decision of 11 March 2020, Supreme Court of Japan, *unpublished*

Legal Gender Recognition Case, Case no. 2020 (Ku) 638, Decision of 30 November 2021, Supreme Court of Japan, *Hanrei Tamizu* [The Law Times Report] 1495 (2022)

Legal Gender Recognition Case, Case no. 2020 (Ku) 993, Decision of 25 October 2023, Supreme Court of Japan, *Saikō Saibansho Minji Hanreishū* [Supreme Court Reports (civil cases)] 77 (1) (2023)

M/V Guanabara Case, Case no. 2011 (Go Wa) 77, Judgment of 1 February 2013, Tokyo District Court, *unpublished*

Marriage for All Lawsuit in Fukuoka, Case no. 2019 (Wa) 2827 and 2021 (Wa) 47, Judgment of 8 June 2023, Fukuoka District Court, *unpublished*

Marriage for All Lawsuit in Nagoya, Case no. 2019 (Wa) 597, Judgment of 30 May 2023, Nagoya District Court, *unpublished*

Marriage for All Lawsuit in Osaka, Case no. 2019 (Wa) 1258, Judgment of 8 June 2022, Osaka District Court, Hanrei Taimuzu [The Law Times Report] 1507 (2023)

Marriage for All Lawsuit in Sapporo, Case no. 2019 (Wa) 267, Judgment of 17 March 2019, Sapporo District Court, *Hanrei Jihō* [The Hanrei Jiho] 2487 (2019)

Marriage for All Lawsuit in Sapporo, Case no. 2021 (Ne) 194, Judgment of 14 March 2024, *Hanrei Taimuzu* [The Law Times Report] 1524 (2024)

Marriage for All Lawsuit in Tokyo, Case no. 2019 (Wa) 3465, Judgment of 30 November 2022, Tokyo District Court, *Hanrei Taimuzu* [The Law Times Report] 151 (2024)

Marriage for All Lawsuit in Tokyo, Case no. 2021 (Wa) 7645, Judgment of 14 March 2024, Tokyo District Court, *unpublished*

Nationality Act case, Case no. 2006 (Gyo-Tsu) 135, Judgment of 4 June 2008, Supreme Court of Japan (Grand Bench), *Saikō Saibansho Minji Hanreishū* [Supreme Court Reports (civil cases)] 62 (6) (2008)

Nishijin Necktie Case, Case no. 1979 (Wa) 44, Judgment of June 29 1984, Kyoto District Court, *Shōmu Geppō* [Monthly Case Report] 31 (2) (1985)

Obstructing Prisoner's Interviews with Defense Lawyer Case, 1992 (Wa) 268, Judgment of 15 March 1996, Tokushima District Court, *Hanrei Jihō* [The Hanrei Jiho] 1597 (1997)

Otaru Hot Spring Case, Case no. 2001 (Wa) 206, Judgment of 11 November 2002, Sapporo District Court, 2023, *Hanrei Jihō* [The Hanrei Jiho] 1806 (2003)

Pakistan Loan Claim Case, Case no. 2003 (Ju) 1231, Judgment of July 21 2006, Supreme Court of Japan (Second Petty Bench), Case no. 2002 (Ju) 1231, *Saikō Saibansho Minji Hanreishū* [Supreme Court Reports (civil cases)] 60 (6) (2002)

Pork Gate-Price Case, Case no. 2012 (Wa) 496, Judgment of April 10 2013, Chiba District Court, *unpublished*

Pork Gate-Price Case, Case no. 2013 (U) 857, Judgment of November 27 2013, Tokyo High Court, *Kōsai Hanrei Shū* [High Court Reports] 66 (4) (2013)

Prohibition Period on Remarriage Case, Case no. 2013 (O) 1079, Judgment of 16 December 2015, Supreme Court of Japan (Grand Bench), *Saikō Saibansho Minji Hanreishū* [Supreme Court Reports (civil cases)] 69 (8) (2015)

Promissory notes invoice Case against Republic of China, Case no.1928 (Ku) 218, Decision of 28 December 1928, Daishinin Case [Grand Court of Cassation], *Daishinin Minji Hanreishū* [Court of Cassation Civil Reports] 7 (1928)

Same-sex Couple Alimony Case, Case no. 2018 (Wa) 30, Judgment of 18 September 2019, Utsunomiya District Court, *Hanrei Jihō* [The Hanrei Jiho] 2473 (2021)

Same-sex Couple Alimony Case, Case no. 2019 (Ne) 4433, Judgment of 4 March 2020, Tokyo High Court, *Hanrei Jihō* [The Hanrei Jiho] 2473 (2020)

Shiomi Case, Case no. 1985 (Gyo-Tsu) 92, Judgment of 2 March 1989, Supreme Court of Japan, *Saikō Saibansho Saibanshū Minji Hanreishū* [Supreme Court Reports (civil cases)] 156 (1989)

Ship Tedon Case, Case no. 1997 (Wa) 35, Judgment of 15 August 1997, Matsue District Court, Hamada Branch, reprinted in *Hanrei Jihō* [The Hanrei Jiho] 1656 (1998)

Sunagawa Case, Case no.1959 (A) 710, Judgment of 16 December 1959, Supreme Court of Japan (Grand Bench), *Saikō Saibansho Saibanshū Keiji Hanreishū* [Supreme Court Reports (criminal cases)] 13 (13) (1959)

Texada Case, Case no.1974 (U) 1243, Judgment of 19 November 1976, Osaka High Court, *Keiji Saibansho Geppō* [Monthly Bulletin on Criminal Courts] 8 (11/12) (1976)

Zhang Zhenhai case, Case no. 1990 (Te) 37, Decision of 20 April 1990, Tokyo High Court, *Kōtō Saibansho Keiji Hanreishū* [High Court Reports (civil cases)] 43 (1) (1990)

Other Domestic Courts

Attorney-General of Israel v. Eichmann, Judgment of December 11, 1961, Supreme Court of Israel, *International Law Report* 36 (1968)

Chung Chi Cheung v. The King, Judgment of 2 December 1938, Judicial Committee of the Privy Council, *The American Journal of International Law* 33 (2) (1939)

Comfort Women Case, Case no. 2016 (GaHap) 505092, Judgment of 8 January 2021, Seoul Central District Court

Distomo Case, Judgment of June 23 2003, Bundesgerichtshof [German Supreme Court], *International Legal Material* 42 (2003)

E.R. Croft v. Sylvester Dunphy, Appeal no. 131 of 1931, Judgment of 28 July 1932, Supreme Court of Canada

Ferrini Case, Case no. 5044, Judgment of 11 March 2004, Corte di Cassazione [The Supreme Court of Cassation], Joint Sections

In re Yamashita, Case no. 61 Misc, Decision of February 4 1946, US Supreme Court, 327 US 1

J. H. Rayner (Mincing Lane) Ltd v. Department of Trade and Industry, Judgment of 26 October 1989, House of Lords, 2 A.C. 418

Motorola Mobility LLC v. AU Optronics Case. Motorola Mobility LLC v. AU Optronics Corp. et al., Judgment of March 27, 2014, 7th Cir., *746 F.3d 842*.

International Cases

Permanent Court of International Justice

The Case of the S.S. Lotus (France v. Turkey), [1927] PCIJ, Judgment of 7 September 1927, *Publications of the PCIJ* Series A (10) (1927)

International Court of Justice

Case concerning the Continental Shelf (Libyan Arab Jamahiriya/Malta), [1985] ICJ, Judgment of 3 June 1985, *ICJ Reports*. 1985

Case concerning the Sovereignty Over Pedra Branca/Pulau Batu Puteh, Middle Rocks and South Ledge (Malaysia v. Singapore), [2008] ICJ, Judgment of 23 May. 2008, *ICJ Reports*. 2008

Fisheries Jurisdiction Case (United Kingdom v. Iceland),[1974] ICJ, Judgment of 25 July 1974, *ICJ Reports*. 1974

In Question of the Delimitation of the Continental Shelf between Nicaragua and Colombia beyond 200 nautical miles from the Nicaraguan Coast (Nicaragua v. Colombia) case, [2023] ICJ, Judgment of 13 July 2023, 29

Jurisdictional Immunities of the State (Germany v. Italy: Greece intervening), [2012] ICJ, Judgment of 3 February 2012, *ICJ Reports*. 2012

Legality of the Threat or Use of Nuclear Weapons (Submitted by the UN General Assembly), Advisory Opinion, [1996] ICJ, Advisory Opinion of 8 July 1996, *ICJ Reports*. 1996

Maritime Delimitation in the Area between Greenland and Jan Mayen (Denmark v. Norway), [1993] ICJ, Judgment of 14 June 1993, *ICJ Reports*. 1993

Maritime Delimitation in the Black Sea (Romania v. Ukraine), [2009] ICJ, Judgment of 3 February 2009, *ICJ Reports*. 2009

Maritime Delimitation in the Indian Ocean (Somalia v. Kenya) case, [2021] ICJ, Judgment of 12 Oct. 2021, ICJ *Reports*. 2021

Military and Paramilitary Activities in and against Nicaragua (Nicaragua v. United States of America), [1986] ICJ, Judgment of 27 June 1986, *ICJ Reports*. 1986

North Sea Continental Shelf (Federal Republic of Germany/Denmark and Federal Republic of Germany/Netherlands), [1969] ICJ, Judgment of 20 February 1969, *ICJ Reports*. 1969

The Minquiers and Ecrehos Case (France v. United Kingdom), [1953] ICJ, Judgment of 17 November 1953, *ICJ Reports*. 1953

Western Sahara Case (Requested by the UN General Assembly), Advisory Opinion, [1975] ICJ, Advisory Opinion of 16 October 1975, *ICJ Reports*. 1975

Whaling in the Antarctic (Australia v. Japan, New Zealand intervening), [2014] ICJ, Judgment of 31 March 2014, *ICJ Reports*. 2014

International Tribunal for the Law of the Sea

Delimitation of the maritime boundary in the Bay of Bengal (Bangladesh/Myanmar), [2012] ITLOS, Judgment of 14 Mar. 2012, *ITLOS Reports*. 2012

Dispute concerning Delimitation of the Maritime Boundary between Ghana and Côte d'Ivoire in the Atlantic Ocean (Ghana v. Côte d'Ivoire), [2017] ITLOS, Judgment of 23 September 2017, *ITLOS Reports*. 2017

Hoshinmaru Case (Japan v. Russian Federation) Prompt Release, [2005] ITLOS, Judgment of 6 August 2007, *ITLOS Reports*. 2007

Land Reclamation in and around the Straits of Johor (Malaysia v. Singapore) Provisional Measures, [2003] ITLOS, Order of 8 October 2003, *ITLOS Reports*. 2003

MOX Plant Case (Ireland v. United Kingdom), Provisional Measures, [2001] ITLOS, Order of 3 December 2001, *ITLOS Reports*. 2001

Request for an Advisory Opinion submitted by the Commission of Small Island States on Climate Change and International Law (COSIS), Advisory Opinion, [2024] ITLOS, Advisory Opinion of 21 May 2024

Request for an Advisory Opinion Submitted by the Sub-Regional Fisheries Commission (SRFC), Advisory Opinion, [2015] ITLOS, Advisory Opinion of 2 April 2015, *ITLOS Reports*. 2015

Southern Bluefin Tuna Cases (New Zealand v. Japan; Australia v. Japan), Provisional Measures, [1999] ITLOS, Order of 27 August 1999, *ITLOS Reports*. 1999

Tomimaru Case (Japan v. Russian Federation), Prompt Release, [2007] ITLOS, Judgment of 6 August 2007, *ITLOS Reports*. 2007

Arbitral Tribunal Constituted under Annex VII of the UNCLOS

In the matter of the Bay of Bengal Maritime Boundary Arbitration between The People's Republic of Bangladesh and The Republic of India case, [2014] Arbitral Tribunal constituted under Annex VII of the UNCLOS, Award of 7 July 2014, *Reports of International Arbitral Awards*, XXXII (2019)

Southern Bluefin Tuna Cases (Australia v. Japan; New Zealand v. Japan), Jurisdiction and Admissibility, [2000] Arbitral Tribunal constituted under Annex VII of the

UNCLOS, Decision of 4 December 2000, *Report of International Arbitral Awards* vol. XXIII (2006)

The Arbitration regarding the Delimitation of the Maritime Boundary between Guyana and Suriname, [2007] Arbitral Tribunal constituted under Annex VII of the UNCLOS, Award of 17 September 2007, *Report of International Arbitral Awards* XXX (2012)

The South China Sea Arbitration (The Republic of Philippines v. The People's Republic of China), [2016] Arbitral Tribunal constituted under Annex VII of the UNCLOS, Award of 12 July 2016, *Report of International Arbitral Awards* XXXIII (2020)

Other Arbitral Tribunals

Japanese House Tax (Germany, France, and Great Britain v. Japan), [1905] PCA, Award of 21 May 1905, *Report of International Arbitral Awards* vol. XI (1961)

Delimitation of the Continental Shelf between the United Kingdom of Great Britain and Northern Ireland, and the French Republic (UK v. France), [1978] Arbitration, Decision of 14 March 1978, *Report of International Arbitral Awards* vol. XVIII (1981)

Second stage of the proceedings between Eritrea and Yemen (Maritime Delimitation), [1999] PCA, Award of 17 December 1999, *Report of International Arbitral Awards* vol. XXII (2006)

Sovereignty and Maritime Delimitation in the Red Sea (Eritrea/Yemen), [1998] PCA, Award of 9 October 1998, *Report of International Arbitral Awards* vol. XXII (2006)

World Trade Organization

Colombia – Anti-Dumping Duties on Frozen Fries from Belgium, Germany and the Netherlands (Colombia v. European Union), [2022] Arbitration under Article 25 of the DSU, Award of 21 December 2022, WT/DS591/ARB25

Japan – Measures Affecting Agricultural Products (Japan v. United States), [1999] Appellate Body Report, Report of 22 February 1999, WT/DS76/AB/R

Japan – Taxes on Alcoholic Beverages (Japan v, European Communities; Japan v. Canada; Japan v. United States), [1996] Appellate Body Report, Report of 4 October 1996, WT/DS8/AB/R, WT/DS10/AB/R, WT/DS11/AB/R

Korea – Import Bans, and Testing and Certification Requirements for Radionuclides (Republic of Korea v, Japan), [2018] Panel Report, Report of 22 February 2018, WT/DS495/R

Korea – Import Bans, and Testing and Certification Requirements for Radionuclides (Republic of Korea v, Japan), [2019] Appellate Body Report, Report of 11 April 2019, WT/DS495/AB/R

Turkey – Certain Measures concerning the Production, Importation and Marketing of Pharmaceutical Products,(Turkey v. European Union), [2022] Arbitration under Article 25 of the DSU, Award of 25 July 2022, WT/DS583/ARB25

United States – Certain Measures on Steel and Aluminium Products (United States v. China), [2019] WTO Panel, Report of 9 December 2022, WT/DS512/R

Others

A.P., Garçon and Nicot v. France, [2017] ECHR, Judgment of 6 April 2017, Applications nos. 79885/12, 52471/13 and 52596/13

Conciliation Commission on the Continental Shelf Area between Iceland and Norway: Report and Recommendations to the Governments of Iceland and Norway, Decision, [1981] Conciliation Commission, Decision of June 1981, *Report of International Arbitral Awards* vol. XXVII (2006)

Gender Identity, and Equality and Non-Discrimination of Same-Sex Couples (Requested by the Republic of Costa Rica), Advisory Opinion, [2017] IACHR, Advisory Opinion of 24 November 2017, OC-24/17

Joslin et al. v. New Zealand, [2002] HRC, Views of 17 July 2002, UN Doc. CCPR/C/75/D/902/1999

Oliari and Others v. Italy Case, [2015] ECHR, Judgment of 21 July 2015 (Final Judgment of 21 of October 2015), Applications Nos. 18766/11 and 36030/11

Timor Sea Conciliation (Timor-Leste v. Australia), Report and Recommendations of the Compulsory Conciliation Commission between Timor-Leste and Australia in the Timor Sea, [2018] Conciliation Commission under ANNEX V to the UNCLOS, Report of 9 May 2018, Reports of International Arbitral Awards vol. XXXVI (2022)

Toonen v. Australia, [1994] HRC, Views of 31 March 1994, UN Doc. CCPR/C/50/D/488/1992

X v. Colombia, [2007] HRC, Views of 30 March 2007, UN Doc. CCPR/C/89/D/1361/2005

Young v. Australia, [2003] HRC, Views of 6 August 2003, UN Doc. CCPR/C/78/D/941/2000

Japanese Laws

Year	English name	Japanese name
1896	Civil Code, Act No. 89 of 1896	民法
1907	Penal Code, Act No. 45 of 1907	刑法
1910	Customs Tariff Act, Act No. 54 of 1910	関税定率法
1918	Wildlife Protection and Hunting Law, Act No. 32 of 1918	鳥獣保護及狩猟ニ関スル法律
1946	The Constitution of Japan (Constitution 1946)	日本国憲法
1948	Financial Instruments and Exchange Act, Act No. 25 of 1948	金融商品取引法
1948	Agricultural Chemicals Regulation Act, Act No. 82 of 1948	農薬取締法
1949	Foreign Exchange and Foreign Trade Act, Act No. 228 of 1949	外国為替及び外国貿易法
1949	Fishery Act, Act No. 267 of 1949	漁業法
1949	Navigational Aids Act, Act No. 99 of 1949	航海標識法
1950	Act on Services Related to Waterways, Act No. 102 of 1950	水路業務法
1950	Law for the Protection of Cultural Properties, Act No. 214 of 1950	文化財保護法
1950	Nationality Act, Act No.147 of 1950	国籍法
1951	Quarantine Act, Act No. 201 of 1951	検疫法
1951	Immigration Control and Refugee Recognition Act, Cabinet Order No. 319 of 1951	出入国管理及び難民認定法
1951	Public Housing Act, Act No. 193 of 1951	公営住宅法
1951	Cocoon and Raw Silk Price Stabilization Act, Act No. 310 of 1951	繭繭価格安定法
1951	Act on the Protection of Fishery Resources, Act No. 313 of 1951	水産資源保護法
1953	Act of Extradition, Act No. 68 of 1953	逃亡犯罪人引渡法
1954	Customs Act, Act No. 61 of 1954	関税法

1954	Public Cleansing Law, Act No. 72 of 1954	清掃法
1954	Self-Defense Forces Act, Act No. 165 of 1954	自衛隊法
1954	Customs Act, Act No. 61 of 1954	関税法
1955	Atomic Energy Basic Act, Act No. 186 of 1955	原子力基本法
1957	Natural Parks Act, Act No. 161 of 1957	自然公園法
1957	Act on the Regulation of Nuclear Source Material, Nuclear Fuel Material and Reactors, Act No. 166 of 1957	核原料物質、核燃料物質及び原子炉の規制に関する法律
1958	Water Quality Control Law, Act No. 181 of 1958	公共用水域の水質の保全に関する法律
1958	Factory Effluent Control Law, Act No. 182 of 1958	工場排水等の規制に関する法律
1959	Patent Act, Act No. 121 of 1959	特許法
1960	Act on Securing Quality, Efficacy and Safety of Products Including Pharmaceuticals and Medical Devices, Act No. 145 of 1960	医薬品、医療機器等の品質、有効性及び安全性の確保等に関する法律
1962	Smoke and Soot Regulation Law, Act No. 146 of 1962	ばい煙の排出の規制等に関する法律
1965	Corporation Tax Act, Act No. 34 of 1965	法人税法
1967	Act on Regulation of Fishing Operation by Foreign Nationals, Act No. 60 of 1967	外国人漁業の規制に関する法律
1967	Basic Law for Environmental Pollution Control, Act No. 132 of 1967	公害対策基本法
1968	Air Pollution Control Act, Act No. 97 of 1968	大気汚染防止法
1970	Act on Prevention of Marine Pollution and Maritime Disaster, Act No. 136 of 1970	海洋汚染及び海上災害の防止に関する法律
1970	Act on Punishment of Crimes to Cause Pollution Harmful to Human Health, Act No. 142 of 1970	人の健康に係る公害犯罪の処罰に関する法律

1970	Water Pollution Control Law, Act No. 138 of 1970	水質汚濁防止法
1970	Waste Management and Public Cleaning Law, Act No. 137 of 1970	廃棄物の処理及び清掃に関する法律
1971	Marine Resources Development Promotion Act, Act No. 60 of 1971	海洋水産資源開発促進法
1972	Maritime Traffic Safety Act, Act No. 115 of 1972	海上交通安全法
1972	Nature Conservation Act, Act No. 85 of 1972	自然環境保護法
1973	Act on the Regulation of Manufacture and Evaluation of Chemical Substances, Act No. 117 of 1973	化学物質の審査及び製造等の規制に関する法律
1977	Act on the Prevention of Collision at Sea, Act No. 62 of 1977	海上衝突予防法
1977	Act on Provisional Measures relating to the Fishing Zone, Act No. 31 of 1977	漁業水域に関する暫定措置法
1977	Law on the Territorial Sea, Law No. 30 of 1977	領海法
1980	Act on International Assistance in Investigation and Other Related Matters, Act No. 69 of 1980	国際捜査共助等に関する法律
1984	Telecommunications Business Act, Act No. 86 of 1984	電気通信事業法
1986	National Security Council Establishment Act, Act No. 71 of 1986	国家安全保障会議設置法
1988	Act on the Protection of the Ozone Layer through the Control of Specified Substances, etc. and Other Measures, Act No. 53 of 1988	特定物質等の規制等によるオゾン層の保護に関する法律
1991	Act Concerning Special Provisions for the Narcotics and Psychotropics Control Act, etc. and Other Matters for the Prevention of Activities Encouraging Illicit Conducts and Other Activities Involving Controlled Substances through International Cooperation, Act No. 94 of 1991	国際的な協力の下に規制薬物に係る不正行為を助長する行為等の防止を図るための麻薬及び向精神薬取締法等の特例等に関する法律

1992	Act on Conservation of Endangered Species of Wild Fauna and Flora, Act No. 75 of 1992	絶滅のおそれのある野生動植物の種の保存に関する法律
1992	Law for the Control of Export, Import and Others of Specified Hazardous Wastes and Other Wastes, Act No. 108 of 1992	特定有害廃棄物等の輸出入等の規制に関する法律
1992	Act on Cooperation with United Nations Peacekeeping Operations and Other Operations, Act No. 79 of 1992	国際連合平和維持活動等に対する協力に関する法律
1993	Basic Act on the Environment, Act No. 91 of 1993	環境基本法
1996	Act on the Preservation and Control of Living Marine Resources, Act No. 77 of 1996	海洋生物資源の保存及び管理に関する法律
1996	Act on the Exercise of the Sovereign Right on Fishing Operations in the Exclusive Economic Zone, Act No. 76 of 1996	排他的経済水域における漁業等に関する主権的権利の行使等に関する法律
1996	Law on Exclusive Economic Zone and the Continental Shelf, Act No. 74 of 1996	排他的経済水域及び大陸棚に関する法律
1996	Law on the Territorial Sea and Contiguous Zone, Law No. 73 of 1996	領海及び接続水域に関する法律
1997	Environmental Impact Assessment Act, Act No. 81 of 1997	環境影響評価法
1997	Act relating to Protection of the Environment in Antarctica, Act No. 61 of 1997	南極地域の環境の保護に関する法律
1998	Act on Promotion of Global Warming Countermeasures, Act No. 117 of 1998	地球温暖化対策の推進に関する法律
1999	Act on Special Measures against Dioxins operates for the reduction of releases from unintentional generated dioxins, Act No. 105 of 1999	ダイオキシン類対策特別措置法
1999	Act for Establishment of the Ministry of Foreign Affairs, Act No. 94 of 1999	外務省設置法

1999	Act on Punishment of Organized Crimes and Control of Proceeds of Crime, Act No. 136 of 1999	組織的な犯罪の処罰及び犯罪収益の規制等に関する法律
1999	Act on the Assessment of Releases of Specified Chemical Substances in the Environment and the Promotion of Management Improvement, Act No. 86 of 1999	特定化学物質の環境への排出量の把握等及び管理の改善の促進に関する法律
1999	Act concerning Measures to Ensure Peace and Security of Japan in Situations that gravely affect the Peace and Security of Japan, Act No. 60 of 1999	重要影響事態に際して我が国の平和及び安全を確保するための措置に関する法律
2000	Basic Act on Establishing a Sound Material-Cycle Society, Act No. 110 of 2000	循環型社会形成推進基本法
2001	Act on Rational Use and Appropriate Management of Fluorocarbons, Act No. 64 of 2001	フロン類の使用の合理化及び管理の適正化に関する法律
2001	Waste Management Law and the Act on Special Measures Concerning Promotion of Proper Treatment of PCB Wastes, Act No. 65 of 2001	ポリ塩化ビフェニル廃棄物の適正な処理の推進に関する特別措置法
2001	Domestic Violence Prevention Act, Act No. 31 of 2001	配偶者からの暴力の防止及び被害者の保護等に関する法律
2002	Act on Punishment of Financing to Offences of Public Intimidation, Act No. 67 of 2002	公衆等脅迫目的の犯罪行為のための資金等の提供等の処罰に関する法律
2002	Protection and Control of Wild Birds and Mammals and Hunting Management Act, Act No. 88 of 2002	鳥獣の保護及び管理並びに狩猟の適正化に関する法律
2002	Soil Contamination Countermeasures Act, Act No. 53 of 2002	土壌汚染対策法
2003	Act on the Conservation and Sustainable Use of Biological Diversity through Regulations on the Use of Living Modified Organisms, Act No. 97 of 2003	遺伝子組換え生物等の使用等の規制による生物の多様性の確保に関する法律
2003	Act of Special Handling of the People with Gender Identity Disorder (The GID Act), Act No. 111 of 2003	性同一性障害者の性別の取扱いの特例に関する法律

2003	Act on the Peace and Independence of Japan and Maintenance of the Nation and the People's Security in Armed Attack Situations, etc., Act No. 79 of 2003	武力攻撃事態等及び存立危機事態における我が国の平和と独立並びに国及び国民の安全の確保に関する法律
2004	Act on Penal Sanctions against Grave Breaches of the International Humanitarian Law, Act No. 115 of 2004	国際人道法の重大な違反行為の処罰に関する法律
2004	Act on the Prevention of Adverse Ecological Impacts Caused by Designated Invasive Alien Species, Act No. 78 of 2004	特定外来生物による生態系等に係る被害の防止に関する法律
2004	Act on Measures Conducted by the Government in Line with U.S. Military Actions in Armed Attack Situations, etc., Act No. 113 of 2004	武力攻撃事態等及び存立危機事態におけるアメリカ合衆国等の軍隊の行動に伴い我が国が実施する措置に関する法律
2004	Act on the Use of Specific Public Facilities, etc. in Armed Attack Situations, etc., Act No. 114 of 2004	武力攻撃事態等における特定公共施設等の利用に関する法律
2004	Act on the Restriction of Maritime Transportation of Foreign Military Supplies in Armed Attack Situations, Act No. 116 of 2004	武力攻撃事態及び存立危機事態における外国軍用品等の海上輸送の規制に関する法律
2004	Act on the Treatment of Prisoners of War and Other Detainees in Armed Attack Situations, Act No. 117 of 2004	武力攻撃事態及び存立危機事態における捕虜等の取扱いに関する法律
2007	Basic Act on Ocean Policy, Act No. 33 of 2007	海洋基本法
2007	Act on the Establishment of Safety Water Areas concerning Artificial Structures in the Oceans, Act No. 34 of 2007	海洋構築物等に係る安全水域の設定等に関する法律
2007	Act on Cooperation with the International Criminal Court, Act No. 37 of 2007	国際刑事裁判所に対する協力等に関する法律
2008	Basic Act on Biodiversity, Act No. 58 of 2008	生物多様性基本法
2008	Act on Navigation of Foreign Ships through the Territorial Sea and Internal Waters, Act No. 64 of 2008	領海等における外国船舶の航行に関する法律

2009	Law on Punishment of and Measures against Acts of Piracy, Act No. 55 of 2009	海賊行為の処罰及び海賊行為への対処に関する法律
2009	Special Measures for Compensation of Minamata Disease, Act No. 81 of 2009	水俣病被害者の救済及び水俣病問題の解決に関する特別措置法
2009	Act on the Civil Jurisdiction of Japan with respect to Foreign States, Act No. 24 of 2009	外国等に対する我が国の民事裁判権に関する法律
2015	Act on Preventing Mercury Pollution of the Environment, Act No. 42 of 2015	水銀による環境の汚染の防止に関する法律
2015	International Peace Support Act, Act 77 of 2015	国際平和共同対処事態に際して我が国が実施する諸外国の軍隊等に対する協力支援活動等に関する法律
2017	Act for Ensuring Sustainable Use of Whales, Act No. 76 of 2017	鯨類の持続的な利用の確保に関する法律
2018	Climate Change Adaptation Act, Act No. 50 of 2018	気候変動適応法
2018	Act on Ship Inspection Operations in Situations that gravely affect the Peace and Security of Japan, Act No. 145 of 2018	重要影響事態等に際して実施する船舶検査活動に関する法律
2019	Act on Promoting Measures to Realize a Society in Which the Pride of the Ainu People Is Respected, Act No. 16 of 2019	アイヌの人々の誇りが尊重される社会を実現するための施策の推進に関する法律
2020	Act on Ensuring the Proper Domestic Distribution of Specified Aquatic Animals and Plants, Act No. 79 of 2020	特定水産動植物等の国内流通の適正化等に関する法律
2022	Act for the Promotion of Ensuring National Security through Integrated Implementation of Economic Measures, Act No. 43 of 2022	経済施策を一体的に講ずることによる安全保障の確保の推進に関する法律
2024	Act on the Protection and Utilization of Important Economic Security Information, Act No. 27 of 2024	重要経済安保情報の保護及び活用に関する法律

Notes on Contributors

Yumiko Kaneto
graduated from Kyoto University of Foreign Studies and at the same time completed her study at Université de Mons in Belgium in 1995. After graduation, she worked as a civil servant at Osaka University for 8 years, including a one-year stay in Canada for a working internship program at McGill University. She graduated from the Faculty of Law, Chuo University in 2004. She obtained a master's degree in law at Graduate School of Law, Chuo University in 2006 and Master in European law at Université de Strasbourg in 2008. She received a Doctoral Degree in law at Chuo University in 2013. She is currently a lecturer at several universities in Japan mainly in charge of international environmental law, European environmental law, and French constitutional law.

Masahiro Kato
is a career diplomat and currently serving as First Secretary at the Japanese Embassy in Vienna. He holds a master's degree in law from Chuo University and an LL.M. from Heidelberg University. Before his current position, he served among others as an officer at the International Legal Affairs Division, the ICJ Whaling Case Division and the International Trade and Investment Dispute Settlement Division of the Ministry of Foreign Affairs of Japan.

Satoshi Kodera
is a professor at the Faculty of Law in Seinan Gakuin University, Fukuoka, Japan. His research focuses specifically on public international law, international economic law, international law of development, and psychology of international law. He is a co-author of *The Introduction to WTO and FTA Law*, 2nd ed. (Horitsu Bunkasha, 2021, in Japanese). He has also published numerous articles including "Evolution of the Organic Japanese Agricultural Standard Systems: A 20-year History," in B.C. Goh and R. Price (eds.), *Regulatory Issues in Organic Food Safety in the Asia Pacific* (Springer, 2020); "Dynamics Between Multilateralism and Regionalism in Relation to Trade Liberalization and Culture," *Public Policy Review*, Vol. 16, No. 5 (2020); "A Critical Stream in the French Doctrine of International Law: Charles Chaumont and the Reims School," *Yearbook of World Law*, No. 40 (2021, in Japanese).

Chie Kojima

is a professor of international law at the Faculty of Law, Chuo University, Tokyo. She holds Bachelor, Master and Ph.D. degrees in law from Chuo University, and an LL.M. and a J.S.D. from Yale Law School. She previously served as a Professor of International Law at Musashino University in Tokyo, an Assistant Professor of Maritime Law and Policy at World Maritime University in Malmö and a Senior Research Fellow at Max Planck Institute for Comparative Public Law and International Law in Heidelberg. Her recent publications focus on the protection of the marine environment, maritime security, and human rights at sea. She is a member of the Editorial Boards of *Ocean Development and International Law* (ODIL), *Asia-Pacific Journal of Ocean Law and Policy* (APJOLP), and *The Law & Practice of International Courts and Tribunals* (LPICT).

Maki Nishiumi

is a professor of international law at the Faculty of Law, Chuo University. His main research focus is in the fields of culture, development, and humanitarian issue. His publications include: « Le droit international comme théâtre d'enjeux » (in French), E. Jouannet, H. Ruiz Fabri, J-M Sorel eds., *Regards d'une génération sur le droit international*, Pedone, 2008; « Réception et application du droit international moderne par le Japon: son Attitude évolutive de 1858 à 1945 » (in French), H. Ruiz Fabri ed., *Selected Proceedings of the European Society of International Law*, Hart Publishing, 2010; "Cultural Aspects of Sustainable Development" (in English), *Japanese Yearbook of International Law*, vol. 57, 2015. *Contemporary International Law – Development, Culture and Humanitarian* (in Japanese), Institute of Comparative Law in Japan, 2016. *Les résistances à la mondialisation* (ed. in French and Japanese), Institute of Social Sciences of Chuo, 2022.

Yuko Osakada

is a professor at the Chuo Law School. She holds master's degrees in law from Utrecht University (the Netherlands), and in Human and Environmental Studies from Kyoto University (Japan). She received her Ph.D. in Human and Environmental Studies from Kyoto University (Japan). She was the alternate of the International Law Association's Committee on the Implementation of the Rights of Indigenous Peoples. Her publications include: "An examination of arguments over the Ainu Policy Promotion Act of Japan based on the UN Declaration on the Rights of Indigenous Peoples", *The International Journal of Human Rights*, Vol. 25 Issue 6 (2021);

"Indigenous Peoples as Actors in International Law-Making: Focusing on International Environmental Law", in K. N. Scott et al. (eds.), *Changing Actors in International Law*, Brill, 2020.

Kuniko Ozaki
is a professor of international law, Chuo University Faculty of Law (2021–present). She holds a B.A. in International Relations (1978, Tokyo University) and a M.Phil. in International Relations (1982, Oxon.). She previously served as a Judge of International Criminal Court (2010–2019) and Second Vice-President of International Criminal Court (2015–2018). Prior to joining the ICC, she served as Director for Treaty Affairs for the United Nations Office on Drugs and Crime (2006–2009). Earlier in her career, she worked for the Japanese government in a number of positions, including Ambassador and Special Assistant to the Foreign Ministry (2009), Director for Human Rights and Humanitarian Affairs in the Foreign Ministry (1991-2001), Director for Refugees in the Justice Ministry (1998–1999) and Specialist to the Criminal Affairs Bureau of the Justice Ministry (1995–1998). She has also taught international law at the Tohoku University Graduate School of Law and at other universities and has written extensively on international criminal law, refugee law and law of human rights.

Ryo Sasaki
is an associate professor of international human rights law at the Department of International Studies in the University of the Sacred Heart (USH) in Tokyo. Before joining USH in 2019, he was an adjunct lecturer in Atomi University in Saitama and Tokyo (2014–2018), and non-tenured assistant professor at the Center for International Exchanges in Shimane University (2018–2019). He studied international law and human rights in a Master's (2009–2011) and doctoral (2011–2019) programmes at the Graduate School of Law in Chuo University, and York Law School, University of York in the UK (2014–2015). He holds an LL.M. in International Human Rights Law and Practice from the University of York and Ph.D. in Law from Chuo University. His research interests focus on international human rights law, especially domestic implementation of international human rights law, equality and non-discrimination principle, and human rights protection in a multicultural society. His publications include; "Discrimination on the Right to Education and Burden of Proof: D. H. and Others v the Czech Republic" in: K. Tonami et al. (eds.), *Essential Cases of the European Court of Human Rights*, Shinzansha, 2019, 429–433; "The Right to Education in

Japan: A Consistent Interpretation of the Constitution of Japan, Educational Acts and Human Rights Conventions", Giovanni Pampanini (ed.), *Right to Education and Democracy* (CUECM, 2013), 141–148.

Akari Takeuchi
is a professor at Sojo University, Kumamoto, Japan. She is an expert of International Law of the Sea and gender studies. She also has extensive working experience at a research institution (Ocean Research Policy Foundation), Japanese Government (Ministry of Foreign Affairs of Japan and Cabinet Office of Japan), as well as teaching experience at several universities. She has published several articles regarding the United Nations Convention of the Law of the Sea.

Masatoshi Takeuchi
is a professor of international law and international relations at the Faculty of Global Communications, Toyo Gakuen University, Tokyo. He holds bachelor's and master's degrees in policy studies and law respectively from Chuo University. He has served as Adjunct Professor in various universities. Recent publications include areas of interdisciplinary theory of International Law and International Relations. He is a member of the Japanese Society of International Law (JSIL), Asian Society of International Law (AsianSIL) and Japanese Association of International Relations (JAIR).

Hiroyuki Taniguchi
is a professor of law and gender/sexuality, Faculty of Law, Aoyama Gakuin University. His research focuses on issues related to gender and sexuality that are often marginalized, such as LGBTQ and sex workers, and international human rights policies. In 2016, he was appointed as a member of the Science Council of Japan and working as Chief Secretary of LGBTI Division. He published many books and articles, such as "*Case Book on Sexual Minorities*" [in Japanese] (2011), "*Law and Society concerning LGBT*" [in Japanese] (2019), and "*Sexual and Gender Minorities in International Human Rights Law: Jurisprudence of the European Convention on Human Rights*" [in Japanese] (2022) among others.

CHAPTER 1

Japan and Modern International Law

Maki Nishiumi

1 Introduction

Today, several European internationalists are interested in clarifying the "European" character of modern international law and how their predecessors at the end of the nineteenth century saw the colonization process that was then taking place on a global scale.[1] This author would like to join this trend and present a non-European viewpoint on the subject.[2]

The "European" characterization of modern international law has, in turn, piqued the interest of historians and jurists in Asian countries, including Japan, who are interested in the process by which modern international law has been received and applied in these countries.[3] This chapter aims to clarify Japan's attitude to modern international law since Japan opened its doors to foreign trade and diplomatic relations, i.e. from the second half of the nineteenth century, until the end of World War II. Japan's attitude to modern international law has not been consistent but rather evolutionary and ambivalent. In my view, it resembles certain Japanese intellectuals' attitude towards Europe whereby on the one hand, he or she adores and readily

1 For example, Jouannet E., "Structure intellectuelle de la pensée internationaliste classique et colonialisme européen", Report at the inaugural ESIL Conference in Florence, 2004, published as: "Colonialisme européen et néo-colonialisme contemporain (Notes de lecture des manuels européens du droit des gens entre 1850 et 1914)", *Baltic Yearbook of International Law* 6 (2006); Koskenniemi M., *The Gentle Civilizer of Nations: the Rise and Fall of International Law 1870–1960* (Cambridge University Press, 2002).

2 Anghie A., "Finding the Peripheries: Sovereignty and Colonialism in 19th Century International Law," *Harvard International Law Journal* 40 (1999); Onuma Y., "When Was the Law of International Society Born?" *Journal of the History of International Law* II 2 (2000); Matsui Y., "Kindai Nihon to Kokusaihō (1)(2) [Japan and Modern International Law vol. 1, 2]" (Japanese), *Kagaku to Shisō* [Science and Thought] 13 and 14 (1974).

3 Higashi Ajia ni okeru Bankoku Kōhō no Juyō to Tekiyō [Reception and Application of the Law of Nations in East Asia] (Japanese), *Higashi Ajia Kindaishi* [Modern History of East *Asia*] 2 (Yumani Shobou,1999); Ajia ni okeru Kindai Kokusaihō [Modern International Law in Asia] (Japanese), *ibid.*, 3 (Yumani Shobou, 2000). Several Japanese and Korean historians and internationalists have contributed on these subjects.

 | DOI:10.1163/9789004548824_002

accepts European values, but on the other, also challenges and even rejects such values.[4]

This chapter will consider, firstly, the international environment during which Japan was obliged to receive modern international law, secondly, Japan's alleged contradictory attitude towards Western powers and neighboring countries, such as China and Korea, during the drafting of bilateral treaties, thirdly, the discriminatory nature of modern European international law and the significance of Japan's attitude to modern international law, and finally, the *Daitōwa-Kyōeiken* project (The Greater East Asia Co-Prosperity Sphere) and the perspectives of Japanese internationalists towards the project.

2 The International Environment during Which Japan Was Obliged to Receive Modern International Law

The year 2008 marks the 150th anniversary of the establishment of diplomatic relations between Japan and five Western countries: France, USA, UK, Russia and the Netherlands. In 1858, Japan concluded, or more precisely was obliged to conclude, treaties of peace, friendship and trade with these countries.[5] By the mid-nineteenth century, these Western countries had, through their industrial revolutions, completed a rapid process of modernization. They were looking for new markets and were beginning to expand into Asia. Under these treaties, Japan promised these Western countries free trade and opened the ports of Hakodate, Kanagawa, Nagasaki, Niigata and Hyogo to facilitate this.[6]

Previously, Japan had adopted a policy of isolation known, in Japanese, as "Sakoku", whereby the Japanese people were forbidden to leave Japan

4 This mentality can be seen in the novels of Soseki Natsume, Shusaku Endo and others.

5 Since 1854, Japan had concluded friendship treaties with the United States, the United Kingdom, Russia and the Netherlands. These treaties were transformed into Peace, Friendship and Trade Treaties in 1858.

6 "The cities and ports of Hakodate, Kanagaoua and Nagasaki will be open to French trade and subjects from August 15, 1859, and the cities and ports whose names follow will be open at the times determined below…" (Art. 3 of the Treaty between France and Japan, *signed at* Edo *on* October 9, 1858. Ratification exchanged at Edo, September 22, 1859, in *Teimei kakkoku Jōyaku Ruisan – Treaties and Conventions concluded between Empire of Japan and Foreign Nations*, Tokyo Nisshusha, 1874); "In all ports of Japan open to commerce, French subjects will be free to import from their own country or from foreign ports, and to sell, buy and export for their own ports or for those of other countries, all kinds of merchandise which are not contraband…" (Art. 8 of the said treaty).

and foreigners were forbidden to enter Japan. Diplomatic relations and foreign trade were limited to a few countries, such as the Netherlands and China. The main reason for this policy was to prevent Catholic evangelization, which, according to the Shogunate government of the time, threatened its authority. Spanning over two centuries, the era of "Sakoku" witnessed a state of internal peace within Japan, which, in turn, fostered the remarkable growth of Japanese culture, industry, and finance.

However, starting from the late eighteenth century, the rise of global capitalism in the Western world caused countries like Russia and the USA to begin pressuring Japan to open its borders and domestic market. As a result, in 1858, the era of "Sakoku" came to an end, with the conclusion of the Peace, Friendship and Trade Treaties mentioned above.[7]

In Japan, these treaties have often been described as "unequal" due to three main reasons. Firstly, they offered no power to set customs tariffs freely; Japan did not have the right to unilaterally and sovereignly set these taxes. During this time, the WTO did not exist; therefore, each sovereign country had the right *a priori* to determine the rates of tariffs. Japan, however, was bound by these treaties to consult its partners beforehand and could only set its taxes after obtaining their consent.[8] The second reason concerns consular jurisdiction. Japan had no jurisdiction over the accused nationals of foreign countries. Thus, criminals from European countries who had committed felonies or misdemeanors on Japanese territory, or merchant debtors from these European countries, were all tried according to the laws of their country of origin and by the consuls of each country resident in Japan.[9] The final reason relates to the non-reciprocal

7 *150ème Anniversaire des relations Franco-Japonaises, revue officielle 1858–2008*, 24–25.

8 Articles regulating trade were annexed to the treaty. According to Article IX of the said treaty, the French diplomatic agent in Japan, together with such officials as may be designated for the purpose by the Japanese government, had the power to make such regulations as might be necessary to carry out the stipulations of the articles regulating trade. Indeed, Class IV of the trade regulations states that "five years after the opening of the port of Kanagawa, import and export duties may be modified, if either of the two Governments of France and Japan so desires." It therefore appears that Japan did not have the sovereign right to decide unilaterally on tariff rates.

9 "All disputes which may arise between Frenchmen concerning their rights, their property or their persons, in the domains of His Majesty the Emperor of Japan, shall be submitted to the jurisdiction of the French authorities constituted in the Country". (Art. V of the said treaty); "French subjects who are guilty of any crime against the Japanese or against individuals belonging to other nations, will be brought before the French Consul and punished in accordance with the laws of the French Empire." (Art. VI of the said treaty); "Any French subject who has a complaint against a Japanese, must go to the French Consulate

most-favored-nation clause. Under these treaties, Japan was compelled to accept a non-reciprocal most-favored-nation clause, granting partner countries privileges that Japan itself did not receive in return.[10] These treaties essentially relegated Japan to the status of a non-civilized country, thereby denying it the rights of a fully sovereign country.[11]

Hence, changing these unequal treaties was a primary diplomatic objective of the Meiji government.[12] To achieve this objective, Japan needed to be recognized by Western countries as a civilized country. Such recognition was also essential if Japan was to maintain its independence and avoid being colonized by these countries. As a result, Japan set about modernizing itself through the intensive introduction of modern technologies and industries, political, economic and military institutions, and Western cultures, including law and, by extension, international law.

During the negotiation of the Peace, Friendship and Trade Treaty with the United States, Japanese representatives openly and naively admitted their lack of familiarity with international diplomatic law to their American partners.[13] This revealed that Japan had little exposure to modern international law at the time. The Shogunate did, however, dispatch young scholars, namely, Shusuke Nishi and Shin'ichiro Tsuda, to the Netherlands. There,

---

and present his complaint. The Consul will examine the merits of the complaint and seek to settle the matter amicably..." (Art. VII of the said treaty); "... [I]f any French subject fraudulently conceals or fails to pay his debts to a Japanese, the French authorities will likewise do everything in their power to bring the delinquent to justice and force him to pay what he owes." (Art. XVIII of the said treaty).

10 "It is expressly stipulated that the French Government and its subjects shall enjoy, freely, from the day on which the present Treaty is brought into force, all the privileges, immunities and advantages which have been or which would in the future be guaranteed by His Majesty the Emperor of Japan to the Government or subjects of any other nation." (Art. XIX of the said treaty).

11 There's another article that also reveals the asymmetry of Franco-Japanese relations. This is Article XXI. According to this article, all official communications addressed by the French diplomatic agent to the Japanese authorities shall be written in French. However, to facilitate the prompt dispatch of business, these communications will, for a period of five years, be accompanied by a Japanese translation. This is a linguistic inequality which, it seems to me, has not been expressly pointed out until now.

12 We have a Japanese calendar (*Gengō*) which was instituted in the 7th century, following the example of the Chinese calendar. It is fixed at the enthronement of the new emperor and revised at the time of succession. The *Gengō* at that time was Meiji.

13 Cosenza E. M. ed., *The Complete Journal of Townsend Harris: first American consul and minister to Japan* (C.E. Tuttle Company, 1959) (translated into Japanese by Sakata S., *Harris Nihon Taizaiki* [Harris in Japan] (1)(2)(3) (Iwanami Shoten, 1953)), 97–98, 120–121 of (3).

they studied international law in Leiden and upon their return to Japan in 1866, they commenced teaching international law for the first time in Japan at State Institutes in Edo (Tokyo). Their teachings were primarily based on the doctrines of Simon Vissering, a professor at Leiden University.[14] Despite these efforts, Japan, towards the end of the Edo period, had yet to fully grasp international law due to the emergence of xenophobia and internal political conflicts.

Following its establishment in 1868, the newly formed Meiji government declared that diplomatic relations should be regulated by the law of nations and by the treaties previously established under the Shogunate.[15] An important contribution to the understanding of international law came in the form of the translation of American internationalist Henry Wheaton's work, *Elements of International Law,* Initially translated into Chinese in 1864, it was later translated into Japanese the following year. This translation proved invaluable, as it was widely read and greatly influenced many Japanese intellectuals and practitioners of that time.[16]

3 Japan's Alleged Contradictory Attitude towards Western Powers and Neighboring Countries Such as China and Korea during the Drafting of Bilateral Treaties

The Sino-Japanese War (1894–95) and the Russo-Japanese War (1904–05) presented significant opportunities to show that Japan had become a civilized country capable of fully observing the rules of the law of war. To deal with the various problems that arose during armed conflicts, the Japanese Army and Navy had renowned internationalists accompany them as jurisconsults. These were Nagao Ariga of the Army, who had studied in Berlin and Vienna, and Sakue Takahashi, of the Navy, who had studied in London. Upon their return to Japan, Ariga became a professor of international law at the Army University, while Takahashi assumed a similar position at Tokyo Imperial University.

Ariga published two notable works in French: *La guerre sino-japonaise au point de vue du droit international* (Pedone, 1896) and *La guerre russo-japonaise au point de vue continental et le droit international* (Pedone, 1908).

14 Ito F., "International Law [Kokusaihō]" (Japanese), in Aomi J. (ed.), *Kindai Nihonshi Taikei* [System of Modern Japanese History] (Japanese) (Yuhikaku, 1979), 461–462.

15 Declaration of the Meiji Government dated February 8, 1868.

16 Ito (n 14), 463–464.

Similarly, Takahashi's *Cases on International Law during the Chino-Japanese War* (Cambridge University Press, 1899) gained recognition. It included a preface by T. E. Holland and an introduction by J. Westlake, both esteemed international legal scholars who affirmed that Japan had upheld the rules of the law of war and had fulfilled the necessary conditions to be regarded as a civilized country.[17]

These works were highly regarded and played a significant role in demonstrating Japan's adherence to the rules of the law of war. They received frequent citations in European publications, further bolstering Japan's reputation as a nation that respected the laws of war.[18]

The approach taken by Ariga and Takahashi was to acknowledge the advanced nature of European civilization and emphasize Japan's integration into that civilization.[19] Their strategic writing style was well-received among Japanese intellectuals and political elites of the time. Japan's remarkable industrial development and military successes propelled it into a major Asian power. The unequal treaties imposed on Japan were eventually revised at the end of the 19th century and the beginning of the 20th century.[20] Furthermore, Japan's participation as one of the victors, alongside France, USA, UK, and Italy, at the Peace Conference held in Paris after World War I solidified its position on the global stage.

Following the end of the Edo period, the Japanese government had intended to establish trade relations with Korea. This intention was put into effect by the *Kanfado incident* (*Kokato* in Japanese). In 1875, a Japanese vessel, ostensibly engaged in exploring sea routes, sailed along Korea's western shore. Ignoring the protests expressed by the Korean government, the vessel witnessed its canoe being attacked by a battery located on Kanfado Island

17 As to these preface and introduction, see Takahashi S., *ibid.*, vi, xvi.

18 *See* Takahashi S., *Äusserungen über völkerrechtlich bedeutsame Vorkommnisse aus dem chinesisch-japanischen Seekrieg und das darauf bezügliche Werk* (Verlag von E. Reinhardt, 1900). This book includes 15 book reviews about Takahashi's book (1899) and his reply to them. In general, these book reviews give high appreciation to his book (1899). *See* Akashi K., "Nihon no Kokusaihōgaku Taigaihassin no 100-nen [One Hundred Years of External Communication of Japanese International Law]" (Japanese), *Kokusaishakai no Hō to Seiji* [Law and Politics in International Society] (Sanseido, 2001), 211.

19 Yamauchi S., "Meiji Kokka niokeru Bunmei to Kokusaihō [Civilization and International Law in the Meji State]" (Japanese), *Hitotsubashi Ronsō* [The Hitotsubashi Review] 115(1) (1996), 28–31.

20 Japan succeeded in successively modifying the unequal treaties with Western states, first in 1894 in the area of abolishing consular jurisdiction, and then in 1911 in that of re-establishing the right to set customs duties.

and retaliated by destroying the battery. This incident provided Japan with an opportunity to conclude a treaty of friendship with Korea. During the negotiations, Japan employed a policy of coercion. It conveyed a message to the Korean government that unless Korea agreed to the treaty, Japanese troops would be deployed on Korean territory. As a part of this strategy, Japan temporarily withdrew its plenipotentiary, declaring that the negotiations had failed. Ultimately, Japan succeeded in obtaining the acceptance of all its demands, leading to the signing of the Treaty of Friendship between Japan and Korea in 1876.[21]

This treaty falls under the category of unequal treaties. It included provisions such as the opening of the three ports, the settlement of Japanese nationals, the dispatch of Japanese consuls, and the establishment of consular jurisdiction. While the treaty also included provisions for free trade and tax exemption on imports and exports, these seemingly fair and egalitarian clauses masked underlying economic interests. Imports of soybeans, rice and gold into Japan from Korea were crucial for the development of Japanese capitalism. The tax exemption on these imports was, therefore, primarily in Japan's favor. However, for Korea, these exports to Japan led to a rise in grain prices due to the outflow of these resources. This provision thus helped to position Korea as a commodity market, and a supply ground for food resources, for the benefit of Japanese capitalism.[22]

The Western powers' expectation that Japan would open up Korea was thus fulfilled. After concluding this treaty with Japan, Korea was compelled to successively conclude similar treaties with the United States, the United Kingdom, Germany, Italy and France. Through its own experiences with Western nations and the unequal treaties imposed upon it, Japan had gained a clear understanding of the implications and consequences of free trade for less economically developed countries. Ironically, Japan, while seeking to modify its own unequal treaties by attaining the ability to set tariffs independently, imposed a similar unequal treaty upon Korea.[23] By demanding equal international status from the developed Western countries, Japan ended up enforcing dependence on the less developed Asian countries like Korea. In 1896, shortly after the Sino-Japanese War, Japan also concluded an unequal treaty of trade and navigation with China, which included provisions on consular jurisdiction and remained in effect until 1943. In this regard, Japan's approach toward these two countries

---

21 Matsui (2) (n 2), 346–348.

22 *Ibid.*

23 *Ibid.*

mirrored the European countries' treatment of Japan itself. This seemingly contradictory attitude of Japan revealed the inherent nature of modern international law.

4 The Discriminatory Nature of Modern European International Law and the Significance of Japan's Attitude to Modern International Law

Modern European international law originated and evolved within the framework of the capitalist mode of production, with its subjects being primarily civilized European countries (or countries in the Americas sharing the same social composition and economic structures). The primary objective of this body of law was to establish a minimum level of order, predictability and stability, facilitating the movement of people, goods, and capital across the borders of these countries.[24] During the nineteenth century, international legal scholars were convinced that the subjects of international law were restricted to civilized nations. In fact, William Edward Hall stated in his publication, *A Treatise on International Law*, released in 1880, that: "International law is a product of the civilization of modern Europe. It is a highly artificial system which could not be understood by countries belonging to a different civilization. It is therefore obvious that only European countries, the successors of European civilization, can be considered obedient to it".[25]

The discriminatory nature of modern international law becomes evident in various works. In particular, *The Institutes of the Law of Nations* published in 1883 by James Lorimer, Professor of Edinburgh University. In his text, Lorimer put forth the notion that humanity can be categorized into three groups: civilized, barbaric, and savage. According to his classification, European countries and those in North and South America constituted civilized mankind. These countries enjoyed full political recognition and the plenary status of subjects of international law. On the other hand, countries such as China, Turkey, Persia, Japan, and Siam were considered part of the barbaric humanity category. These countries enjoyed only partial recognition and were regarded as partial subjects of international law. Civilized countries entered into unequal treaties with them, as demonstrated above in the case

24 Lissitzyn J. O., *International Law Today and Tomorrow* (Oceana Publications, Inc., 1965), 3–4.

25 Hall W. E., *A Treatise on International Law* (Clarendon Press, 1880), 34–35.

of Japan. Lorimer's perspective implied that for civilized countries, the remaining parts of the world inhabited by savage humanity were considered *terra nullius*, meaning they were considered unoccupied territories to which the theory of occupation could be applied. This viewpoint provided justification for the colonization and subjugation of these territories by the civilized countries.[26]

When examining the history of modern international law, it becomes evident that it has been shaped by the dominance of capitalist countries in Europe and America over the rest of the world. This perspective highlights the fact that international law is inherently influenced by power dynamics and interests. As pointed out by B.V.A. Röling, positive rights in international law often conceal elements of power and self-interest. While rights should not be equated with power or interests, they do reflect the existing balance of power in the world. Consequently, international law tends to serve the interests of the stronger and wealthier nations. Classical international law, which primarily emerged from Europe, is no exception to this pattern and has historically served the interests of wealthy countries.[27]

Japan became the first non-European country to gain full recognition as a civilized nation, and by extension, a plenary subject of international law. However, it is important to understand this achievement within the framework of European hegemony and the structure of modern international law. Rather than challenging the structure of domination and dependence inherent in modern European international law, Japan transitioned from a position of dependence to that of a dominant country within the existing system. In 1896, Japan further solidified its privileged status by concluding a treaty of commerce and navigation with China. During the negotiations, the Chinese plenipotentiary, Li Hung Chang (Ri Kosho), expressed his protest to Japan's then-Prime Minister, Hirobumi Ito, arguing that it was inconsistent to demand China to lower tariff rates while allowing Western countries to increase their tariffs. However, Hirobumi Ito dismissively responded to the protest, considering it a ridiculous and melancholy statement.[28]

After the Meiji Restoration, Japan exhibited a consistent and obedient approach to modern international law. As a result, by the end of the 19th century, many European textbooks on international law positively assessed Japan, recognizing its careful adherence to international legal principles and

26 Lorimer J., *The Institutes of Law of Nations* 1 (William Blackwood & Sons, 1883), 101–103.

27 Röling B.V.A., *International Law in an Expanded World* (Djambatan, 1960), 15.

28 Mutsu M., *Kenkenroku* (Japanese) (1895), 231 and 233.

acknowledging its contributions to the development of international law. However, alongside this seemingly automatic and uncritical obedience to the content of that law, it is in my view that there existed a negation of international law and a belief in power politics. This perspective can be observed in the writings of Yukichi Fukuzawa, one of the leading thinkers of the Meiji period, who stressed the importance of Japan becoming a great modern power in order to maintain its independence from the European powers. In his article "Tsūzoku Kokken Ron", Fukuzawa took a nihilistic view of international law. He argued that international law was merely a ceremonial façade, and that the relations between States were basically driven by the pursuit of self-interest and hegemony of each country. According to Fukuzawa, a hundred volumes of international law could not outweigh a few batteries. Peace treaties could not prevail over a few munitions, and the purpose of guns and ammunition was not to maintain and protect existing reason but to create deception.[29]

Indeed, this critical perspective towards international law was not limited to certain thinkers but was also reflected in the behavior of the Meiji Government itself. When it came to accepting the compulsory jurisdiction of international courts for legal disputes, the Meiji Government consistently displayed reluctance. On the surface, it appeared that the government was demonstrating loyalty to international law. However, beneath this outward display, there was a growing and indelible sense of distrust towards international law.[30] This underground trend emerged in the 1940s.

5 The *Daitōwa-Kyōeiken* Project (the Greater East Asia Co-prosperity Sphere) and the Perspectives of Japanese Internationalists towards the Project

Following the experiences mentioned above, Japan's approach to modern international law underwent a radical transformation. In the 1940s, after the creation of Manchuria and the outbreak of war with China, the Japanese government initiated the project to build *Daitōwa-kyōeiken* (The Greater

29 Fukuzawa Y., "Tsūzoku Kokken Ron [Popular Discourse on National Rights]" (Japanese), *Fukuzawa Yukichi Zenshū* [Collected Edition of Fukuzawa Yukichi] 4 (Iwanami Shoten, 1959), 637.

30 Ishimoto Y., "Meijiki ni okeru Chūsai Saiban no Senrei [International Arbitral Jurisprudence in Meiji Period]" (Japanese), *Hōgaku Zasshi* [Journal of Law and Politics of Osaka City University] 9 (3/4) (1962), 182–183.

East Asia Co-Prosperity Sphere). This project aimed to establish, under Japanese leadership, a new order or sphere of co-prosperity in East and Southeast Asia, with the objective of liberating the region from the colonial domination of Western countries.[31] This project was inspired by Carl Schmitt's notion of *Grossraum*.[32] However, in practice, it served as a slogan and ideological framework used by the Japanese government to justify and advance its war efforts, including the Pacific War and the war against China. The primary objective was to create an economic community centered around Japan, China, and Manchuria, with Southeast Asia serving as a resource supply base for Japan's industrial needs.

Within the context of the Greater East Asia Co-Prosperity Sphere project, a number of internationalists actively participated in developing a new theory of the International Law of Greater East Asia and sought to modify modern international law to align with their objectives.[33] Three

31 The construction of this sphere began with the establishment of Manchuria, which Japan recognized in the Protocol between Japan and Manchuria of 1932. Japan established the Wāng Zhàomíng Government in Nanjin and endorsed it in the Japan-China Fundamental Relations Treaty of November 30, 1940. On the same day, a joint declaration by Japan, China and Manchuria was proclaimed, affirming "the common ideas of building a new order based on morality in East Asia". On July 26, 1940, the Council of Ministers adopted a decision entitled "Essential Points of Fundamental State Policies." This decision stated, "Japan's policy, in order to realize world peace, is to build a new *Daitōwa* order at the center of which is Japan, based on the alliance of Japan, China and Manchuria." *Daitōwa* has no precise scope or foundation of its own. It was formed as Japan's war of aggression expanded. Nevertheless, Japanese leaders of the time were commonly aware that the "old regime" was characterized by the aggression of Western powers towards Asian countries, including Japan. The common awareness of being victims of Western aggression, and the consequent thought of liberation for the nations of Asia, led almost necessarily to the thought of taking hegemony in Asia from European imperialism. *See* Matsui Y., "Gurōbaruka Suru Sekai ni okeru Fuhen to Chiiki – *Daitōwa Kyōeiken*ron ni okeru Fuhenshugi Hihan no Hihanteki Kentō [The Universal and the Regional in the Globalized World – Critical Consideration of the Critique of Universalism in *Daitōwa kyōeiken* Theory]" (Japanese), *Kokusaihō Gaikō Zassi* [The Journal of International Law and Diplomacy] 102 (4) (Bunsei Shoin, 2004), 2–6.

32 Schmitt C., *Völkerrechtliche Großraumordnung mit Interventionsverbot für raumfremde Mächte: Ein Beitrag zum Reichsbegriff im Völkerrecht* (Duncker & Humblot, 1939) (translated by Okada I., "Ikigai Rekkyō no Kanshō Kinshi wo Tomonau Kokusaihōteki Kōkuiki Chitsujo - Kokusaihōjō no Reich Gainen heno Kiyo [International Legal Broad Order with Prohibition of Interference by Extraterritorial Powers - Contribution to the Reich Concept in International Law]" (Japanese), *Nazis to Schmitt* (Bokutakusha, 1976)).

33 In 1942, the Japanese Society of International Law began joint research aimed at studying the problems that would be reflected in the process of building *Daitōwa*, accelerating the development of its international law regime, and contributing to the

notable figures in this regard were Kaoru Yasui, Masatoshi Matsushita, and Shigejiro Tabata.

Kaoru Yasui, a professor at Tokyo Imperial University, played a significant role in presenting and analyzing Carl Schmitt's theory of *Grossraum* international law. Yasui argued that East Asia was positioned on the periphery of the European-centric world, and the international law of ancient régime had developed in this context, as evidenced by the unequal treaty regime imposed upon East Asian nations. He proposed the concept of European *Grossraum* international law as a counter to the universalism of the British Empire. The historical significance of this new international law lies in the fact that it accelerates the end of the global domination of European international law from within. With this in mind, Japan first freed itself from the international law of the old regime and then set about emancipating all the nations of East Asia. East Asia was to be constituted as a sphere of independent co-prosperity, with Japan at its center. *Daitōwa* international law was created and henceforth governed the sphere's external and internal relations in accordance with Japan's vision as the leader of the sphere. Yasui's focus was primarily on the conceptual framework of *Grossraum* international law and Marxist international law, which he critiqued as alternatives to liberal international law theory. Whether he personally favored *Grossraum* or Marxist international law was not explicitly stated. However, his thinking was coherent in the sense that it aimed to dismantle the old Anglo-Saxon order and liberate the nations of Asia.[34]

Masatoshi Matsushita, a professor at Rikkyo University, said that the legal nature of *Daitōwa-kyōeiken* can be explained neither by conventional relations nor as an extension of States. He argued that the co-prosperous sphere should not be viewed as a formal collection of equal States but as an organic association of unequal States. Matsushita described the co-prosperous sphere as an association that guarantees the right to live of each member State, representing an association of destiny that transcends spontaneous wills. As a result, each member of this sphere would not have the option to withdraw from the sphere but would possess a certain degree of freedom within the limits imposed by the right to live. Consequently, he proposed

establishment of a new world order and the improvement of world international law. To this end, *Daitōwa sōsho* (*Daitōwa* international law collection) was published, with the participation of four internationalists, including Yasui and Matsushita, mentioned below.

34 Yasui K., *Oshū Kōiki Kokusaihō no Kiso Rinen* [Fundamental Ideas of International Law of Great Area] 1 (Japanese) (Yuhikaku, 1942).

the need to redefine the notion of sovereignty in international law to accommodate this unique arrangement. Rejecting the principle of equality among States, Matsushita argued that it was unfounded as it attempted to apply a theory of equality to States that were inherently unequal. Instead, he advocated for the principle of equity, which he expressed as "*sorezore ni sono tokoro wo eshimuru*", meaning to provide each nation with the status that is appropriate to it. In this way, he sought to establish the legal status of the governing State within and beyond the co-prosperous sphere.[35]

Shigejiro Tabata, a professor at Kyoto Imperial University, emphasized that modern international law did not consist of a truly unified order but of pluralist orders that presupposed diverse values and ideas. In his view, the international law of the *Grossraum* was an important step towards justifying the plurality of international legal orders because the notion of the *Grossraum* was perceived as a concrete and unified historical and political entity rather than a natural given such as race or people. Tabata emphasized the inherent incompatibility between leadership within the co-prosperous sphere and the traditional principle of State equality. He conducted historical research to trace the origins of this principle and concluded that equality among States within the sphere would not be absolute but rather relative. The recognition of equality would be based on the objective criterion of the sphere's values and ideas, which aimed to provide each nation with the status it deserved. Consequently, Tabata argued against the notion of absolute equality and instead advocated for achieving a relative equality, where nations with the same capacities would be treated equally.[36]

Their critique of Eurocentrism in world history remains relevant today, as they highlighted how modern international law has often served the imperialistic interests of Western oligarchic countries. They emphasized the need for a pluralist construction of the international legal order that can accommodate diverse values and perspectives. In questioning the notion of State equality, they challenged the prevailing norms and structures of international relations. However, it is important to acknowledge that they paid little attention to the realities and consequences of Japan's actions during its

35 Matsushita M., *Daitōwa Kokusaihō no Shomondai* [Problems of Daitōwa International Law] (Japanese) (Nihon Hori Kenkyukai, 1942).

36 Tabata S., "Kokusaihō Chitsujo no Tagenteki Kōsei [Pluralist Composition of International Legal Orders]" (Japanese), *Hōgakuronsō* [Kyoto Law Review] 47–3, 48–2 and 6 (1942/1943); "Kindai Kokusaihō ni okeru Kokka Byōdō no Gensoku ni tsuite [On the Principle of Equality of States in Modern International Law]" (Japanese), *Hōgakuronsō* [Kyoto Law Review] 50–3 (1944).

expansionist endeavors in China, Manchuria, the Philippines, Burma, Indochina, and other regions. They either consciously or unconsciously supported Japan's aggression against these countries. What they decisively lacked was a self-critical point of view as they were highly critical of European imperialism but failed to critically examine Japanese imperialism itself.[37]

6 Conclusion

This author has attempted to offer a comparative point of view to appreciate modern international law and its influence on non-European countries, in this case, Japan. This country, or *my* country, does not fit neatly into the dichotomous pattern of European and American domination of Asian countries. Japan dominated and invaded neighboring countries while skillfully and painstakingly avoiding colonization by Western powers. Japan adapted perfectly to modern international law and consequently gained recognition as a civilized nation. In the 1940s, as part of justifying the *Daitōwa War*, Japanese internationalists challenged modern international law and tried, albeit in vain, to create a new legal framework for Greater East Asia, by drawing on Carl Schmitt's concept of *Grossraum international law* and also by questioning the established international legal order, especially its principle of State equality.

What this author cannot decide is the responsibility of the internationalists that were intensively involved in this enterprise. While there were speeches promoting ultra-nationalism, they were not representative of the majority. Most articles written by Japanese internationalists about the *Daitōwa-kyōeiken* project were objective and academic in nature, with a sincere pursuit of realizing the project as a means of emancipating Asian nations from Western domination. As stated earlier, this project was cloaked in an ideology that concealed Japan's aggression against its Asian neighbors. That is why the work of internationalists who contributed to this project is scarcely taken into consideration today. Yet one may wonder whether we should remain categorical in reproaching them for having consciously or unconsciously supported Japanese aggression on the theoretical level of international law.

---

37 Matsui (n 31), 12, 21.

That being said, is there not a certain merit to their theses, such as their critique of European international law, the pluralist composition of the international legal order, or the questioning of the principle of the equality of States? It is impossible for us to recognize all the elements of any given period. This is an intrinsic limitation of living human beings.[38] The appreciation of social facts is necessarily polyhedral, and within the inherent limit of human cognitive capacity, if a researcher did her or his best in her or his academic life, there may be room to appreciate her or his work in a relatively positive way. But we must, of course, assume that there is a difference in perspective between the aggressor and the aggrieved. What we can do for the moment is simply stress the importance of maintaining a critical perspective on government speeches and actions. As scientists, we internationalists also bear a social responsibility.[39]

---

38 After the war, Yasui was forced to leave Tokyo University by decision of the Minister of National Education. He then published an essay entitled "Science and Freedom of Conscience" in a journal of this university, where he wrote as follows: "Japan's position towards East Asia has had a dual aspect: liberation and aggression. How to resolve this contradiction, the tragedy of nations? It was an urgent mission that approached me. Motivated by an irresistible inner demand from my heart, I tried to scientifically establish the ideas of East Asian liberation, knowing the limit of my intellectual capacity. This effort was unsuccessful because of the great wave of that time, I admit. But it would be against freedom of conscience to equate my discourse with cooperation in a war of aggression, and to stigmatize me as militarist or ultra-nationalist. I cannot absolve myself of my responsibility. I deeply regret that my works have been so seriously lacking. I have already reflected on myself several times, but on this occasion, I reflect even more severely on myself." (*Tokyo University Journal*, 1948).

39 Matsui (n 31), 21–22.

CHAPTER 2

Incorporation of International Law into the Domestic Legal System of Japan

Ryo Sasaki

1 Introduction

This chapter deals with how international law, including treaties and customary international norms, is incorporated into and applied in the domestic legal system of Japan. While international law primarily regulates the relationship between sovereign States, domestic law regulates the relationship between citizens or a State and its citizens. Popular discussions on how international law is applied in domestic legal systems often begin with two different approaches: monism and dualism. Japanese law is understood as belonging to the latter, where international and domestic laws operate separately and independently. Following the dualistic approach, international law is required to be translated into the national legal system through mechanisms such as the adoption of national legislation and application in domestic courts.

As domestic implementation of international law is a constitutional issue, it varies from State to State. The main aim of this chapter is to discuss how Japan coordinates its domestic laws with international law. It explores the process of ensuring compatibility through national legislation and the application of international law in domestic courts through a critical examination of the attitudes exhibited by domestic courts towards the implementation of international law.

2 Relationship between International and Domestic Law

Little attention has been given to examining the relationship between national and international law as, until the beginning of the nineteenth century, international law primarily dealt with the conduct of States and the relationship among them. During the era of despotic monarchy in Europe, domestic law was perceived as an order issued by the monarch, while international law was seen as a contract made between monarchs. Both

 | DOI:10.1163/9789004548824_003

domestic law and international law were recognized as belonging to a singular legal system. As international law expanded its scope of regulation in the nineteenth and twentieth century, overlapping realms where both national and international law regulated increased. Hence, concerns over the overlap between national and international law emerged in the field of international legal studies at the beginning of the nineteenth century. International legal doctrines concerning the relationship between international and domestic law can generally be categorized into two main approaches: dualism and monism.

2.1 *Dualism*

Among international legal scholars supporting dualism, Heinrich Triepel, a German scholar, pioneered the theoretical analysis of the relationship between international and domestic law. He stood on the position of dualism, which considers international and domestic law as separate legal systems independent of each other. He highlighted that international law, which regulates the relationship between sovereign States, arises from the will of multiple States, whereas domestic law, which regulates the relationship among private actors and the relationship between private actors and the State, can be enacted based on the will of a single State. Triepel focused on the distinctions in subject and rationale between these two legal systems to support dualism.[1] Other jurists such as Lassa Francis Lawrence Oppenheim and Dionisio Anzilotti also endorsed the dualist perspective.[2] In the same period, dualism was also supported by leading international legal scholars in Japan such as Sakutaro Tachi and Mitsuo Maehara.[3]

2.2 *Monism*

Monism posits that international and domestic law are part of a single legal system. Therefore, the issue of supremacy arises, which involves determining whether international law or domestic law holds superiority. Within this framework, two positions can be proposed:

1 Triepel H., *Völkerrecht und Landesrecht* (C.L. Hirschfeld, 1899), 271.

2 Oppenheim L. F. L. (H. Lauterpacht ed.) *International Law* 1, 8th ed. (Longmans, Green & Co., 1955), 37; Anzilotti D., *Corso di diritto internazionale* (Italian), 3rd ed. (Cedam, 1928), 49–65.

3 Tachi S., *Heiji Kokusaihō Ron* [Outline of International Law in Peacetime] (Japanese), 3rd ed. (Nippon Hyoron sha, 1933), 27–29; Maehara M., *Kokusaihō Kōgi (Jō)* [Lecture on International Law (Vol. 1)] (Japanese) (Rikkosha, 1936), 33–34.

One variant of monism in international legal studies argues that domestic law is superior to international law. Under the influence of Hegelian legal philosophy, it emphasized the sovereignty of the States and the principal definition of international law as an agreement between sovereign States. German jurists at the end of the 19th century, such as Karl Magnus Bergbohm and Max Wenzel, supported this position. They characterized international law as being part of domestic law which regulates a State's foreign relations. According to this view, international law is seen as subordinate to domestic law because the legal effectiveness of international law is derived from the will of States, which is contingent upon the constitutional order of each State.[4] This position is not supported today because it underestimates the significance of international law and does not account for the continued legally binding effect of treaties even after a state's constitutional order or government undergoes reforms.

On the other hand, another group of monism asserts the superiority of international law over domestic law. This position was widely supported by jurists of the Vienna School (*wiener Schule*), such as Hans Kelsen and Alfred Verdross. Hans Kelsen, a prominent jurist known for the "*Reine Rechtslehre*" (*Pure Theory of Law*), adopted a strict legal positivist stance. He argued that both positions within dualism, which place international law as superior to domestic law or vice versa, and monism can be theoretically valid. The determination of which position is more appropriate, according to Kelsen, cannot be resolved through legal reasoning alone but depends on one's ethical and political values. Kelsen argues that placing international law above domestic law may enable the States to coexist under the same international legal order, whereas placing domestic law above international law may allow arbitrary interpretation of the law by individual States.[5] Therefore, it can be inferred that Kelsen advocates for the former position wherein international law is superior to domestic law.[6]

The Vienna School had a significant influence on contemporary international lawyers in Japan, including Akira Osawa and Kisaburo Yokota. Osawa, inspired by Verdross, argued that the domestic legal order of each State can

---

4 Bergbohm C., *Jurisprudenz und Rechtsphilosophie* (Duncker & Humblot, 1882); Wenzel M., *Juristische Grundprobleme* (German) (Dümmler, 1920), 403–407.

5 Kelsen H., *Das Problem der Souveränität und die Theorie des Völkerrechts* (Mohr, 1920).

6 Verdross A., *Die Einheit des rechtlichen Weltbildes auf Grundlage der Völkerrechtsverfassung* (Mohr, 1923).

possess a legal existence with equal status. According to his viewpoint, as domestic law legally exists under the authority of international law, international law should be considered superior to domestic law.[7] Yokota, on the other hand, explained that the validity of domestic law within the territory of each State is sustained by international law. He drew an analogy from Kelsen's argument on the hierarchical structure of law, where the validity of legal norms derives from the validity of superior law. In this context, Yokota viewed international and domestic law as components of a singular legal system, with international law holding superiority over domestic law.[8]

2.3 *Influence of Legal Positivism*

Despite the extensive doctrinal history of international law's relationship with domestic law, both dualism and monism fall short of fully explaining the practices of States. As will be discussed below, contemporary international society is witnessing an increase in situations where both international law and domestic law apply to the same facts. This challenges the traditional dualistic view that perceives international and domestic law as independent entities, as it no longer aligns with the realities of international law.

On the other hand, the monist perspective also faces issues when examining the historical development of legal systems. Systems of government and conflict resolution based on law have existed since ancient times before the emergence of modern international law. Some States have a long history beyond modern international law of conducting governance under domestic law, even if it significantly differs from contemporary legal systems. In this sense, the argument of monism that the validity of domestic law depends on the authorization by international law does not correspond to historical facts.

To bridge the gap between traditional theories and the realities of international society, doctrines in recent days have adopted a more legal-positivist approach, aiming to empirically describe this issue. A leading scholar on this issue, Gerald Fitzmaurice agrees with an assumption of dualism in that international and domestic law belong to different realms of the legal system. According to Fitzmaurice, there is, *a priori*, no supremacy or inferiority

---

7 Osawa A., *Kokusaihō Chitsujo Ron: Tōitsuteki Chitsujo no Naka ni Okeru Kokusaihō Chitsujo no Hōritsuteki Chii ni Tsuite* [On International Legal Order: The Legal Status of International Legal Order in the Unified Order] (Japanese) (Iwanami Shoten, 1931), 174–188.

8 Yokota K., *Kokusaihō no Kiso Riron* [Fundamental Theory of International Law] (Japanese) (Yuhikaku, 1949), 97–99.

between those legal systems themselves. Thus, domestic legal rules that violate international law are not automatically invalidated. However, when a State's conduct, based on its national legal rules, conflicts with international law, the scope of application of the national and international legal rules is coordinated in a way that examines the opposability of domestic law as well as the State's international responsibility.[9] Sōji Yamamoto, a noted Japanese scholar in this area of international law, supports Fitzmaurice's theory, calling it "coordination theory (*Chōsei Riron*)" or "coordinate theory (*Tōi Riron*)".[10] While "coordination theory" or "coordinate theory" may be seen to substantially remain in a category of dualism, it is recognized as "neo-dualism"[11] as it overcomes traditional theoretical confrontation between monism and dualism by explaining the relationship between international and domestic law based on positivist observations of the application of international law.[12]

The validity of the "coordination theory" or "coordinate theory" can be seen in international jurisprudence. In the *Fisheries Jurisdiction* case, for instance, the International Court of Justice (ICJ) concluded that "the Icelandic Regulations of 14 July 1972 establishing a zone of exclusive fisheries jurisdiction extending to 50 nautical miles from baselines around the Coast of Iceland are not opposable to the United Kingdom".[13] This case illustrates that, in the international sphere, the scope of application of domestic law can be restricted by international law. However, even if domestic legislation is deemed "not opposable" to another State, its legal effect within the domestic

---

9 Fitzmaurice G., "The General Principles of International Law Considered from the Standpoint of the Rule of Law," *Recueil des Cours* 92 (1957), 80–97.

10 Yamamoto S., *Kokusaihō* [International Law] (Japanese) New ed. (Yuhikaku, 1994), 85.

11 *See*, Yokota Y., "Kokusaihō to Kokunaihō no Kankei ni Kansuru Shin Nigen Ron no Kanōsei: ILO 88gō Jōyaku no Nihon heno Tekiyō no Jirei no Kentō [The Validity of Neo-Dualism regarding the Relationship between International Law and Municipal Law: In case of Application of ILO Convention No. 88 in Japan]" (Japanese), *Chuo Law Journal* 13(4) (2017), 3–21.

12 *E.g.*, Tanaka T., "Kokusaihō to Kokunaihō no Kankei o Meguru Shogakusetsu to Sono Rironteki Kiso [Doctrines and Their Theoretical Foundations regarding the Relationship between International and Domestic Law]" (Japanese) in Hirobe K. and Tanaka T. (eds.), *Kokusaihō to Kokunaihō: Kokusai Kōeki no Tenkai* (*Yamamoto Sōji Sensei Kanreki Kinen*) [International Law and Domestic Law: The Development of International Public Interest (Festschrift for Prof. Sōji Yamamoto for His 60th Anniversary)] (Keiso Shobo, 1991), 31–56, 49; Sugihara T., *Kokusaihōgaku Kōgi* [Lectures on International Law] (Japanese), 2nd ed. (Yuhikaku, 2013), 110.

13 *Fisheries Jurisdiction* case (*United Kingdom v. Iceland*), Judgment of July 25, 1974, ICJ, *ICJ Reports* 1974, 3, para. 67.

sphere is not negated. The ICJ's decision in the *Fisheries Jurisdiction* case indicates that the scope of application of domestic legislation can be restricted by reason of its incompatibility with international law. It implies that international and domestic law can relate to each other. Thus, it challenges the traditional dualistic view that international or domestic law can exist independently or that domestic legal rules violating international law are automatically invalidated, as argued by monism. As such, "coordination" or "coordinate" theory can be seen to give an explanation of the contemporary practice in international society.

In the new trend of research on the relationship between international law and domestic law, especially international human rights law and constitutional law, it should be noted that the primary beneficiaries should be individuals rather than sovereign States. Both international human rights law and constitutional law aim to realize fundamental rights and freedoms of individuals. Scholars emphasizing pluralistic structure of legal system and multi-layered human rights protection propose new understanding of their relationship such as "trapezium model of legal system" and "transnational source of human rights law."[14]

3 Conclusion of Treaties and Incorporation into Domestic Law in Japan

The Constitution of Japan distributes to the Cabinet the power of concluding international agreements with other States. Article 73 of the Constitution prescribes, "1) The Cabinet, in addition to other general administrative functions, shall perform the following functions; [...] 2) manage foreign affairs; 3) conclude treaties. However, it shall obtain prior or, depending on circumstances, subsequent approval of the Diet."[15] In practice, the Ministry of Foreign Affairs (MOFA), an administrative division under the control of the Cabinet, has the authority of concluding treaties as well as other

---

14 Negishi Y., *Conventionality Control of Domestic Law: Constitutionalised International Adjudication and Internationalised Constitutional Adjudication* (Nomos, 2022), 202–208; Yamamoto H., "'Kokken teki Shii' vs 'Transnational Jinken Hōgen-ron ['Thoughts of National Constitution' vs 'Theory of Transnational Source of Human Rights Law']" (Japanese), *Globalization and Transformation of Law* [Global-ka to Hō no Hen-yō] (Nippon Hyoron sha, 2018), 16–18.

15 The Constitution of Japan, English translation available at the Prime Minister of Japan and his Cabinet, https://japan.kantei.go.jp/constitution_and_government_of_japan/constitution_e.html (accessed March 17, 2023).

international agreements. Article 4 of the Act for Establishment of the Ministry of Foreign Affairs (Act No. 94 of 1999)[16] stipulates that 1) issues related to foreign policy, [...] and 4) interpretation and implementation of treaties and other international agreements, as well as established international legal rules, fall under the purview of the MOFA. Once negotiations with other States are finalized, and the treaty text is determined, the Japanese translation of the treaty or international agreement, along with a bill of legislation for its implementation, is subject to examination by the Cabinet Legislation Bureau (CLB, *Naikaku Hōseikyoku*).[17] Prior to the signing of a treaty or international agreement, the Minister of Foreign Affairs requests a decision in a Cabinet meeting to ensure the authority to conclude an international agreement.[18]

While the administrative section has the authority to sign and ratify treaties, it shall obtain prior or, depending on circumstances, subsequent approval of the Diet. The approval of the Diet is required with respect to democratic control on concluding international agreements, but from the viewpoint of convenience, efficiency, reasonableness and necessity, it is generally recognized that not all treaties require the Diet's approval. In other words, there are some cases where the Cabinet and administrative division can conclude international agreements without the Diet's approval, for example, with respect to managing foreign affairs as provided for in Article 73(2) of the Constitution. These kinds of agreements, usually taking the form of an exchange of notes, are called "*gyōsei torikime* (executive agreements)". As treaties requiring Diet approval and executive agreements are both legally-binding treaties under international law, the distinction is maintained in the domestic sphere for constitutional purposes.[19]

Under administrative practice in Japan, the government has established a categorization system for treaties that determines whether they require approval from the Diet. This system is known as the "*Ōhira San-Gensoku* (Ohira principles)", named after a statement made by Foreign Minister Masayoshi Ohira during a Committee on Foreign Affairs session in the House of Representatives in 1974. The *Ōhira San-Gensoku* classifies treaties

16 Translated by the present author.

17 Mori T., "The Current Practice of Making and Applying International Agreements in Japan", in Bradley, C. A. (ed.), *The Oxford Handbook of Comparative Foreign Relations Law* (Oxford University Press, 2019) 191–204, 193–194.

18 *Ibid.*, 194.

19 Iwasawa Y., *International Law, Human Rights, and Japanese Law: The Impact of International Law on Japanese Law* (Clarendon Press, 1998), 19–20.

requiring Diet approval into three categories:[20] 1) international agreements including "legislative issues", which require Japan to take legislative measures for implementation, such as the United Nations Convention on the Law of the Sea,[21] which required the National Diet to pass eight bills for approval of ratification in 1996; 2) international agreements including "budgetary issues", which require fiscal expenditure as a measure for implementation such as the Agreement between Japan and the Republic of Korea concerning the Settlement of Problems in regard to Property and Claims and Economic Cooperation;[22] and 3) other important international agreements, which do not require legislative or budgetary issues but are considered as politically so important as to influence fundamentals of international relationship between Japan and other States, such as the Treaty of Peace and Friendship between Japan and the People's Republic of China.[23]

In practice, even though Japan adopts an incorporation system for treaty implementation, it often enacts or amends domestic laws and regulations to align with the provisions of the treaties it enters into. For instance, Japan amended the Nationality Act (Act No. 147 of 1950) in 1985 when ratifying the Convention on the Elimination of All Forms of Discrimination Against Women (CEDAW),[24] to provide women with equal rights as men in relation to acquiring, changing or retaining their nationality (Article 9). Before the amendment, children could only obtain Japanese nationality at birth if his/her father had Japanese nationality. After the amendment, children became eligible to obtain Japanese nationality at birth if his/her mother and/or father were of Japanese nationality. Additionally, in response to the ratification of the CEDAW, Article 10(b), which focuses on equal access to

---

20 Mori (n 17) 194–195; *see also* Hirobe K., "The Japanese Practice Concerning International Treaties," *Archiv des Völkerrechts* 25(1) (1987), 39–57, 41; Nakauchi Y., "Kokkai no Shōnin wo Yōsuru 'Jōyaku' no Han-i: Genzai no Un-yō to Kokkai de Giron to Natta Jirei no Kōsatsu [The Scope of 'Treaties' Requiring the Diet's Approval: An Analysis on the Operation Today and Examples of Discussions at the Diet]" (Japanese), *Rippō to Chōsa* [Legislation and Research], 429 (2020), 17–35, 19–24.

21 United Nations Convention on the Law of the Sea, *signed on* December 10, 1982, *entered into force on* November 16, 1994, 1833 UNTS 397.

22 Agreement on the Settlement of Problems concerning Property and Claims and on Economic Cooperation, *signed on* June 22, 1965, *entered into force on* December 18, 1965, 583 UNTS 173.

23 Treaty of Peace and Friendship between Japan and the People's Republic of China, *signed on* August 12, 1978, *entered into force on* October 23, 1978.

24 Convention on the Elimination of All Forms of Discrimination against Women, *signed on* December 18, 1979, *entered into force on* September 3, 1981, 1249 UNTS 13.

education, the course of study of secondary education was amended in the 1993 fiscal year. Both girls and boys were given the opportunity to learn industrial arts and housecraft. Before the amendment, girls typically took a housecraft class while boys took industrial arts at junior high schools (former-secondary education). Moreover, housecraft was a compulsory module for girls only in high schools (late-secondary education). The amendment ensured equal access to these subjects for both genders. When Japan joined the Convention relating to the Status of Refugees[25] and its Protocol,[26] the Immigration Control Order (Cabinet Order No. 319 of 1951) was amended for the purpose of including provisions on refugee recognition and changed its name to Immigration Control and Refugee Recognition Act. Furthermore, Japan enacted the Act on Cooperation with the International Criminal Court (Act No. 37 of 2007) in 2007 upon becoming a State party to the Rome Statute of the International Criminal Court.[27] The country also enacted the Act on Preventing Mercury Pollution of the Environment (Act No. 42 of 2015) and partially revised the Air Pollution Control Act (Act No. 97 of 1968) to comply with the Minamata Convention on Mercury in 2017.[28]

4 Implementation of International Law in Japan

4.1 *Incorporation of International Law into Domestic Law*

Under international law, States are under the obligation to comply with international legal rules which bind them. This principle is derived from the general principle of law known as "*pacta sunt servanda*" (agreements must be kept). Given the decentralized structure of international society, international legal norms can be primarily executed through incorporation into the domestic legal system. As more areas are subject to regulation by both international and domestic law, domestic constitutional systems now operate within a transnational legal environment.

The process of incorporating international legal rules into domestic law and the status of international law incorporated in the domestic legal

25 Convention relating to the Status of Refugees, *signed on* July 28, 1951, *entered into force on* April 22, 189 UNTS 187.

26 Protocol relating to the Status of Refugees, *signed on* January 31, 1967, *entered into force on* October 4, 1967, 606 UNTS 267.

27 Rome Statute of the International Criminal Court, *signed on* July 17, 1998, *entered into force on* July 1, 2002, 2187 UNTS 3.

28 Minamata Convention on Mercury, *signed on* October 10, 2013, *entered into force on* August 16, 2017, 3201 UNTS I-54669.

system vary between States and are usually an issue of constitutional law. These different approaches are generally classified into two systems: the "transformation" system and the "incorporation" system.

In principle, under the "transformation" system, international law is implemented through parliamentary legislation that mirrors the content of international law. Therefore, international legal rules themselves do not have direct application in the domestic sphere. The United Kingdom is a notable example of a State that follows this system, where the constitutional principle of "parliamentary sovereignty" or "supremacy of the parliament" is widely known. Under the UK's jurisprudence, international law is regarded as "simply another system of law which regulates the relations between states".[29] "A treaty may be incorporated into and alter the laws of the United Kingdom by means of legislation".[30] Customary international law is also recognized as a fundamental aspect of English law provided that it is consistent with a statutory and common law.[31] Even if it is "in contravention generally acknowledged principles of international law, [legislation of the Parliament] is binding upon and must be enforced by the [domestic] Courts".[32]

On the other hand, under the "incorporation" system, treaties, as well as customary international law, hold direct legal effect within the domestic legal system. Many civil law countries, such as Germany and France adopt this system. The Japanese legal system is also classified under this system. When it comes to the incorporation of international legal rules into domestic law, 1) the status of international law under the domestic legal system and 2) the applicability of international legal rules under the domestic legal system become an issue.

4.2 *Status of International Law under the Japanese Legal System*

Under the "incorporation" system, when international legal rules can be applied in a domestic sphere, their status in the hierarchical structure of the domestic legal system is important. In other words, their relationship with the Constitution and statutory acts needs to be considered. Typically, international legal rules that are incorporated into domestic law hold a

---

29 *J. H. Rayner (Mincing Lane) Ltd v. Department of Trade and Industry* [1990] 2 A.C. 418, at 463.

30 *Ibid.*, at 476 (by Lord Templeman).

31 *Chung Chi Cheung v. The King* [1939] AC 160.

32 *E. R. Croft v. Sylvester Dunphy* [1933] AC 156.

higher or equivalent status to parliamentary legislation but a lower status than the Constitution.

In the case of Japan, the status of international law in the domestic sphere is not explicitly provided for in the Constitution. As a result, there are diverging scholarly views on the status of international law in Japanese legal system due to the ambiguity of constitutional provisions.[33] Some scholars, taking a minority position, deny the legal effect of international law in the domestic sphere, arguing that Article 98(2) of the Constitution stipulates the "faithful observance of treaties" only under international law.[34] However, the prevailing view in Japan is that treaties ratified by the country do have legal effect in the domestic legal system of Japan after they are published in the official government gazette (*kampō*). Scholars supporting this view agree that international law is incorporated into the domestic legal order of Japan by means of Article 98(2) of the Constitution. It is also noted that the Japanese government consistently maintains the position that ratified treaties have legal effect in Japanese law by means of Article 98(2) of the Constitution.[35]

Although ratified treaties have legal effect in the domestic sphere, neither its relationship with domestic law nor the Constitution is prescribed in the Constitution of Japan. Regarding the relationship between international law and statutory acts, the predominant view is that treaties hold a superior to statutes. This view is supported by the provision in Article 98(2) of the Constitution, which states that "[t]he treaties concluded by Japan and established laws of nations shall be faithfully observed". In practical application, this means that if a domestic statute is found to be incompatible with a ratified treaty, the provisions of the treaty take precedence, and the domestic statute's applicability may be excluded. An example illustrating this principle can be seen in a case involving the Law on Territorial Sea and Contiguous Zone (Law No. 73 of 1996) and the Agreement on Fisheries between

---

33 Iwasawa Y., *Jōyaku no Kokunai Tekiyō Kanōsei: Iwayuru "Self-Executing" na Jōyaku ni Kansuru Ichi Kōsatsu* [Domestic Applicability of Treaties: A Study on So-Called "Self-executing" Treaties] (Japanese) (Yuhikaku, 1985), 27–32.

34 Iwasawa (n 19), 29.

35 Shūgiin Kempō Chōsakai [Committee on Investigation of the Constitution, House of Representative], Kempō to Kokusaihō (tokuni Jinken no Kokusai-teki hoshō) ni Kansuru Kisoteki Shiryo [Basic Materials on Constitution and International Law (in particular Human Rights Protection)] (Japanese), 11–12, https://www.shugiin.go.jp/internet/itdb_kenpou.nsf/html/kenpou/chosa/shukenshi050.pdf/$file/shukenshi050.pdf (accessed March 17, 2023).

Japan and the Republic of Korea.[36] The Hamada Branch of the Matsue District Court held that applicability of the Territorial Sea Law should be excluded by reason of its incompatibility with the Japan-Korea Fisheries Agreement.[37]

The relationship between international law and the constitution in Japan is not explicitly specified in the Constitution itself. Some have suggested that treaties could be considered superior to the constitution based on the principles of sincere observance of international law and international cooperation (Preamble, Article 98(2)). Additionally, the lack of reference to treaties in the examination of the constitutionality (Articles 81 and 98(1)) has been cited as a supporting factor. However, the widely accepted view is that treaties are placed below the Constitution in the hierarchy.

One of the prevailing explanations for this hierarchy centers on procedures prescribed in Article 61 and Article 98 (amendments of the Constitution). Article 61, with reference to Article 60(2), requires Diet approval for the conclusion of treaties when the House of Councillors makes a decision different from that of the House of Representatives and when no agreement can be reached even through a joint committee of both Houses, provided for by law, or in the case of failure by the House of Councillors to take final action within thirty days [...], the decision of the House of Representatives shall be the decision of the Diet. Article 96 of the Constitution outlines the amendment procedure, requiring a concurring vote of two-thirds or more of all the members of each House of the National Diet, followed by ratification through a majority vote of all votes cast in a national referendum. Comparing these provisions, Diet approval for the conclusion of treaties requires a less strict procedure than what is required to amend the Constitution. In the light of a rigid constitution, under which, in principle, a more strict procedure is required to establish, abolish or amend a norm in a higher place in the domestic legal system, it becomes evident that the Constitution, which has a stricter procedure for amendment, is placed more superior than treaties. Furthermore, Article 98(1) explicitly stipulates that Constitution shall be the supreme law of the nation which emphasizes its superiority above treaties and other domestic laws.

Even when a treaty is found to breach the Constitution, the treaty is not automatically invalidated. When the constitutionality of Treaty of Mutual

36 Agreement on Fisheries between Japan and the Republic of Korea, *signed on* June 22, 1965, 583 UNTS 51.

37 *Ship Tedon* case, Judgment of August 15, 1997, Matsue District Court, Hamada Branch, reprinted in *Hanrei Jihō* 1636 (1998), 59.

Cooperation and Security between Japan and the United States of America (the Japan-U.S. Security Treaty)[38] was dealt with in *Sunagawa* case, the Supreme Court did not reach a definitive conclusion on the constitutionality of the Japan-U.S. Security Treaty declaring that "unless the [Japan-U.S. Security] treaty is obviously unconstitutional and void, it falls outside the purview of the power of judicial review granted to the court".[39] The prevailing doctrine explains it as "act of government theory (*tōchi-kōi ron*)" that highly political issues affecting the fundamental elements of the State governance should not be reviewed by the judicial organ but rather be dealt with by legislative and administrative organs, drawing inspiration from the French theory of "*acte de gouvernement*" or the American theory of "political question theory."[40] In this regard, it is crucial to note that the Supreme Court of Japan implicitly indicated that the Japan-U.S. Security Treaty is not unconstitutional or void by holding that "unless unconstitutional and void, it falls outside the purview of the power of judicial review".[41]

4.3 *Applicability of International Law and Judicial Review*

As discussed earlier, international legal rules binding Japan are incorporated into its domestic legal system without additional procedures under the 'incorporation' system by way of Article 98(2) of the Constitution, which provides that "[t]he treaties concluded by Japan and established laws of nations shall be faithfully observed". While it is generally true that provisions of treaties ratified by Japan are legally binding in the domestic sphere, in numerous cases, they are not always directly applied. Furthermore, many treaties do not include detailed provisions on implementation, leaving it to domestic legislation. When an issue arises concerning a violation of

38 Treaty of Mutual Cooperation and Security between the United States and Japan, *signed on* January 19, 1960, *entered into force on* July 23, 1960, 11 UST 1632.

39 *Sunagawa* case, Judgment of December 16, 1959, Supreme Court (Grand Bench), *Saikō Saibansho Saibanshū Keiji Hanreishū* [Supreme Court Reports (criminal cases)] 13 (13), 3225, English translation available at Courts in Japan, https://www.courts.go.jp/app/hanrei_en/detail?id=13 (accessed 17 March 2023).

40 Matsuda H., "International Law in Japanese Courts", in Bradley, C. A. (ed.) (n 17), 537–547, 539; Takahashi K., *Rikken-Shugi to Nihonkoku-Kempō* [Constitutionalism and the Constitution of Japan] (Japanese), 5th ed. (Yuhikaku, 2020), 458–459.

41 Matsuda, *ibid.*, 539. In addition, it should be criticized in a strong term that the government of Japan depended on *Sunagawa* judgment to explain the constitutionality of exercising the right of collective self-defense, which was decided through the change of constitutional interpretation by the Cabinet without enough extent of democratic dialogue.

international law in the domestic sphere, careful consideration is needed on how to apply international law in domestic courts.

It is worth noting that the courts in Japan adopt a highly restrictive approach to constitutional review. This is primarily due to a judicial practice known as *kanzen-tampo-shugi* (literally, implementing legislation perfectionism). Under this practice, the CLB meticulously checks the compatibility and consistency of proposed legislation with the Constitution, existing laws, and international obligations and, if necessary, will propose amendments when the Diet establishes a statute. This serves as a "pre-reviewing" system, enabling the legislature to eliminate any potential unconstitutionality or unconventionality in statutes beforehand.[42]

The obligation imposed on the State from Article 98(2) to observe treaties ratified by Japan and customary international law applies to the State as a whole, encompassing all sectors – legislative, administrative and judicial. In this context, it is essential to differentiate between the domestic legal force of international law and its direct applicability. While ratified treaties generally obtain legal effect in the domestic sphere, not all of them can be directly applied.[43]

4.3.1 Direct Applicability

In Japan, the direct applicability of international law in the domestic sphere should be examined in two stages.[44] First, it is essential to determine whether the parties to a treaty intended to exclude its direct applicability, which can be inferred from the treaty's text or *travaux préparatoires*. Second, it is necessary to ascertain whether the international legal rule is precise and complete enough to the extent that no implementing legislative measures by the State authorities is required.[45]

The courts in Japan tend to misconstrue the "obligation of progressive implementation" provided by the International Covenant on Economic, Social and Cultural Rights (ICESCR)[46] as being aligned with the political aims of the government, resulting in the denial of the direct applicability of

42 *Ibid.*, 541.

43 Iwasawa (n 19), 44–45.

44 Iwasawa emphasizes whether an international legal rule is directly applicable in a domestic sphere is a question of domestic law (*ibid.*, 48).

45 *Ibid.*, 46–47.

46 International Covenant on Economic, Social and Cultural Rights, *signed on* December 16, 1966, *entered into force on* January 3, 1976, 993 UNTS 3.

certain provisions. For instance, in the *Shiomi* case, the Supreme Court denied the direct applicability of Article 9 of the ICESCR, stating that it does not provide "a concrete right to be granted to individual immediately".[47] In contrast, provisions of the International Covenant on Civil and Political Rights (ICCPR)[48] are often considered to be directly applicable. For example, in the *Breaching Cannabis Control Act and Customs Act* case, the Tokyo High Court ruled that, even if the right of the accused in a criminal trial to the assistance of interpreter without a fee, prescribed in Article 14 (3)(f), had not previously been known in Japanese law, the requirement of that provision is unconditional and absolute. Therefore, it was not permitted to order the criminal defendant to pay the cost of the interpreter.[49] Another instance is the case of *Obstructing Prisoner's Interviews with Defense Lawyer*, where a prisoner who had been physically abused by prison guards, sought State compensation against the State responsible for managing the prison. However, lawyers representing the prisoner faced obstacles in accessing their client. The prison in Tokushima limited their interview time to within 30 minutes and interrupted their meeting with the presence of prison staff. Tokushima District Court determined that limiting the time of the interview was illegal and beyond the prison director's discretionary power or an abuse of it. The court further stated that the prison/State had breached Article 14(3)(b) of the ICCPR, which guarantees "adequate time and facilities for the preparation of the defense and to communicate with counsel".[50]

---

47 *Shiomi* case, Judgment of March 2, 1989, Supreme Court, *Saikō Saibansho Saibanshū Minji Hanreishū* [Supreme Court Reports (Civil Cases)] 156, 271, English translation referred from Iwasawa (n 19), 47.

48 International Covenant on Civil and Political Rights, *signed on* December 16, 1966, *entered into force on* March 23, 1976, 999 UNTS 171.

49 *Breaching Cannabis Control Act and Customs Act* case, Judgment of February 3, 1993, *Tokyō Kōtō Saibansho Keiji Hanketsu Jihō* [Tokyo High Court Criminal Casebook], 44 (1–12), 11, case summary in English available at: Webster, T., "International Human Rights Law in Japan: The View at Thirty", *Columbia Journal of Asian Law* 23(2) (2010), 241–268, 253–254.

50 *Obstructing Prisoner's Interviews with Defense Lawyer* case, Judgment of March 15, 1996, Tokushima District Court, *Hanrei Jihō* 1597 (1997), 115; English translation available at: *Japanese Annual of International Law* 40 (1997), 118. In higher courts' rulings, Takamatsu High Court advocated the District Court's judgment (Judgment of November 25, 1997, Takamatsu High Court, *Hanrei Jihō* 1653 (1998), 117; English translation available at: *Japanese Annual of International Law* 41 (1998), 87), but the Supreme Court dismissed (Judgment of September 7, 2000, Supreme Court, *Shūmin* 199, 371, reprinted in *Hanrei Jihō* 1728 (2001), 17).

4.3.2 Consistent Interpretation of Domestic Law with International Law

In practice, many treaties grant the State authority some discretion in determining their implementation, which means that treaty provisions are often not as precise and concrete as required by the *Shiomi* case. Critics argue that this strict requirement of preciseness and concreteness, especially in the context of international human rights law, may hinder the intended protection of individuals' rights.[51]

As the obligation to implement international law extends to all sectors of the State, including legislative, administrative and judicial branches, the State can fulfill this obligation through various means, such as adopting new legislation, administrative regulations, or interpreting existing domestic law consistently with international law.[52] Even if treaties are not directly applicable in the domestic sphere, it does not mean that their domestic legal force has dissolved, rather they still bind the State authorities as valid norms of positive law. Therefore, the State must ensure consistent interpretation of domestic law with international law, which can be categorized into the interpretation of statutory law and constitutional law.[53] In this regard, the term of "indirect application" is often used in Japan to mean "applying international law in the domestic legal system" and both concepts, "consistent interpretation" and "indirect application" are sometimes confused. Here, the author uses "consistent interpretation" with consideration that it is domestic law which is applied and the courts interpret the domestic legal rules consistently with relevant international legal rules. The cases related to the "consistent interpretation" can be categorized into those on legality of acts taken by administrative organs and those on torts between private entities. In the former, international law functions as restricting discretion of administrative agencies while in the latter, international law is indirectly applied to civil affairs.[54]

---

51 Shin H., "Jinken Jōyaku no Chokusetsu Tekiyō Kanōsei: Kokunai Saibansho no Shihōken to Jōyaku Kihan [Direct Applicability of Human Rights Treaties: Judicial Power of National Courts and Treaty Norms]" (Japanese), in Shin, H., *Jinken Jōyaku no Gendaiteki Tenkai* [Contemporary Development of Human Rights Treaties] (Shinzansha, 2009), 211–283, 214–217.

52 Matsuda H., *Kokusaihō to Kempō Chitujo: Kokusai Kihan no Jisshi Kengen* [International Law and Constitutional Legal System: The Competence to Implement International Norms] (Japanese) (University of Tokyo Press, 2020), 186–188.

53 Matsuda (n 40), 542.

54 Yamada S. "Kokunai-hō no Kokusai-hō Tekiōteki Kaishaku to Kenryoku Bunritsu: Beikoku ni okeru Charming Betsy Canon no Shōkai o Chūshin ni [Consistent

In the context of consistent interpretation of statutes with international law, each State agency is obligated to interpret laws in a manner consistent with the faithful observance of international law, as prescribed by Article 98(2) of the Constitution, even in cases where the treaty does not stipulate a concrete obligation for the State's action.[55] An example of this can be seen in the *Kitami Road* case, where the Sapporo District Court ruled that the Convention on Biological Diversity[56] can serve as interpretative guidelines for relevant domestic legislation, such as the Basic Act on the Environment (Act No. 91 of 1993), the Environmental Impact Assessment Act (Act No. 81 of 1997), and the Act on Conservation of Endangered Species of Wild Fauna and Flora (Act No. 75 of 1992), etc. to restrict the discretion of State authorities. It is important to note that, in the jurisprudence of the Japanese judicial system, treaties do not directly regulate the relationship between private persons because they primarily function as agreements between States.

In the context of private relationships, international law is rarely directly applied, and domestic civil law primarily governs such matters. However, domestic civil law must be interpreted consistently with international law to ensure compliance. For example, in the *Otaru Hot Spring* case, the Sapporo District Court pointed out that when an act of a private person violates other persons' rights and freedoms beyond the socially-permitted extent, it is contrary to the restriction on private autonomy (Article 1) and public policy (Article 90) of the Civil Code (Act No. 89 of 1896). Although neither the ICCPR nor International Convention on the Elimination of All Forms of Racial Discrimination (ICERD)[57] can be directly applied to the relationship between private persons, they can be taken into consideration when interpreting relevant provisions in civil law.[58] Similarly, in the *Kyoto Korean*

Interpretation of Domestic Law to International Law and Divison of Powers: How Charming Is the Charming Betsy Canon?]" (Japanese), Okayama Daugaku Hōgakkai Zasshi [Okayama Law Review] 65 (3–4) (2016), 415–416.

55 Matsuda (n 52), 188.

56 Convention on Biological Diversity, *signed on* June 5, 1992, *entered into force on* December 29, 1993, 1760 UNTS 79.

57 International Convention on the Elimination of All Forms of Racial Discrimination, *signed on* March 7, 1966, *entered into force on* March 12, 1969, 660 UNTS 195.

58 *Otaru Hot Spring* case, Judgment of November 11, 2002, Sapporo District Court, website of Courts in Japan, https://www.courts.go.jp/app/hanrei_jp/detail4?id=8644 (accessed March 17, 2023); English translation available at: Webster T. (trans.), "*Arudou v. Earth Cure*: Judgment of November 11, 2002, Sapporo District Court," *Asian-Pacific Law & Policy Journal* 9(2) (2008), 297–321.

Elementary School case, the Kyoto District Court determined tort law in Article 709 of the Civil Code to be consistent with the ICCPR and ICERD, ordering compensation for hate speech to fulfill the purpose of ICERD, which aims to eliminate racial discrimination.[59]

In contrast, interpreting the Constitution consistently with international law is more complex due to the Constitution's superior status to international law in Japan's domestic legal system. While States are not allowed to "invoke the provisions of its internal law as justification for its failure to perform a treaty",[60] interpreting the Constitution inconsistently with international law may result in breaching international obligations.[61] Therefore, States are expected to interpret the Constitution consistently with international law in the international sphere. However, the extent to which such interpretation is accepted under the domestic constitutional order needs scrutiny.[62] In the *Nationality Act* case, Judge Izumi discussed this point in his concurring opinion. In this case, Article 3(1) of the Nationality Act, which did not allow a child born out of wedlock to a Japanese father and foreign mother to acquire Japanese nationality without the legal marriage of his/her parents, was regarded as a breach of Article 14 of the Constitution which provides for equality before the law. In his concurring opinion, Judge Izumi strictly analyzed the authority of legislative and judicial sectors, declaring that the essence of Article 3(1) of the Nationality Act should be maintained even if a part of the provision, "marriage of the parents", is found unconstitutional. This interpretation aligns with Article 24(3) of the ICCPR and Article 7(1) of the Convention on the Rights of the Child (CRC).[63] Furthermore, he pointed out that it

59 *Kyoto Korean Elementary School* case, Judgment of October 7, 2013, Kyoto District Court, website of Courts in Japan, https://www.courts.go.jp/app/files/hanrei_jp/675/083675_hanrei.pdf (accessed March 17, 2023); Osaka High Court (appeal trial) also took similar interpretation of the Civil Code in consideration of the ICERD (Judgment of July 8, 2014, Osaka High Court, *Hanrei Jihō* 2232 (2014), 32), and the Supreme Court advocated the judgments of the lower courts (Decision of December 9, 2014, Supreme Court, unpublished); Case summary available at: Hatano A., "The Internalization of International Human Rights Law: The Case of Hate Speech in Japan", *New York University Journal of International Law and Politics* 50(2) (2018), 637–654.

60 Article 27 of Vienna Convention on the Law of Treaties, *signed on* May 23, 1969, *entered into force on* January 27, 1980, 1155 UNTS 331.

61 Matsuda (n 51), 192–193.

62 *Ibid.*, 193.

63 Convention on the Rights of the Child, *signed on* November 20, 1989, *entered into force on* September 2, 1990, 1577 UNTS 3.

falls with the legislative authority of the Diet to amend the Nationality Act to resolve the uncons-titutionality.[64]

4.3.3 Referring to International Law as "Persuasive Authority"

When interpreting legal rules, State authorities, such as judicial organs, can make reference to various materials, including non-legally binding documents, such as legislation and case law from foreign countries. On certain occasions, Japanese courts have cited the trend of legislation in foreign jurisdictions and international legal instruments, including non-legally binding advisory documents, as a supporting factor to justify their interpretation of domestic law. These sources are commonly referred to as "persuasive authorities".[65]

In the *Nationality Act* case mentioned above, the Supreme Court of Japan referred to the legislative situations in other countries and international human rights conventions like the ICCPR and CRC to conclude that the provision in the Nationality Act constituted discriminatory treatment against children born out of wedlock, which was inconsistent with Article 14(1) of the Constitution.[66] Similarly, in the *Prohibition Period on Remarriage* case, the constitutionality of Article 733 of the Civil Code at the time was questioned as it prohibited only women from remarrying within six months of divorce. The Supreme Court of Japan ruled that this part of the provision, which prohibited women from remarriage beyond 100 days after divorce, violated Article 14(1) (equality before law) and Article 24 (respect for family life) of the Constitution. The Court also referred to recommendations provided in the concluding observations of the Committees on Civil and Political Rights and Elimination of All Forms of Discrimination against Women.[67] Following these rulings, the Diet amended the Civil Code in

64 *Nationality Act* case, Judgment of June 4, 2008, Supreme Court (Grand Bench), *Minshū* 62 (6), 1367; English translation available at: *Japanese Yearbook of International Law* 52 (2009), 648–657.

65 Matsuda (n 52), 203–208; Ejima A., "A Gap between the Apparent and Hidden Attitudes of the Supreme Court of Japan towards Foreign Precedents," in Groppi T., Ponthoreau M.C. (eds.), *The Use of Foreign Precedents by Constitutional Judges* (Hart Publishing, 2013) 273–300; Yamamoto H., "Foreign Precedents in Constitutional Litigation in Japan," in Okada N., Sasada E., Hasebe Y. (eds), *Kempō no Kitei to Kempōron: Shisō, Seido, Un-yō* (*Takami Katsutoshi Sensei Koki Kinen*) [Fundamentals of the Constitution and Constitutional Theory: Thoughts, Institutions and Practice (Festschrift for Prof. Katsutoshi Takami for His 70th Anniversary)] (Shinzansha, 2015), 781–814.

66 *Nationality Act* case (n 64).

67 *Prohibition Period on Remarriage* case, Judgment of December 16, 2015, Supreme Court (Grand Bench), *Minshū* 69 (8), 2427; As to recent cases declaring unconstitutionality of family law in Japan including summary of this case in English, Tsuji Y., "Decisions That

2016 to reduce the prohibiting period for women's remarriage to 100 days. Then, in December 2022, the bill to eliminate the prohibition period of remarriage after divorce in the Civil Code was passed by the Diet and came into effect in April 2024.[68]

5 Conclusion

The relationship between international and domestic law has been analyzed in this chapter. As is shown in Section 2 of this chapter, the traditional theories, whether dualism or monism, tried to explain it on a conceptual level. Both theories include the inadequacy in explaining the practices of the contemporary international society. Under the influence of the legal positivism approach, the reality of international law can be understood by an eclectic position between dualism and monism such as the "coordination" or "coordinate theory."

In the domestic sphere, we can see more cases where international legal rules are applied and implemented. As is discussed in Section 4, as Japan adopts the "incorporation" system, under which incorporation of international law into domestic law comes into question from two aspects, status of international law in the domestic legal system and its applicability. In the Japanese legal system, international law has been understood to be placed higher than or equivalent to parliamentary legislations but lower than the Constitution, and incorporated international legal rules are, in principle, applicable in domestic courts. In practice, however, Japanese courts tend not to apply international law directly in their rulings, so it is necessary to consider how the obligations imposed by the incorporated international legal rules are implemented in the domestic sphere. Obligations based on international law can be implemented in the domestic sphere even when international legal rules are not directly applied. On this point, this chapter considered the classification of applicability of international into "direct applicability," "consistent interpretation of domestic law with international law" and "referring to international law as 'persuasive authority.'"

Declared Laws Unconstitutional and Their Impact on Japanese Families," *ILSA Journal of International and Comparative Law* 24–1 (2017), 139–180, esp. 168ff.

68 *See*, Ministry of Justice of Japan, Mimpō no Ichibu wo Kaisei Suru Hōritsu nitsuite [About the Act Partially Amending the Civil Code] (Japanese), January 13, 2023, https://www.moj.go.jp/MINJI/minji07_00315.html (accessed March 17, 2023).

CHAPTER 3

Japan's Practice on State Recognition

Masahiro Kato

1 Introduction[1]

While the recognition of State is a much-debated subject overall, discussion of the Japanese practice on State recognition remains a rarity. This might be due, among other reasons, to Japan only rarely disclosing its position on State recognition to the outside world, whether through Diet discussions or through ministerial statements at press conferences which detail specific instances of State recognition, such as those covered in this chapter. One valuable reference for understanding Japan's domestic procedures for and implementation of State recognition is the volume *State Recognition*[2] published as part of the series "*Kokusaihō Jirei Kenkyū*" [Case Studies in Japanese International Law] by the *Kokusaihō Jirei Kenkyūkai* [International Law Case Study Group] in cooperation with the Ministry of Foreign Affairs more than 30 years ago.

This chapter is based on a report the author compiled on the occasion of a conference while serving as an officer at the International Legal Affairs Division of the International Legal Affairs Bureau of the Ministry of Foreign Affairs in charge of State recognition from late 2011 until early 2015. The purpose of said report was to give an introduction to Japan's practice on State recognition. It partially supplemented and updated the contents of the above-mentioned publication (in particular Yozo Yokota's contribution "Domestic Procedures in Japan Concerning State Recogni-

1 This chapter is mainly an English translation of my article with some corrected figures and updated references, "Nihon no Kokka Syōnin Jitsumu [Japan's Practice on Recognition of States]" (Japanese) *Tokyo Review of International Law* 5 (2017) 141–154. It is a partially revised version of the author's report made at the 2015 Conference of the Japanese Society of International Law, whose main theme was "'Transformations' in the System of Sovereign States". It should be noted that the views expressed in this paper are the author's and do not necessarily reflect the Ministry of Foreign Affairs' views.

2 Kokusaihō Jirei Kenkyūkai (ed), *Kokka Shōnin* [Recognition of States] (Japanese) (Nihon Kokusai Mondai Kenkyujo, 1983).

 | DOI:10.1163/9789004548824_004

TABLE 3.1 Examples of states recently recognized by Japan

Country name	Independence declared	Recognized by Japan	Diplomatic relations established
Niue	–	15 May 2015	5 August 2015
South Sudan	9 July 2011	9 July 2011	9 July 2011
Cook Islands	–	25 March 2011	16 June 2011
Kosovo	17 February 2008	18 March 2008	25 February 2009
Montenegro	3 June 2006	16 June 2006	24 July 2006
Timor-Leste	20 May 2002	20 May 2002	20 May 2002
Federal Republic of Yugoslavia	27 April 1992	20 May 1997	20 May 1997
Bosnia and Herzegovina	–	23 January 1996	9 February 1996
Palau	1 October 1994	1 October 1994	2 November 1994
Macedonia	18 September 1991	21 December 1993	1 March 1994
Eritrea	24 May 1993	24 May 1993	1 September 1993
Andorra	14 March 1993	7 December 1993	20 October 1995
Czech Republic and Slovakia	1 January 1993	1 January 1993	29 January 1993 (Czech Republic) 3 February 1993 (Slovakia)
Georgia	9 April 1991	3 April 1992	3 August 1992
Croatia and Slovenia	25 June 1991	17 March 1992	5 March 1993 (Croatia) 12 October 1992 (Slovenia)
Ukraine[a]	24 August 1991	28 December 1991	26 January 1992
Estonia[b]	20 August 1991	6 September 1991	10 October 1991
Yemen	22 May 1990	23 May 1990	25 May 1990
Namibia	21 March 1990	21 March 1990	21 March 1990

a Apart from Ukraine, Japan also recognized Armenia, Azerbaijan, Belarus, Kazakhstan, Kirgizstan, Moldova, Tajikistan, Turkmenistan and Uzbekistan on December 28, 1991.

b Apart from Estonia, Japan recognized Latvia and Lithuania on September 6, 1991.

tion"[3]) by making use of the State recognitions Japan had granted since the publishing of the above-mentioned work, in particular since the 1990s, as a database. The objective of the present chapter remains the same.

2 Current Status of State Recognitions Granted by Japan

To illustrate the current status of State recognitions granted by Japan, a brief introduction to several examples from recent years should be helpful.

The table above lists states recognized by Japan since 1990.[4] The large number of cases in the 1990s (26 cases or approx. 82 percent of the total number of cases since 1990) is due to the collapse of the former Soviet Union and the Socialist Federal Republic of Yugoslavia, which led to the creation of a multitude of new states during this period.

Two additional points should be mentioned in this context: Japan did not recognize Russia as a state as it considers it the same state as the former Soviet Union with continuity.[5] Likewise, at the time of the unification of Germany in 1990, Japan did not recognize the unified Germany as a state, as the former West Germany (the Federal Republic of Germany) annexed the former East Germany (the German Democratic Republic) based on an agreement.

With the recognition of Niue as a state in May 2015, the number of states recognized by Japan has reached 195. Since the total number of UN member states is currently 193,[6] the number of states Japan recognizes exceeds the number of UN member states by two. This is because Japan recognizes Kosovo, the Cook Islands, Niue and the Vatican State, which are not UN members, while not recognizing North Korea, which is a UN member. Four (Kosovo, the Cook Islands, Niue and the Vatican State) minus two (North Korea and Japan) therefore equals a difference of two countries (see Figure 3.1 below).

---

3 Yokota Y., "Kokka Shōnin ni kansuru Wagakuni no Kokunai Tetsuzuki" (Japanese), in Kokusaihō Jirei Kenkyūkai (ed.), *Kokusaihō Jirei Kenkyū* (*Kokka Shōnin*) (Nihon Kokusai Mondai Kenkyujo, 1983) 175–185.

4 Compiled by the author based on information from the Ministry of Foreign Affairs' website and other sources. Dates impossible to confirm are marked by a dash (–).

5 Gaimu Iinkai Gijiroku [Minutes of the Foreign Affairs Committee] (Japanese), 2 (February 26, 1992) 4–5; Komatsu I., *Jissen Kokusaihō* [Praxis of International Law] (Japanese), 3rd ed. (Shinzansha, 2022) 307.

6 Homepage of the United Nations at https://www.un.org/en/about-us/growth-in-un-membership (accessed Jan. 1, 2023).

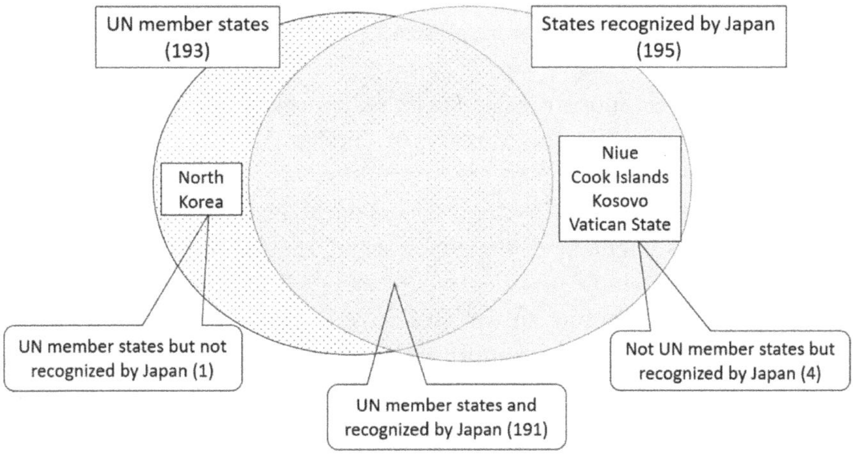

FIGURE 3.1 Relationship between UN Member States and states recognized by Japan (by author)

3 Review Process for State Recognition

State recognition falls under the jurisdiction of the Ministry of Foreign Affairs, and is defined in the Act for Establishment of the Ministry of Foreign Affairs based on the National Government Organization Act.

Article 4 of the Act for Establishment of the Ministry of Foreign Affairs, defining the Ministry of Foreign Affairs' scope of jurisdiction, stipulates in item 2, as one of the domains that the Ministry is responsible for, the handling of "negotiations and cooperation with foreign governments on behalf of the Government of Japan and other matters concerning the management of political affairs related to foreign countries".[7] This provision clarifies that the Ministry is charged with handling bilateral relations on behalf of the Japanese government through negotiations and cooperation with foreign governments, and it is understood that the granting of State recognitions is

7 Act for Establishment of the Ministry of Foreign Affairs [Gaimushō Settchihō] (Japanese), Act No. 94 of 1999 (excerpt):

Article 4

The Ministry of Foreign Affairs […] shall be responsible for the following matters:

4.1. […]

4.2. Negotiations and cooperation with foreign governments on behalf of the Government of Japan and other matters concerning the management of political affairs related to foreign countries (This shall mean a country or region outside the territory of Japan. The same shall apply hereinafter.) […].

(Translation by the author)

included as part of the "management of political affairs related to foreign countries".[8]

When Japan intends to recognize an entity as a State, a draft decision is first formulated within the Ministry of Foreign Affairs to request among others a Cabinet decision on the recognition of said entity as a state by Japan.[9] The draft is issued by the Division of the regional Bureau within the Ministry that is in charge of the region where the country to be recognized is located. For example, the Central and South Eastern Europe Division of the European Affairs Bureau was in charge for the recognition of Kosovo, the First Africa Division of the African Affairs Department was in charge for South Sudan, and the Oceania Division of the Asian and Oceanian Affairs Bureau for Niue and the Cook Islands. After review by the International Legal Affairs Bureau and other relevant departments within the Ministry, the draft is submitted for final approval to the Foreign Minister.[10]

At this point, a brief explanation of the terminology used here regarding the organization of the Ministry of Foreign Affairs might be helpful. Simply put, there are two main types of departments within the Ministry: regional Bureaus in charge of managing certain regions, and functional Bureaus responsible for specific matters. While regional Bureaus such as the Asian and Oceanian Affairs Bureau, the Latin American and Caribbean Affairs Bureau or the North American Affairs Bureau are in charge of Japan's overall foreign policy with regard to their respective region, functional Bureaus such as the International Legal Affairs Bureau, the Consular Affairs Bureau or the Economic Affairs Bureau oversee specific matters rather than regions. The European Affairs Bureau comprises the Central and South Eastern Europe Division mentioned above, as well as the Russian Division and the Western Europe Division, among others.[11]

Circling back to the review process for State recognition, it must be noted that the regional Bureau issuing the draft decision for State recognition focuses on the relationship between Japan and the region in question. However, depending on the specifics of the case, the impact of Japan granting State recognition to an entity may not be limited solely to the relationship between Japan and the region in question alone. In fact, such cases are

8 The same applies to the recognition of governments.

9 *See also* "6. Timing of State Recognition".

10 Yokota (n 3), 177.

11 For further information on the organization of the Ministry of Foreign Affairs, see its website at https://www.mofa.go.jp/about/hq/org.html (accessed Jan. 1, 2023).

rather the exception nowadays. The Foreign Policy Bureau is therefore also involved in the approval process in order to assess the impact of the proposed State recognition from the viewpoint of Japan's overall foreign policy, beyond the limits of the mere regional frameworks. Thus, the regional Bureau, which is in charge of the relationship between Japan and the region where the entity to be recognized is located; the International Legal Affairs Bureau, which examines State recognition under international law; and the Foreign Policy Bureau, which is responsible for Japan's overall foreign policy, are all included in the review process for State recognition from the perspective of their respective jurisdictions.

4 Criteria for State Recognition

This section shall examine specific criteria for State recognition. First of all, the Government of Japan has clarified in its answer to a written inquiry submitted by a member of Parliament that in order to be granted State recognition, an entity must meet the required conditions of Statehood under general international law, *i.e.* the entity must have established effective political authority within a defined territory to govern the population of that territory. In addition to these conditions, Japan also takes into consideration whether the entity is willing and able to comply with international law.[12] It can therefore be said that Japan's decision on State recognition is based on the following two criteria: "whether or not the entity meets the conditions of Statehood" and "whether or not the entity has the will and ability to comply with international law".[13]

When Japan considers granting State recognition, it must therefore determine whether an entity meets these criteria by examining the facts of each individual case. Regarding the second criterion, i.e., "whether or not the entity has the will and ability to comply with international law," Japan bases its decision-making process on the following considerations: the will to comply with international law is often expressed in the constitutional

12 Diet Inquiry 164/322 (June 16, 2006).

13 *See* for example *Gaimu Iinkai Gijiroku* (Japanese), 9 (April 16, 1997) 8. The former is sometimes referred to as the "objective requirement" of State recognition, while the latter is called the "subjective requirement." *See also* Sugihara T. et al., *Gendai Kokusaihō Kōza* [Lectures on Modern International Law] (Japanese), 5th ed. (Yuhikaku, 2012) 41–42.

provisions or proclamation of independence of the entity declaring secession or independence.[14] Thus, in many cases, the existence of such a will is determined in light of the contents of these documents. In other cases, the entity requested to be recognized as a state by Japan via letter, and expressed above-mentioned will in said letter.

In order to determine whether an entity seeking recognition has "the ability to comply with international law", Japan examines for example if an agreement exists between the "parent country" of an entity concerning the latter's secession from said "parent country". Furthermore, if an international agreement exists between the entity and another country that has already recognized the entity as a state prior to recognition by Japan, it is likewise taken into consideration whether the terms of this agreement have been fulfilled.

Thus, after comprehensive examination of the relevant circumstances in each individual case, Japan determines whether the entity seeking recognition has the will and ability to comply with international law.

5 Policy Factors of State Recognition

As described earlier, when considering whether to grant an entity State recognition, Japan first examines if said entity meets the criteria for State recognition. However, as the recognition of state is a unilateral act of the party granting recognition, there is no legal duty to do so if the criteria are fulfilled.[15] The next part of this chapter shall therefore review a number of past cases to identify which other factors apart from the criteria for State recognition Japan has considered in its practice.

Regarding Niue, the most recent case of State recognition by the government of Japan, the Foreign Minister at that time stated the following in a press conference:

> Niue is a state with a population of around 1,500 people situated 2,400km northeast of New Zealand, and so far 12 countries have given it state recognition. It is also a member of 34 international organizations.

---

14 Article 98, paragraph 2 of the Constitution of Japan (1946) stipulates that "[t]he treaties concluded by Japan and established laws of nations shall be faithfully observed." This can be considered an indication of Japan's will to comply with international law."

15 *See* for example *Gaimu Iinkai Gijiroku* (Japanese), 3 (October 2, 1991) 22.

> The Government of Japan has decided to give it state recognition, with a view to cooperation in the international arena in the future.[16]

Thus in the case of Niue, in addition to meeting the criteria for State recognition, "cooperation in the international arena in the future" was likewise taken into consideration.

In the context of granting State recognition to Palestine, the Foreign Minister stated the following during the debate in the Diet:

> [...] As to whether or not Japan recognizes Palestine as a state, it is of course important to consider the perspective of international law. However, we must also consider whether [our recognition of Palestine] would contribute to advancing the peace process. We will examine these points comprehensively, and consider Japan's response from the perspective of advancing the peace process and direct negotiations.[17]
>
> Translation by the author

> [...] We have been working from the standpoint that, *in addition* to perspectives on international law, it is equally important to consider whether [State recognition] will contribute to advancing the peace process.[18]
>
> Translation and emphasis by the author

As evidenced by the Minister's answer, the question of whether recognition of Palestine as a State by Japan would "contribute to advancing the peace process" between Israel and Palestine is examined "*in addition* to perspectives on international law" (emphasis added).[19]

---

16 Press Conference by Foreign Minister Fumio Kishida (May 15, 2015), at https://www.mofa.go.jp/press/kaiken/kaiken4e_000166.html (accessed Jan. 1, 2023); *Gaimu Iinkai Gijiroku* (Japanese), 3 (March 11, 2016) 11.

17 *Gaimu Iinkai Gijiroku* (Japanese), 6 (April 17, 2015) 18. *See also Gaimu Iinkai Gijiroku* (Japanese), 14 (July 27, 2011) 29.

18 *Ibid.* (emphasis added by author).

19 In response to the recent Israeli-Palestinian situation, Foreign Minister Kamikawa stated the following in response to a question from a reporter during a press conference on the recognition of Palestine as a State by Japan: "Japan voted in favor of the draft Security Council resolution on full UN membership for Palestine as a comprehensive decision, recognizing that Palestine meets the criteria for admission to the UN membership, while also taking into account the perspective of promoting the establishment of a Palestinian state through peaceful negotiations for the realization of peace in the Middle East. Nevertheless, our vote in favor of the Security Council

Whenever Japan granted an entity State recognition in the past, including the case of Niue mentioned above, the following factors were considered depending on the specific circumstances of each case:

- Contribution to resolution of conflicts and regional stability
- Developments in neighboring countries in the affected region (including the "parent country" in the case of secession[20]) and in the international community
- Acceptance of the entity in question in international organizations
- Potential for cooperation and mutual support at international level

Furthermore, in some past cases "the importance of trade and economic relations with Japan" was likewise taken into consideration.[21]

It should be noted that these factors are examined separately from the criteria for State recognition itself, as evidenced by the wording "in addition to international law considerations" in the Minister's answer on Palestine

---

resolution on Palestine's admission to UN membership and recognition of Palestine as a state are two separate issues, and the position of Japan has not changed. Japan will continue to support a 'two-state solution' and understand the wish of the Palestinians to establish an independent state, and supports Palestine's efforts toward that." (Press Conference by Foreign Minister Yoko Kamikawa (May 10, 2024), at: https://www.mofa.go.jp/press/kaiken/kaikenwe_000001_00066.html (accessed July 1, 2024).

20 The recognition of an entity that seceded and declared independence against the will of the 'parent country' may negatively impact the relationship between Japan and said country, and it is therefore paramount to minimize such adverse effects. For example, at the time of Kosovo declaring independence, its 'parent country' Serbia strongly opposed Kosovo's independence, and Japan was concerned recognizing Kosovo as a State would worsen bilateral relations with Serbia. Japan therefore issued a statement by the Foreign Minister upon extending State recognition to Kosovo, emphasizing that Japan had traditionally enjoyed friendly relations with Serbia, that it was not Japan's intention to have these friendly relations with Serbia disrupted by the recognition of the Republic of Kosovo, and that it hoped friendly relations with Serbia would continue to be maintained. *See* Statement by the Foreign Minister, "Kosobo Kyōwakoku no Shonin ni tsuite [About the Recognition of the Republic of Kosovo]" (Japanese) (March 18, 2008), http://www.mofa.go.jp/mofaj/press/danwa/20/dkm_0318.html (accessed Jan. 1, 2023).

Serbia reacted by temporarily recalling the Serbian ambassador to Japan to Serbia in protest (a decision revoked in October of the same year), as it had done with the ambassadors of other countries which had recognized Kosovo as a State. Japan, however, made the conscious decision not to reciprocate by recalling its ambassador to Serbia to Japan. These two measures are considered as government's response aimed at limiting the negative impact of Japan's recognition of Kosovo on bilateral relations with Serbia.

21 Yokota (n 3), 182–183.

mentioned earlier. This means that recognition based on an entity meeting these factors cannot be accepted as premature recognition if the conditions for State recognition itself are not met.

International law does not require States to take above-mentioned factors into account when considering State recognition, and thus recognition becomes a policy decision of each State. In 1991, for instance, the then EC agreed on "Guidelines on the Recognition of New States in Eastern Europe and in the Former Soviet Union," establishing uniform instructions on which aspects to consider when recognizing states. However, the factors listed above are classified inductively based on previous cases in which Japan had granted State recognition, and there is no obligation to examine them when considering recognition.[22] In other words, unlike the EC, Japan does not have guidelines on factors to be considered when recognizing States.[23]

6 Timing of State Recognition

When an entity secedes or attains independence in a peaceful manner, Japan usually recognizes it as a State in a relatively swift manner. This is likely due to the consideration that in the event of peaceful secession, maintaining said State as unrecognized (*i.e.* having no diplomatic relations with

22 For the text of the guidelines, *see European Journal of International Law* 4 (1993) 72. It may be argued that Japan had established guidelines similar to those of the EC in relation to State recognition for countries created by the collapse of the former Soviet Union (Talmon S. "The Constitutive Versus the Declaratory Theory of Recognition: Tertium Non Datur?" *British Yearbook of International Law* 75–1 (2004) 109, n 46). However, this example of Japanese practice refers, strictly speaking, to the context of establishing diplomatic relations rather than recognizing States. As will be discussed later (*see* "6. Timing of State recognition"), while granting of State recognition and establishment of diplomatic relations often occur in close proximity, they are indeed different. In this sense, it would not be accurate to say that "Japan also prepared such guidelines (author's note: guidelines for recognition declared by the EC in 1991) for recognition" (*see* Komatsu (n 5), 64–65).

23 "[...] The criteria of international law having been met [by an entity] does not mean that each country is obligated to grant recognition. [The decision] is left to the judgment of each individual country [...]. [...] to answer the question, not in terms of international law, but in terms of what kind of political standards Japan is applying, I can only say that a decision is made on a case-by-case basis" (translation by the author), *Gaimu Iinkai Gijiroku* (Japanese), 15 (May 21, 1997) 10, Answer by Foreign Minister Ikeda.

Japan[24]) for a needless long period would be undesirable for Japan. State recognition is a unilateral act of the party according recognition and therefore does not equal the establishment of diplomatic relations,[25] which is a mutual act based on mutual consent by both parties. However, Japan usually opens diplomatic relations with a country at the same time as recognizing its Statehood or within a few months thereafter,[26] and only in very few cases no diplomatic relations have been established despite recognition for a prolonged period of time.

As shown in the table above, Japan recognized South Sudan, Timor-Leste, Palau, Eritrea, the Czech Republic, Slovakia and Namibia on the very day these declared independence; Montenegro and Bosnia and Herzegovina within one month after their declaration of independence; and Kosovo and Yemen about one month after their declaration of independence. When the Japanese government recognizes a state, the Cabinet is to make a decision on the recognition of said state at a Cabinet meeting approximately one week to ten days before the state's date of independence. The decision follows a thorough consideration of the time period leading to the date of independence, as well as diplomatic deliberations such as the impact of Japan's recognition of said state on other states.[27]

In some cases, however, it took Japan longer to recognize a state after it had declared independence. The decision to grant State recognition is usually based on relevant information sent to the Ministry of Foreign Affairs in Tokyo sporadically by Japanese embassies or consulates-general in the region where the entity in question is located. Therefore, if no such outpost existed in the area in question, a mission consisting of officials from nearby Japanese diplomatic missions had to be dispatched in order to gather information relevant to understanding the situation on site, which took a considerable amount of time.

---

24 On the contrary, the absence of diplomatic relations with a state does not necessarily mean it is not recognized as a state (*see* list on page 37).

25 Komatsu (n 5), 64–65 and 313.

26 *See* list on page 37. In some cases, no embassies are established due to personnel or budgetary reasons, among others. However, this does not necessarily mean an absence of diplomatic relations between Japan and the country in question. In some cases, Japanese embassies in neighboring countries extend their jurisdiction to said country, such as for instance the Embassy of Japan in Austria, which is likewise responsible for Kosovo (*see* Art. 5 of the Vienna Convention on Diplomatic Relations).

27 For this purpose, the regional Bureau prepares in advance a draft decision stating that, among others, a Cabinet resolution on State recognition is to be sought and circulates it within the Ministry for approval (*see* "3. Review process for State recognition").

In other cases, armed conflicts were continuing in the region that had declared independence and the situation remained unstable. As a result, further assessment was necessary.

In cases where an entity gained independence peacefully through a referendum, Japan recognized the newly independent country after reviewing the results of relevant meetings held immediately after said entity attained independence by countries which had played a leading role in organizing the independence referendum, in order to assess said countries' reaction. As a result, Japan recognized the entity as a state shortly after the date of their declaration of independence.

In one case, however, the seceding entity's "parent country" was in turmoil resulting from emotional backlash against countries that had recognized the entity as a state. Japan therefore decided to wait before granting recognition to the entity in question until after the emotional upheaval among citizens opposing the secession in the "parent country" and the situation in said country in general had calmed down to some extent.

7 Types of State Recognition

It is well known that recognition of States can be granted either explicitly or implicitly. In case of explicit recognition, Japan unambiguously states that it "recognizes" an entity as a state. One possible form of expressing this intent is by a letter issued by the Foreign Minister or the Prime Minister, which commonly includes a phrase in the character of "I have the honor to inform Your Excellency that the Government of Japan recognizes XXX as a state as of DD/MM/YY." Furthermore, in cases of explicit State recognition, a public notice by the Ministry of Foreign Affairs is published in the Official Gazette approximately one week to ten days after the date of the recognition, stating that the government of Japan has recognized the entity in question as a state and the date of said recognition.[28]

In contrast, implied recognition refers to cases in which for certain reasons, it is not desirable for a recognizing state to express its recognition of an entity's Statehood to the outside world, for example out of consideration for the "parent state" the entity seceded from. In such cases, the recognizing state does not use the term "recognition", however tacitly recognizes the

28 For recent examples, *see Kanpō* (Japanese) 4796 (March 27, 2008) 4, for Kosovo; *Kanpō* (Japanese) 5527 (April 1, 2011) 6, for the Cook Islands; *Kanpō* (Japanese) 5601 (21 July 2011) 3, for South Sudan; and *Kanpō* (Japanese) 6538 (May 25, 2015) 3, for Niue.

entity by an act that assumes State recognition, for example the establishing of diplomatic relations. Japan has granted implied recognition in the past in cases where the circumstances of independence were complicated in relation to the "parent state" or where the country in question had a special background relating to Japan due to gaining independence as a result of World War II.[29]

More than 30 years ago, the book "Case Studies in Japanese International Law" referred to at the beginning of this chapter stated that at the time of publication, "with the end-of-war process of implied recognition of divided states almost complete, implied recognition according to Japanese practice seemed to have almost reached the end of its historical role".[30] In fact, Japan has granted explicit State recognition in the majority of cases ever since.[31]

8 Conclusion

In the absence of a central authority in the international community in charge of recognizing entities as states in a competent manner, the decision on act of recognition is left to the discretion of each existing state individually. In this regard, the current situation in which "transformations" in the system of sovereign states are discussed, remains the same as that of the end of the 18th century, when the United States of America gained independence from Great Britain and the question of State recognition first arose. It therefore remains vital to examine the national practice in each country individually when discussing State recognition.

Based on this understanding, the present chapter, as mentioned at its outset, aimed to partially fill the information gap on Japan's practice on State recognition more than 30 years after the publication of the volume "State Recognition" in the "Case Studies in Japanese International Law" series by discussing, albeit briefly, cases of state recognition since 1990. The

---

29 Yokota (n 3), 184–185.

30 Yokokawa S., "Mokuji no Kokka Shōnin to Nihon no Kokka Jikkō" (Japanese), in *Kokusaihō Jirei Kenkyūkai* (ed.), *Kokusaihō Jirei Kenkyū* (*Kokka Shōnin*) (Nihon Kokusai Mondai Kenkyujo, 1983) 201 (Translation by the author).

31 While due to its nature, implied State recognition is rarely made public as such, past cases of implied recognition that were discussed in the Diet include among others the Socialist Republic of Vietnam (*see Gaimu Iinkai Gijiroku* (Japanese) 1 (July 9, 1976) 11), the German Democratic Republic (East Germany) (*see Gaimu Iinkai Gijiroku* (Japanese) 18 (May 30, 1973) 2) and the Republic of Korea (*see* Komatsu (n 5), 75–77).

chapter presented the current status of State recognitions granted by Japan, and covered the country's practice relating to the review process, criteria, policy factors, timing as well as types of State recognition.

While the chapter is based on a conference report compiled in 2015, its contents should nevertheless still be relevant given its nature as an introduction to past cases of State recognition by Japan, and the absence of new cases since then.

CHAPTER 4

Japan's Practice of Jurisdiction and Immunity

Masatoshi Takeuchi

1 Introduction

As one of the early incidents of the global COVID pandemic, the cruise ship *MS Diamond Princess* attracted a considerable amount of attention. It was substantially the first case of COVID-19 clusters and quarantine measures in the Japanese media. Though the attention certainly included a political and social dimension, the legal (and international legal) dimension had to be emphasized to explain why certain measures could (not) be taken by the Japanese government while the passengers and crew (a vast amount were Japanese) suffered from poor conditions. In this case, the flag State (and the nationality of the owner) of *MS Diamond Princess* was the UK, and it was managed by a US company. The crew and passengers were from various nations. The vessel entered the Yokohama port on 3 February, and the Japan Ministry of Health, Labour and Welfare (informed of a COVID positive passenger found in Hong Kong) boarded for quarantine and other measures on 5 February. Though the measures were largely led by the Japanese side, some confusion was found in which state (Japan or the UK) should be responsible. The rights of port-coastal states (in this case, Japan) can be traced to sovereignty over internal waters. However, the obligations of the port-coastal state (and their relations to the flag State) during pandemics were unclear in this case, which caused confusion to the overall operation. As found in this case, not every case is obvious as to which state's responsibility a particular issue may fall.[1] As asserted by several authors, an

1 "Michi no Kansenshō Kōkai Imamo (Unknown Infectious Diseases, Unsolved Regrets)" *Nikkei* (Tokyo, February 3, 2021) (late ed.). For more legal analysis on this incident, *see also* Seta M., "Kansenshō -hasseiji-niokeru-gaikokuseki-Cruise-sen-nitaisuru-nauiseuien-gannkoku-no-taiō [Coastal State Responses against Foreign Cruise Vessels in Internal Waters during the Pandemic: Towards a New System]" (Japanese), *Kokusaiho Gaiko Zassi* [The Journal of International Law and Diplomacy] 120 (2021) 120–130, Kanehara A., "'Pandemic-*Kokusaihō*' niokeru-Kaiyohō: Diamond Princess-gō nikakaru Kikōchisochi ["'Pandemic International Law' and the Law of the Sea: The Diamond Princess and Port State Measures]" (Japanese), *Kokusaimondai* [International Affairs] 699 (2021) 5–16; Schultz S., "The Buffet Doesn't Stop until COVID-19 Walks In: How the Hands-Off Approach of Flag

 | DOI:10.1163/9789004548824_005

important function of international law has been to coordinate jurisdiction of states to avoid conflicts.[2] For example, the United Nations Convention on the Law of the Sea (UNCLOS) provides elaborate categories that decide the rights and obligations of the coastal state and the flag state of a vessel. This issue may be traced back to concepts like territorial sovereignty and sovereign equality.

This chapter considers a major representation of sovereignty: state jurisdiction. It first provides an overview of the basic concept and the approaches that Japanese law has adopted. Taking Japanese criminal law as an example, the reader shall discover various principles such as territoriality, nationality, protective jurisdiction, and universal jurisdiction in the Japanese legal system. Then, the issue of immunity shall be discussed as an exception to state jurisdiction. As other states, Japan has taken a long journey from absolute immunity to a more restrictive approach. Focusing on state immunity, it shall go over famous cases such as the *Pakistan Loan Claim* case to describe how the Japanese adapted to the changing environment of the international society and to the establishment of the Act on the Civil Jurisdiction of Japan with respect to a Foreign State. Finally, this chapter shall consider the recent conflict between Japan and South Korea regarding the 2021 "comfort women" case by the Seoul Central District Court. By making comparisons with international cases such as the *Jurisdictional Immunities of the State* (*Germany v. Italy: Greece intervening*) in the International Court of Justice, it shall see how each state sought to examine the limits of state jurisdiction.

2 Foundations and Scope of State Jurisdiction

In line with any other textbook of international law, state jurisdiction in Japanese textbooks refers to "the competence of a State to make, apply and enforce law on people, property, and acts. It is based upon sovereignty, equal right, and nonintervention obligations."[3] Types of this competence are

States Exposed Legal Nightmares Onboard Cruise Ships during a Global Pandemic and Why Changes Must Be Made," *George Mason International Law Journal*, 13 (2022) 132–174.

2 Yamamoto S., *Kokusaihō* [International Law] (Japanese) (Yuhikaku, 1995) 231.

3 Iwasawa Y., *Kokusaihō* [International Law] (Japanese), 2nd ed. (University of Tokyo Press, 2023) 170.

often referred to as legislative (prescriptive) jurisdiction, juridical jurisdiction, and executive jurisdiction, coinciding with the three main branches of a modern government.

As the modern notion of a sovereign state is based upon a "defined territory[4]," which is the extent to state jurisdiction may reach. The limit of state jurisdiction has been the limit of its territory. However, in some instances, the reach of a state may constitute what is referred to as extra-territorial jurisdiction, where a state may seek to exercise legislative jurisdiction to events taking place on foreign soil and/or committed by foreign nationals in the absence of any prohibition by international law. As the Permanent Court of International Justice stated in the famous *SS Lotus* case (*France v Turkey*), "Far from laying down a general prohibition to the effect that States may not extend the application of their laws and the jurisdiction of their courts to persons, property and acts outside their territory, it leaves them in this respect a wide measure of discretion which is only limited in certain cases by prohibitive rules [...] .[5]" The so-called approach of "Lotus rule", with its emphasis on legislative (and not enforcement) jurisdiction can be seen in articles of serious crimes such as insurrection, counterfeiting of currency or acts of terrorism under Japanese Law.[6] Regarding crimes committed outside its territory governed by treaties, Japan has traditionally established or amended domestic law each time it entered such a treaty.[7] This was primarily to maintain integrity with the principle of *nulla poena sine lege* (no punishment without law). Such ado to comply with treaties changed in 1987 by the insertion of Article 4.2, which states "this Code also applies to anyone who commits those crimes outside the territory of Japan prescribed under Part II which are governed by a treaty even if committed outside the

4 Art. 1, Montevideo Convention on the Rights and Duties of States, *signed on* Dec. 26, 1933, *entered into force on* Dec. 26, 1934, 165 LNTS 19.

5 *Lotus* Judgment No 9, PCIJ Series *A* No. 10 19.

6 For example, Carlos Ghosn (former-Nissan CEO) was investigated and apprehended for charges of violating the Financial Instruments and Exchange Act (Act No. 25 of 1948) but fled to Lebanon in 2019. Without the consent or cooperation (or any criminal extradition treaty) of Lebanon's government, the criminal court proceedings cannot advance. In other words, though Japan is asserting juridical jurisdiction, it lacks the enforcement jurisdiction to attain Mr. Ghosn for proceedings. *See* JSIL Expert Comment of Prof. Megumi Ochi "The Issue of Mr. Carlos Ghosn's Flight" (Japanese) No. 2023-2, https://jsil.jp/wp-content/uploads/2023/04/expert2023-2.pdf (accessed August 18, 2023).

7 One example of such practice is the 1970 Hague Hijacking Convention and the Act on Punishment of Unlawful Seizure of Aircraft. As asserted in Komatsu, I., *Jissen Kokusaihō* [Praxis of International Law] (Japanese), 3rd ed. (Shinzansha, 2022) 132.

TABLE 4.1 Different principles in the Japanese Penal Code

Principles	Basic idea	Examples	Examples of statutes within Japanese Penal Code
Territoriality principle	Any crime committed within Japanese territory	Ordinary crimes	Art. 1.1 Article 1.1 This Code applies to anyone who commits a crime within the territory of Japan.
Active personality principle	Specific crimes committed by a Japanese national	Arson, forcible sexual intercourse, homicide, robbery	Art. 3 Article 3 This Code applies to any Japanese national who commits one of the following crimes outside the territory of Japan.
Passive personality principle	Specific crimes when a Japanese national is the victum	Forcible sexual intercourse, homicide, kidnapping, robbery	Former Art. 3 (retracted) and new Art. 3.2 Article 3.2 This Code applies to any non-Japanese national who commits one of the following crimes against a Japanese national outside the territory of Japan.
Protective principle	Specific, serious crimes against the state which may be committed by any national at any region	Insurrection, instigation of foreign aggression, counterfeiting of currency	Art. 2
Universal jurisdiction	Specific, serious crimes against the international community which may not have relation to Japan	Piracy, unlawful seizure of aircraft, acts of terror	Law on Punishment of and Measures against Acts of Piracy, etc.

territory of Japan".[8] This provision also forms a foundation to comply with treaties concerning international terrorism. In civil cases, the *Braun Tube Cartel case* (Supreme Court), claimed an extra-territorial jurisdiction that "though the cartel may be agreed out of state, if it infringes the free competitive economic order" the Japanese Anti-Monopoly act should be applied.[9] Such an approach may resemble the 'effects' doctrine first developed in the context of US antitrust law.[10]

Thus, territoriality and nationality (with some variants) are the two primary pillars to determine the link between the State and the act in question for jurisdiction to be exercised. With due respect to sovereign equality, states seek other bases which offer different logic for the need for extra-territorial jurisdiction as found in Table 4.1. Table 4.1 takes Japanese criminal law as an example found in the Japanese approach to jurisdiction.[11]

2.1 *Territoriality Principle*

As the case with other States, Japanese criminal law takes the territoriality principle as the base to cover all ordinary crimes committed "within the territory of Japan" (Art. 1.1). Because a state is basically a territorial based entity, most would agree that states "have jurisdiction over the people, property and acts within its own territory."[12] Thus, even in cases of transnational crimes, where the offence was allegedly initiated in Japan (subjective territoriality principle) or completed in Japan (objective territoriality principle),

8 An exception to this would be treaties where contracting States have the discretion to exercise jurisdiction, as in the case of piracy. Under the United Nations Convention on the Law of the Sea Art. 105, states "may seize a pirate ship or aircraft, or a ship or aircraft taken by piracy and under the control of pirates, and arrest the persons and seize the property on board. The courts of the State which carried out the seizure may decide upon the penalties to be imposed, and may also determine the action to be taken with regard to the ships, aircraft or property, subject to the rights of third parties acting in good faith." To comply with this procedure, Japan enacted the Law on Punishment of and Measures against Acts of Piracy (Act No. 55 of 2009).

9 CRT *Cartel case*, Judgment of December 12, 2017, Supreme Court Third Petty Bench, Case No. 233(Gyo-Hi) of 2017, *Saikou Saibansho Minji Hanreishu* [Supreme Court Reports (civil cases)] 71(10) 1958.

10 Japan, along with some other European states, was initially opposed to this approach, which focuses on the economic effect as the basis of jurisdiction. However, over the years, the Japanese government (Japan Fair Trade Commission) has hinted at a trend toward this approach, which can be found in amicus briefs such as in that of the *Motorola Mobility LLC v. AU Optronics case*. *Motorola Mobility LLC v. AU Optronics Corp.* et al., Judgment of March 27, 2014, 7th Cir., 746 F.3d 842.

11 *See also* Chapter 12.

12 Iwasawa (n 3) 171.

Japan may exercise its jurisdiction. For example, two unidentified vessels (suspected to be used for espionage by North Korea) were in Japanese territorial waters near the Noto Peninsula on 23 March 1999.[13] When given orders to stop by the Coast Guard, the vessels fled, which led to a pursuit by the Coast Guard and the Japan Maritime Self Defense Force. This was the first time in post-war Japan to engage in seaborne policing action (*Kaijo Keibi Kodo*) under the Self-Defense Act Article 82. In this incident, Japan legitimized its pursuit by asserting violation of Law on Territorial Sea and Contiguous Zone and the subjective territorial jurisdictions.[14]

Also, note Article 1.2 states that the same shall apply to crimes committed "on board a Japanese vessel or aircraft outside the territory of Japan." The idea of this article is under another principle; known as the flag State principle. The Diamond Princess incident was a case where port State jurisdiction was apparently in conflict with flag State jurisdiction.

2.2 *Active Personality Principle*

Nationality is another major principle which determines the link between a State and an act taken outside its territory. The main feature of this principle can be found in "recognizing states have jurisdiction over the acts and property of their nationals outside the territory of Japan."[15] Again, in the case of criminal law, there can be two variations of the this principle where the national of a given state is the perpetrator (active nationality (or personality) principle) or the victim (passive nationality (or personality) principle). Both, under Japanese law, consider a situation where a Japanese national commits a crime outside the territory.[16] The active nationality principle (or just nationality principle) has been standard practice for States to set provisions for the crimes of nationals committed abroad. Article 3 of the Japanese Penal Code makes clear it "applies to any Japanese national who commits one of the following crimes outside the territory of Japan"; listing crimes as arson (Arts. 108 and 109(1)), damage to inhabited buildings by flood (Art. 119), crimes related to counterfeiting documents (Arts. 159 through 161), counterfeiting or unauthorized use of private seals (Art. 167),

13 Japan Coast Guard, *Kaijō Hōan Hakusho* [Japanese Coast Guard White Paper] (Japanese) (1999), https://www.kaiho.mlit.go.jp/info/books/h11haku/1-1.htm (accessed April 30, 2023).

14 *Ibid.*

15 Iwasawa (n 3) 174.

16 Under the Penal Code, such perpetrators are designated as a *kokugai-han* (criminals outside Japan) in Art. 2 as opposed to *kokunai-han* (criminals within Japan) in Art. 1.

forceful sexual intercourse (Arts. 176 through 181), active bribery (Art. 198), homicide (Art. 199) and attempted homicide, injury and injury causing death (Arts. 204, 205), crimes related to abortion (Arts. 214 through 216), abandonment (Arts. 218, 219), unlawful capture and confinement (Art. 220, 221), kidnapping (Arts. 224 through 228), defamation (Art. 230), theft, robbery and other related crimes (Arts. 231 through 236, Arts. 238 through 240, paragraphs (1) and (3) of Art. 241, Art. 243), crimes related to fraud (Art. 246), embezzlement in the pursuit of social activities (Art. 253), and acceptance of stolen property (Art. 256(2)).

It should be noted that the phrase "outside the territory of Japan" includes not only foreign territory, but vessels or aircraft on/above the high seas. Another variant of the personality principle assumes a case where the national is the victim of a crime on foreign soil.

2.3 *The (Re)Installment of Article 3.2 and Passive Personality Principle*

Pre-war Japanese Penal Code Article 3.2 stated that the law shall apply to "Foreigners who commit crimes against Imperial subjects outside the Imperial territory." This statute was retracted in the reforms of 1947, with due respect to the practice of other states and concern for infringement of other state's sovereignty.[17] However, a similar sub article was inserted in 2003 after the 2002 *Tanker Tajima* incident.

2.3.1 The Tanker *Tajima* Incident

The *Tajima* was a tanker ship enlisted in Panama, with a Japanese owner, operated by a Japanese Company, and with a Japanese and Filipino crew. A Japanese crewman was killed by two Filipino crewmen while on high sea. The captain of the vessel arrested the two offenders and contacted the Japanese Coast Guard for help. The Japanese Coast Guard did conduct an investigation but did not arrest the offenders due to the concern that Japan lacked provisions for crimes committed on a foreign vessel on the high seas, and the perpetrators were not Japanese. The Japanese government took action to coordinate with Panama (the flag State). This limitation as a coastal

17 In a recent event, Japan took issue with an alleged existence of covert Chinese facilities within Japan. These protests were based upon claims by a Spanish NGO report that "Tokyo is unwittingly hosting a so-called Chinese overseas police station, believed to monitor and threaten Chinese citizens abroad." If true, this would be an exercise of extra-territorial application of enforcement jurisdiction, which the Foreign Minister Hayashi describes as "infringement upon Japan's sovereignty", https://www.mofa.go.jp/mofaj/press/kaiken/kaiken24_000150.html#topic6 (accessed June 10, 2025).

State stirred controversy to reinstate the passive personality principle for certain crimes.

> Article 3.2 (Crimes Committed by Non-Japanese Nationals outside Japan)
>
> This Code applies to any non-Japanese national who commits one of the following crimes against a Japanese national outside the territory of Japan:

Toshiaki Hiwatari (then Director of Criminal Affairs Bureau, Ministry of Justice) emphasized the necessity of such provision in the Penal Code as follows in the House of Councilors.

> However, as of now, not all States have similar legal systems. And because the State where the crime has been committed may not necessarily exercise proper punitive authority, it may not be valid from the perspective of protection of our nationals to not be able to apply Japanese criminal law in cases where the life and body of Japanese nationals outside the territory of Japan may be seriously infringed by a crime. We sought urgently to prepare statues for crimes committed outside Japanese territory when Japanese nationals are victims of serious crimes against their life and body such as homicide. [...] In essence, internationalism, international cooperation is significant. However, such damages do exist, and we thought it necessary to have a statute as a foundation to rectify situations where no state may be able to prosecute.[18]

Though the article may seem to cause controversy in coordinating with another state's jurisdiction, a recent treatise edited by members of the Japanese Ministry of Foreign Affairs comments the operation of Article 3.2 will seek to be "principally in a careful manner."[19]

2.4 *Protective Principle*

The protective principle enables extra-territorial jurisdiction to acts committed outside Japan by non-nationals. Such a principle is legitimized by the

18 Statement by Toshiaki Hiwatari, July 10, 2003, 156th National Diet Session, House of Councilors, Committee on Judicial Affairs. Vol. 21., https://kokkai.ndl.go.jp/txt/115615206X02120030710/31 (Japanese) (accessed Aug. 18, 2023).

19 Komatsu (n 7) 37.

fact that the state of the act or the home state of the perpetrator may not be interested in the act. Article 2 of the Japanese Penal Code states that it "applies to any Japanese national who commits one of the following crimes outside the territory of Japan," listing serious crimes as: insurrection and crimes related to insurrection (Arts. 77 through 79), instigation of foreign aggression, assistance to the enemy (Arts. 81, 82, 87, 88), counterfeiting of currency (Art. 148), counterfeiting state, imperial, official documents, and related crimes (Arts. 154, 155, 157, 158, 161, 162), counterfeiting securities and uttering counterfeit securities (Arts. 162, 163), crimes related to unauthorized payment cards (Arts. 163-2 through 163-5), and counterfeiting or usage of unauthorized state, imperial, official documents, and related crimes (Arts. 164 through 166). Also, art. 4 enables the protective principle to exercise jurisdiction over crimes committed by public employees outside Japan. Crimes under Article 4 include: assistance in escape by a guard, making of false official documents, abuse of authority by public employees (Art. 193), assault and cruelty by specialized public employees (paragraph (2) of Art. 195) and acceptance of bribes; acceptance on a request; acceptance in advance; passing of bribes to a third party; aggravated acceptance of bribes (Arts. 197 through 197-4; acceptance after resignation of office; acceptance for exertion of influence), and abuse of authority causing death or injury by specialized public employees (Art. 196) and related crimes in paragraph (2) of Article 195. In the case of bribery and other crimes of corruption by public servants, the prevailing interpretation of Article 4 is taking the protective principle to complement the territoriality principle. However, some have argued that the assertion of Article 4 to apply "to any public employees of Japan" should be understood as a combined use of both nationality and protective principles.[20]

2.5 *Universal Jurisdiction*

The last principle asserts that States may exercise state jurisdiction upon crimes (usually defined by treaties) regardless of territory or nationality due to significance in the international society. Crimes related to terrorism (such as killing diplomats or taking embassy workers as hostages) or piracy (described as *hostis humani generis*) are major examples of this line of thought. On ratifying the 1973 "Convention on the Prevention and Punishment of Crimes against Internationally Protected Persons, including Diplomatic Agents," Japan partially amended the Penal Code to insert Article 4.2

20 Oya M., *Keihō Kōgi Sōron* [General Lecture of the Penal Code] (Japanese), new ed., (Seibundo, 2000) 81 and accompanying texts.

(Crimes Committed outside Japan Governed by a Treaty) to cover crimes that cannot be covered by Articles 2 through 4, but which Japan is nevertheless obliged by treaty to comply with.[21] However, in some cases, Japan has enacted new criminal legislation to cope with treaty provisions or UN resolutions. An example of this would be the issue of piracy. UNCLOS states in Article 105 that the "courts of the State which carried out the seizure may decide upon the penalties to be imposed, and may also determine the action to be taken with regard to the ships, aircraft or property, subject to the rights of third parties acting in good faith," though the Japanese Penal Code holds no provision for piracy. Also, Article 4.2 of the Japanese Penal Code, which states to apply "to anyone who commits those crimes outside the territory of Japan [...] governed by a treaty", does not cover piracy, as Article 105 of UNCLOS does not impose any obligation. To coordinate UNCLOS, domestic law as the 2007 Japanese Basic Act on Ocean Policy[22], and UN Security Council Resolutions as S/Res/1816(2008) paragraph 7(b) which allows States to "[u]se, within the territorial waters of Somalia, in a manner consistent with action permitted on the high seas with respect to piracy under relevant international law, all necessary means to repress acts of piracy and armed robbery," Japan enacted the 2009 Law on Punishment of and Measures against Acts of Piracy.[23] Under this act, Japan put two Somalians on trial before the Tokyo District Court in 2013.[24] In the High Court ruling of the same case, the court explicitly stated that "pirates have been known as the common enemy of mankind which threatens international maritime traffic from ancient times. Article 105 recognizes the right on the high seas, or in any other place outside the jurisdiction of any State, every State may seize a pirate vessel and arrest the persons. It is relevant to understand this with the premise that the intent of any State being able to arrest pirates on high sea is not just to recognize administrative arrest, but with the premise

21 *Ibid.*

22 Art. 21 of this act provides that "it is essential to secure the development and use of the marine resources, the safety of the maritime transport and others as well as to maintain the order in the oceans, with regard to the oceans, ... to take necessary measures to secure the peace and safety of our State as well as to secure the maritime safety and public order."

23 *See* Tatematsu S., "Kaizoku Taishohō no Seitei [The Enactment of the Piracy Act]" (Japanese), *Toki no Hōrei* 1847 (2009) 43–54.

24 *M/V Guanabara case*, Case no. 2011 (Go Wa) 77, Judgment of February 1, 2013, Tokyo District Court, unpublished. *See also* "Somalia-Moto Shōnen ni Jikkei Kaizoku Jiken de Tokyo Chisai Hanketsu [Former-Juvenile Sentenced to Jail for the Crime of Piracy by Tokyo District Court]" (Japanese) *Nikkei* (Tokyo, April 13, 2013).

to apply the basis of penal provisions for this arrest to pirates. Taking the wording of Article 100 in the context of the entire convention, acts of piracy should be seen consolidated under the fundamental idea of the State parties' universal jurisdiction."[25]

3 State Immunity as an Exception of State Jurisdiction

As mentioned above, the principles of state jurisdiction had been set to avoid conflict and overlapping jurisdiction as much as possible. However, with due respect to other states' sovereignty (more specifically, the principle of *par in parem non habet imperium* ("equals have no sovereignty over each other"), there are certain exceptions where state jurisdiction may not be realized. Thus, juridical immunity may include heads of state, naval vessels, diplomatic missions, and the state itself. In addition, immunity may be provided to individuals under treaties such as the Agreement under Article VI of the Treaty of Mutual Cooperation and Security between Japan and the United States of America, Regarding Facilities and Areas and the Status of the United States Armed Forces in Japan.[26] Such exceptions from jurisdiction are known as state (or sovereign) immunity. According to a Japanese dictionary of international law, sovereign immunity is to examine that "States and its property (for example public

25 *M/V Guanabara* case, Case no. 2013 (U) 578, Judgment of December 18, 2013, Tokyo High Court, 66(4) Kosai Hanrei Shu 6 (translation by the author).

26 According to Art. 16 of this treaty, it is the duty of US forces to "to respect the law of Japan." However, due to the nature of their activities, they enjoy immunity during public duty. In other cases, Art. 17.1 holds that "the military authorities of the United States shall have the right to exercise within Japan all criminal and disciplinary jurisdiction conferred on them by the law of the United States over all persons subject to the military law of the United States." Also, the same clause also provides "the authorities of Japan shall have jurisdiction over the members of the United States armed forces, the civilian component, and their dependents with respect to offenses committed within the territory of Japan and punishable by the law of Japan." Since US military personnel and civil employees may be interpreted to include both "all persons subject to the military law of the United States" and "members of the United States armed forces, the civilian component," a situation may arise where jurisdiction overlap. Previous criminal cases where the Japanese side could not claim jurisdiction have created a sense of unfairness within Japanese society.

Cases of concurrent jurisdiction have been particularly evident in Okinawa, where the majority of US forces are stationed. Though several modifications have been made to secure a stable criminal procedure, it remains a complicated issue between the Japanese and the US.

vessels) generally do not fall under the juridical jurisdiction of a foreign state in international law".[27]

Two different approaches to immunity have been discussed in academia: absolute and restrictive immunity. From a historical perspective, absolute immunity assumes the Sovereign and the State to be synonyms and thus immune from civil suit, as the accepted doctrine. In such cases, the issue would be whether the defendant was a state (or state agencies, state corporations, etc.) or not. The restrictive principle distinguishes sovereign acts (*acta jure imperii*) from private acts (*acta jure gestionis*) with recognized immunity only for the prior. In a court which takes this doctrine, the issue would not be the nature of the entity, but the objective or nature of the act in question.

As described in Table 4.2, the trend of state immunity has shifted from absolute immunity (with domestic cases such as the *Schooner Exchange v. McFaddon* being the leading case) toward restrictive immunity (with the 1962 "Tate Letters".[28] to be a turning point) in general. Article 2.2 of the UN Convention of State Immunity defines "commercial act" in a way that "reference should be made primarily to the nature of the contract or transaction, but its purpose should also be taken into account if the parties to the contract or transaction have so agreed, or if, in the practice of the State of the forum, that purpose is relevant to determining the non-commercial character of the contract or transaction".

Japan has been active in applying the international legal principle of state immunity to domestic cases. As one author puts it, "perhaps the problem was that it was too active" in recognizing immunity.[29] Contrary to the international trend, it has persisted to the doctrine of absolute immunity, which has brought domestic criticism to assert that "our policy is obsolete".[30] Historically, the law of immunity developed gradually from domestic court rulings, domestic law to customary international law, regional treaties, and then to the UN Convention on State Immunity.[31] In

27 Taijudo K. and Yakushiji K., "Shuken Menjo [Sovereign Immunity]" (Japanese), *Kokusai Kankeihō Jiten* [Dictionary of International Relations Law], 2nd ed. (Sanseido, 2005) 456.

28 *U.S. Dept. St. Bull.*, XXVI (1952) 984.

29 Mizushima T., "Shuken Menjo (Sovereign Immunity)" (Japanese), *Jurist* 1321 (2006) 37–44, at 37.

30 Taijudo K., "Kokka no Saibanken Menjo [The Jurisdictional Immunity of States]" (Japanese), *Kokusaihō no Kihonteki Mondai* [Basic Issues of International Law] (Yuhikaku, 1986) 126.

31 For example, *see* Fox H. and Philippa W., *The Law of State Immunity,* 3rd ed. (Oxford Univ. Press, 2015).

TABLE 4.2 Timeline of events relevant to the development of state immunity

Year	Case/events	
1812	The Schooner Exchange v. McFaddon and others (US Supreme Court)	One of the first leading case of Absolute Immunity
1928	Matsuyama v. Republic of China, Daishin-in (Japanese former Supreme Court)	Most cited case in the issue of sovereign immunity until the 2006. (Absolute Immunity)
2000	Distimo Case (Greek Supreme Court)	Decided that States do not have immunity to acts agains *jus cogens*
2004	United Nations Convention on Jurisdictional Immunities of States and their Property	First universal convention, though not in effect as of 2023 (Restrictive Immunity)
2006	Tokyo Sanyo Trading Co Ltd v. Islamic Republic of Pakistan (Japanese Supreme Court)	Japanese Surpreme Court changed its position to Restrictive Immunity. (Restrictive Immunity)
2009	The Act on the Civil Jurisdiction of Japan over Foreign States	Domestic law enacted to take position of Restrictive Immunity. (Restrictive Immunity)
2012	Jurisdictional Immunities of the State (Germany v. Italy: Greece intervening) (ICJ)	Decided that act of the military (States) do have immunity in regard to the Distimo cases
2021	'Comfort Women' Case (Seoul Central District Court, South Korea)	Ordered the Japanese government for compensation for acts during . Though the court recognized the act as sovereign, it denied immunity on similar logic as the Distimo Case

the most recent form, the Act on the Civil Jurisdiction of Japan with respect to Foreign States (hereafter: Japanese State Immunity Law) Article 4, holds that a foreign state "will have immunity from jurisdiction (meaning the civil jurisdiction of Japan." The rest of this chapter will be dedicated to describing the historical context of state immunity in Japanese courts and academia.

3.1 *Historical Precedents*

Two cases shall be mentioned in this section as precedents to describe the Japanese approach to state immunity; the *Daishin-in* case and the *Pakistan Loan Claim case.*

3.1.1 *Daishin-in* Case (*Matsuyama v. Republic of China*) and Intermediate Cases

In 1928, a historical precedent was set by the Japanese *Daishin-in* (predecessor of the Supreme Court). The court dismissed an appeal in relation to a promissory note billing exchange case to the Republic of China based on absolute immunity. The court argued that all States are entitled to juridical immunity except for special cases when (1) the State waives its immunity or (2) cases regarding real estate.[32] This precedent was repeatedly referred in the subsequent cases to legitimize the government's position on immunity. However, this does not mean that the Japanese courts or academia were blind to the international trend toward restrictive immunity.

In the *Yokota Air Base* case, residents demanded the suspension of night flight exercises by the US on the basis of personal rights. The Japanese Supreme Court dismissed the case based on treaties with the US and the fact that "the night flight exercises of aircraft of the United States forces at Yokota base are essentially official acts of US forces stationed in Japan. From the objective and nature of the act, it is obvious that this is a sovereign act. Thus, it shall enjoy immunity from civil jurisdiction under international customary law".[33] It should be noted that the reasoning here emphasizes the sovereign "act" and not the feature of the entity.

3.1.2 *Pakistan Loan Claim* Case

The turning point toward restrictive immunity arrived in the *Pakistan Loan Claim case* when a state-owned company infringed a contract with a Japanese

32 *Daishinin Case*, Judgment of December 28, 1928, Grand Court of Cassation, Case No. 218 (Ku), *Daishinin Minji Hanreishu* [Court of Cassation Civil Reports] 7 1128 et seq. AD 1927–1928, No. 107, 168–169. *See also* "Promissory notes invoice case against the Republic of China" in *Hanrei Kokusaihō* [Cases of International Law] (Japanese), 3rd ed. (Toshindo, 2019) 88–90.

33 *Demands for No-Night-Flight Hours at Yokota Air Base case*, Judgment of April 12, 2002, Supreme Court Second Petty Bench, No. 1999(O)887, *Saikou Saibansho Minji Hanreishu* [Supreme Court Reports (civil cases)] 56(4) 729.

company when it refused to deliver payment for a supercomputer.[34] The Japanese Supreme Court expressly stated its change of position to restrictive immunity. Also, this case took the position of examining the nature of the act to distinguish whether the act is *acta jure imperii* or *acta jure gestionis*. After this case, Japan ratified the UN State Immunity Convention by parliamentary approval on June 10, 2009, and enacted its own state immunity law (Act on the Civil Jurisdiction of Japan with respect to Foreign States, Act No. 24 of April 24, 2009) in the same year (enforced from 2010). The Japanese state immunity law takes a similar position as the UN treaty, which allows the treaty to be substantially effective.[35]

3.2 *The Comfort Women Case and the Response by the Japanese Government*

In this section, the position taken by the Japanese government regarding certain human rights issues rooted in history and State immunity. The 2021 Seoul Central District Court rendered a judgment of the "comfort women" case represented a series of tension between Japan and South Korea over the recent years in both social and political spheres.[36] Some of the other flashpoints included the miscommunication between the two States regarding the General Security of Military Information Agreement (GSOMIA), an incident in which a Japanese Naval Aircraft was targeted by a South Korean naval vessel with targeting radars, the territorial conflict regarding the island of Takeshima (Dokdo), criticism toward discharging contaminated water from the TEPCO Dai-ichi Nuclear Facility, which are all contemporary in nature. However, the "comfort women" case is rooted in a more historical

34 *Pakistan Loan Claim case*, Case no. 2003 (Ju) 1231, Judgment of July 21, 2006, Supreme Court (Second Petty Bench), no. 2002 (Ju) 1231, *Saikō Saibansho Minji Hanreishū* [Supreme Court Reports (civil cases)] 60(6) 2542.

35 For an overview of this act, see for example, Yakushiji K., "Legislation of the Act on Civil Jurisdiction over Foreign States, Acceptance of the UN Convention on Jurisdictional Immunity of States and Their Property, and Their Possible Effects upon the Jurisprudence of Japanese Domestic Courts on State Immunity", *Japanese Yearbook of International Law* 53 (2010) 202–42; Kawajiri E. and Nishiwaki E., "Hourei Kaisetsu Tai Gaikoku Minji Saibankenhō (Shuken Menjyohō) no Seitei [The Enactment of the Act on Civil Jurisdiction over Foreign States]" (Japanese) *Toki no horei* 1847 (2009) 6–24.

36 For the general Japanese (MOFA) reaction to the issue of comfort women, see MOFA, "Japan's Efforts on the Issue of Comfort Women" (accessed Aug. 18, 2023). https://www.mofa.go.jp/policy/postwar/page22e_000883.html (accessed Sept. 30, 2024).

Japan-Korean relationship after WWII. Thus, some background information may be useful to understand this conflict from a legal perspective.

The Seoul Central District Court confirmed a judgment filed by former "comfort women" and others to the Japanese government on January 23, 2021.[37] This judgment ordered the Japanese government to compensate to the plaintiffs for the damages by acts during WWII. It was Japan's position that "this lawsuit (…) must be dismissed because it is not acceptable for the Government of Japan to be subject to the jurisdiction of the Republic of Korea in accordance with this principle of State immunity in international law." Though the court recognized the acts in question as sovereign, the court dismissed the argument of state immunity as an exception in which the act was contrary to *jus cogens* of international law.

The official position of the Japanese government has been that Japan-South Korean relations had been normalized by the 1965 Treaty on Basic Relations Between Japan and the Republic of Korea. A subsequent treaty, the Agreement on the Settlement of Problem concerning Property and Claims and on the Economic Co-operation between Japan and the Republic of Korea of 1965 provides all issues of compensation "concerning property, rights and interest (…) and their nationals" (i.e., including that of "comfort women") would be settled "completely and finally."[38] On the other hand, issues such as the "comfort women" have remained as a historical, moral issue. As a legal issue, the Japanese government has taken the position that it has already been solved by the treaties mentioned above. Thus, several Prime Ministers have made statements (such as the "Kono Statement", 1993) or "Letters of Apology"' (1996, 2001) to former victims.[39] Also, the Asian Women's Fund, a Government Oriented NGO was established to compensate for the moral responsibilities towards the victims.

The Korean perspective took a rather different path. In sum, the Korean discourse toward this issue can be described as historical and legal (with emphasis on human rights). First, the historical argument stresses the

37 *Comfort Women case*, Judgment of January 8, 2021, Seoul Central District Court, Case no. 2016 (Kahap) 505092. For this chapter, the author cites a Japanese translation by Seita Yamamoto, http://justice.skr.jp/koreajudgements/30-1.pdf (accessed May 5, 2023).

38 However, it should be noted that regardless of this treaty, some issues remain, such as 1. the effectivity of the Japanese-Korean treaties predating 1910, 2. territorial issues, 3. issues regarding property rights and claims, 4. issues regarding the legal status of Korean nationals in Japan, 5. issues regarding fisheries, and 6. issues regarding the restoration of Korean cultural assets.

39 MOFA, "Statement by the Chief Cabinet Secretary," August 4, 1993, https://www.mofa.go.jp/a_o/rp/page25e_000343.html (accessed May 5, 2023).

illegality of the Japanese occupation and its rule prior to 1945. The validity of the 1910 Japan-Korea Annexation Treaty (and the subsequent rule by Japan) was a question the parties could not agree upon during the post-war normalization talks. As a result, art. 2 of the Japan-Korea Basic Relations Treaty confirms that "all treaties or agreement concluded between the Empire of Japan and the Empire of Korea on or before August 22, 1910 are *already null and void*" (emphasis added). This wording "already null and void" was due to the difference of historical interpretation. Japan asserts the forceful annexation was legal according to the international law at the time, while Korea's position was to consider it an imperialistic occupation, annexation and anything founded upon it to be null and void. This difference of interpretations has also been the focal point of discussion in both States to take a legal and historical perspective on the comfort women issue. If "comfort women," along with forced labor and other unresolved issues, are a historical issue of imperialism (non-legal), so would be the approach and language toward reconciliation. Thus, some of the Korean public opinion regarding the January 2021 judgment seemed to have been toned on this manner.[40]

The second strand of arguments (mostly found in the court) employs the language of international law and Korean law. Domestic cases regarding comfort women have been raised in other States including Japan in the past. In fact, this was the first case in which the plaintiff's argument was recognized. The Seoul District Court cited Art. 27 of the Korean Constitution and the Universal Human Rights Declaration and asserted that "if remedies cannot be secured, the Constitutional right to justice shall be in vain."[41] Thus, the court denied the state immunity of the Japanese government in the January 2021 decision. As mentioned above, the Korean courts all

40 For example, the dismissal of the January judgment in April 2021 and the public discourse toward this seems to represent this well. In an editorial of the *Hankyōrei* titled "Court's dismissal of 'comfort women' lawsuit disregards victims' dignity," the paper states that "To ensure that *the historical record* […] understand that the comfort women system fundamentally represented wartime sexual violence that trampled on the victims' humanity, we need not only diplomatic efforts but also manifest rulings by the courts" (emphasis added), April 22, 2022, https://www.hani.co.kr/arti/english_edition/e_editorial/992195.html (accessed August 18, 2023); the Chosun also put forth an editorial on the same day which stated that "the January judgment gave in to *the logic of the national sentiment,* and this judgment gave in to the logic of the World Court," as cited by "Kankoku no Shihō: Futatsu no Chōryū [The Judiciary of Korea, Two Strands of Approaches]" (Japanese), *Asahi Shimbun* (Tokyo, April 25, 2021) (emphasis added).

41 Yamamoto (n 37).

recognized the acts by the Japanese government as sovereign. Then, how could state immunity be denied? This is the second argument that substantiates the first lawsuit's logic. To broaden our perspective, it may be useful to find similar domestic cases in recent years. Such cases assert that state action which constitutes serious human rights violations such as genocide or torture may not enjoy immunity. Thus, as Article 53 of the 1969 Vienna Convention on the Law of Treaties declares treaties to be "void if, at the time of its conclusion, it conflicts with a peremptory norm" or *jus cogens*, some domestic courts have sought to rule over sovereign acts. Leading cases of such are the *Distomo* case (2000)[42] and the *Ferrini* case (2004).[43] In both cases, the acts of the German Reich during World War II were both regarded as *acta jure imperii*, but denied of State immunity. The International Court of Justice summarizes this logic in the following passage in the *Jurisdictional Immunities of the State case*:

> Since *jus cogens* rules always prevail over any inconsistent rule of international law, whether contained in a treaty or in customary international law, so the argument runs, and since the rule which accords one State immunity before the courts of another does not have the status of *jus cogens*, the rule of immunity must give way.[44]

However, the ICJ has been negative to this logic, saying that it is "noticeable that there is no limitation of State immunity by reference to the gravity of the violation or the peremptory character of the rule breached in the European Convention, the United Nations Convention or the draft Inter-American Convention."[45] It should be noted that such arguments were discussed in the United Nations International Law Commission and then to the Working Group of the Sixth Committee of the General Assembly. However, the Working Group found that "it did not seem to be ripe enough for the Working Group to engage in a codification exercise over it."

Japan's position on the issue of state immunity and *jus cogens* coincides with that of the ICJ. On Nov. 23, 2023, Masataka Okano, then Vice-Minister of MOFA, summoned the Korean Ambassador to protest that "it is extremely

42 *Distomo* Case, Judgment of June 23, 2003, Bundesgerichtshof [German Supreme Court], 42 *ILM* 1030.

43 *Ferrini* Case, Judgment of March 11, 2004, Corte di Cassazione, Joint Sections, No. 5044.

44 *Jurisdictional Immunities of the State Case*, Judgment of February 3, 2012, ICJ Rep 140, para. 92.

45 *Ibid.*, 138, para 89.

regrettable that, in a lawsuit filed by former comfort women and others against the Government of Japan, the Seoul High Court had rendered a judgment in favor of the plaintiffs, denying the application of the principle of State immunity under international law."[46] Based on this position, the Japanese government did not appear before the court in this case.

As seen from the above, Japan approached the case as an issue of traditional state immunity, while South Korea (in the initial January judgment) took a different approach closer to the *Distomo* case and *Ferrini* case. Considering the above, the judgment of the Seoul Central District Court is not peculiar in the international trend of domestic courts. However, the ruling of the ICJ and the position of the Japanese government do not share this perspective.

4 Conclusion

As a conclusion, the author of this chapter would like to emphasize how the Japanese approach has adapted to the ever-changing international environment and coming in line with the prominent theories of state jurisdiction.

Whether it be basic principles of state jurisdiction, approaches to state immunity, or issues with *jus cogens*, Japanese law and cases (though with different historical settings and implications) have been compatible with the Western approach.

---

46 MOFA, "Communication to the Government of the Republic of Korea on Japan's Position regarding a Lawsuit in the Republic of Korea Filed by Former Comfort Women and Others", https://www.mofa.go.jp/press/release/press1e_000488.html (accessed Sep. 30, 2024). See also, statement by FM Yoko Kamikawa with similar wording, "Regarding the Judgment of the Seoul High Court of the Republic of Korea in the Lawsuit Filed by Former Comfort Women and Others", https://www.mofa.go.jp/press/release/press1e_000489.html (accessed Sep. 30, 2024). Also, note that these statements were issued regarding a subsequent ruling by the Seoul High Court.

CHAPTER 5

Japan's Ocean Law and Policy: Maritime Zones

Chie Kojima

1 Introduction

Japan is an active participant in the making and development of the law of the sea because of its extensive use of the oceans and their resources for economic, security, societal, and cultural reasons, which is enhanced by scientific and technological advantages. Japan's State practice in the law of the sea is closely linked to its vital interests in the oceans, as pushed forward by the government, maritime stakeholders, and fishing communities within the Japanese society. These interests also arise from Japan's geographical features with the coastline of 35,268 km[1] and 14,125 islands.[2]

First, Japan has a distinctive profile as a maritime State. It not only relies on maritime transport for 99.6 percent of its imports and exports[3] but also has maritime industries, namely shipping and shipbuilding industries, which maintain international competitiveness. Second, Japan is a fishing State. Despite the continuing decrease of fish stocks resulting in decreases in fish consumption, as well as the decline of the Japanese fishery industry, Japan continues to seek options for the sustainable use of marine living resources through its participation in all relevant Regional Fisheries Management Organizations (RFMOs), and by revising relevant domestic laws to prevent further overfishing and to protect marine living resources. The sustainable management of marine living resources is at the center of Japan's ocean policies for the food security of the entire Japanese population, the protection of traditional food culture, and the maintenance of economic security for both the fishing industries and communities whose livelihood depends on fisheries.

1 Ministry of Land, Infrastructure, Transport and Tourism, Kaigan Tōkei, 2023.

2 Geospatial Information Authority of Japan, the Number of Islands in Japan, available at: https://www.gsi.go.jp/kihonjohochousa/islands_index.html (accessed Nov. 27, 2024) (Japanese).

3 The information is available from the website of the Ministry of Land, Infrastructure, Transport and Tourism at: https://www.mlit.go.jp/maritime/ (accessed Nov. 27, 2024) (Japanese).

 | DOI:10.1163/9789004548824_006

This chapter first gives a historical overview of the Japanese government's ocean policies in the development of the international law of the sea, namely those policies promoted during the United Nations Conferences on the Law of the Sea (hereinafter referred to as UNCLOS I, II, and III), and examines a series of Japanese laws incorporating the maritime zones stipulated under the United Nations Convention on the Law of the Sea (UNCLOS).[4] Second, it focuses on the Japanese regulation and State practice on the navigation of foreign vessels in the Japanese territorial sea and exclusive economic zone (EEZ) as well as on piracy.

2 Historical Overview of Japan's Ocean Policies and Maritime Zones

Japan's major claims during UNCLOS I, II, and III arose from Japan's policy upholding the freedom of navigation and the freedom of fishing. Although Japan's vision of a narrow territorial sea and broad high seas was not realized in the final text of UNCLOS, the essence of these claims still exist in Japan's ocean policy today.

2.1 *Japan and the United Nations Conferences on the Law of the Sea*

Japan's major claims submitted during the UNCLOS I, II, and III involved the claim to categorize sedentary fisheries in the high sea fisheries (*i.e.*, not to include them in the regime of the continental shelf) and the claim to maintain the 3 nm territorial sea. Japan's 3 nautical miles (nm) territorial sea was first established when Japan opened its ports to the Western powers in the 19th century.[5]

2.1.1 The Claim Related to Sedentary Fisheries

Shortly after World War II, when the international community started to expand its territorial sea limit and declare sovereign rights over the continental shelf, Japan first confronted Australia with regard to the sedentary fisheries on the continental shelf. Since before World War II, Japanese fishermen had been engaged in pearl fisheries in the Arafura Sea near Australia. The declaration on the continental shelf by Australia in the early 1950s excluded these Japanese fishermen from the ocean area, which led the

4 United Nations Convention on the Law of the Sea, *signed on* December 10, 1982, *entered into force on* November 16, 1994, 1833 UNTS 3

5 Yanai S. and Asomura K., "Japan and the Emerging Order of the Sea: Two Maritime Laws of Japan", *Japanese Annual of International Law* 21 (1977) 48.

Japanese Government to protest against the measures taken by Australia. Japan argued that pearl fisheries belong to high sea fisheries, therefore, they should be subject to the freedom of fishing by all States.

The controversies over sedentary fisheries existed also during the codification process of the law of the sea at the United Nations. It was in 1953 when the International Law Commission (ILC), which once excluded sedentary fisheries from the meaning of "natural resources" of the continental shelf, changed its position and concluded that the term "natural resources" must be retained, as distinguished from "mineral resources", on the ground that sedentary fisheries should not be outside the scope of the continental shelf regime. It was also noted that the coastal State exercising its exclusive rights over sedentary fisheries must respect the existing rights of nationals belonging to other States over those fisheries.[6]

The discussions concerning the scope of sedentary species remained controversial even after the adoption of the 1958 Convention on the Continental Shelf, which integrated the notion of sedentary fisheries to the "natural resources" on the continental shelf over which coastal States can exercise their sovereign rights. In 1960, the United States Department of State stated: "clams, oysters, abalone, etc. are included in the definition, whereas shrimp, lobsters, and finny fish are not".[7] Japan also protested that Alaskan king crabs in the eastern Behring Sea are a high sea fishery resource and should not be included in the definition of sedentary fisheries of the continental shelf. Similarly, France protested against Brazil's jurisdiction over lobster fishing in the Atlantic, having claimed that lobsters are capable of swimming and therefore belong to the high sea fisheries. While Japan did not oppose the notion of continental shelf itself and supported the sovereign rights over mineral resources of the continental shelf, it remained as a non-contracting party to the Convention on the Continental Shelf.

2.1.2 The Claim Related to the 3 nm Territorial Sea

Another major claim made by Japan was the maintenance of the 3 nm territorial sea. The claim to retain a narrow territorial sea and broad high seas was based on the long history of fishing by Japanese fishermen within the areas of 200 nm from the coast of other States. Therefore, during UNCLOS I and II, Japan insisted on its position that the areas beyond the 3 nm

---

6 [1953] Vol. II UNYBILC 214. *See also*, Kojima C., "Fisheries, Sedentary", in Wolfrum R. (ed.), *Max Planck Encyclopedia of Public International Law* IV (Oxford Univ. Press, 2012) 84–89.

7 Hearing on the Law of the Sea Conventions before the Committee on Foreign Relations, U.S. Senate, 86th Cong, 2d Sess. (1960) 82, 88.

territorial sea should be the high seas, which belong to all human beings and all States can enjoy the freedom of fishing. In the 1960s, while the international community increasingly expanded the territorial sea limit to 12 nm, Japan still maintained the 3 nm territorial sea for its own waters and objected to the establishment of a 12 nm territorial sea by other States including that of New Zealand. In the early 1970s, Japan appeared isolated from the rest of the world because of its persistent 3 nm territorial sea claim.

Japan proposed an alternative approach at the Colombo meeting of the Asian–African Legal Consultative Organization in 1971. The proposal suggested that, beyond the 12 nm territorial sea, the coastal State that is a developing country could have priority access to fishing. At its Lagos meeting in 1972, Japan officially submitted its proposal on the fishing regime on the high seas, which emphasized the priority of the coastal State's fishing rights and the importance of the conservation of the marine living resources on the high seas. However, this proposal did not gain support from Asian and African States because instead of priority access to fishing on the high seas with conservation obligations, exclusive fishing rights within their own waters was preferred by the developing countries.

During UNCLOS III, the establishment of a 200 nm economic or fishery zones by a number of States not only excluded Japanese fisherman from fishing within 200 nm from the coast of those States, but also resulted in increased fishing by nationals of other distant sea fishing nations such as the Soviet Union and the Republic of Korea (ROK) outside the 3 nm territorial sea of Japan. The Japanese fishing industry faced difficulties since its distant sea fishing in the 200 nm zones of foreign countries amounted to more than one third of Japan's total catch at that time.[8] The Japanese coastal fishing industry also demanded the Government to extend the territorial sea to 12 nm for protection against the large-scale fishing operations of foreign fishing vessels in waters off the coasts of Japan.[9]

From the need to protect coastal fisheries, the Japanese Delegation finally expressed its acceptance of the concept of a 12 nm territorial sea in the Caracas Session in 1974 and that of the 200 nm economic zone in the Fourth Session in 1976.[10] It was against this background that Japan promulgated new laws, provisionally introducing the 12 nm territorial sea and 200 nm fishery zone for Japan in 1977.[11]

8 Yanai and Asomura (n 5), 49 (footnote 3).

9 *Ibid.*, 49.

10 *Ibid.*, 48 n 2.

11 Law on the Territorial Sea, Law No. 30 of 1977; Act on Provisional Measures relating to the Fishing Zone, Act No. 31 of 1977.

2.2 *Legislation Related to Maritime Zones*

Japan signed UNCLOS on February 7, 1983, and ratified it on June 20, 1996, by revising the 1977 laws simultaneously. The Convention entered into force for Japan on July 20, 1996. Further legislative efforts have been made in order for the relevant existing laws to be applied to activities and incidents that occur in the newly introduced maritime zones. The responsibility to implement ocean-related laws and policies has been entrusted to different government ministries and agencies of Japan. The enactment of the 2007 Basic Act on Ocean Policy[12] became a turning point for Japan to advance and implement its ocean policy in a more systematic way within the framework of UNCLOS. A Headquarters for Ocean Policy, for which the Prime Minister of Japan serves as the Director-General, was established under the Basic Act. The Basic Act also facilitates and enhances the cooperation and coordination among different government ministries and agencies; and it also promotes the formulation of ocean policies in light of changing domestic and international circumstances. The promulgation of the Basic Act also precipitated the making of other related laws such as the 2007 Act on the Establishment of Safety Water Areas concerning Artificial Structures in the Oceans[13] and the 2008 Act on Navigation of Foreign Ships through the Territorial Sea and Internal Waters.[14]

2.2.1 Territorial Sea

The 1977 Law on the Territorial Sea consisted of two provisions stipulating the 12 nm limit (and baselines respectively) of the territorial sea. It omitted to provide the details necessary for its implementation such as the right of innocent passage, relevant enforcement jurisdiction, and penalties. The reason why the Law included only a few provisions was that Japan had incorporated other relevant rules into the domestic law by becoming a party to the 1958 Convention on the Territorial Sea and the Contiguous Zone.[15] The following Cabinet Order No. 210 of 1977 provided specific details of the baselines such as the closing baselines of the Seto Inland Sea (Seto Naikai), which was explicitly recognized as internal waters under Article 2(1) of the 1977 Law on the Territorial Sea.[16] The Law also made an exception to the

12 Act No. 33 of 2007.

13 Act No. 34 of 2007.

14 Act No. 64 of 2008.

15 Yanai and Asomura (n 5), 53.

16 The mouths of the three channels connecting the Seto Island Sea to the outer seas (Kii Suidō, Bungo Suidō and Kanmon Kaikyō) are narrower than 24 nm. See for more details on the Seto Inland Sea, *ibid.*, 56–58. The Osaka High Court also interpreted in its 1976 judgment that the Seto Inland Sea is historic waters recognized as customary

five straits[17] to which 3 nm territorial sea limit was kept provisionally pending the outcome of the UNCLOS III.

The 1977 Law was amended and renamed as the Law on the Territorial Sea and Contiguous Zone in 1996 (hereinafter referred to as 1996 TS Law),[18] in which new rules concerning straight baselines, the right of hot pursuit, and the contiguous zone are established by referring to specific provisions under UNCLOS. The 3 nm territorial sea for the five straits remains in the new Law. Based on this 1996 TS Law, the Cabinet Order No. 206 of 1996 establishes straight baselines in 15 areas including the four main islands, Ryukyu Islands, and the Northern Territories.

Through the introduction of straight baselines under the 1996 TS Law, the Japanese territorial sea expanded in some ocean areas, which triggered international conflicts. On June 9, 1997, a Korean fishing vessel was arrested in the expanded territorial sea of Japan off the coast of Shimane prefecture. The area in question was, however, an area where Korean nationals were allowed to fish under the 1965 Agreement between Japan and the ROK concerning Fisheries.[19] The ROK condemned Japan by stating that under Article I of the agreement, both parties to the agreement have the right to establish a 12 nm fishery zone, but in a case where either party "uses the straight base line for the establishment of its fishery zone, the straight base line shall be determined through consultation" with the other party. No such consultation took place before Japan enacted the 1996 TS Law. Under the 1965 agreement, the place of the arrest in question is outside the exclusive fishery zone and the agreement explicitly stipulated, under Article IV(1), that "the right of control (including the right to halt and inspect vessels) and jurisdiction in waters outside the exclusive fishery zone shall be exercised only by the High Contracting Party to which the ship belongs". Both Japan and the ROK were parties to UNCLOS at the time of the incident.

After the incident, the captain of the arrested fishing vessel was brought before the Matsue District Court for violating the Act on Regulation of

---

international law and that Japan exercised its jurisdiction in the Seto Inland Sea as internal waters for a long time, which was not met by any objections from other States. Judgment of November 19, 1976, 8(11/12) *Keiji Saibansho Geppō* [Monthly Bulletin on Criminal Courts] (Japanese) 465, 470.

17 The five straits include the Sōya Strait, the Tsugaru Strait, the eastern and western channels of the Tsushima Strait, and the Ōsumi Strait. The 3 nm territorial sea for these five straits is still kept today.

18 Law No. 73 of 1996.

19 Agreement between Japan and the Republic of Korea concerning Fisheries, *signed on* June 22, 1965, 583 UNTS 51.

Fishing Operation by Foreign Nationals.[20] On August 15, 1997, the Matsue District Court stated that the notion of straight baselines was already adopted under the 1958 Convention on the Territorial Sea and the Contiguous Zone, and that there was no special change of circumstances after entering into the force of UNCLOS in 1994.[21] The Court also emphasized the importance of "waters of mutual interest" referred in the Preamble of the 1965 Agreement,[22] which was not merely referring to the "high seas" as argued by the prosecutor. Article II of the 1965 Agreement explicitly stipulated a joint control zone, which excluded the then territorial waters and the ROK's fishery zone. The Court held its opinion that a unilateral adoption of straight baselines virtually invalidates the 1965 Agreement and, therefore, ruins the purpose of concluding the agreement. The Court dismissed the case by concluding that Japan does not have jurisdiction since the place of the arrest was outside the 12 nm fisheries zone under the 1965 Agreement.

The Hiroshima High Court, in its judgment of September 11, 1998, remanded the case to the Matsue District Court by stating that the place of the arrest was within the territorial sea of Japan established in accordance with international law.[23] The Court stated that exercising sovereign rights within the territorial sea is an established principle under international law and, considering the background when the 1965 agreement was concluded,[24] the purpose of the agreement is to solve fishery disputes on the high seas and not to regulate activities in the territorial seas of the contracting parties. The phrase "waters of mutual interest" in the preamble of the 1965 agreement, therefore, refers to the high seas and not the specific water areas comprising the territorial seas. The Court further ruled that the expansion of the territorial sea of Japan by the 1996 TS Law is in accordance with UNCLOS to which the ROK is also a party and that it is not the expansion of the "fishery zone" under the 1965 agreement.[25]

---

20 Act No. 60 of 1967. The Act prohibits foreign nationals from fishing in the territorial waters of Japan.

21 Judgment of 15 Aug. 1997, *Saikō Saibansho Keiji Hanreishū* [Supreme Court Reports (Criminal Cases)] (Japanese) 53(8), 1101.

22 The Preamble provides "[d]esiring that the maximum sustained productivity of the fishery resources in waters of mutual interest be maintained … ".

23 Judgment of 11 September 1998, *Saikō Saibansho Keiji Hanreishū* [Supreme Court Reports (Criminal Cases)] (Japanese) 53(8), 1108.

24 The Court refers to the fishery disputes between Japan and the Republic of Korea triggered by the Republic of Korea's drawing of the Syngman Rhee Line in 1952.

25 Art. I(1) of the 1965 Agreement provides: "The High Contracting Parties mutually recognize that each High Contracting Party has the right to establish a sea zone (hereinafter

On November 30, 1999, the Supreme Court of Japan dismissed the Hiroshima High Court's decision on the ground that the establishment of the straight baselines in question are not in conformity with UNCLOS as well as Article 98(2) of the Constitution of Japan, which stipulates that "[t]he treaties concluded by Japan and established laws of nations shall be faithfully observed".[26] The Court also noted that the Japanese Government had concluded a new Fisheries Agreement with the ROK in 1998 and condemned the Government's unilateral enactment of the 1996 TS Law as well as its enforcement measures, which not only denied the effect of the 1965 agreement but also violated good faith in the international community.

This case involved the question of a conflict of treaties since both Japan and the ROK are parties to the 1965 agreement and UNCLOS. While the maxim *lex specialis derogat legi generali* could allow the 1965 agreement, a solution for the transitional period between the old and new law of the sea regimes, to prevail over UNCLOS, one could possibly argue that both Japan and the ROK agreed with the new regime under UNCLOS by becoming a party to it. Yet the question of conflicting treaties cannot be answered only by comparing substantive provisions concerning the "fishery zone" under the 1965 agreement or the "territorial sea" under UNCLOS. The contracting parties' procedural duty to go through consultation provided under Article 1(1) of the 1965 agreement is a part of the obligations arising from the agreement, which are compatible with UNCLOS. Obviously, UNCLOS does not alter such obligations (Art. 311(2) of UNCLOS) and Japan was under this obligation even after UNCLOS took effect.

2.2.2 Exclusive Economic Zone

Under the 1977 Law on Provisional Measures relating to the Fishing Zone, foreign nationals were prohibited to engage in fishing within the 200 nm fishing zone measured from the baselines of Japan. The Law also stipulated Japan's exclusive jurisdiction over fishing activities within the 200 nm fishing zone, the need to obtain fishing licenses for foreign vessels to engage in fishing within the fishing zone, and Japan's jurisdiction over anadromous

"fishery zone"), extending not more than 12 nautical miles from its respective coastal base line, over which it will have exclusive jurisdiction with respect to fisheries. However, in case either High Contracting Party uses the straight base line for the establishment of its fishery zone, the straight base line shall be determined through consultation with the other High Contracting Party."

26 Judgment of November 30, 1999, *Saikō Saibansho Keiji Hanreishū* [Supreme Court Reports (Criminal Cases)] (Japanese) 53(8), 1045(587).

species beyond the fishing zone if the species spawn in the fresh waters of Japan. Foreign nationals did not need to obtain permissions where the fishing is targeted on highly migratory species, where the fishing was associated with scientific research approved by the Minister of Agriculture and Forestry, and where the fishing was of an insignificant nature (Art. 6).

On one hand, the 1977 Law was enacted as a countermeasure to the fishery zones established by the United States and the former USSR, which eliminated Japanese fishing vessels from the zones.[27] On the other hand, the Japanese Government desired to maintain its fishery relations with the ROK and the People's Republic of China (PRC) as Japanese fishing vessels had been engaged in fishing in the waters off the coasts of the ROK and PRC under the fishery agreements concluded in 1965 and 1975 respectively; and these two neighboring States had not established a 200 nm zone at the time.[28] The Cabinet Order of 1977 issued for the enforcement of the 1977 Law, therefore, made exceptions to the areas of interests including the East China Sea and the Yellow Sea where no 200 nm fishing zone was established (Art. 1 of the Cabinet Order). The order further made exceptions that the nationals of the PRC and ROK were exempted from the application of the 1977 Law, *i.e.*, they were free to fish in any part of Japan's then fishery zone beyond the 12 nm territorial sea (Art. 6 of the Cabinet Order).

Upon ratifying UNCLOS, Japan promulgated the Act on the Exercise of the Sovereign Right for Fishery in the Exclusive Economic Zone (hereinafter referred to as the 1996 EEZ Act)[29] and the Law on Exclusive Economic Zone and Continental Shelf.[30] The 1996 EEZ Act establishes necessary measures for the exercise of sovereign rights in the EEZ and revises the 1977 Law. Major modifications include the deletion of the highly migratory species exception (Art. 5 of the 1996 EEZ Law) and the prohibition of transshipment and the loading of fish catches or products within the prohibited area (Art. 4(2) of the 1996 EEZ Law). Article 14 of the Law newly stipulates that Articles 3 to 13, which are concerned with the prohibition of fishing by foreign nationals without permissions in the EEZ, apply *mutatis mutandis* to the exploration and exploitation of sedentary fisheries on the continental shelf of Japan beyond the 200 nm EEZ. The 1996 Cabinet Order following

27 Yanai and Asomura (n 5), 72. Both the United States and the former USSR established the 200 nm fishery zone in 1976.

28 *Ibid.*, 73–76.

29 Act No. 76 of 1996.

30 Law No. 74 of 1996.

the 1996 EEZ Law maintains the exceptions for the nationals of the PRC and the ROK, and allows them to freely fish in the designated areas of the EEZ of Japan; however, it does not make any exceptions to the East China Sea and the Yellow Sea like the 1977 Cabinet Order. According to the Law on Exclusive Economic Zone and Continental Shelf, the relevant Japanese laws apply when exercising jurisdiction over the exploration, exploitation, conservation and management of EEZ resources, the protection and preservation of the marine environment, marine scientific research, and the establishment and use of artificial islands, installations and structures.

The establishment of EEZ around Oki-no-Tori Shima Island, the southernmost island of Japan, has met protests from PRC and the ROK in recent years. They argue that Oki-no-Tori Shima Island is a rock under the definition given by Article 121(3) of UNCLOS and, therefore, has no EEZ or continental shelf.

With regard to the disputed areas between Japan and the ROK, the provisional joint fishery zones have been established, ignoring the maritime delimitation issues under the bilateral agreement.[31] The fishery agreement between Japan and the PRC, on the contrary, leaves the disputed area untouched and sets up a provisional fishery zone in the north of the disputed area.[32] These agreements can be regarded as "provisional arrangements" under Article 74(3) of UNCLOS.

In order to control and preserve marine living resources within the EEZ of Japan, Japan also enacted the Act on the Preservation and Control of Living Marine Resources.[33] According to the Act, the Minister of Agriculture, Forestry and Fisheries were designated to establish a basic plan on the preservation and control of living marine resources in the exclusive economic zone, including the total allowable catch (TAC) for each category of fisheries based on the trends of those fisheries. The concept of TAC was introduced into Japanese Law for the first time as a new method by this Act. Traditionally, Japan controlled fishing activities by the "size and number of vessels, fishing seasons, types of fishing gear, areas and periods of operation".[34] The Act was integrated into and then abolished by the 2018 amendment of the

31 Agreement between Japan and the Republic of Korea concerning Fisheries, *signed at Kagoshima on* November 28, 1998, *entered into force for Japan on* January 22, 1999.

32 Agreement between Japan and the People's Republic of China concerning Fisheries, *signed at Tokyo on* November 11, 1997, *entered into force for Japan on* June 1, 2000.

33 Law No. 77 of 1996.

34 Hayashi M., "Japan: New Law of the Sea Legislation," *International Journal of Marine and Coastal Law* 12 (1997) 570, 577.

Fishery Act.[35] Under the amended Fishery Act, TAC became the basic method for fishery management, and the Fisheries Agency of Japan expressed its intention to use TAC as a management tool by increasing the TAC from 56 percent to 80 percent of capture production. Moreover, the 2018 amendment included the increase of fines in cases of fishing activities conducted without a license or in violation of the fishing right conferred under the Fishery Act, as well as the introduction of new offences such as the offence of catching and collecting designated aquatic animals and plants without a license or in violation of a fishing right and the offence of distributing seafood from IUU fishing deliberately.

2.2.3 Continental Shelf

The Law on the Exclusive Economic Zone and Continental Shelf stipulates sovereign rights over resources on the continental shelf as defined under UNCLOS. The Law also provides that, when there is an overlapping EEZ or continental shelf with another State opposite from the coast of Japan, a median line should be the limit of the EEZ or continental shelf (Art. 2).[36]

With regard to the continental shelf extending beyond the 200 nm, Japan made its submission to the Commission on the Limits of the Continental Shelf (CLCS) on November 12, 2008, in accordance with Article 76(8) of UNCLOS. The submission consisted of continental shelves of seven separate regions.[37] On that occasion, the PRC and the ROK requested the CLCS not to examine the submission concerning the continental shelf claim around Oki-

35 Act No. 267 of 1949.

36 In this regard, Japan's position differs from the PRC insisting on the natural prolongation of its continental shelf to be the delimitation line. In relation to the ROK, the two countries agreed on the median line for the delimitation of continental shelf of the northern overlapping area and established a joint development zone for the southern overlapping area for the period of 50 years: these agreements are the Agreement between Japan and the Republic of Korea concerning the Establishment of Boundary in the Northern Part of the Continental Shelf Adjacent to the Two Countries (*signed at Seoul on* January 30, 1974, *entered into force for Japan on* June 22, 1978) and the Agreement between Japan and the Republic of Korea concerning Joint Development of the Southern Part of the Continental Shelf Adjacent to the Two Countries (*signed at Seoul on* January 30, 1974, *entered into force for Japan on* June 22, 1978). For the methods of maritime delimitation and discussions related to undelimited maritime areas, *see* Chapter 8.

37 The Southern Kyushu-Palau Ridge region (KPR), the Minami-Io To Island region (MIT), the Minami-Tori Shima Island region (MTS), the Mogi Seamount region (MGS), the Ogasawara Plateau region (OGP), the Southern Oki-Daito Ridge region (ODR), and the Shikoku Basin region (SKB).

no-Tori Shima Island because the legal status of the Island is questionable under Article 121(3) of UNCLOS.[38] Japan communicated with CLCS that the PRC and the ROK have no direct interest in the legal status of the Island and, therefore, the objection cannot be considered as a land or maritime dispute between Japan and those States.[39] The United States and the Republic of Palau each submitted that there are potential overlaps between Japan's continental shelf claims and their claims over KPR, MIT, and OGP, but they confirmed that they would not object to Japan's request to the extent that CLCS's recommendations are without prejudice to the establishment of the outer limits of their continental shelf by the United States and the Republic of Palau respectively, or any final delimitation of the continental shelf between Japan and those countries.[40]

The CLCS gave its recommendations with regard to the submission made by Japan on April 19, 2012. In the recommendations, the CLCS accepted Japan's submission related to four regions (MIT, OGP, ODR, and SKB). The CLCS recommended Japan not to establish the outer limits of the continental shelf in both MTS and MGS as the foot of the continental slope points in these regions did not satisfy the test of appurtenance. Furthermore, the CLCS decided not to take action in relation to the Southern Kyushu-Palau Ridge Region (KPR) due to possible overlaps with the continental shelves of the U.S. and Palau, as well as objections from ROK and PRC regarding Oki-no-Tori Shima Island. The CLCS Commission considered that it would not be in a position to take action to make recommendations on the KPR until the dispute over the legal status of Oki-no-Tori Shima Island has been resolved.[41] In 2014, based on Article 2(2) of the Law on the Exclusive

38 Communication dated February 6, 2009, by the Permanent Mission of the People's Republic of China to the United Nations, http://www.un.org/Depts/los/clcs_new/submissions_files/jpn08/chn_6feb09_e.pdf (accessed May 20, 2023); Communication dated February 27, 2009 by the Permanent Mission of the Republic of Korea to the United Nations, http://www.un.org/Depts/los/clcs_new/submissions_files/jpn08/kor_27feb09.pdf (accessed May 20, 2023).

39 Communication dated April 9, 2012 by the Permanent Mission of Japan to the United Nations, http://www.un.org/Depts/los/clcs_new/submissions_files/jpn08/jpn_09apr12.pdf (accessed May 20, 2023).

40 *E.g.*, Communication dated June 15, 2009 by the Permanent Mission of the Republic of Palau to the United Nations, http://www.un.org/Depts/los/clcs_new/submissions_files/jpn08/plw_15jun09.pdf (accessed May 20, 2023).

41 Commission on the Limits of the Continental Shelf, Summary of the Recommendations of the Commission on the Limits of the Continental Shelf in regard to the Submission made by Japan on November 12, 2008.

Economic Zone and Continental Shelf as well as the recommendations from the CLCS, a cabinet order was adopted by which Japan expanded its continental shelf in the SKB and ODR.[42] This cabinet order was revised in 2024[43] in light of the declaration made by the United States on 19 December 2023[44] over its extended continental shelf, which partly overlaps with OGP and stipulated that ODR excluding the overlapping area is the excluded continental shelf of Japan. Japan simultaneously expresses its willingness to negotiate with the United States over the overlapping area. It is viewed that, because the United States is not a party to UNCLOS, its claim based on customary international law cannot receive recommendations from the CLCS and therefore cannot be considered as "final" under Article 76(8) of UNCLOS.[45] It is not entirely impossible that Japan and the United States sign a maritime delimitation agreement over the overlapping extended continental shelf before the United States becomes a party to UNCLOS, but the area to be agreed by both States without receiving a recommendation from the CLCS would not be opposable to the third State.[46]

Japan's claims to an EEZ and continental shelf have been partially disputed in respect of their possible overlaps with the claims of other States, namely the PRC, the ROK, Russia, the United States (Northern Mariana Islands), and the Philippines. The only successful delimitation agreement is the 1974 Agreement between Japan and the ROK concerning the establishment of a partial boundary in the northern part of the continental shelf adjacent to the two countries. The maritime delimitation disputes with the neighboring countries are discussed in Chapter 8 and territorial disputes over islands, namely Senkaku Islands (referred to by PRC as "Diaoyu" Islands), Takeshima (referred to by ROK as "Dokdo"), and the Northern Territories (referred to by Russia as "South Kuril Islands"), respectively, are discussed in Chapter 7.

---

42 Cabinet Order No. 302 of September 12, 2014.

43 Cabinet Order No. 230 of July 20, 2024.

44 U.S. Department of State, The Outer Limits of the Extended Continental Shelf of the United States of America, Executive Summary 2023, available at: https://www.state.gov/wp-content/uploads/2023/12/ECS_Executive_Summary.pdf (accessed Nov. 28, 2024).

45 Nishimoto K., "Nihon no Tairikudana no Genkai Settei to Kyōkai Kakutei" [Demarcation and Delimitation of the Japanese Continental Shelf] (Japanese), in Sakamoto S. et al. (eds.), *Nihon no Kaiyōhō Seido no Tenbō* [The Prospects of the Japanese Legal System on the Law of the Sea] (Yushindo, 2024), 201.

46 *Ibid.*, 202.

3 Navigation of Foreign Vessels

The 1996 TS Law did not provide the right of innocent passage, nor what constituted innocent or non-innocent passage. The government only took the position that Article 19(2) of UNCLOS was illustrative, not exhaustive. Japan subsequently took legislative action to give its interpretation to the meaning of passage under Article 18(2) of UNCLOS. The 2008 Act on Navigation on Foreign Ships through the Territorial Sea and Internal Waters prohibits the stopping, anchoring, mooring, and hovering of foreign ships within the territorial sea and internal waters of Japan, unless there are otherwise legitimate reasons to do so, such as reasons of force majeure or distress, for the purpose of rendering assistance to persons, ships or aircraft in danger or distress, or unavoidable reasons in accordance with relevant Japanese laws and ministerial ordinances. This is an example of Japan's ocean policy being implemented in a unique balance between its exclusive and inclusive interests, *i.e.*, protecting against maritime security threats while upholding the freedom of navigation. Similarly, Japan's commitment to the suppression of piracy and the enactment of the 2009 Law on the Punishment of and Measures against Piracy indicate its interests in ensuring the safety of Japanese vessels and maintaining the public order of the oceans as a valued member of the international community.

3.1 *Navigation of Foreign Vessels in the Territorial Sea and Exclusive Economic Zone of Japan*

3.1.1 Passage of Foreign Vessels in the Territorial Sea

Different laws regulate the activities of foreign ships navigating the territorial sea of Japan. Those laws include the Act on the Prevention of Collision at Sea,[47] Maritime Traffic Safety Act,[48] Navigational Aids Act,[49] Telecommunications Business Act,[50] Fishery Act, Act on Regulation of Fishing Operation by Foreign Nationals,[51] Act on Prevention of Marine Pollution and Maritime Disaster,[52] Act on Services Related to Waterways,[53] Customs Act,[54] Foreign Exchange and Foreign Trade Act,[55] Immigration Control and

47 Act No. 62 of 1977.
48 Act No. 115 of 1972.
49 Act No. 99 of 1949.
50 Act No. 86 of 1984.
51 Act No. 60 of 1967.
52 Act No. 136 of 1970.
53 Act No. 102 of 1950.
54 Act No. 61 of 1954.
55 Act No. 228 of 1949.

Refugee Recognition Act,[56] and Quarantine Act.[57] These laws correspond to the areas of laws and regulations relating to innocent passage permitted under Article 21(1) of UNCLOS.

The enactment of the 2008 Act on Navigation on Foreign Ships through the Territorial Sea and Internal Waters facilitated controlling so-called "suspicious vessels" (*fushin-sen*) in the Japanese territorial sea and internal waters. According to the 2008 Act, the navigation of foreign ships through the Japanese territorial sea and some areas of internal waters which expanded by adopting straight baselines under the 1996 TS Act (hereinafter referred to as "new internal waters") shall be continuous and expeditious, as prescribed under Article 18(2) of UNCLOS.[58] Ships may only stop, anchor, moor, or hover when they have legitimate reasons such as force majeure, distress or for the purpose of rendering assistance to persons, ships or aircraft in danger or distress.[59] They may also stop, anchor, moor or hover when they have a compelling reason in compliance with the 1977 Act on the Prevention of Collisions at Sea and other relevant laws and regulations of Japan.[60] Foreign ships stopping, anchoring, mooring, or hovering are otherwise prohibited to navigate in the territorial sea and internal waters of Japan.[61] Foreign ships are not allowed to navigate through internal waters, except for the new internal waters, if they do not intend to enter a Japanese port.[62] If foreign ships have legitimate reasons to engage in any of these acts, they must submit prior notification to the Japan Coast Guard (JCG).[63]

The 2008 Act has enforcement mechanisms including sanctions on foreign vessels. Article 6 of the 2008 Act allows Coast Guard officers to inspect foreign vessels. If the captain and crew of a foreign vessel refuse, disturb or avoid an inspection or remain silent or give false statements to questions asked by the Coast Guard officers, the captain or crew will be imprisoned

---

56 Cabinet Order No. 319 of 1951.

57 Act No. 201 of 1951.

58 Act on Navigation of Foreign Ships through the Territorial Sea and Internal Waters (n 14), Art. 3.

59 *Ibid.*, Art. 4(1).

60 *Ibid.*

61 *Ibid.*

62 *Ibid.*, Art. 4(2).

63 *Ibid.*, Art. 5. In the past, Japan had requested foreign vessels entering the territorial sea by force majeure or distress to give a prior notification to Japan Coast Guard, but only half of approximately 4,000 followed this procedure. This resulted in a number of accidents such as damaging fishing nets, etc., Kobashi M., "Ryōkai Tō ni okeru Gaikoku Senpaku no Kōkō ni Kansuru Hōritsu nitsuite [On the Law concerning the Navigation of Foreign Vessels in the Territorial Sea etc.]" (Japanese), 11(3) *Unyu Seisaku Kenkyu* 41 (2008), 43.

for less than 6 months or pay a fine no less than JPY 300,000.[64] If the Coast Guard officers found no legitimate reasons to stop, anchor, moor, or hover in the territorial sea and internal waters of Japan, the JCG may order the captain of the foreign vessel to leave the territorial sea.[65] If the captain of the vessel does not follow the JCG's order, he or she will be charged with a maximum of one year of imprisonment or a maximum fine of JPY 500,000.[66]

Article 18(2) of UNCLOS stipulates that stopping and anchoring, which are "incidental to ordinary navigation", are considered to be within the meaning of "passage". Although the phrase leaves room for interpretation, the scope of foreign ships' right to passage in the territorial sea under UNCLOS appears broader than that under the 2008 Act, which only permits vessels to stop and anchor in the case of force majeure, distress or the rendering of assistance to persons, ships or aircraft in danger or distress and when there is a compelling reason.

3.1.1.1 *Foreign Warships*

Japan allows foreign warships to exercise the right of innocent passage in the territorial sea of Japan in principle.[67] Self-Defense Forces may take necessary actions based on the prime minister's decision in accordance with government's policies and procedures expressed in the 1996 and 2015 Cabinet Decisions for cases when foreign submarines remain submerged and do not fly a flag, as well as for foreign warships in the territorial sea and internal waters of Japan whose navigation is considered to be non-innocent under international law.[68]

Japan prohibits the passage of foreign warships carrying nuclear weapons in its territorial sea because of its domestic policy based on the "Three Non-Nuclear Principles" of not possessing nuclear weapons, not producing them and not permitting their entry into the country.[69] When ratifying UNCLOS in 1996, Japan made it clear that passage of vessels carrying nuclear weapons

64 *Ibid.*, Art. 13.

65 *Ibid.*, Art. 8.

66 *Ibid.*, Art. 12.

67 Sugihara T., et al., *Gendai Kokusaihō Kōgi* [*Lectures of International Law*] (Japanese), 5th ed. (Yuhikaku, 2012), 124.

68 The explanation note can be found at http://www.cas.go.jp/jp/gaiyou/jimu/pdf/gaikokugunkantaisho.pdf (available only in Japanese, accessed May 20, 2023).

69 Statement of December 11, 1967 by former Prime Minister Eisaku Sato, http://www.mofa.go.jp/policy/un/disarmament/nnp/index.html (accessed May 20, 2023).

through the territorial sea cannot be considered "innocent".[70] The Japanese government justifies its position based on Article 19(1) of UNCLOS stipulating that "[p]assage is innocent so long as it is not prejudicial to the peace, good order or security of the coastal State".[71]

This may raise a question as to whether this Japanese policy is consistent with Article 23 of UNCLOS, which allows the innocent passage of foreign nuclear-powered ships and ships carrying nuclear or other inherently dangerous or noxious substances as long as they carry documents and observe special precautionary measures established for such ships by international agreements. In fact, an example of a non-innocent passage of a nuclear-powered ship occurred in 1980 when a Soviet nuclear-powered submarine navigated through the Japanese territorial sea in spite of warnings given by a Japanese patrol boat.

On August 21, 1980, a Soviet nuclear-powered submarine was discovered afire on the high seas about 110 kilometers east of Okinawa. The JCG together with the Maritime and Air Self-Defense Forces took measures for rescue. The Ministry of Foreign Affairs of Japan made inquiries to the Soviet Embassy concerning the risk of radioactive pollution and reiterated its Three Non-Nuclear Principles, as well as the prohibition of the passage of nuclear-powered ships through its territorial sea. The USSR responded that there was no risk of radioactive pollution from the accident and that, in view of force majeure, it was desirable to shorten the submarine's course of navigation by towing it across Japanese territorial waters and into the East China Sea.[72]

When the submarine towed by a tugboat of the Soviet navy approached the Japanese territorial sea, the Japanese patrol boat warned: "the four Soviet ships including the nuclear-powered submarine will trespass in the Japanese territorial sea if you go on along this course. We do not consider that you will be exercising the right of innocent passage on the basis of the international Convention on the Territorial Sea and the Contiguous Zone, so we

70 Takata T., "The Conclusion by Japan of the United Nations Convention on the Law of the Sea (UNCLOS) and the Adjustment of Maritime Legal Regime," *Japanese Annual of International Law* 39 (1996) 133.

71 Komatsu I., *Jissen-Kokusaihō* [Praxis of International Law] (Japanese) 2nd ed. (Shinzansha, 2015) 126. In this context, the Japanese government interprets that Article 19(2) is illustrative.

72 Nakamura K., "The Passage through the Territorial Sea of Foreign Warships Carrying Nuclear Weapons: An Interpretation of the Convention on the Territorial Sea and the Contiguous Zone and Its Application to the Broken Soviet Nuclear-Powered Submarine," *The Japanese Annual of International Law* 25 (1982) 3.

warn you not to trespass in the Japanese territorial sea".[73] The Soviet convoy ignored the warning and entered the Japanese territorial sea. The Ministry of Foreign Affairs gave a second warning to the Soviet Embassy, but the Soviet ships continued their course and passed through the territorial sea around the Okinawa islands en route to the East China Sea. This incident led the Japanese government to file a diplomatic protest with the USSR.[74]

Another example of harmful passage of a foreign warship can be found in a case of disguised submarine passing through the territorial waters of Japan; such a passage obviously violates Article 20 of UNCLOS. On November 10, 2004, an unidentified submarine did not show its flag when it entered Japan's territorial waters of Okinawa near Sakishima Guntō and navigated without surfacing.[75] A maritime security operation was formed based on Article 82 of the Self-Defense Act and tracked the submarine until it reached 500 kilometers northwest of an Okinawa Island. The unidentified submarine turned out to be a Chinese nuclear submarine. This was the first time that Japan applied Cabinet Decision of December 24, 1996, which enabled the Self-Defense Forces to promptly chase a submerged foreign submarine that does not fly a flag.

The Japanese government also considered the entry of a Chinese naval reconnaissance vessel into the Japanese territorial water on June 15, 2016, as not innocent.[76] A Maritime Self-Defense Force P-3C patrol aircraft identified the vessel entering into the Japanese territorial waters west of Kuchinoerabu Island and warned it to exit the waters. Unlike in the case of the disguised submarine in 2004, no order was issued for the Self-Defense Forces to take maritime security measures because the vessel left the waters south of Yakushima Island in one and a half hours. On that occasion, the Defense Minister of Japan expressed his view that "[p]rior notifications should be made for a warship's entry into territorial waters".[77]

---

73 *Ibid.*, 4.

74 *Ibid.*

75 Hamamoto Y., "The Incident of a Submarine Navigating Underwater in Japan's Territorial Sea," *The Japanese Annual of International Law* 48 (2005) 123; State Practice of Japan, 11 *Asian Yearbook of International Law* 187 (2003–2004) 194–5. Article 20 of UNCLOS requires submarines and other underwater vehicles to navigate on the surface and to show their flag in the territorial sea.

76 "Chinese naval ship enters Japan's territorial waters," *The Japan Times* (Tokyo, June 16, 2016).

77 "China says it does not need Japanese permission to sail ships through Tokara Strait," *The Japan Times* (Tokyo, June 18, 2016).

Regarding the disputed maritime areas, Japan continuously condemns the intrusion by Chinese Coast Guard vessels into the territorial sea established by Japan surrounding the Senkaku Islands.[78] The intrusion intensified since the ownership of three of the Senkaku Islands (Uotsuri, Kitakojima, and Minamikojima Islands) was transferred from private citizens to the Government of Japan. The Japanese government let patrol boats from the Japan Coast Guard demand the Chinese vessels leave its territorial waters and made protest through diplomatic routes. There are academic views that Japan should enact law concerning the safety of navigation under Article 21(1) of UNCLOS and recognize the intrusion of Chinese vessels as violating such law.[79] However, the navigation of the Chinese vessels and the law enforcement by the Japan Coast Guard vessels in these instances are better discussed from the perspective of the peaceful settlement of dispute under international law in the first place. From the perspective of the law of the sea, what Japan and the PRC could do in the disputed maritime areas have to be judged under the so-called obligation of self-restraint, *i.e.*, the obligation to make every effort to enter into provisional arrangements of a practical nature and the obligation not to jeopardize or hamper the reaching of the final agreement stipulated under Articles 74(3) and 83(3) of UNCLOS.[80]

3.1.1.2 *"Suspicious Vessels"*

Foreign vessels are sometimes identified as "suspicious vessels" (*fushin-sen*) in the Japanese territorial sea. The term "suspicious vessels" does not appear in Japanese law, but it is widely used in government documents and by the media. Suspicious vessels are often disguised with vessel names, flags, or un-

78 Ministry of Foreign Affairs, Trends in China Coast Guard and Other Vessels in the Waters Surrounding the Senkaku Islands, and Japan's Response, November 1, 2024, available at: https://www.mofa.go.jp/region/page23e_000021.html (accessed Nov. 28, 2024). Japan maintains that "[t]here exists no issue of territorial sovereignty to be resolved concerning the Senkaku Islands." *See*, https://www.mofa.go.jp/region/asia-paci/senkaku/index.html (accessed Nov. 28, 2024).

79 Sakota A., "Ryōkai ni okeru Gunkan, Hishōgyō-teki Seifusenpaku no Kōdō ni taisuru Engankoku no Sochi [Coastal States Measures against Acts of Warships and Ships operated for Non-commercial Purposes]" (Japanese), in Sakamoto S., et al. (eds), *Nihon no Kaiyōhō Seido no Tenbō* [The Prospects of the Japanese Legal System on the Law of the Sea] (Yushindo, 2024), 151.

80 *See* Nishimoto K., "The Obligation of Self-Restraint in Undelimited Maritime Areas," 3(1) *Japan Review* 28 (2019), available at: https://www.jiia-jic.jp/en/japanreview/pdf/JapanReview_Vol3_No1_07_Nishimoto.pdf (accessed Nov. 28, 2024).

necessary equipment on board and navigate in a suspicious manner. The navigation of these vessels is considered to be non-innocent in practice.

On March 23, 1999, two fishing vessels were found suspiciously hovering within the internal waters of the Noto Peninsula and were chased by Japanese patrol boats. The vessels disguised themselves by having Japanese fishing boat names but they were equipped with unnecessary antennas.[81] The Japanese authorities chased the vessels on the grounds that they refused the inspection required under Article 74(3), of the Fishery Act.[82] The patrol boats used warning shots but the suspicious vessels eventually escaped from Japanese waters.

This incident precipitated the revision of the Japan Coast Guard Act in order to allow JCG officers to use arms directly against foreign vessels in certain situations. The JCG and the Japan Maritime Self-Defense Force held joint training and created a manual for joint actions, which acknowledged the primary role of the JCG in reacting to suspicious vessels and the supporting role of the Japan Maritime Self-Defense Force in taking measures when the JCG faces difficulties in reacting.[83]

3.1.2 Passage of Foreign Vessels in the Exclusive Economic Zone

Japan established its 200 nm EEZ under the 1996 Act on the Exclusive Economic Zone and Continental Shelf.[84] Article 3(1), which corresponds to Article 56(1) of UNCLOS, stipulates that relevant Japanese law and the punishment stipulated thereby applies to the exploration, exploitation, conservation and management of natural resources, the establishment and use of artificial islands, installations and structures, the protection and preservation of the marine environment, and marine scientific research in the EEZ and continental shelf. The Act, therefore, regulates the navigation of foreign vessels by their types of activities. Unlike the territorial sea, there is no law regulating certain manners of foreign vessels navigating in the EEZ.

An example of the relevant Japanese laws applicable to foreign vessels' activities in the EEZ is the 1996 Act on the Exercise of Sovereign Rights on

81 Kanehara A., "The Japanese Legal System concerning Innocent Passage of Foreign Vessels," *Japanese Annual of International Law* 42 (1999) 92.

82 Art. 74(3) of the Fishery Act stipulates that fisheries surveillance officers may inspect the vessel and ask the person concerned questions when they considered necessary.

83 Okuzono J., "Kaijyōhoanchō: Kaijyō Jieitai Kankei no Henka to Kaizoku Taishohō [The Japan Coast Guard: Changes of the Relationship with Maritime Self-Defense Force and the Counter-Piracy Act]" (Japanese), in *Kaizokutaishohō no kenkyu* [Studies on the Japanese Act on Punishment of and Measures against Piracy] (Yuishindo, 2016), 185.

84 Act No. 74 of 1996.

Fishing Operations in the Exclusive Economic Zone.[85] Article 3(1) of the Act states that the Act is applicable to fishing, sampling, and exploration activities by foreign nationals in the EEZ. However, under Article 3(2), the application of the Fishery Act to foreign nationals in the EEZ is excluded except for Article 74 (Fisheries Supervising Public Officers), Article 141 (punishment of a person who violated the Act), and Article 145 (punishment of a juridical person). Article 141 of the Fishery Act states that the person who violated the Act be punished "by imprisonment with work for no more than six months or a fine of not more than 300,000 yen".

With regard to marine scientific research conducted by foreign vessels in the EEZ, Japan issued the Guideline for Conducting Marine Scientific Research in Areas under the National Jurisdiction of Japan in 1996.[86] According to the guideline, "any foreign nationals or foreign institutions, whether private or public, are requested to obtain consent of the Government of Japan prior to conducting marine scientific research in the territorial sea or in the exclusive economic zone or on the continental shelf of Japan". This request for consent will be made through diplomatic channels to the Ministry of Foreign Affairs of Japan. If the research project involves catching, taking or the exploration of marine animals and/or plants in the EEZ of Japan, a separate approval from the Ministry of Agriculture, Forestry and Fisheries of Japan under the 1996 EEZ Act is necessary.

The Guideline is a soft instrument and does not impose penalties on foreign vessels, which conduct marine scientific research without Japan's consent or without meeting the conditions set for approval. Problems remain in the implementation of the guideline in areas where the EEZs and continental shelf have not been delimited between Japan and the PRC, and Japan and the ROK. Japan and the PRC exchanged notes verbales in 2001 to establish a prior notification system on marine scientific research in the East China Sea areas, which simplified the procedures.

The Act on Prevention of Marine Pollution and Maritime Disaster[87] applies to foreign vessels navigating in the EEZ of Japan under certain conditions.[88] The Act establishes a centralized mechanism for the protection of

85 Act No. 76 of 1996.

86 Ministry of Foreign Affairs of Japan, The Guideline for Conducting Marine Scientific Research in Areas under National Jurisdiction of Japan of July 20, 1996, Law of the Sea Bill 33 (1997) 38.

87 Act No. 136 of 1970.

88 The Cabinet Order concerning the Application of the Act concerning the Prevention of Marine Pollution and Maritime Disaster in the Exclusive Economic Zone (Cabinet Order No. 102 of June 26, 1996, *last amended by* Cabinet Order No. 297 of Dec. 12, 2012)

the marine environment from various sources of marine pollution. The Act prohibits the discharge of oil[89] and noxious liquid substances[90] as well as the dumping of wastes into the sea from ships, offshore facilities and aircrafts. The Act also obliges ship owners and owners/managers of offshore facilities to take preventive and responsive measures against marine pollution from substances and wastes. It further stipulates administrative sanctions (monetary penalties) in cases of violation.

3.2 *Piracy*

Following the Security Council's resolutions calling for States to enact necessary domestic laws for the suppression of piracy off the coast of Somalia, Japan enacted a special criminal law called the Law on the Punishment of and Measures against Acts of Piracy[91] in order to punish acts of piracy committed both within and beyond the territorial waters of Japan. The Law also enables the Japan Coast Guard and the Self-Defense Forces of Japan to react against piracy in emergency situations.

Although a number of States have explicit provisions in their Penal Code regarding piracy,[92] the Japanese Penal Code does not have a special provision applicable to piracy. This means, in the case where a pirate was

excludes certain kinds of foreign vessels conducting exploration and exploitation activities on the continental shelf of Japan and those navigating between Japanese ports from the application of the Act relating to the Prevention of Marine Pollution and Maritime Disaster.

89 "Oil" includes crude oil, heavy oil, lubricating oil, light oil, kerosene, volatile oil, and other oils and oily mixture containing these oils. *See* Art. 3(2) of the Act on Prevention of Marine Pollution and Maritime Disaster.

90 "Noxious liquid substances" includes liquid substances other than oil, which is carried as liquid cargo in bulk by a ship, and water ballast, tank washing water, and other unnecessary liquid substances which has been generated in a ship containing these substances (excluding such substances as liquid petroleum gas and other substances that are not liquid at the normal temperature and excluding liquid substances loaded on a ship for the purpose of throwing and combustion for disposal in the sea area). *See* Art. 3(3) of the Act on Prevention of Marine Pollution and Maritime Disaster.

91 Law No. 55 of 2009.

92 *E.g.*, Section 316c of the German Criminal Code stipulates assaults against sea traffic. Paragraph 1 of Section 316c stipulates that whoever applies force to or assaults the freedom of decision of a person or engages in other machinations in order to thereby gain control of, or influence the navigation of a ship employed in civil sea traffic, or uses firearms or undertakes to cause an explosion or a fire, in order to destroy or damage such an aircraft or ship or the cargo which exists on board thereof, shall be punished with imprisonment for not less than five years. Strafgesetzbuch [StGB][Criminal Code] (German), *first enacted on* May 15, 1871, *last promulgated on* November 13, 1998 Bundesgesetzblatt [BGBl.] I, 3322, *as amended*, official translation available at: http://www.gesetze-im-internet.de/englisch_stgb/index.html (accessed May 20, 2023).

arrested before the enactment of the above Law, the general provisions under the Japanese Penal Code – such as robbery, kidnapping, or murder – had to be applied. All the offences provided under the Japanese Penal Code apply not only to offences committed within the Japanese territory but also to offences committed in Japanese vessels or airplanes (Article 1(2) of the Penal Code). The Japanese Penal Code applies also to certain offences committed by foreign nationals outside the territory of Japan, such as murders, injuries, forcible imprisonment, trafficking of persons, and robberies (Article 3bis of the Penal Code).

Under the Law on the Penalization of Acts of Piracy and Measures against Acts of Piracy, acts of piracy are defined as offences committed for private ends by any person on board a ship (except warships and ships owned or operated by a State) on the high seas (including the exclusive economic zone as provided under UNCLOS), in the territorial sea or internal waters of Japan (Article. 2). The offences consist of seizing another navigating ship, controlling the navigation of another ship by forcing the persons on board such ship to be unable to resist by using violence, threat or other means, robbing property on board the ship and gaining unlawful benefits from the property or enabling another to gain such benefits, abducting persons on board the ship for the purpose of taking hostages in order to demand a third person the delivery of property or other acts, demanding a third person to deliver property by taking hostages from persons abducted from another navigating ship, trespassing on or destroying another navigating ship for the purpose of committing acts of piracy, approaching or tracking another navigating ship or preventing such ship from navigation by operating a ship for the purpose of committing acts of piracy, and preparing weapons and operating a ship for the purpose of committing acts of piracy (Article 2, paras 1–7). Articles 3 and 4 of the Law penalize those offences under Article 2: ranging from imprisonment for less than 3 years, life imprisonment to the death penalty. The Law also stipulates measures to be taken by the JCG against acts of piracy as well as measures to be taken by the Self-Defense Forces of Japan against acts of piracy in emergency situations. Both the JCG and the Self-Defense Forces of Japan are allowed to use weapons if the person committing acts of piracy did not obey their orders and there is a reasonable reason to believe that no other means exists (Articles 6 and 8).

In 2013, the Tokyo District Court rendered its first judgment applying the Law on the Penalization of Acts of Piracy and Measures against Acts of Piracy.[93] The case involved two Somali piracy suspects who attempted to

93 Tokyo District Court, Judgment of February 1, 2013.

commit acts of piracy over a tanker flying the flag of the Bahamas which was owned by a Japanese shipping company. The two Somalis were caught by the US navy and handed over to the Japanese authorities. The two Somalis were sentenced to 10 years imprisonment by the court's judgment. In the judgment, the District Court interpreted the definition of piracy under the Law as an application of universal jurisdiction as provided under Article 105 of UNCLOS. The two Somalis appealed to the Tokyo High Court in the same year, in which the court dismissed the case by confirming that every State is entitled to exercise its jurisdiction against acts of piracy.[94]

4 Conclusion

Japan establishes large maritime areas including the EEZ and continental shelf based on its baselines in accordance with UNCLOS, but challenges remain, such as other States, in relation to climate change. Because a number of islands are used as basepoints for the straight baselines of Japan,[95] the effects of the sea level rise on these islands may seriously affect Japan's entitlements in its maritime areas. On February 6, 2023, Mr. Hayashi Yoshimasa, then Minister for Foreign Affairs of Japan, held a meeting with the delegation of the Pacific Islands Forum (PIF) and stated that "Japan would strengthen its support to the Pacific Island countries region in the area of climate change" and that "with regard to climate-change-related sea-level rise, Japan has decided to take the position that it is permissible to preserve the existing baselines and maritime zones established in accordance with the United Nations Convention on the Law of the Sea (UNCLOS), notwithstanding the regression of coastlines and the PIF side welcomed Japan's decision."[96] Japan maintained the same position at the open debate held at the Security Council of the United Nations and supported the Small Island Developing States (SIDS) as follows:

94 Tokyo High Court, Judgment of December 18, 2013, *Kosai Hanrei Shu* 66(4), 6. For more analyses, *see* Ishii Y., "M/V Guanabara: Japan's First Trial on Piracy under the Anti-Piracy Act," M*aritime Safety and Security Law Journal* 1 (2015) 45.

95 "Japan Coast Guard publicizes maps of straight baselines of Japan," available at: https://www1.kaiho.mlit.go.jp/ryokai/kakudai/itiran.html (accessed Nov. 27, 2024) (Japanese).

96 Ministry of Foreign Affairs of Japan, Press Releases, Foreign Minister Hayashi's Meeting with the Delegation of the Pacific Islands Forum (PIF), available at: https://www.mofa.go.jp/press/release/press1e_000369.html (accessed Nov. 27, 2024).

> … [L]egal stability and predictability are the necessary foundation for the island nations as well as for coastal states of continents that are exposed to various uncertainties due to sea level rise. In this context, I would like to make clear Japan's position that it is permissible for coastal countries to preserve the existing baselines and maritime zones established under the UNCLOS, notwithstanding the regression of coastlines caused by climate change. We are confident that this interpretation is legitimate and will ensure legal stability and predictability in particular for SIDS.[97]

This position expressed by the Japanese government since 2023 is seen as a shift of policy as the 1996 TS Law adopts the low-water line as baseline for measuring the breath of the territorial sea, as in Article 5 of UNCLOS, and therefore considered to follow the ambulatory theory.[98] However, it is unclear if such policy change expressed towards the international community may effectively constitute a new interpretation of the TS Law or the Law requires an amendment to fix the maritime zones regardless of the sea level rise.[99]

---

97 See the statement publicized on the website of the Permanent Mission of Japan to the United Nations available at: https://www.un.emb-japan.go.jp/itpr_ja/ishikane021423.html (accessed Nov. 27, 2024).

98 TS Law, Art. 2(1). *See*, Honda Y., "Kaimen Jyōshō ga Nihon no Ryōkai Kisen ni oyobosu Hōteki Eikyō [Legal Effects of the Sea Level Rise on Japan's Territorial Sea Baselines]" (Japanese), in Sakamoto S. et al. eds, *Nihon no Kaiyōhō Seido no Tenbō* [The Prospects of the Japanese Legal System on the Law of the Sea] (Yushindo, 2024), 16.

99 *Ibid.*, 17–18.

CHAPTER 6

Japan's Ocean Law and Policy: Protection and Preservation of the Marine Environment

Chie Kojima

1 Introduction

Japan has long embraced the idea of harmony with nature as found in Shintoism. However, the rapid economic growth after World War II caused severe pollution and harm to human health, which precipitated the development of environmental law in Japan as described in Chapter 14. The economic growth also led to a growth in the fishery industry, which not only operated fishing within its territorial sea and exclusive economic zone (EEZ), but also operated in the high seas and in the EEZ of other States with license. As discussed also in Chapters 5 and 15, such extensive fishing by Japanese vessels sometimes caused disputes with other States. Japan's whaling has also been at the center of controversies due to its scale compared to other States' practices in whaling.

Japan establishes a large EEZ comprising an area of approximately 4,470,000 km^2 in accordance with the United Nations Convention on the Law of the Sea (UNCLOS).[1] Within the Japanese EEZ, there are not only several transboundary stocks shared with the Republic of Korea (ROK), the People's Republic of China (PRC), and the Russian Federation, but also highly migratory stocks controlled under relevant Regional Fisheries Management Organizations (RFMOs). Japan is generally willing to cooperate with other States on the protection and conservation of marine living resources. On the one hand, Japan not only concluded bilateral fisheries agreements with these neighboring States, notwithstanding the ongoing maritime delimitation disputes, but also ratified the 1995 Fish Stocks Agreement and actively participated in the relevant RFMOs. On the other hand, Japan's withdrawal from the International Convention for the Regulation of Whaling (ICRW) and non-participation in the Convention on the Conservation of Migratory Species of Wild Animals (CMS) are exceptional. Japan's non-participation in

1 Hydrographic and Oceanographic Department, Japan Coast Guard, available at: https://www1.kaiho.mlit.go.jp/ryokai/ryokai_setsuzoku.html (accessed May 20, 2023).

 | DOI:10.1163/9789004548824_007

these conventions indicates that the sustainable use of marine living resources based on scientific information is vital to its interests and that the moratorium under the ICRW and the complete ban of taking certain species under the CMS are not compatible with Japan's domestic policies.

At the domestic level, the statistics indicating a decrease of fish stocks within the Japanese EEZ forced Japan to revise its Fishery Act in 2018.[2] The revised Act aims to overcome the weaknesses of fishers' self-management, which was based on their common fishing rights, by strengthening catch control measures and by introducing a mechanism to mobilize fishers' motivation to comply with such measures. This chapter discusses Japan's law and policy related to the Marine Protected Areas (MPAS), illegal, unreported and unregulated (IUU), whaling, and the discharge of Advanced Liquid Processing System (ALPS) treated water from the Fukushima Daiichi nuclear power plants in light of relevant international rules and principles.

2 Marine Protected Areas

Although MPAs have been introduced in Japan based on several laws, none of them provide a definition of MPA. The 2011 Marine Biodiversity Conservation Strategy adopted by the Ministry of the Environment, however, recognizes the definition of MPA adopted by the Seventh Ordinary Meeting of the Conference of the Parties to the Convention on Biological Diversity (CBD)[3] and by the International Union for Conservation of Nature and Natural Resources (IUCN).[4] The Strategy states:

> [I]nternationally recommended marine protected areas today could be seen as an effectively set and clearly defined protected area in

2 *See* Chapter 5, 2.2.2.

3 COP adopted the following definition: "A marine and coastal protected area means any defined area within or adjacent to a marine environment, together with its overlying waters and associated flora, fauna and historical and cultural features, which has been reserved by legislation or other effective means, including customs, with the effect that its marine and/or coastal biodiversity enjoys a higher level of protection than its surroundings." Originally the definition was adopted by the Ad Hoc Technical Expert Group on Marine and Coastal Protected Areas in 2003. Doc. unep/cbd/sbstta/8/inf/7 (Feb. 13, 2003).

4 IUCN adopted the following definition: "A protected area is a clearly defined geographical space, recognized, dedicated and managed, through legal or other effective means, to achieve the long-term conservation of nature with associated ecosystem services and cultural values."

> specified marine areas with the main objective of conserving marine biodiversity or ecosystems. Measures for such protection are decided flexibly according to their objectives, and include non-legislative measures such as local customs. Also the sustainable use of ecosystem services cannot be separated from the conservation of biodiversity, and is achieved by conserving biodiversity. Thus, aiming for the sustainable use of any of the ecosystem services could also be regarded as marine protected areas.[5]

Accordingly, the strategy adopts a definition of MPA as "[m]arine areas designated and managed by law or other effective means, in consideration of use modalities, aimed at the conservation of marine biodiversity supporting the sound structure and function of marine ecosystems and ensuring the sustainable use of marine ecosystem services." [6]

The law and policy related to MPAS in Japan are developing progressively. One of the characteristics of MPAS in Japan that had been established before the Aichi Target was adopted at COP10 in 2010 is that their primary purpose is to protect aquatic animals and plants that are of commercial value. Especially, the Marine Resources Development Promotion Act[7] in 1971 and the Fishery Act in 1949, under which the majority of MPAS were established, protect only aquatic animals and plants with commercial value. For instance, Article 5(1) of the 1971 Act stipulates that prefectural governments can designate areas which are considered appropriate to promote fisheries' production including the promotion of aquatic animals and plants as well as aquaculture. Additionally, under Article 12 of the Act, areas designated by the prefectural governments and the cabinet can also designate areas that are important for fisheries' production because of natural conditions such as seabed features, ocean currents, and feed organisms.

Another characteristic of previously established Japanese MPAS is that they are established, managed, and implemented in a decentralized manner. They include: (1) No-bottom trawling zones based on the Fishery Act and the Act of the Protection of Fisheries Resources,[8] (2) Protected waters based on the Act on the Protection of Fisheries Resources, (3) Special marine

5 Ministry of the Environment, Marine Biodiversity Conservation Strategy, March 2011, available at: http://www.env.go.jp/nature/biodic/kaiyo-hozen/pdf/pdf_eng_honbun.pdf (accessed May 20, 2023), 33 [hereinafter, "Conservation Strategy"].

6 *Ibid.*, 34.

7 Act No. 60 of 1971.

8 Act No. 313 of 1951.

areas and protected areas based on the Nature Conservation Act,[9] (4) Marine parks based on the Natural Parks Act,[10] (5) Fisheries resources development areas and designated areas based on the Marine Resources Development Promotion Act, (6) Special protection areas, and wild birds and mammals protection areas based on the Protection and Control of Wild Birds and Mammals and Hunting Management Act,[11] and (7) Common fishing right areas based on the Fishery Act. The first six types of MPAS can be categorized as the centralized type of MPAS for the conservation of the environment, namely the conservation of scenery and endangered species. The last type of MPAS is the community-based type of MPAS for the sustainable management of fisheries based on a self-regulation system under the Fishery Act.

Different ministries, including the Ministry of the Environment and the Fisheries Agency, as well as local governments exercise their authorities in planning, establishing and managing top-down types of MPAS. Since fishery areas are included in national parks, "consensus-building with local stakeholders is a prerequisite" in establishing such MPAS. The regulations implemented in these MPAS include the prohibition of bottom trawling, the use of certain types of fishing gears, certain harvesting activities, land reclamation, digging, taking of soil, and artificial constructions. The community-based MPAS exist for different purposes: the most common purpose is to manage fishery resources and to conserve marine ecosystems and biodiversity. Examples of activities associated to these MPAS include the artificial seeding of seagrasses, the extermination of sea urchins for the recovery of seagrass beds, sand refill, the cleaning up of drift dusts for tidal lands, the extermination of *Acanthaster planci*, and the prevention of soil coverage for coral reefs.

The protection and conservation of marine biological diversity has attracted more attention after the adoption of Aichi Target in 2010. Besides the 2011 Marine Biodiversity Conservation Strategy adopted by the Ministry of the Environment, the Third Basic Plan on Ocean Policy[12] adopted by the Cabinet in 2018 stated that, in accordance with the Sustainable Development Goals, Convention on Biological Diversity (CBD), and other international instruments, the government should implement measures for the conservation and sustainable use of biodiversity. In accordance with the ecologically and

9 Act No. 85 of 1972.

10 Act No. 161 of 1957.

11 Act No. 88 of 2002.

12 Third Basic Plan on Ocean Policy, available at: https://www8.cao.go.jp/ocean/policies/plan/plan03/pdf/plan03.pdf (available only in Japanese, accessed May 20, 2023).

biologically important marine zones identified by the Ministry of the Environment in 2016, the Basic Plan encouraged both the Ministry of Agriculture, Forestry and Fisheries and the Ministry of the Environment to promote the establishment of MPAS to meet the target of appropriately preserving and managing 10 percent of the jurisdictional waters by 2020 in accordance with the Aichi Target. When the Target was set, Japanese MPA covered only 8.3 percent of its jurisdictional waters, but the protected areas increased to 13.3 percent in 2020.[13] The following Fourth Basic Plan on Ocean Policy[14] adopted in 2023 further requested these Ministries to establish MPAS and Other Effective area-based Conservation Measures (OECM) in order to protect 30 percent of the jurisdictional waters by 2030 in accordance with the target "30 by 30" included in the Kunming-Montreal Global Biodiversity Framework.[15] These Basic Plans described MPAS as one of the management measures that contribute to the sustainable use of fisheries resources and thus recognizes that marine areas managed autonomously by fishers for the purpose of managing resources sustainably and conserving biodiversity may be considered as effective MPAS.

Along with these developments, on April 24, 2018, the Japanese Diet unanimously approved a bill to amend the Nature Conservation Act, which enables the Minister of the Environment to designate, manage and implement MPAS in offshore seabed areas of Japan. The amended Act was promulgated on April 26, 2019. The purpose of the amendment was to protect and conserve ecosystems and living marine resources existing around cold vents, hydrothermal vents, deep-sea trenches, and seamounts on the ocean floor. Under the amended Nature Conservation Act, the offshore areas include internal waters and territorial seas that are deeper than 200 meters,

---

13 *See*, https://policies.env.go.jp/nature/biodiversity/30by30alliance/documents/flyer30by30.pdf (only in Japanese, accessed Nov. 29, 2024).

14 Fourth Basic Plan on Ocean Policy, available at: https://www8.cao.go.jp/ocean/policies/plan/plan04/pdf/keikaku_honbun.pdf (available only in Japanese, accessed Nov. 29, 2024).

15 Target 3 concerns the conservation of 30 percent of Land, Waters and Seas and describes as follows: Ensure and enable that by 2030 at least 30 percent of terrestrial and inland water areas, and of marine and coastal areas, especially areas of particular importance for biodiversity and ecosystem functions and services, are effectively conserved and managed through ecologically representative, well-connected and equitably governed systems of protected areas and other effective area-based conservation measures, recognizing Indigenous and traditional territories, where applicable, and integrated into wider landscapes, seascapes and the ocean, while ensuring that any sustainable use, where appropriate in such areas, is fully consistent with conservation outcomes, recognizing and respecting the rights of Indigenous peoples and local communities, including over their traditional territories.

the EEZ, and the continental shelf of Japan. In 2020, four offshore seabed areas are designated as such protected areas under the revised Act.[16] It has been pointed out that the four areas are selected by considering the seabed areas whose mineral resources are likely to be exploited, which is in line with the practices of the International Seabed Authority (ISA).[17] The amendment, however, addresses only the conservation of ecosystems in offshore seabed areas and not ecosystems in the water column above. Therefore, the amendment is criticized as lacking an ecological approach.[18]

3 Illegal, Unreported and Unregulated Fishing

While UNCLOS does not include the notion of Illegal, Unreported and Unregulated (IUU) Fishing, the adoption of a series of binding and non-binding instruments on IUU fishing aim to strengthen the responsibilities of States under UNCLOS and all stakeholders in the sustainable management and control of marine living resources. Such instruments include the International Plan of Action to Deter, Prevent and Eliminate Illegal, Unreported and Unregulated Fishing (IPOA-IUU) by the Food and Agriculture Organization (FAO) in 2001. The IPOA-IUU is a voluntary instrument addressed to all States, entities, and fishers, but it has become an influential soft law instrument in international fisheries law. Under the IOPA-IUU, States are encouraged to take measures to prevent IUU fishing including flag State measures, port State measures, coastal State measures, market-related measures, and measures to ensure that nationals do not support or engage in IUU fishing.[19] These international trends, followed by the practice of other States, precipitated the Japanese government to take more active domestic measures such as the enactment of the Act on Ensuring the Proper Domestic Distribution of Specified Aquatic Animals and Plants, which was promulgated on December 11, 2020[20] and the 2018 amendment of the Fishery Act mentioned above.

---

16 Ministry of the Environment, Press Releases, available at: https://www.env.go.jp/press/108741.html (available only in Japanese, accessed Nov. 29, 2024).

17 Sato C., "Wagakuni no 'Kaiyō Hogoku' Seido no Tokuchō to Kadai" [Features and Challenges in Japan's System on Marine Protected Areas] (Japanese), in Sakamoto S. et al. (eds.), *Nihon no Kaiyōhō Seido no Tenbō* [The Prospects of the Japanese Legal System on the Law of the Sea] (Yushindo, 2024), 232.

18 *Ibid.*

19 Food and Agriculture Organization of the United Nations, International Plan of Action to Prevent, Deter and Eliminate Illegal, Unreported and Unregulated Fishing (2001), para. 9.3.

20 Act No. 79 of 2020.

Other efforts of Japan to tackle IUU fishing include its accession to the FAO Agreement on Port State Measures to Prevent, Deter and Eliminate Illegal, Unreported and Unregulated Fishing[21] on May 19, 2017.

The enactment of the 2020 Act on Ensuring the Proper Domestic Distribution of Specified Aquatic Animals and Plants, which was promulgated on December 11, 2020, was praised by groups of seafood companies and NGOs and seen as Japan's good faith effort to fulfil its responsibility to promote sustainable fishery management globally as one of the biggest importers of seafood in the world.[22] Similar market measures have already been taken by the other biggest seafood importers, namely the European Union and the United States. The Act is comprised of regulations to prevent illegally caught aquatic animals and illegally collected plants from being distributed in the Japanese market and regulations for preventing the importation of seafood related to IUU fishing. The Act further stipulates that the government conduct inspections that are necessary for the enforcement of the Act. It also penalizes violators of the regulations with a fine or imprisonment of not more than one year. Accordingly, the Act introduces an enforceable mechanism for the traceability of seafood in their distribution processes, which not only prevents illegally caught seafood from being distributed in the domestic market but also identifies existing inappropriate distribution of seafood in the Japanese fishery sector.

4 Whaling

The history of whaling in Japan dates back to the 12th century.[23] Whale meat became common to the population during the Edo era. While the importance of whale meat as a source of nutrition decreased significantly,

---

21 Agreement on Port State Measures to Prevent, Deter and Eliminate Illegal, Unreported and Unregulated Fishing, *adopted on* Nov. 11, 2009, *entered into force on* June 5, 2016, 3161 UNTS 377.

22 *See* "Global seafood coalition applauds Japanese government on actions to eliminate IUU fishing; calls for further collaboration between industry and governments," available at: https://www.globaltunaalliance.com/global-seafood-coalition-applauds-japanese-government-on-actions-to-eliminate-iuu-fishing-calls-for-further-collaboration-between-industry-and-governments/ (accessed May 20, 2023); Joint Statement on Japan's "Act on Ensuring the Proper Domestic Distribution and Importation of Specified Aquatic Animals and Plants," available at: https://iuuwatch.jp/wp/wp-content/uploads/2021/03/210315_EN_Asia_Joint_Statement.pdf (accessed May 20, 2023).

23 Japan Whaling Association, History of Whaling, available at: https://www.whaling.jp/english/history.html (accessed Nov. 29, 2024).

eating whale meat as a food tradition, worshipping whales in religious ceremonies, and treating whales as symbols in local festivals and arts continue to today.[24] This section focuses only on Japan's policy change after the *Whaling in the Antarctic* case before the International Court of Justice (ICJ).[25]

On December 26, 2018, the Japanese government announced that it decided to withdraw from the International Convention for the Regulation of Whaling (ICRW)[26], which it had acceded to in 1951, and resumed commercial whaling in its territorial waters and exclusive economic zone in July 2019 when the withdrawal came into effect.[27] The Chief Cabinet Secretary of Japan stated that Japan would remain "committed to international cooperation for the proper management of marine living resources", notably for "the science-based sustainable management of whale resources".[28] The government explained that its decision to withdraw from the ICRW was based on the assessment that the International Whaling Commission (IWC) was unable to function as it was supposed to under the ICRW. During the 67th meeting of the IWC, the Japanese delegation argued that the IWC in its current form was inconsistent with the objectives of the ICRW, namely "to provide for the proper conservation of whale stocks and thus make possible the orderly development of the whaling industry".[29] For over 30 years, Japan has promoted, as a Member of the IWC, the sustainable use of whale species based on scientific evidence, i.e., the sustainable use of whale species whose abundance is scientifically proven. However, the failure of the member

24 *Ibid.*

25 *Whaling in the Antarctic* (*Australia v. Japan: New Zealand intervening*), Judgment of March 31, 2014. For the details of the case, *see* Chapter 15.

26 International Convention for the Regulation of Whaling, *signed on* Dec. 2, 1946, *entered into force on* Nov. 10, 1948, 161 UNTS 72.

27 Since the resumption of commercial whaling, TAC has been set for whaling based on the amended Fishery Act. The allocation of TAC is disclosed at https://www.mofa.go.jp/policy/economy/fishery/whales/japan.html (accessed May 20, 2023). In 2024, the Fisheries Agency of Japan decided to include North Pacific fin whales in the total allowable catch for its commercial whaling. *See*, Fisheries Agency, Catch limits for western North Pacific fin whales calculated in line with the IWC's Revised Management Procedure (RMP), Doc. RW/S23/02, available at: https://www.jfa.maff.go.jp/j/whale/attach/pdf/index-71.pdf (accessed Nov. 22, 2024).

28 Statement by Chief Cabinet Secretary (Dec. 26, 2018), available at: https://www.mofa.go.jp/ecm/fsh/page4e_000969.html (accessed May 20, 2023), para. 5.

29 Japan's Opening Statement to the 67th Meeting of the International Whaling Commission, available at: https://www.mofa.go.jp/mofaj/files/000400198.pdf (accessed May 20, 2023).

States of the IWC to agree on the notion of sustainable use of cetacean resources has ended up leaving the moratorium in place, in spite of the terms of the moratorium set forth under paragraph 10(e) of the Schedule under the ICRW.[30]

Prior to the decision to withdraw from the ICRW, Japan proposed an IWC reform and presented a resolution on the "Way Forward of the IWC" at the 67th meeting of the IWC in September 2018.[31] In the proposed resolution, the Japanese government tried to pursue a fair approach to achieving both conservation and development and recommended the establishment of the Sustainable Whaling Committee. The proposed committee's tasks would be to make recommendations to the IWC on catch limits for whaling, irrespective of the type of whaling, based on the best scientific evidence available; to make recommendations to the IWC on any management issues contributing to sustainable whaling; to implement activities that the IWC may request in relation to sustainable whaling; and to elaborate its Rules of Procedure to properly conduct its work for the promotion of sustainable whaling based on the best scientific evidence available.[32] The resolution was rejected by a vote of 27 in favor, 41 against, with 2 abstentions.

Even though Japan withdrew from the ICRW, it remains as a contracting party to UNCLOS. Articles 65 and 122 of UNCLOS oblige Japan to cooperate with other States and to work through the appropriate international organizations for the conservation, management, and study of marine mammals. Since cetaceans are listed as highly migratory species in Annex I of UNCLOS, Japan is also under the duty to cooperate with other States in the region, directly or through international organizations, to ensure the conservation and promotion of the objective of optimum utilization of whale species both with and within the exclusive economic zone. In addition, Japan has to comply with Part XII of UNCLOS on the protection and preservation of the marine environment. According to Article 193 of UNCLOS, States have

---

30 Paragraph 10(e) of the Schedule reads:

> Notwithstanding the other provisions of paragraph 10, catch limits for the killing for commercial purposes of whales from all stocks for the 1986 coastal and the 1985/86 pelagic seasons and thereafter shall be zero. This provision will be kept under review, based upon the best scientific advice, and by 1990 at the latest the Commission will undertake a comprehensive assessment of the effects of this decision on whale stocks and consider modification of this provision and the establishment of other catch limits.

31 Resolution on Way Forward of the IWC, available at: https://www.mofa.go.jp/files/000393952.pdf (accessed May 20, 2023).

32 *Ibid.*

the sovereign right to exploit their natural resources pursuant to their environmental policies and in accordance with their duty to protect and preserve the marine environment. Article 194(5) stipulates that the measures to protect and preserve the marine environment include those necessary to protect and preserve rare or fragile ecosystems as well as the habitat of depleted, threatened, or endangered species and other forms of marine life.[33]

The duty to cooperate is generally considered as an obligation of conduct and not an obligation of result. One view is that the cooperation obligation under Articles 65 and 120 does not require a State to become a member of an international organization and can be fulfilled by "positive acts on the part of a State to further the work or goals of an appropriate international organization". Japan may fulfill this obligation by participating in the Scientific Committee, following the case of Canada which withdrew from the ICRW in 1982. Japan may also fulfill this obligation through a new regional organization following the case of Iceland, which participated in the North Atlantic Marine Mammal Commission during the period it was a not a party to ICRW between 1992 and 2002. In this regard, the Japanese government chooses to participate in the IWC as an observer.[34]

Japan's responsibility and accountability towards the international community in taking measures for the conservation of marine mammals are critically evaluated. Under the 2017 Act for Ensuring Sustainable Use of Whales with the 2019 amendment,[35] commercial whaling in Japan is conducted within Japan's territorial sea and its EEZ. Since the resumption of commercial whaling, the total allowable catch (TAC) has been set for whaling based on the amended Fishery Act. According to the government, TAC is calculated in line with the method adopted by the IWC, but it is viewed that

33 Most cetaceans are listed as threatened in Appendix I of the Convention on International Trade in Endangered Species of Wild Fauna and Flora.

34 Ministry of Foreign Affairs of Japan, Frequently Asked Questions on Whaling, March 2023, available at: https://www.mofa.go.jp/files/000518768.pdf (accessed May 20, 2023).

35 Act No. 76 of June 23, 2017, *amended by* Act No. 73 of Dec. 11, 2019. Article 3 of the Act provides fundamental principles regarding scientific whale research and measures pertaining to whale fishery. The latter includes: (a)whale fishery will be operated within the catch limits ("catch limits" means the number of whales calculated for each species of target whales as the maximum number of whales that can be caught in one year for sustainable use of whales, based on findings of scientific whale research and other scientific evidence [...]); (b)whale fishery will be operated in accordance with treaties and other international agreements concluded by Japan, as well as in accordance with established international law; and (c)whale fishery will be operated smoothly with appropriate support, considering the circumstances surrounding whale fishery.

Japan's duty to cooperate with IWC remains as a challenge.[36] The decision of June 11, 2024, by the Fisheries Agency of Japan to include 59 fin whales in the TAC for its commercial whaling is questioned from the fact that the IWC stated that there are insufficient data to assess the status of North Pacific fin whales.[37]

5 Discharge of ALPS Treated Water into the Sea

The release and leaking of radioactive water from the Fukushima Daiichi nuclear power plants into the Pacific Ocean, following the accidents caused by the earthquake in March 2011, provoked concerns among the international community. This experience led Japan's neighbors to protest the Japanese government's decision to discharge the ALPS treated water[38] into the Pacific Ocean, which started in August 2023.[39] Although the ALPS treated water satisfied safety standards and proved to have no harmful effects on human health or the environment, concerns about unknown cumulative effects of the water to marine ecosystems and human health as well as its unknown trans-generational and trans-boundary effects remained. The fishery sector, which suffered reputational damage by the release of radioactive waters in 2011, protested the release of ALPS treated water.

There were differences in countries' positions as to whether the discharges of ALPS treated water fall within the meaning of dumping under

36 The allocation of TAC is disclosed at https://www.mofa.go.jp/policy/economy/fishery/whales/japan.html (accessed May 20, 2023).

37 As of November 2024, the IWC states on its website: "There are insufficient data to assess their present status. For the eastern North Pacific, partial estimates show around 3,000 (2013) whales in the Gulf of Alaska, 1,000 (2010) on the eastern Bering Sea shelf, around 400 (2009–2014) along the Canadian continental shelf, more than 8,000 (2014) in California, Oregon, and Washington waters"(https://iwc.int/about-whales/population-status). *See also*, Wold C. "Japan Expands Its Whale Hunt to Include Fin Whales and Violates Its Duty to Cooperate,"*EJIL Talk!* (2024).

38 ALPS means Advanced Liquid Processing System. It is explained as a "system that removes multiple radionuclides from water." *See*, Ministry of Foreign Affairs of Japan, "What Is 'ALPS Treated Water'?," available at: https://www.mofa.go.jp/dns/inec/alps_navi01.html (accessed May 23, 2024).

39 For more information on the definition of the ALPS treated water and its discharge, *see* Kanehara A., "Japan's Discharge of ALPS Treated Water Containing Tritium," 66 *Japanese Yearbook of International Law* (2023) 413. Kanehara explains that the ALPS treated water is purified from contaminated water, which meet the regulatory standards with an exception of tritium.

the 1972 London Convention and its 1996 Protocol or, because the discharges originated from land-based facilities, whether they were outside the scope of the aforementioned instruments.[40] On these arguments, the Secretariat of the London Convention and its Protocol stated that "[i]t is not certain that such disposal [disposal from land through pipelines] would fall within the scope of the treaty" and "nothing would prevent the Contracting Parties to the London Convention/London Protocol from adopting a new instrument covering land-based dumping into the sea and thereby filling a space currently unoccupied by other instruments."[41]

Operational releases of low-level radioactive wastewater into the ocean, as opposed to accidental releases, occur all over the world.[42] These land-based releases come from nuclear fuel-cycle installations, particularly spent fuel reprocessing plants, as well as nuclear power plants. According to the joint studies conducted by several international organizations including the IMO, UNEP, FAO, and IAEA, as long as these releases are well-operated and regulated by the respective countries, they present relatively minor risks to human health on a regional or global scale.[43] Countries operating those installations and plants have the primary responsibility to control their operations properly under their laws and regulations.

5.1 *Protection of the Marine Environment from Radioactive Substances in Japan*

Measures to prevent radioactive pollution from accidents were covered under the Atomic Energy Basic Act[44] but not under the relevant legislation for the protection of the environment in Japan before the Fukushima accidents occurred in 2011. The laws aiming to protect the environment from pollution, such as the Water Pollution Prevention Act,[45] included exception clauses indicating pollution caused by radioactive substances are excluded

40 *Ibid.*, 419–420. The ROK, PRC, and Canada expressed their positions that the discharge of ALPS treated water fell under the scope of the London Convention and its Protocol, while France and Japan held their positions that the discharge from land-based facilities are not covered under these instruments.

41 Report of the Forty Fourth Consultative Meeting and the Seventeenth Meeting of Contracting Parties, IMO Doc. LC/44/11, 5, paras 20–21.

42 Kanehara (n 39), 426–428.

43 GESAMP 2001, A Sea of Troubles, IMO/FAO/UNESCO/WMO/IAEA/UN/UNEP Joint Group of Experts on the Scientific Aspects of Marine Environmental Protection and Advisory Committee on Protection of the Sea, Studies No: 70, Publ. UNEP, Nairobi.

44 Act No. 186 of 1955.

45 Act No. 138 of 1970.

from the scope of application. The Fukushima incidents, however, precipitated lawmakers to introduce the environmental approach to radioactive pollution in Japan. Consequently, the measures to prevent air pollution, water pollution and soil contamination caused by radioactive substances were placed under the scope of the Basic Environment Act[46] through necessary revisions. Furthermore, by a cabinet decision on 19 April 2013, exception clauses were removed from several special environmental laws such as the Air Pollution Control Act,[47] Water Pollution Prevention Act, Environmental Impact Assessment Act,[48] and the Act relating to Protection of the Environment in Antarctica.[49] The exception clauses in other special laws remain unchanged to date.

The Act relating to the Prevention of Marine Pollution and Maritime Disaster[50] (hereinafter referred to as the "Marine Pollution Act") is one of the special laws which maintains the exception clause; Article 52 of the Act excludes the prevention and control of marine pollution by radioactive materials from its application. After the Fukushima incident, the Central Environment Council of the Ministry of the Environment suggested that the Marine Pollution Act was one of the laws for which removing the exception clause should be considered, since the Act is the law implementing the London Convention and its Protocol.[51]

The Marine Pollution Act mainly regulates discharge of oil and noxious liquid substances, as well as the dumping of wastes into the sea from ships, offshore facilities, and aircraft. Under the Act, the Ministry of Land, Infrastructure, Transport and Tourism (MLIT) is responsible for controlling marine pollution by oil and noxious liquid substances and is obliged to issue ministerial ordinances providing necessary measures for implementation. These include technical standards, such as the equipment required on board ships or the method for discharging ballast water from a segregated ballast tank. Under the Act, the Ministry of the Environment is responsible

46 Act No. 91 of 1993.

47 Act No. 97 of 1968.

48 Act No. 81 of 1997.

49 Act No. 61 of 1997.

50 Act No. 136 of 1970.

51 Central Environment Council, Ministry of the Environment, "On Legislation Related to the Environmental Laws concerning Clauses Excluding the Application of Radioactive Substances in Light of the Revision of the Basic Environment Act" (in Japanese), Doc No. 687 (Nov. 30, 2012), available at: https://www.env.go.jp/council/content/i_08/900430926.pdf (accessed May 19, 2024). The Council submitted its opinion to the then Minister of the Environment.

for assessing unknown liquid substances to be carried by sea, as well as for controlling the dumping of wastes.

From a formal point of view, there appears to be a gap between the Marine Pollution Law excluding radioactive materials from its application and the London Convention and its Protocol, which prohibit dumping of radioactive wastes or other radioactive matter into the ocean. This gap, however, is filled by other Japanese laws including the Atomic Energy Basic Act and the Basic Environment Act as well as special laws governing nuclear energy. In particular, Article 62 of the Act on the Regulation of Nuclear Source Material, Nuclear Fuel Material and Reactors,[52] explicitly prohibits the discharge of nuclear materials into the ocean as follows:

(1) Nuclear source material, nuclear fuel material, or material contaminated by these materials must not be discharged to sea; provided, however, that this does not apply to cases that are inevitable for ensuring the safety of human life, vessel, aircraft, or artificial marine structure.

(2) The term "discharged to sea" as used in the preceding paragraph means the disposal of material from a vessel, an aircraft, or an artificial marine structure into the sea, or the combustion of materials on a vessel or an artificial marine structure for the purpose of disposing of the material; provided, however, that this does not apply to the disposal of material that is generated from the operation of the vessel, aircraft, artificial marine structure, or their equipment from the vessel, aircraft, or artificial marine structure into the sea, or to the combustion of material that is generated from the operation of the vessel, artificial marine structure, or their equipment on a vessel or an artificial marine structure for the purpose of disposing of the material.

With the combination of these laws, Japan complies with its obligations under the London Convention and its Protocol regarding the prohibition of dumping of radioactive material into the sea from vessels, aircraft, platforms, and other artificial marine structures at sea.

5.2 *International Instruments Governing the Protection of the Marine Environment from the Disposal of Radioactive Wastes*

There is no comprehensive international law regime which governs the disposal of radioactive wastes into the ocean. While the dumping of radioactive wastes into the ocean from vessels, aircraft, platforms, and other man-made structures at sea is explicitly prohibited under the London

52 Act No. 166 of 1957.

Convention, the discharge of radioactive wastes into the ocean from land-based facilities is not.

An early indication of the prohibition of dumping of radioactive wastes can be found in Article 25 of the 1958 Convention on the High Seas. Paragraph 1 stipulates that "[e]very State shall take measures to prevent pollution of the seas from the dumping of radioactive waste, taking into account any standards and regulations which may be formulated by the competent international organizations." Paragraph 2 obliges all States to "cooperate with the competent international organizations in taking measures for the prevention of pollution of the seas or air space above, resulting from any activities with radioactive materials or other harmful agents." Under the 1972 London Convention and its 1996 Protocol, "radioactive wastes or other radioactive matter" are listed under Annex I, and dumping (*i.e.*, deliberate disposal) of those listed substances from vessels, aircraft, platforms, or other man-made structures at sea is prohibited.

Nothing in international law, however, prohibits the discharge of radioactive wastes from the land or from land-based facilities. It is clear from customary international rules on the sovereignty of States that States have the freedom to decide its domestic matters, including its energy policy and the operation of nuclear facilities within its territories. Under international nuclear law, the release of radioactive substances into the environment is permitted as long as the safety standards and requirements adopted by the IAEA are met. While the standards and requirements of the IAEA are adopted in non-binding instruments, whether the discharging State complies with the regulations is crucial in assessing if that State fulfills its due diligence obligation. The obligation of due diligence is an inevitable part of the obligation to prevent transboundary harm in international environmental law.

Despite the lack of binding instruments addressing the release of radioactive wastewater from the land, there are non-binding instruments which are inclined towards the reduction and elimination of radioactive waste as a source of land-based marine pollution. There are two instruments that are important: one is the Montreal guidelines in 1985,[53] which list "radioactive materials" as part of a blacklist of pollution that States should eliminate. The other is the UNEP Global Programme of Action (GPA) in 1995,[54] the

53 Montreal Guidelines for the Protection of the Marine Environment against Pollution from Land-Based Sources, Governing Council of UNEP, Decision 13/18/II (May 24, 1985).

54 Global Programme of Action for the Protection of the Marine Environment from Land-Based Activities (GPA), UNEP(OCA)/LBA/IG.2/7 (Dec. 5, 1995).

only universal instrument to address land-based marine pollution, which lists radioactive substances as one of the sources against which action will be necessary towards reduction or elimination. Under the GPA, States should not promote or allow the storage or disposal of high level, intermediate-level, and low-level radioactive wastes near the marine and coastal environment unless they determine on the basis of scientific evidence and the appropriate application of the precautionary approach that the storage or disposal poses no unacceptable risk to people and the marine and coastal environment or does not interfere with other legitimate uses of the sea.[55]

5.3 *Obligations under the United Nations Convention on the Law of the Sea*

5.3.1 Definition of "Pollution of the Marine Environment" and Relevant Obligations under UNCLOS Concerning Dumping and Pollution from Land-Based Sources

Article 1(1)(4) of UNCLOS stipulates that "pollution of the marine environment means the introduction by man, directly or indirectly, of substances or energy into the marine environment, [...] which results or is likely to result in such deleterious effects as harm to living resources and marine life, hazards to human health, hindrance to marine activities, including fishing and other legitimate uses of the sea, impairment of quality for use of sea water and reduction of amenities". The broad definition of marine pollution under UNCLOS is interpreted and applied evolutionarily under the present-day conditions by the International Tribunal for the Law of the Sea.[56] Considering that the exposure to radioactive substances is considered as hazardous to human health and the environment, the definition may well cover the discharge of nuclear wastewater from reprocessing plants or nuclear power plants, be they accidental or operational.[57]

If the discharge of nuclear wastewater falls under the definition of pollution of the marine environment, a series of obligations under UNCLOS Part XII become relevant. As for dumping, Article 210 stipulates legislative jurisdiction of

55 *Ibid.*, para. 111.

56 *E.g.*, Request for an Advisory Opinion Submitted by the Commission of Small Island States on Climate Change and International Law (May 21, 2024).

57 Nishimoto writes that the definition does not include the level of deleterious effects, it is difficult to interpret that ALPS treated water does not fall within the meaning of the pollution of the marine environment under Article 1(1)(4) of UNCLOS even if the tritium contained in the ALPS treated water is lower than the safety standards. Nishimoto K., "Fukushima Daiichi Genshiryoku Hatsudensho karano Hōshutsu to Kokusaihō" [Discharge of Treated Water from Fukushima Daiichi Nuclear Power Plants and International Law] (Japanese), 496 *Hogaku Kyoshitsu* 43 (2022) 45.

States to prevent, mitigate, and control marine pollution from dumping. Article 216 stipulates enforcement jurisdiction of States on the same matter. While there is consensus among scholars that the prohibition of dumping of radioactive wastes under the London Convention and its Protocol can be integrated into the "international rules and standards" under Article 210 and "applicable international rules and standards" under Article 216, it is less clear whether customary rules as well as safety requirements under international nuclear law can be integrated into UNCLOS through these repeated phrases.

It is also unclear what could inform the content of "internationally agreed rules, standards and recommended practices and procedures" under Article 207(1) and "applicable international rules and standards established through competent international organizations or diplomatic conference" under Article 213, both of which are related to measures to prevent, reduce and control pollution of the marine environment from land-based sources. One may refer to environmental principles within the corps of international law, such as considerations of safety, human health, and the protection of the environment, that have the potential to be part of the umbrella obligations under Part XII of UNCLOS, notably the obligation of due diligence expressed under Article 194. There might also be room to consider the continuing process of soft rules turning into customary international rules. From these perspectives, one cannot underestimate the potential that non-binding standards and guidelines such as requirements adopted under the IAEA and non-binding instruments on land-based marine pollution might influence the content of Articles 207(1) and 213 in the future.

At the same time, since the reference to radioactive wastes in non-binding instruments, such as GPA is limited, States would remain committed, under Article 207(4), to establish global and regional rules, standards and recommended practices and procedures to prevent, reduce and control land-based marine pollution.

5.3.2 Other Environmental Obligations under UNCLOS

Besides specific obligations related to dumping and pollution from land-based sources, the general obligations under Part XII of UNCLOS continue to apply to States discharging nuclear wastewater into the ocean for the entire period of each discharging plan. The following three obligations are particularly important.

First, the discharging State is under the obligation of due diligence enshrined under Article 192 (general obligation to protect and preserve the marine environment) and Article 194 (obligation to take all measures to prevent, reduce and control pollution of the marine environment from any source). The obligation derives from a customary rule in international environmental law, under which States have the obligation to take necessary measures to prevent significant transboundary harm or at any event, minimize the risk thereof arising out of activities.[58] The standard of due diligence must be proportionate with the degree of hazard of the activity in question.[59]

Second, the discharging State is under the obligation of cooperation. The obligation to cooperate is repeatedly referred to as "a fundamental principle in the prevention of pollution of the marine environment" under Part XII UNCLOS and under general international law by the International Tribunal for the Law of the Sea and the arbitral tribunals constituted under Annex VII of UNCLOS.[60] Article 197 (obligation to cooperate on a global or regional basis), Article 198 (notification of imminent or actual damage), and Article 199 (contingency plans against pollution) are especially relevant for the discharging State.

Third, the discharging State is required to assess the potentially harmful effects of a planned discharge prior to its execution and to disseminate the obtained results under Article 204 (monitoring of the risks or effects of pollution), Article 205 (publication of reports), and Article 206 (assessment of potential effects of activities). The obligation to conduct EIAS is recognized as a direct obligation under UNCLOS as well as a general obligation under customary international law in the Advisory Opinion *Responsibilities and obligations of States with respect to activities in the Area* and the arbitral award of the *South China Sea Arbitration*.[61] Although Article 206 contains an element of discretion for States as expressed in the terms "reasonable" and "as far as practicable," the South China Sea Arbitral Tribunal opined that the obligation to communicate reports of the results of the assessments was "absolute."

---

58 2001 draft article on Prevention of Transboundary Harm from Hazardous Activities.

59 Takamura Y., "Release of Radioactive Substances into the Sea and International Law: The Japanese Experience in the Course of Nuclear Disaster," in Caron D. D., Kelly M. J., and Telesetsky A. (eds.), *The International Law of Disaster Relief*, Cambridge University Press, 2014, 103.

60 *MOX Plant* (*Ireland v. United Kingdom*), Provisional Measures, Order of Dec. 3, 2001, ITLOS Reports 2001, 95, para. 82; *Land Reclamation in and around the Straits of Johor* (*Malaysia v. Singapore*) Provisional Measures, Order of Oct. 8, 2003, ITLOS Reports 2003, 10, para. 92; *Request for an Advisory Opinion Submitted by the Sub-regional Fisheries Commission* (*SRFC*), Advisory Opinion of April 2, 2015, ITLOS Reports 2015, 4, para. 140; *South China Sea Arbitration* (*Republic of the Philippines v. The People's Republic of China*), Award of July 12, 2016, PCA Case No. 2013–19, para. 946.

61 *Ibid.*, SFRC Advisory Opinion, para. 145; South China Sea Arbitration Award, para. 948.

The 2024 Advisory Opinion of ITLOS on climate change and international law, emphasized that the duty under Article 206 applies to any planned activity under the jurisdiction or control of the State concerned and that "[l]and-based activities as well as those at sea are included."[62] The ITLOS went a step further to describe the content of an EIA in the Advisory Opinion on climate change and international law as follows:

> Concerning the content of an environmental impact assessment, the Tribunal considers that the broad wording of article 206 of the Convention *does not preclude such assessment from embracing not only the specific effects of the planned activities concerned but also the cumulative impacts of these and other activities on the environment.* In the context of pollution of the marine environment from anthropogenic GHG emissions, planned activities may not be environmentally significant if taken in isolation, whereas they may produce significant effects if evaluated in interaction with other activities. Moreover, the broad wording of article 206 does not preclude the assessment from including the socio-economic impacts of the activities concerned (emphasis added).[63]

This Advisory Opinion is particularly illuminating in the case of nuclear waste disposal, as the cumulative impacts of purified nuclear wastewater on the marine environment, even if the water itself meets the safety standard, are unknown.

6 Conclusion

An overview of Japan's State practice in the protection and preservation of the marine environment analyzed in this chapter indicate that, while Japan remains as a strong economic actor whose interests support the economic activities at sea, including fishing and whaling activities, the trends in protecting and preserving the marine environment, including ecosystems, have pushed Japan to adopt, amend, and abolish its laws and policies over time. The amendment of the Fishery Act and Nature Conservation Act are such examples. At the same time, Japan's emphasis on the conservation and

62 *Request for an Advisory Opinion submitted by the Commission of Small Island States on Climate Change and International Law*, Advisory Opinion of May 21, 2024, para. 360.

63 *Ibid.*, para. 365.

sustainable use of marine living resources based on the best available scientific information in its diplomacy has led to international disputes and might lead to future disputes as much is still unknown in ocean-related science. How Japan could reconcile its interests with the international trends in integrating various principles of international environmental law, including the precautionary approach and ecosystem approach, into the law of the sea remains as a challenge.[64]

Regarding the discharge of ALPS treated water, one has to also consider other policies related to energy and the environment. There are differences in opinion as to whether nuclear energy should be promoted for sustainable development and reducing greenhouse gas emissions. At UNFCCC COP 28, twenty-two governments, including Japan, launched a declaration recognizing the key role of nuclear energy and proposing that tripling nuclear energy is crucial to reach net zero greenhouse gas emissions by 2050 and keeping the 1.5 degree goal.[65] The experiences of Japan, however, provide other States to choose an option to reduce nuclear energy to avoid nuclear disasters and ensure a clean and healthy environment. Whether the international community can uniformly choose between the two opposing policies towards the common goal of ensuring the human right to a clean and healthy environment for sustainable development remains a challenge that is yet to be solved.

---

64 *See*, Kojima C., "Integration of General Principles of International Environmental Law into the Law of the Sea: Assessment and Challenges," *Marine Policy* 149 (2023) 105497.

65 Endorsing countries include the United States, Armenia, Bulgaria, Canada, Croatia, Czech Republic, Finland, France, Ghana, Hungary, Jamaica, Japan, Republic of Korea, Moldova, Mongolia, Morocco, Netherlands, Poland, Romania, Slovakia, Slovenia, Sweden, Ukraine, United Arab Emirates, and United Kingdom. *See* UNFCCC, Summary of Global Climate Action at COP 28, available at: https://unfccc.int/sites/default/files/resource/Summary_GCA_COP28.pdf; U.S. Department of Energy, Declaration Recognizes the Key Role of Nuclear Energy in Keeping Within Reach the Goal of Limiting Temperature Rise to 1.5 Degrees Celsius, available at: https://www.energy.gov/articles/cop28-countries-launch-declaration-triple-nuclear-energy-capacity-2050-recognizing-key (accessed Nov. 29, 2024).

CHAPTER 7

Territorial Disputes between Japan and Neighboring Countries

Maki Nishiumi

1 Introduction

In general, the background for territorial disputes between states is complex as States do not only rely on international law when claiming disputed territories as their own. In addition to international law, various other factors such as history, politics, economics, society, culture, and public opinion are mobilized to justify their claims. This also applies to Japan's current territorial disputes. A firm grasp of the international legal aspects of territorial disputes remains a prerequisite for resolving them. In this context, the following section deals with the international legal aspects of three territorial disputes that Japan is involved in with its neighbors: the Northern Territories dispute (with Russia), the Takeshima dispute (with South Korea) and the Senkaku Islands dispute (with China).

2 Northern Territories Issue

Since the end of World War II, no peace treaty has yet been concluded between Japan and Russia. This is due to the dispute between the two countries over the so-called Northern Territories (the four islands of Habomai, Shikotan, Kunashiri and Etorofu).

2.1 *History*

The Matsumae clan recognized the four northern islands as its territory from the beginning of the 17th century and began to govern these areas, effectively controlling them at the beginning of the 19th century at the latest.[1] The 1855 Treaty of Friendship between Japan and Russia established the border between Japan and Russia as between Etorofu and Uruppu.

1 Wada H., *The Northern Territories Issue* (The Asahi Shimbun, 1999), 34–38.

 | DOI:10.1163/9789004548824_008

As a result, Etorofu belonged to Japan and the Kuril Islands north of Uruppu belonged to Russia. On the other hand, the treaty on Sakhalin did not define the boundary between the two countries, but allowed the free passage and residence of both peoples, and made it the common land of both countries.[2] The 1875 Treaty of Exchange of Sakhalin and Kuril Islands made all of Sakhalin Russian territory, and all of the Kuril Islands Japanese territory.[3] Subsequently, the 1905 Treaty of Portsmouth (the peace treaty of the Russo-Japanese War) ceded the area of Sakhalin south of 50°N to Japan.[4]

In February 1945, at the end of World War II, the US, Britain, and the USSR concluded the Yalta Agreement, under which the USSR was promised that the South Sakhalin and all the Kuril Islands would be handed over to the USSR in return for the USSR's participation in the war against Japan.[5] Under the agreement, the Soviet Union entered the war against Japan on August 9th, 1945 shortly before Japan's surrender, and by early September of the same year, the Soviet Union had occupied South Sakhalin, the Kuril Islands, and parts of Hokkaido, including the islands of Habomai and Shikotan, and incorporated them into its territory in February the following year. On the other hand, the Allies made the principle of non-aggression which is the basic policy for dealing with post-war territories in the Atlantic Charter of 1941 and the Cairo Declaration of 1943.[6] The Cairo Declaration further stated that Japan would also be expelled from all other territories which she has taken by violence and greed.[7] Japan accepted the Potsdam Declaration on August 14th, 1945, which required Japan to surrender. The Potsdam Declaration stipulates that the Cairo Declaration must be implemented, and that Japanese sovereignty is limited to Honshu, Hokkaido, Kyushu, Shikoku, and such islands as the Allies may determine.[8] Under the 1951 Treaty of Peace with Japan (San Francisco Treaty), Japan renounced its territorial rights over the Kuril Islands and Minami Karafuto.[9] In the 1956 Soviet-

2 Article 2 of the Russo-Japanese Treaty of Friendship, *signed on* February 7, 1855, *entered into force on* August 7, 1855.

3 Articles 1 and 2 of the Treaty of Exchange of Sakhalin and Kuril Islands, *signed on* May 7, 1875, *entered into force on* August 22, 1875.

4 Article 9 of the Treaty of Portsmouth, *signed on* September 5, 1905.

5 Articles 2 and 3 of the Yalta Agreement, *signed on* February 11, 1945.

6 Atlantic Charter, *released on* August 14, 1941, para. 1; Cairo Declaration General Statement, *released on* December 1, 1943, para. 3.

7 Cairo Declaration General Statement, *ibid.*

8 Potsdam Declaration, *released on* July 26, 1945, para. 8.

9 Article 2(c) of the Treaty of Peace with Japan, *signed on* September 8, 1951, *entered into force on* April 28, 1952, 136 UNTS 45.

Japanese Joint Declaration, the USSR agreed to hand over to Japan the territories of Habomai and Shikotan after the conclusion of a peace treaty between the two countries.[10] However, this has never been implemented.[11] In 2020, the Russian Constitution was revised and the prohibition of cession of Russian territory was clearly stated. In the same year, the Russian Criminal Code was also revised, stipulating sentences of up to four years imprisonment for those who call for the cession of territory and up to 10 years imprisonment for those who violate the prohibition on ceding territory.[12] These legal revisions have brought the Northern Territories negotiations to a halt.

2.2 *Claims of Both Governments*

2.2.1 Japanese Government Claims

The Japanese governments claims are as follows. "The Kuril Islands renounced by the Treaty of Peace with Japan do not include the islands of Habomai, Shikotan, Kunashiri, and Etorofu. The islands of Habomai and Shikotan were originally attached to Hokkaido and are not included in the Kuril Islands. Kunashiri and Etorofu became Japanese territory peacefully under the Treaty of Friendship between Japan and Russia. These four northern islands have never been claimed by Russia and in that sense are inherently Japanese territory. The Cairo Declaration states that Japan must be rid of areas 'plundered by the Japanese nation through violence and greed', but the four northern islands do not fall into this category in view of their historical background. Japan is not a party to the Yalta Agreement and is therefore not bound in any way by that agreement, which stipulates the handover of the entire Kuril Islands to the Soviet Union. Under the Treaty of Peace with Japan, Japan renounced Minami Sakhalin and the Kuril Islands, but the Treaty follows the principle of non-extension of territory as stated in the Cairo Declaration and the Potsdam Declaration. Therefore, the

10 Joint Declaration of the Soviet Union and Japan, *signed on* October 19, 1956, para. 9.

11 Article 67(2) of the Russian Constitution as revised in 2020. However, the same paragraph is supplemented by the phrase "except for boundary demarcation, demarcation work and re-demarcation work between the Russian Federation and neighboring countries".

12 Articles 280-1 and 280-2 of the Russian Criminal Code, as amended in 2020, with the addition of the words "except for boundary demarcation, demarcation work and re-demarcation work between the Russian Federation and neighboring states" to these sections.

Kuril Islands referred to in said treaty, do not include the four northern islands as Japan's inherent territory."[13]

2.2.2 Claims of the Soviet and Russian Governments

The Soviet/Russian Government's claims are, in summary, as follows. "The Soviet Union's territorial rights over the southern half of Sakhalin, the adjacent islands, as well as the Kuril Islands, which are now under Soviet sovereignty, are undisputed."[14] "The Soviet Union agreed to hand over the islands of Habomai and Shikotan to Japan. However, these islands were to be handed over after the conclusion of a peace treaty between Japan and the USSR".[15] "The Soviet Government, considering that the new treaty signed by the Japanese Government is directed towards the USSR and the People's Republic of China, cannot allow that the handing over of these islands (Habomai and Shikotan) to Japan will facilitate the expansion of the territory used by foreign troops. Only on condition of the withdrawal of all foreign troops from Japanese territory and the signing of the Soviet-Japan Peace Treaty, will the islands be handed over to Japan[16]" In essence, President Putin explained his thoughts as, "I want to develop relations between Japan and Russia, but I will not do anything that violates the Russian Constitution."[17]

2.2.3 Legal Assessment

The Japanese government maintains that the four northern islands are inherent to Japan and that they are not part of the Kuril Islands, which Japan abandoned under the Treaty of Peace with Japan. However, the Japanese government's attitude on this point has not been consistent. In September 1951, then Prime Minister Shigeru Yoshida in his acceptance speech of the treaty stated the following "the two islands in the southern part of the

13 Reply by Parliamentary Vice-Minister for Foreign Affairs Morishita at the House of Representatives Committee on Foreign Affairs held on 11 February 1956, International Law Case Study Group (Kokusaihō Jirei Kenkyūkai), *Territory* (Keio Tsushin, 1990), 108.

14 Speech by Gromyko, representative of the Soviet Union at the San Francisco Peace Conference, 5 September 1951, cited in Serita K., *Nihon no Ryōdo* [Japan's Territory] (Japanese) (Chuokoron Shinsha, 2002), 75–76.

15 Joint Declaration of the Soviet Union and Japan, *signed on* October 19, 1956, para. 9.

16 Memorandum from the Government of the USSR to the Government of Japan, dated 27 January 1960, International Law Case Study Group (n 13).

17 Remarks by President Putin on 10 February 2021, Nihon Keizai Shimbun, 19 February 2021, https://www.nikkei.com/article/DGXZQOGR18EV10Y1A210C2000000/ (accessed Jan. 28, 2024).

Kuril Islands, Kunashiri and Etorofu" and "the northern Kuril Islands, north of Uruppu" and thus acknowledged that Kunashiri and Etorofu were included in the Kuril Islands abandoned under the Treaty of Peace with Japan, although in the context of protesting against having been forced to abandon the Kuril Islands[18]. In addition, in October 1951, when the scope of the Kuril Islands referred to in the Treaty of Peace with Japan was questioned during deliberations in the House of Representatives, Kumao Nishimura, Director-General of the Treaty Bureau of the Ministry of Foreign Affairs, clearly stated that the Kuril Islands abandoned under the Treaty included the Southern Kuril Islands (Kunashiri and Etorofu).[19]

The Northern Territories theory that the territories of Habomai, Shikotan, Kunashiri, and Etorofu are inherent to Japan and not included in the Kuril Islands renounced under the Treaty of Peace with Japan was first put forward during the negotiations for the conclusion of the Soviet-Japanese Peace Treaty, which began in 1955.[20] However, this theory is not internationally persuasive because, as the author mentioned just above, the Japanese Government acknowledged clearly, during acceptance of the Treaty of Peace and in the deliberations of the House of Representatives, that Japan renounced all the Kuril Islands, including Kunashiri and Etorofu under the Treaty of Peace with Japan.[21]

In light of this, the Japan should point out to Russia that the Kuril Islands clause in the Yalta Agreement and in the Peace Treaty with Japan are contrary to the principle of non-extension of territory confirmed in the Cairo Declaration and the Potsdam Declaration, withdraw the Northern Territories theory which lacks historical and legal foundations, propose a review of Japan's renunciation of all the Kuril Islands and the Soviet Union's possession of all the Kuril Islands, and negotiate territorial issues with Russia by relying on the Treaty of Amity between Russia and Japan and also on the Treaty of Exchange of Karafuto (Sakhalin) and Kuril Islands, both of which peacefully established the territories of these two countries.

After the revision of the Constitution and Criminal Code (2020) and Russia's invasion of Ukraine (2022), there is no momentum for the time being, to resolve the Northern Territories issue. We can only hope that in the

18 Speech of 7 September 1951 by Prime Minister Shigeru Yoshida on the acceptance of the Treaty of Peace with Japan, Ministry of Foreign Affairs, Treaties Bureau, Legal Affairs Division, "Record on the Conclusion of the Peace Treaty VII," 118–122.

19 Wada (n 1), 203, 225–226.

20 International Law Case Study Group (n 13). This was the unified view of the Japanese Government at the time on this issue.

21 *See* Wada (n 1), 203, 225–226.

future the two governments, having rebuilt trust, will resolve this territorial issue politically and in good faith.

3 Takeshima Issue

Takeshima is located off the coast of Shimane Prefecture and consists of two small islands (Otokojima and Onnajima) and numerous reefs. Japan is in dispute with South Korea over the territorial rights to Takeshima. Takeshima is currently effectively controlled by South Korea.

3.1 *History*

According to Korean sources, Takeshima was discovered by Koreans in the mid-15th century. However, from then until the end of the 19th century, there was confusion over the names of Takeshima and its neighboring islands, and there is no evidence of any clear claim to Takeshima as their territory on the part of either country.[22]

In the early 20th century, Oki Islanders overhunted the sea lions on Takeshima and a fisherman concerned about this, applied to incorporate the island into Japan and lease it to prevent overfishing. In response, the Japanese government made a cabinet decision on January 28th, 1905 to declare Takeshima an island belonging to Japan and under the jurisdiction of Shimane Prefecture's Oki Affairs Department.[23] On the other hand, under the Korean Annexation Treaty signed on August 22nd, 1910, Korea was annexed to Japan.[24]

After World War II, an Allied directive issued in November 1945 followed the Potsdam Declaration and limited Japanese sovereignty to Honshu, Hokkaido, Kyushu, Shikoku, and islands determined by the Allies.[25] A General Headquarters memorandum issued in January 1946 suspended Japanese administrative authority over Ulleungdo, Jeju Island, and Takeshima.[26]

22 International Law Case Study Group (n 13), pp. 166–169; Serita (n 14), 149–152; Sakamoto Y., *Rekishi kara himotoku Takeshima/Dokdo mondai* [Taleshima/Dokdo Issues from a Historical Perspective] (Japanese) (Shimizu Shoin, 2021), 83–86.

23 International Law Case Study Group (n 13), 170–171; Sakamoto (n 22), 113; Official Documents, 29 ed. 1905, affiliated with the National Archives of Japan.

24 Article 1 of the Treaty regarding Annexation of Korea to the Empire of Japan, *signed on* August 22, 1910, *entered into force on* August 29, 1910.

25 "Early Basic Directives to the Supreme Commander of the Allied Powers for the Occupation and Administration of Japan after the Surrender," International Law Case Study Group (n 13), 172.

26 "Memorandum of Governmental and Administrative Separation of Certain Outlying Areas from Japan," SCAPIN-677 of 29 January 1946, cited in Sakamoto (n 22), 114.

Furthermore, an Allied General Headquarters memorandum issued in June of the same year prohibited Japanese ships from entering within 12 miles of Takeshima.[27] However, the January 1946 memorandum stated that these series of measures should not be interpreted as the final disposition of Japanese territory by the Allies.[28]

Under the Treaty of Peace with Japan (signed on September 8th, 1951 and entered into force on April 28th, 1952), Japan recognized Chosun's independence and renounced its rights, title and claims over Chosun, including Cheju, Geomundo and Ulleungdo.[29] On January 18th, 1952, just before the Peace Treaty entered into force, Korean President Syngman Rhee issued the Declaration of Maritime Sovereignty[30] and unilaterally declared sovereignty over the waters including Takeshima, establishing a fishing protection zone and regulating the fishing activities of foreign ships (the Syngman Rhee Line). In response, the Japanese government immediately protested that the Korean government's territorial claim to Takeshima was unacceptable. The Treaty of Peace with Japan did not specify Takeshima as an area that Japan had abandoned, so when the treaty came into effect, Takeshima was placed under the jurisdiction of the Oki Branch Office of Shimane Prefecture as before. However, Korea continues to occupy Takeshima to this day. The Japanese government proposed the Korean government to settle the dispute by the International Court of Justice, but the Korean government rejected the proposal.[31]

27 "Memorandum of the Allied General Headquarters on the Area Authorised for Japanese Fishing and Whaling," SCAPIN-1033, 22 June 1946, cited in Sakamoto, *ibid.*, 115.

28 SCAPIN-677 (n 26), para 6. International Law Case Study Group (n 13), 172.

29 Article 2(a) of the Treaty of Peace with Japan, *signed on* September 8, 1951, *entered into force on* April 28, 1952, 136 UNTS 45.

30 For the contents of the Declaration, *see*, Ministry of Foreign Affairs of the Republic of Korea, Reference Documents on Korea-Japan Relations, 1958, 155–156, Hyeon Dae-song (Translation), Database "World and Japan" (represented by Tanaka A.) Database on Japanese Politics and International Relations, National Graduate Institute for Policy Studies and Institute of Oriental Culture, University of Tokyo, https://worldjpn.net/documents/texts/JPKR/19520118.O2J.html (accessed Jan. 27, 2024).

31 The Japanese Government proposed to the Korean Government to settle this dispute at the International Court of Justice by oral statement on 12 September 1954, but the Korean Government rejected the proposal by memorandum on 28 October of the same year. International Law Case Study Group (n 13), 178.

3.2 *Claims of Both Countries*

3.2.1 Japanese Government Claims

The Japanese government's argument is summarized as follows. "The quotations of historical documents and facts relied upon by the Korean government are inaccurate and their interpretations are full of misunderstandings."[32] "International law did not apply to Japan before the opening of the country to the outside world, and it is sufficient for Japan to consider and treat Takeshima as its territory and claim it as such if no other country disputes it."[33] "Prior to the annexation of Japan and Korea, the Japanese government incorporated the island into the jurisdiction of the Oki Islands Office belonging to Shimane Prefecture. It met the requirements for territorial acquisition as required by modern international law. The measure to incorporate Takeshima into Japanese territory has nothing to do with the Japan-Korea Protocol or the Japan-Korea Agreement. Since the incorporation of Takeshima into Japanese territory, the island has been effectively managed by the Japanese people and during this period, the ownership of the island by other countries has never been an issue. The Treaty of Peace with Japan does not call for the cession to Korea of any territory that was Japanese territory before the annexation of Japan and Korea."[34] "The measures taken by the Allied General Headquarters against Japan under SCAPIN-677, 1033 have nothing to do with the ownership of Takeshima, as stated in SCAPIN-677, paragraph 6."[35]

3.2.2 Korean Government Claims

The Korean government's argument is summarized as follows. "In light of the historical and geographical background, and in view of international law's conception of land ownership, Takeshima is part of Korean territory."[36] "Japan's incorporation measure of Takeshima is based on the legal principle of *occupatio*, but this measure is invalid because Takeshima was not unclaimed land but Korean territory at the time. Japan's declaration of its territorial intention in the form of Shimane Prefecture's notification was made in secret and was not notified to the Korean government, so it is invalid. Even if the Korean government was aware of this fact, it was not in a

32 *Ibid.*, 176.
33 Serita (n 14), 159.
34 Opinion of the Ministry of Foreign Affairs, 13 July 1953. International Law Case Study Group (n 13), 175.
35 *See*, n 28 of this chapter.
36 International Law Case Study Group (n 13), 175.

position to challenge the Japanese government due to the Japan-Korea Protocol and the First Japan-Korea Agreement. Japan's actions after the incorporation measures were carried out as part of the invasion of Korea and therefore cannot be regarded as a continuing act of territorial control under international law."[37] "SCAPIN-677, 1033 suspended Japan's exercise of administrative authority over Takeshima and prohibited access to the island. This is an agreement and confirmation by the Allied General Headquarters of Korea's demands for Takeshima."[38]

3.2.3 Legal Assessment

The Korean government claims that Takeshima belonged to Silla in the early 6th century, according to the history book Samguksagi, but Samguksagi was written in the 12th century, and 12th century geographical perceptions do not necessarily match those of the 6th century. It is also unlikely that Silla's rule in the 6th century extended to Takeshima, which is still essentially uninhabited.[39] On the other hand, the Edo Shogunate recognised the Korean ownership of Ulleungdo Island, located to the west of Takeshima, at the end of the 17th century and issued a ban on passage to the island, but took no clear stance on the ownership of Takeshima.[40] The Meiji government then made a decision in 1877 that Ulleungdo and Takeshima were outside of Japan's territory.[41] The Korean government issued an imperial decree in 1900, upgrading Ulleungdo to Uldo County and including Takeshima within its jurisdiction.[42] However, this cannot be said to be an effective incorporation of Takeshima into Korean territory as the royal decree did not specify the region in terms of exact latitude and longitude, nor did it specify the attribution of Takeshima to its jurisdiction.[43]

In 1905, the Japanese government made a Cabinet decision to incorporate Takeshima into Japanese territory, and the Shimane Prefecture Notification No. 40, which followed this decision, stated that Takeshima was "under the jurisdiction of the Oki Island Office". This notification accurately indicated

37 Serita (n 14), 152–153.
38 International Law Case Study Group (n 13), 174.
39 Sakamoto (n 22), 83.
40 *Ibid.*, 86.
41 Grand Council Directive, cited in Sakamoto *ibid.*, 87.
42 "Royal Decree 41," cited in Sakamoto, *ibid.*, 88.
43 *Ibid.*

the latitude and longitude of the region, had administrative procedures in place, and met the requirements for *occupatio* under international law.[44]

Therefore, from a formal and legal point of view, Takeshima's claim to be Japanese territory has an advantage. However, such an understanding alone cannot resolve this dispute. In the late 19th and early 20th centuries, Japan was under unequal treaties in its relations with Europe and the US, which it overcame through victory in the Sino-Japanese and Russo-Japanese wars and subsequent treaty revisions. On the other hand, Japan adopted an imperialist and coercive attitude towards Asian countries. The biggest victim of this was the Korean empire and the Korean people. Without this heavy fact, it is impossible to resolve the territorial disputes and other issues between Japan and Korea. The Japan-Korea Joint History Study Committee should be reopened, and a final solution would be reached through political discussions based on listening to each other's opinions which are both frankly expressed, in light of historical facts.[45]

4 Senkaku Islands Issue

The Senkaku Islands are a group of uninhabited islands in the northern part of the Yaeyama Islands in Okinawa, Japan. They have been disputed between Japan, China and Taiwan since 1968, when scientists announced the possibility of oil fields in the surrounding waters.

---

44 *Ibid.*, 90–91. In this period, among the titles of acquisition of territory, there was *occupatio* according to which the control of free newly discovered territory by a State with no sovereign title to the land entitles this State to acquire the territory. There are four requirements of *occupatio* (*see* note 57). The majority of Japanese international lawyers, including the author himself, acknowledge that the measures taken by the Japanese Government at that time met these requirements.

45 *Ibid.*, 107–108. The Japan-Korea Joint History Research Committee is a joint research committee comprising researchers from both Japan and South Korea with the aim of conducting research and surveys on the history of relations between the two countries. Its establishment was agreed at the Japan-Korea summit meeting in October 2001 and its activities began in May 2002, with the first phase (2002–2005) and the second phase (2007–2010) reports on the results have been published. During this period, the Japanese side proposed dealing with the Takeshima/Dokdo issue, but this was put off due to strong protests from the Korean side. If a third phase is to be initiated, it would be necessary to set rules, such as that committee members should be chosen by the relevant academic societies rather than the Government, and that there should be no restrictions on the theme (*ibid.*, 109, footnote 2).

4.1 *History*

The Senkaku Islands are mentioned as a navigational marker in the Sakuhōshiroku (16th-19th centuries), a record of the Sakuhōshi sent by China to the Ryukyu Islands.[46] A Book written in the 16th century against Japanese pirates includes the islands in their maritime defense zone.[47] On the other hand, there are few references to the Ryukyu Islands in Ryukyuan literature, and a document written by a native Japanese at the end of the 18th century painted the islands in the same cherry blossom colors as mainland China, regarding them as Chinese territory.[48]

In 1879, the Meiji Government annexed the Ryukyu Islands through the Ryukyu Disposition and established the Okinawa Prefecture. On January 14th, 1895, the Meiji Government decided to construct a national marker on the Senkaku Islands. This decision was instructed to the Governor of Okinawa Prefecture on January 21st.[49] In 1896, a county system was established in Okinawa Prefecture and the Senkaku Islands were incorporated into Yaeyama County. Since then, the Senkaku Islands have consistently belonged to Okinawa Prefecture, except for a period under US administration. After the incorporation, civilians were engaged in albatross feather collecting, bird dropping mining and skipjack fishing.[50]

The Peace Treaty with Japan provided that Japan would renounce all rights, titles and claims to Taiwan and the Penghu Islands, and that the US would administer the Southwest Islands south of 29°N for the time being.[51] Thereafter, the islands remained under US administration until 1972, when they were given back under the Okinawa Reversion Agreement.

In 1968, Japanese, Taiwanese, South Korean and US scientists conducted a geophysical survey of the East China Sea and Yellow Sea under the coordination of the UN Economic Commission for Far East Asia (ECAFE). Their findings, published the following year, showed that the area around the Sen-

---

46 Matsui Y., *Kokusaihō Gakusha ga Yomu Senkaku Mondai* [The Senkaku Issue as Read by International Law Scholars] (Nippon Hyoronsha, 2014), 29–30; Harada N., *Senkakushotō – Sakuhō Ryūkyū Shiroku wo Yomu* [The Senkaku Islands: From the reading of Sakuhō Ryūkyū Shiroku] (Japanese) (Yojyu Shorin, 2006).

47 Matsui, *ibid.*, 30; Harada, *ibid.*, 118–120.

48 Matsui, *ibid.*, 33; Inoue K., *Senkakurettō – Uotsurishotō no Shitekikaimei* [The Senkaku Islands: Historical Clarification of Uotsuri Islands] (Japanese) (Gendai Hyoronsha, 1972), 44.

49 Matsui, *ibid.*, 36; Serita (n 14), 133–134.

50 Matsui, *ibid.*, 40; Urano K., *Senkakushōtō, Ryūkyū, Chūgoku* [The Senkaku Islands, Ryukyu, China] (Japanese) (Sanwa Shoseki, 2002), 138.

51 Articles 2(b) and 3 of the Treaty of Peace with Japan, *signed on* September 8, 1951, *entered into force on* April 28, 1952, 136 UNTS 45.

kaku Islands would become a future global oil producing region.[52] In response, Taiwan declared its exercise of sovereignty over the adjacent continental shelf resources in 1969 and officially communicated its sovereignty over the Senkaku Islands to Japan in 1971. The People's Republic of China also officially announced its sovereignty over the islands in 1970. In response, in 1972, the Japanese Ministry of Foreign Affairs announced its basic view that there was no doubt that the islands belonged to Japan.

In 2010, a Chinese trawler collided with a Japanese patrol vessel in territorial waters near the islands, and the Japan Coast Guard arrested the trawler's captain, who was later released pending charges. In 2012, the Japanese Government acquired ownership of three islands in the archipelago for long-term peaceful and stable maintenance[53]. The Chinese Government and people reacted to this with anti-Japanese demonstrations, destruction and looting of Japanese businesses and an escalation of military confrontation.[54]

4.2 *Claims of Both Countries*

4.2.1 Japanese Government Claims

The Japanese Government's claim is, in summary, as follows. The Senkaku Islands have been surveyed repeatedly by the Government of Japan since 1885, including through the authorities of Okinawa Prefecture. After having carefully confirmed that the islands were not only uninhabited but also that there were no traces of Qing rule, a Cabinet decision was made on January 14th 1895 to construct a marker on the site and formally incorporate the islands into Japan's territory.[55] In a separate document, the Ministry of Foreign Affairs explains that "this action is in line with the way to legitimately acquire territorial rights under international law and is based on the doctrine of *occupatio*".[56] *Occupatio* is one of the titles to acquire territory in traditional international law and is an example of *prima facie* acquisition; acquiring territory that does not belong to either State. There are four requirements for *occupatio* to be effective under international law: (i)

52 Matsui (n 46), 43; Ministry of Foreign Affairs of Japan, "About Senkaku Islands", https://www.mofa.go.jp/mofaj/area/senkaku/pdfs/senkaku.pdf (accessed Jan.30, 2024), 7.

53 "On the relevant ministerial meeting on the acquisition and possession of the Senkaku Islands", available at Japan Coast Guard website, https://www.kaiho.mlit.go.jp/info/kouhou/h24/k20120910/k120910-2.pdf (accessed Jan. 27, 2024).

54 Asahi Shimbun, 13 November 2012, evening edition, 21 November 2012; Matsui (n 46), 50.

55 Ministry of Foreign Affairs of Japan, "Basic View on the Senkaku Islands", https://www.mofa.go.jp/mofaj/area/senkaku/kenkai.html (accessed Jan. 27, 2024).

56 Ministry of Foreign Affairs of Japan, "Q&A on the Senkaku Islands Situation, Q2-A2", https://www.mofa.go.jp/mofaj/area/senkaku/qa_1010.html#q2 (accessed Jan. 27, 2024).

the subject of occupation is the State; (ii) the object of occupation is terra nullius (unclaimed land); (iii) the State making occupation has the intention to possess the territory; and (iv) the substantive requirement is effective occupation.[57]

4.2.2 Chinese Government Claims

The Chinese Government's two main claims are as follows. (1) Article 2 of the Sino-Japanese Peace Treaty (Shimonoseki Treaty) states that sovereignty over the following lands shall be ceded to Japan forever: the Liaodong Peninsula, all islands of Taiwan and its attached islands and the Penghu Islands. The Senkaku Islands were ceded to Japan as "the attached islands of Taiwan" as referred to here. Therefore, in accordance with Article 2(b) of the Treaty of Peace with Japan (San Francisco Treaty of 1951), which stipulates that Japan renounces all rights, title and claims to Taiwan and the Penghu Islands, the islands should be returned to China. (ii) When Japan incorporated the Islands into Japan through *occupatio*, the Islands, which had been under Chinese possession for a long time, were not unclaimed lands subject to *occupatio*. Therefore, the Japanese Government's claim that the Islands became Japanese territory through *occupatio* cannot be established.[58]

4.2.3 Legal Assessment

Does Japan's act of incorporating the Senkaku Islands into its territory satisfy the requirement of *occupatio*? There is no question that the actor is a State. As to whether the Senkaku Islands can be said to be unclaimed land, the Chinese Government has relied on various historical titles to argue that the islands have long been Chinese territory and are not subject to *occupatio*. The effect of these historical titles in the international legal order at the end of the 19th century will be examined in the Conclusion, but as far as they stand with regards to traditional international law in force at the end of the 19th century, these historical titles lacked effective control and cannot be regarded as valid titles. As such, the islands were terra nullius. The intention to claim the Islands was expressed by a Cabinet decision to erect a marker there. The Japanese Government has effectively occupied and controlled the Islands through more than ten surveys, land readjustment projects, land numbering, leasing of state-owned land, and collection of land rent and property tax. Therefore, it can be said that Japan's acts of occupation have fulfilled the requirements of *occupatio* imposed by traditional

57 Taijudo K., *International Law of Territorial Attribution* (Toshindo, 1998), 19.

58 Matsui (n 46), 69.

international law and that therefore the Islands have been effectively incorporated into Japan.[59]

On the other hand, in order for the Chinese Government's first claim to stand, it must be proven that the islands are included in the archipelago attached to Taiwan. However, there was no reference to the islands in the negotiation process of the Sino-Japanese Peace Treaty, or at the time of the actual handover of Taiwan and other islands. Furthermore, there are no descriptions in past historical documents to support this.[60] There are also those who argue that the Islands being an archipelago attached to Taiwan is a self-evident fact that does not require proof. This is a preemptive argument and cannot be used in a legal setting.[61]

In its second argument, the Chinese Government states that the islands were already Chinese territory during the Ming dynasty. This was based on the Book of Feudal Emissaries and their incorporation into the maritime defense area. However, the fact that the islands were used as a navigation marker and incorporated into the maritime defense area does not mean that the islands were Chinese territory.[62] Some consider that discovery was also a valid territorial title at the time, but this is not the majority view.[63] Since the decisive factor for the acquisition of territory in traditional international law is effective control, and all of the above grounds lack it, it is difficult to accept the claim that the Islands were Chinese territory.

Furthermore, as neither the Chinese nor Taiwanese governments had any objection to Japan's possession of the Senkaku Islands from 1895 to 1970, and a letter of thanks was issued by the Chinese consul to the islanders who rescued Chinese fishermen in distress in 1919, stating that the islands were Japanese territory, it may be possible to consider that the so-called theory of historical consolidation of territorial titles[64] may have made the Islands Japanese territory.

---

59 *Ibid.*, 100–104.

60 *Ibid.*, 69–73.

61 *Ibid.*, 76–78.

62 *Ibid.*, 78–80.

63 *Ibid.*, 81–83.

64 *Ibid.*, 135–139. Here, the theory of historical consolidation of title refers to the idea that even when the individual requirements of the title to acquire territory, such as *occupatio*, prescription, attachment and cession, are not met, acquisition of territory may still be granted based on a holistic and comprehensive judgment. *See* next. Nakatani K., "An International Legal Consideration of the Memorandum of Understanding between Iran and Sharjah on Abu Musa Island", *Journal of Island Studies*, vol. 9, no. 2, 2020,

The above states that the historical title claimed by the Chinese Government cannot be regarded as a valid title in traditional international law. In East Asia, the hierarchical order centered on China was replaced by the traditional international legal order of European origin (sovereign equality order), at the end of the 19th century. In this case, what effect do the facts, acts and norms of the old order have on the new order? In order to assess the Senkaku Islands dispute more fundamentally, we have to clarify this difficult question of law between legal systems.[65] The above-mentioned assessment was made exclusively from the perspective of the New Order, *i.e.* traditional international law. The attitudes of international precedents have not converged on this issue. There are some that hold that facts, acts and norms of the old order do not have any legal effect in the new order,[66] some that emphasize the principle of effectiveness,[67] some that call for the exercise of sovereignty while respecting the economic and cultural patterns of the old order which are incompatible with the territorial sovereignty of traditional international law,[68] some that recognize the existence of ancient primitive title and so on.[69] The issue of "law between legal systems" is unexplored, and how this is reflected in territorial disputes, including the Senkaku Islands, remains an issue for the future.

---

https://www.spf.org/islandstudies/jp/wp/wp-content/uploads/2020/04/9-2-1_sample_nakatani.pdf (accessed Jan. 27, 2024).

65 Matsui (n 46), 113–114. Tomoko F., "Kokusai Saiban ni okeru 'Zen-Kindai/Hi-Oushū no Ryōiki Shihai' no Enyō to Hyōka" in Yanagihara M., Kanehara A. ed., *Kokusaihō kara mita Ryōdo to Nihon* [Territory and Japan from the Perspective of International Law] (Japanese) (University of Tokyo Press, 2022).

66 Matsui, *ibid.*, 123–125. *The Minquiers and Ecrehos Case*, Judgment of 17 November 1953, *ICJ Reports*, 1953, 56–57. Award of the Arbitral Tribunal in the first stage of the proceedings between Eritrea and Yemen (Territorial Sovereignty and Scope of the Dispute), Decision of 9 October 1998, *RIAA*, vol. 22, at 245, para. 131; *ibid.*, at 268, para. 239.

67 Matsui, *ibid.*, 125–126. Western Sahara, Advisory Opinion of 16 October 1975, *ICJ Reports*, 1975, at 38–39, paras. 79–81; at 41–42, paras. 87–88; at 43–44, paras. 93–95; at 63, paras. 148–149; at 68, para. 162.

68 Matsui, *ibid.*, 127–129. Award of the Arbitral Tribunal in the second stage of the proceedings between Eritrea and Yemen (Maritime Delimitation), Decision of 17 December 1999, *RIAA*, vol. 22, at 244–245, paras. 126–130.

69 Matsui, *ibid.*, 129. *Case concerning Sovereignty Over Pedra Branca/Pulau Batu Puteh, Middle Rocks and South Ledge*, Judgment of 23 May 2008, *ICJ Reports*, 2008, at 33, paras. 52; at 35–37, paras. 60–69.

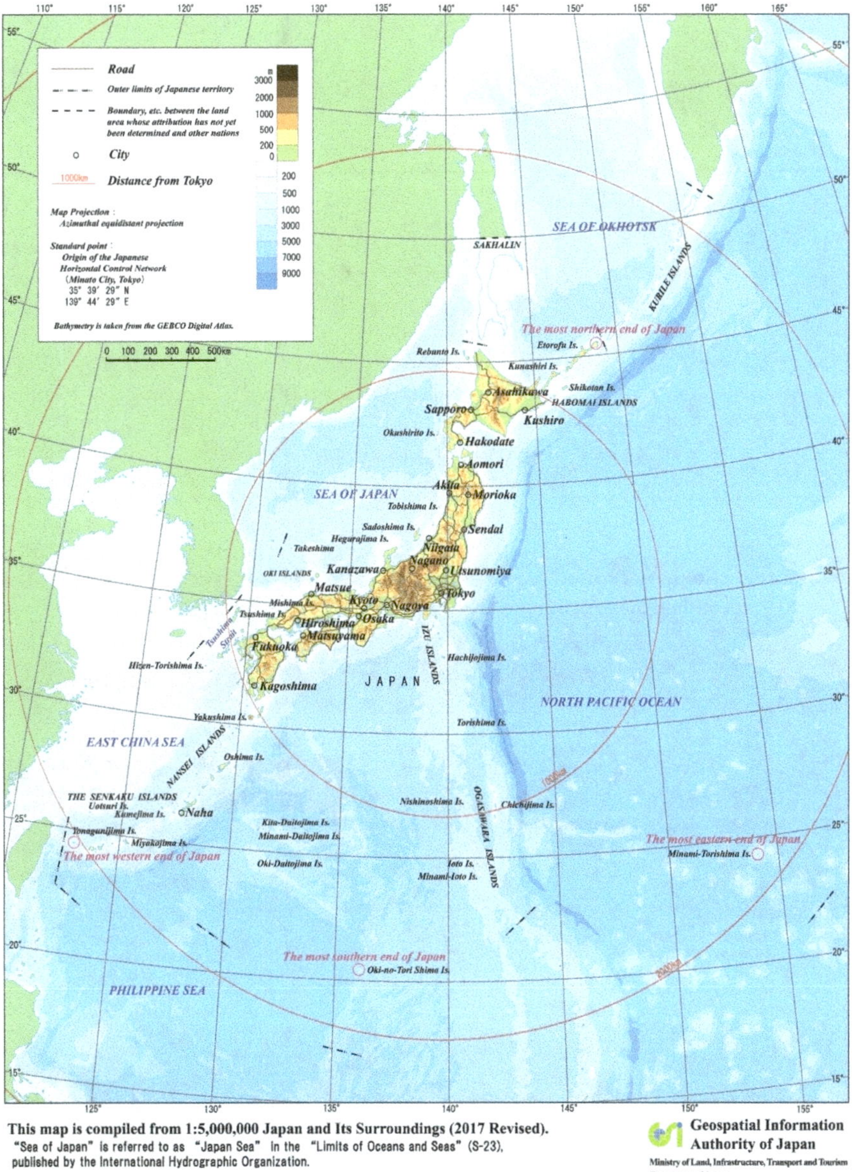

FIGURE 7.1 Japanese territory (https://www.gsi.go.jp/common/000247486.pdf)

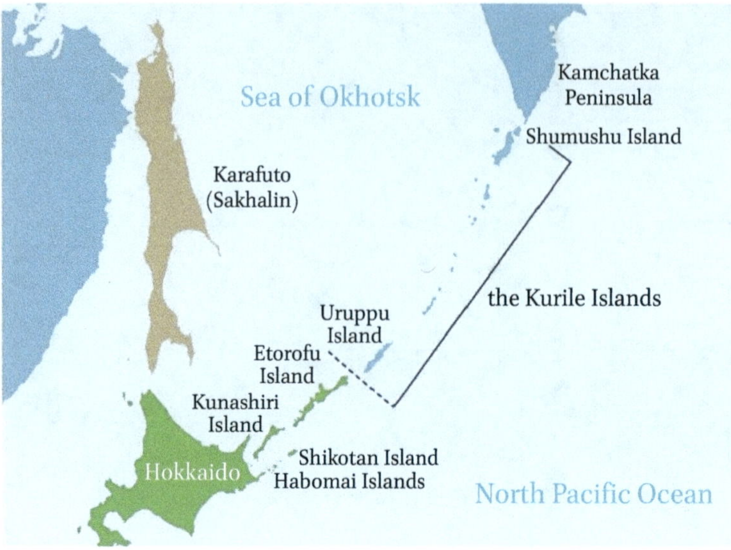

FIGURE 7.2 Northern Territories (https://www.cas.go.jp/jp/ryodo_eg/taiou/hoppou/hoppou01-01.html)

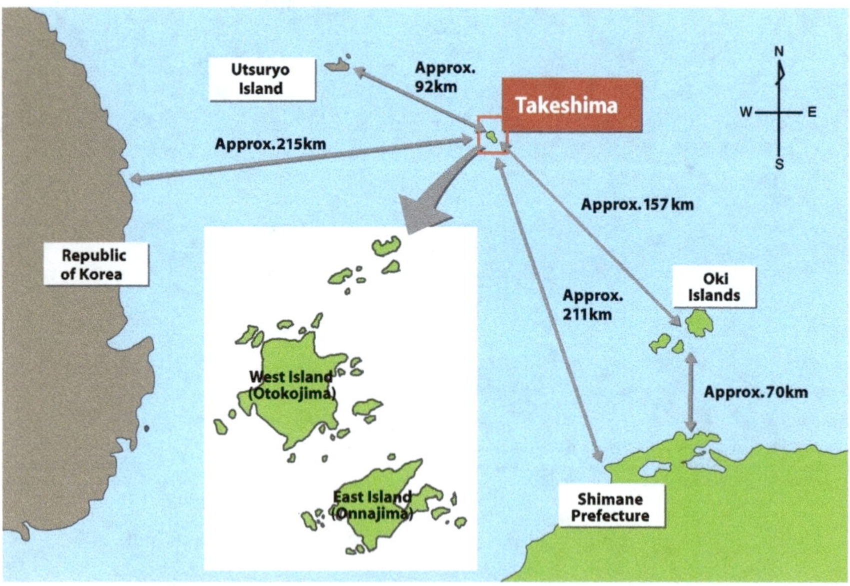

FIGURE 7.3 Takeshima Islands (https://www.eu.emb-japan.go.jp/The_Issue_of_Takeshima.html)

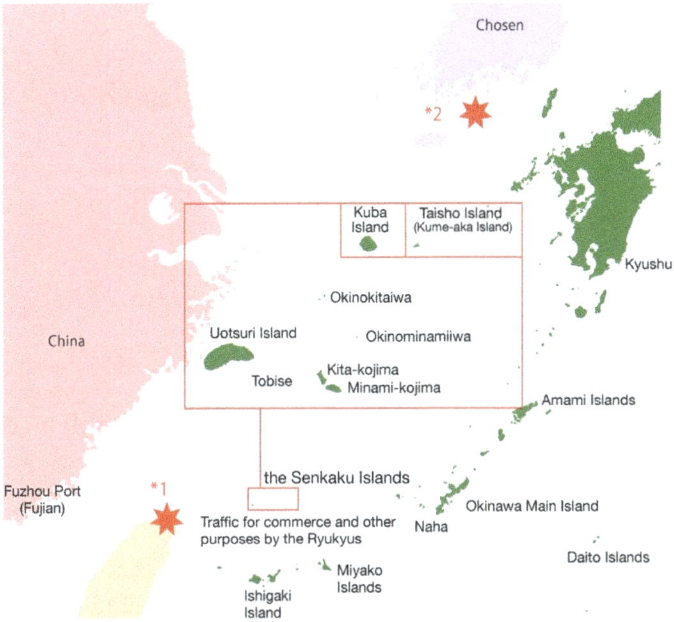

***1 Sino-French War** France and Qing Dynasty China waged war over the suzerainty of Viet Nam from 1883 to 1885

***2 Port Hamilton Incident** The British Navy occupied Port Hamilton, an island south of Korea, in April 1885 (Meiji 18), following the confrontation between the UK and Russia.

FIGURE 7.4 Senkaku Islands (https://www.cas.go.jp/jp/ryodo_eg/taiou/senkaku/senkaku01-01.html)

5 Conclusion

Territorial disputes are multifaceted and have a combination of legal, historical, political, economic and cultural dimensions. While international legal analysis and evaluation of territorial disputes is important, it is not the only way to resolve disputes. In particular, with regard to the Takeshima and Senkaku Island disputes, the Korean and Chinese governments and people see this as part of Japan's imperialistic expansionist policy towards their countries This makes it difficult to resolve the disputes through the objective and dispassionate application of international law. For international law to fulfill its role as an objective standard, it is necessary to face as honestly and faithfully as possible, the historical aspects and contexts of these territorial disputes, thus to foster a confident relationship. The Japanese Government and people, bearing primary responsibility for these aspects and contexts, must make further efforts to build a trusting relationship with them.

CHAPTER 8

Japan and Maritime Boundary Disputes with Neighboring Countries

Akari Takeuchi

1 Introduction

Japan has a vast exclusive economic zone (EEZ) and continental shelf based on the four main islands (Hokkaido, Honshu, Shikoku, and Kyushu) and a number of small islands. The maritime area covers approximately 4.05 million km², ten times larger than the land area.[1] Although the maritime claims overlapped with neighbors, only a small part is delimited. Conflicts often arise between the States over unilateral activities in the undelimited area, such as the natural gas development by the People's Republic of China (PRC) in the East China Sea and the maritime survey by the Republic of Korea (ROK) or Japan around the disputed island, Takeshima/Dokdo. In this chapter, we will first touch on the principles of international law of maritime delimitation, then briefly see the maritime boundary situation around Japan, including the issues of the East China Sea, such as boundary claims, joint development agreements, and unilateral development of natural resources.

2 Principles of Maritime Delimitation

Maritime boundary delimitation can be defined as "a process of establishing lines separating the spatial ambit of coastal State jurisdiction over maritime spaces where the legal title overlaps with that of another State."[2] After World War II, many States faced a situation in which their maritime claims overlapped with those of neighbors' due to the expansion of coastal States'

1 Hydrographic and Oceanographic Department, Japan Coast Guard, "Nihon no Ryōkai tō Gainenzu [Map of Japanese Territorial Sea and Other Maritime Zone]," https://www1.kaiho.mlit.go.jp/JODC/ryokai/ryokai_setsuzoku.html (accessed 9 Mar. 2023).

2 Tanaka Y., *Predictability and Flexibility in the Law of Maritime Delimitation*, 2nd ed. (Hart Publishing, 2019), 6.

 | DOI:10.1163/9789004548824_009

jurisdiction. The United Nations Convention on the Law of the Sea (UNCLOS) states that delimitation of such areas should be done by agreements between the relevant States based on international law (Articles 74 and 83). However, in cases where the States cannot reach agreements, the matter is often referred to international courts and tribunals. Thus, the law on maritime delimitation has developed through treaties such as the 1958 Convention on the Territorial Sea and the Contiguous Zone (TSC), the 1958 Convention on the Continental Shelf (CCS) and UNCLOS, as well as through international judicial decisions and State practices.[3]

2.1 *Maritime Delimitation of Continental Shelf and the EEZ*

2.1.1 The Principle of Equidistance and the Principle of Equity

The 1958 CCS defines the limit of the continental shelf as "to the seabed and subsoil of the submarine areas adjacent to the coast but outside the area of the territorial sea, to a depth of 200 meters or, beyond that limit, to where the depth of the superjacent waters admits of the exploitation of the natural resources of the said area". It stipulates that the continental shelf boundaries shall be delimited basically by agreements. However, if the relevant States fail to reach such agreements, they shall be delimited with equidistance lines modified by special circumstances (the principle of equidistance) (Article 6).

In the case of opposite States, delimitation by the equidistance principle works well in many cases. However, in the case of adjacent States, such delimitation sometimes brings inequitable results. *The North Sea Continental Shelf* case (*Federal Republic of Germany/Denmark; Federal Republic of Germany/Netherlands*) (hereinafter referred to as *the North Sea Continental Shelf* Case) could be an example. In this case, if one applies the principle of equidistance mechanically, Germany, with an indented coastline, can get only a tiny triangle-shaped area, being cut off by the convex coastline of the Netherlands and Denmark. Thus, the International Court of Justice (ICJ) took "the principle of equity" approach while rejecting "the principle of equidistance," which, in the Court's view, had not become customary international law binding the non-party State of CCS (Germany). The ICJ applied the equitable principle by emphasizing the importance of the title of the

3 The law of the sea, long developed as customary law, was codified in 1958 in four sector-specific conventions, including TSC and CSC. Subsequently, in 1982, UNCLOS was adopted to regulate the entire range of maritime issues. The 1958 conventions and UNCLOS cover the same maritime issues, but in case of a conflict of the treaties, UNCLOS prevails between UNCLOS States Parties (UNCLOS Art.311).

continental shelf, that is, the natural prolongation of the land territory (the natural prolongation theory). The ICJ stated that delimitation is to be affected by agreement following equitable principles and taking account of all the relevant circumstances in such a way as to leave as much as possible to each party all those parts of the continental shelf that constitute a natural prolongation of its land territory.[4]

2.1.2 Maritime Delimitation under UNCLOS

In the third United Nations Conference on the Law of the Sea, the participants split into the supporters of each equidistance and equitable principles. As a compromise, the drafters formed UNCLOS that the delimitation of EEZ and continental shelf shall be affected by agreement "on the basis of international law, [...] in order to achieve an equitable solution" (Arts. 74(1) and 83(1)). Neither the terms "equidistance" nor "equitable principle" was adopted so that the provision could be interpreted either way. The ambiguous text left the development of the law of maritime boundary delimitation to the accumulation of judicial cases.[5]

It should also be noted that the influence of the newly evolved regime of the 200 nm EEZ on the law of maritime delimitation. With the adoption of the regime of EEZ to UNCLOS, the outer limits of the continental shelf have been changed to "the outer edge of the continental margin" or "a distance of 200 nautical miles from the baselines." This means the distance criteria has been incorporated int the title of the continental shelf up to 200 nm while the title of the outer continental shelf remains the natural prolongation. Although title and relevant circumstances may differ between EEZ and continental shelf, for practical reasons, there is a general tendency to delimit them as a single boundary delimitation.

2.1.3 Development of the Law of Delimitation; "Equidistance/Relevant Circumstances Method" and "Three-Stage Approach"

To achieve an "equitable result" in maritime delimitation, the Courts have developed a method known as the "equidistant/relevant circumstances method" using the equidistant line modified with the "relevant circumstances." For example, in the 1985 *Case Concerning the Continental Shelf (Libyan*

---

4 *North Sea Continental Shelf (Federal Republic of Germany/Denmark and the Federal Republic of Germany/Netherlands)* case, [1969] ICJ, Judgment of 20 Feb. 1969, *ICJ Rep.* 1969, 53, para. 101.

5 Evans M., "Maritime Boundary Delimitation," in Rothwell D.R., Elferink, A.G.O., Scott K.N., and Stephens T. (eds), *The Oxford Handbook of the Law of the Sea* (Oxford University Press, 2016), 258.

Arab Jamahiriya/Malta) (hereinafter referred to as the *Libya/Malta* case), the ICJ first drew a provisional equidistance line and then moved the boundary line north toward Malta, considering the relevant circumstances such as the ratio of the length of the coastlines of the two States.[6] In this case, geological or geophysical factors of the seabed were not considered as the relevant circumstances since the development of the law of the sea enables a State to claim the continental shelf up to 200 miles from its coast, whatever the geological characteristics of the sea bed. There is no reason to ascribe any role to geological or geophysical factors within that distance either in verifying the legal title of the States concerned or in proceeding to a delimitation between their claims.[7]

In the *Maritime Delimitation in the Black Sea* (*Romania v. Ukraine*) case, the ICJ tried to refine the equidistance/relevant circumstances method into the "three-stage approach." The ICJ first drew a provisional equidistance line, then modified this line with the relevant circumstances to achieve an equitable result, and finally examined whether the maritime area allocated by the line resulted in a significant disproportionality in light of the length of the Parties' coastlines.[8] This approach is followed by cases of other UNCLOS tribunals, such as ITLOS case, the *Delimitation of the maritime boundary in the Bay of Bengal* (*Bangladesh/Myanmar*) (hereinafter referred to as the *Bangladesh/Myanmar* case).[9]

2.1.4 Delimitation of the Extended Continental Shelf beyond 200 nm

In the past decade, the jurisprudence of the delimitation of the Extended Continental shelf beyond 200 nm has been developing through several judicial cases and State practices. In the first judicial case, the *Bangladesh/Myanmar* case, ITLOS adjudged that "the delimitation method to be employed in the present case for the continental shelf beyond 200 nautical miles should not differ from that within 200 nm" since Article 83 does not distinguish inner and Extended Continental Shelf.[10] This judgment is followed by several cases, but it is too hasty to assume that this approach has matured as a legal principle applicable to all situations because *the Bangladesh/Myanmar* case and the following cases up to 2024 are between

6 *Continental Shelf* (*Libyan Arab Jamahiriya/Malta*) case, [1985] ICJ, Judgment of June 3 1985, *ICJ Rep.* 1985, 48–49, paras. 66–68.

7 *Ibid.*, 35, para. 39.

8 *Maritime Delimitation in the Black Sea* (*Romania v. Ukraine*) case, [2009] ICJ, Judgment of 3 Feb. 2009, *ICJ Rep.* 2009, 61, paras. 116–122.

9 *Delimitation of the Maritime Boundary in the Bay of Bengal* (*Bangladesh/Myanmar*), [2012] ITLOS, Judgment of 14 Mar. 2012, *ITLOS Rep.* 2012, 4.

10 *Bangladesh/Myanmar* case, *ibid.*, 117, paras. 454–455.

adjacent States in areas where there is no significant uncertainty as to the existence of a continental margin.[11]

As to the question of whether one State's entitlement to the Extended Continental Shelf can extend to a neighbor State's entitlement to 200 nm maritime zone, ICJ pronounced that, under customary international law, the former may not extend within the latter (*In Question of the Delimitation of the Continental Shelf between Nicaragua and Colombia beyond 200 nautical miles from the Nicaraguan Coast* (hereinafter *Nicaragua v. Colombia* case)).[12] The ICJ led this conclusion firstly based on the interrelationship of the 200 nm continental shelf and the EEZ.[13] To this point, Judge Iwasawa noted that natural prolongation has been replaced by distance as the criterion used to define the continental shelf within 200 nautical miles.[14] Secondly, the ICJ relied on examining the coastal States' submissions of the Extended Continental Shelf to the Commission on the Limits of the Continental Shelf (CLCS), which excluded areas within other States' 200 nm zone from their claims. ICJ believes these State practices are widespread and uniform and may be seen as an expression of opinion juris.[15] The decision received strong criticism, particularly regarding the recognition of customary law, but it could significantly impact the maritime boundaries of States whose Extended Continental Shelf claims and 200 nm overlaps, such as Japan/ROK/PRC.[16]

---

11 *In the Matter of the Bay of Bengal Maritime Boundary Arbitration between the People's Republic of Bangladesh and the Republic of India* case, [2014] Arbitral Tribunal constituted under Annex VII of the UNCLOS, Award of 7 July 2014, *RIAA*, XXXII (2019) 1; *Dispute concerning Delimitation of the Maritime Boundary between Ghana and Côte d'Ivoire in the Atlantic Ocean* (*Ghana/Côte d'Ivoire*) case, [2017] ITLOS, Judgment of Sept. 23, 2017, *ITLOS Rep.* 2017, 4: *Maritime Delimitation in the Indian Ocean* (*Somalia v. Kenya*) case, [2021] ICJ, Judgment of 12 Oct. 2021, *ICJ Rep.* 2021, 206.

For the review of these cases by Japanese researchers, see Tanaka (n 2) 171–184 and Nishimoto K., "Encho Tairiku Dana no Kyokai Kakutei [Delimitation of the Extended Continental Shelf]" (Japanese), *Tohoku Law Review* 5 (2018), 1.

12 *In Question of the Delimitation of the Continental Shelf between Nicaragua and Colombia beyond 200 nautical miles from the Nicaraguan Coast* (*Nicaragua v. Colombia*) case, [2023] ICJ, Judgment of 13 July 2023, 29, para. 79, at https://www.icj-cij.org/sites/default/files/case-related/154/154-20230713-jud-01-00-en.pdf (accessed 9 Mar. 2023).

13 *Ibid.*, 29, paras. 75–76.

14 *Nicaragua v. Colombia* case, separate opinion of Judge Iwasawa, 2. para. 4. at https://www.icj-cij.org/sites/default/files/case-related/154/154-20230713-jud-01-05-en.pdf(accessed 9 Mar. 2023).

15 *Nicaragua v. Colombia* (n 12) 29, para. 77.

16 For the case review, *see* Tanaka Y. "Recent Developments in the Jurisprudence concerning the Delimitation of the Continental Shelf beyond 200 Nautical Miles: Analysis

2.1.5 Relevant Circumstances and Effect of Islands

In the judicial precedents, many of the relevant circumstances addressed were related to geographic factors, including the shape of the coast, the general direction of the coast, and proportionality between the length of the coastline and the maritime area to be allocated to the parties. However, except for the presence of third countries, non-geographic factors, including economic factors such as the location of oil deposits and fishing grounds, historical rights, security, and navigation, are not recognized as relevant circumstances in many cases.[17]

The possible effect of islands on delimitation is often a point of contention. For example, even though a maritime feature is categorized as an "island" under Art.121, it is not always given full EEZ or continental shelf where such areas overlap with other States. As a result, the effect of islands on the boundaries varies, which can be classified into four categories: i) full effect, ii) half effect, iii) partial effect, and iv) enclave solution.[18] In the *Delimitation of the Continental Shelf between the United Kingdom of Great Britain and Northern Ireland, and the French Republic* (*UK, France*), only the 12 nautical miles continental shelf was given for the Channel Islands in proximity to the French mainland, because recognizing the full continental shelf would be disproportionate.[19] The Court also gave half-effect for the Isles of Scilly, 20 nautical miles from the British coast.[20] The treatment of islands varies by case, and no general law has yet been formed. However, in previous judicial prudence, there is a tendency to limit the effect of a small remote island if giving full effect would have a disproportionate impact on the equidistance line.[21]

---

of the Mauritius/Maldives and Nicaragua v. Colombia Cases," *International Law Studies* 103 (2024) 74–111. Woker, H. and Bernard, L., "A New Constraint to the Entitlement of a Continental Shelf beyond 200 Nautical Miles? – Implications of the Recent Case Law," *The International Journal of Marine and Coastal Law* (published online ahead of print 2024), at https://brill.com/view/journals/estu/aop/article-10.1163-15718085-bja10193/article-10.1163-15718085-bja10193.xml (accessed 9 Nov. 2024)

17 Tanaka (n 2), 444–446.

18 *Ibid.*, 274.

19 *Delimitation of the Continental Shelf between the United Kingdom of Great Britain and Northern Ireland, and the French Republic* (*UK, France*), [1978] Arbitration, Decision of 14 Mar, 1978, *RIAA* XVIII (2018), 93–95, paras. 196, 201–202.

20 *Ibid.*, 93–95, paras. 251.

21 Kaye S., "Chapter 20 State Practice as a Factor Impacting Potential East China Sea Boundaries", in Kraska J., Long R., and Nordquist M. H. (eds.), *Peaceful Maritime Engagement in East Asia and the Pacific Region* (Brill Nijhoff, 2023), 330–332. The State Practices Have the Same Tendency: Tanaka (n 2), 275.

2.2 *Obligations of Coastal States in Undelimited Areas*

UNCLOS imposes two obligations on States to avoid exacerbating the conflict and preventing the conclusion of the final agreement (Arts. 74(3) and 83(3)).

2.2.1 Obligation to Make Every Effort to Conclude a Provisional Agreement

This obligation aims to enable economic activities through a provisional arrangement in the undelimited area.[22] This obligation is an obligation of conduct, not of result.[23] This provision imposes States "a duty to negotiate in good faith" and requires them to take "a conciliatory approach to negotiations.[24] UNCLOS does not specify the details of the interim agreement, but it is thought to include establishing provisional boundaries and joint management zones in the disputed area.[25]

The notion of the joint development of continental shelf was firstly mentioned in *The North Sea Continental Shelf* case and incorporated into several agreements including 1974 Japan/ROK Southern CS Agreement, which will be discussed later in this chapter.[26] However, it is not a panacea for delimitation disputes.[27] Successful joint development depends on the following factors: the parties have solid, friendly relations and are willing to share sovereign rights; resource development is paramount to them; and they have a common understanding of the scheme of agreements in detail.[28] Joint

22 *The Arbitration regarding the Delimitation of the Maritime Boundary between Guyana and Suriname,* [2007] Arbitral Tribunal Constituted under Annex VII of the UNCLOS, Award of 17 Sept. 2007, *RIAA* XXX (2012), 130, para. 460.

23 *Ghana/Côte d'Ivoire* case (n 11), 162, para. 604

24 *Guyana v. Suriname* case (n 22), 130, para. 460.

25 British Institute of International and Comparative Law, *Report on the Obligations of States under Articles 74(3) and 83(3) of UNCLOS in respect of Undelimited Maritime Areas* (2016), 13–14, at https://www.biicl.org/documents/29_1192_report_on_the_obligations_of_states_under_articles_743_and_833_of_unclos_in_respect_of_undelimited_maritime_areas.pdf (accessed 9 Mar. 2023).

26 Several joint development agreements position themselves as provisional agreements under UNCLOS Art. 74(3) and 83(3). For example, The Timor Sea Treaty between the Government of East Timor and the Government of Australia (*signed on* 20 May 2002, *entered into force on* 2 Apr. 2003, Australian Treaty Series (2003) ATS 13) (hereinafter 2002 Timor Sea Treaty).

27 Churchill R.R., "Joint Development Zones; International Legal Issues" in Fox H. (ed.), *Joint Development of Offshore Oil and Gas,* vol. II (British Institute of International & Comparative Law, 1990), 67.

28 Townsend-Gault I. and Stormont W., "Offshore Petroleum Joint Development Arrangements: Functional Instrument? Compromise? Obligation?" in Blake G.H., Hildesley W.J., Pratt M.A., Ridley R.J., and Schofield C.H. (eds), *The Peaceful Management of Trans-boundary Resources* (Graham & Trotman/Martinus Nijhoff, 1995), 70–72.

development agreements without these elements may not fulfill the expected function and strengthen dissatisfaction with each other.[29]

2.2.2 Obligation Not to Jeopardize or Hamper the Reaching of the Final Agreement

UNCLOS does not clarify what conduct constitutes a breach of the obligation of "not to jeopardize or hamper the reaching of the final agreement." In *the Arbitration regarding the Delimitation of the Maritime boundary between Guyana and Suriname* (hereinafter referred to as *Guyana v. Suriname* case), the Tribunal adopted a similar standard of the ICJ's provisional measures: the existence of a "permanent physical change to the marine environment." Accordingly, it found that Guyana's authorization of exploration with drilling in the disputed waters constituted a unilateral act that caused "permanent physical change to the marine environment."[30] This "permanent physical change to the marine environment" criteria is confirmed by subsequent ICJ judgment, *Maritime Delimitation in the Indian Ocean (Somalia v. Kenya)* case (hereinafter *Somalia v. Kenya* case)[31]. However, this criterion is not seen as sufficient, as some activities can aggravate relations between the parties even if they do not involve physical changes.[32]

For this point, the International Tribunal of the Law of the Sea (ITLOS) Special Chamber adopted a new approach in the *Dispute concerning*

Maclaren G. and James R., "Negotiating Joint Development Agreements," in Beckman R., Townsend-Gault I., and Schofield C. (eds.), *Beyond Territorial Disputes in the South China Sea: Legal Frameworks for the Joint Development of Hydrocarbon Resources* (Edward Elgar Publishing, 2013), 141–144. Xue S., "Why Joint Development Agreements Fail," *Contemporary Southeast Asia* 41 (2019), 441.

29 The 2002 Timor Sea Treaty may be categorized as an agreement that lacks common understanding in its scheme. Timor-Lest was not satisfied with the borderline of the treaty's joint development zone favorable to Australia; in the end, the States terminated this treaty after the Compulsory Conciliation under UNCLOS. *See* Takeuchi A., "Shima wo Meguru Keisou Suiiki no Kyoudou Kaihatu ni kansuru Itikousatu [Joint Development Agreements in the Disputed Area concerning Islands]" (Japanese), *Tousho Kenkyu Journal* 11 (2021), 58–71.

30 *Guyana v. Suriname* case (n 22), 137 paras. 467, 479–482. Judge Paik pointed out that this classification is too strict since activities that do not involve physical changes to the marine environment may also be the source of severe tension between States. *Ghana/Côte d'Ivoire*, Separate Opinion of Judge Paik, *ITLOS Rep.* 2017, 180, para. 7. *See also* British Institute of International and Comparative Law (n 25), 26.

31 *Somalia v. Kenya* case (n 11), 282, para. 207.

32 British Institute of International and Comparative Law (n 25) 23–26. Nishimoto K., "The Obligation of Self-Restraint in Undelimited Maritime Areas," *Japan Review* 3 (2019), 16–18. Shimoyama K., "Keiso Suiiki deno Kaiyo Chosa ni kansuru Ichikostsu [Marine Research in the Disputed Area]" (Japanese), *Tosho Kenkyu Journal* 13 (2023), 99–107. van Logchem Y., *The Rights and Obligations of States in Disputed Maritime Areas* (Cambridge University Press, 2021), 227–230.

delimitation of the maritime boundary between Ghana and Côte d'Ivoire in the Atlantic Ocean (hereinafter referred to as the *Ghana/Côte d'Ivoire* case). It took this obligation as to act "in a spirit of understanding and cooperation". The Special Chamber viewed the Ghana's suspension of hydrocarbon drilling after the Special Chambers Provisional Order as such cooperative action and pronounced it does not violate this obligation.[33] As to the criterion of the violation of this obligation, Judge Paik, in his separate opinion, noted that no single test must be applied in all situations. He suggested that a key criterion is whether the activities endanger the process of reaching a final agreement which is assessed by considering relevant elements such as "type," "nature," "location," "time of acts," and "the manner in which they are carried out," which depend much on the particular circumstances of each case.[34]

Introducing the contextual criterion of "in a spirit of understanding and cooperation" in the *Ghana/Côte d'Ivoire* case will likely have no small impact on the international community, even if its content has not been considered sufficiently detailed and lacks clarity within the judgment. In disputed waters, coastal States would be required to act in a "spirit of understanding and cooperation", regardless of whether they are involved with drilling activities.[35]

3 Maritime Boundary Situations around Japan

Japan is surrounded by the Sea of Okhotsk, the Sea of Japan/East Sea, the East China Sea, and the Pacific Ocean. Its claims to territorial waters, EEZ, continental shelf, and extended continental shelf overlap with those of Russia, the PRC, the ROK, the United States (Northern Mariana Islands), the Philippines, and Palau, but most of the area of overlaps remain undelimited except a part of the continental shelf in the Sea of Japan/the East Sea. As stated in the introduction of this Chapter, Japan has serious maritime disputes with ROK and PRC.[36]

33 *Ghana/Côte d'Ivoire* case (n 11), 167–169, paras. 629–634.

34 *Ghana/Côte d'Ivoire* case, Separate Opinion of Judge Paik (n 30) 178, 180, paras. 6, 10.

35 Nishimoto (n 32) 22; Shimoyama (n 32), 105.

36 Relationship between Japan and neighboring States other than the ROK and the PRC. (a) Russia: The focus of the dispute is the territorial status of the Northern Territories/ Kuril Islands, and the States are not at the stage of discussing the delimitation of maritime boundaries. (b) Philippines/the United States (Northern Mariana Islands) /Palau: There are possible overlapping continental shelf and extended continental shelf in the

3.1 *Delimitation and Maritime Agreements Situation of Japan and ROK/PRC*

As of 2024, Japan/ROK and Japan/PRC have concluded several maritime agreements, including one continental shelf delimitation agreement, but most of the Sea of Japan/East Sea and the East China Sea remain undelimited; the coastal States try to exploit the seabed resources by joint development agreements pending delimitation, which do not function well. To understand the maritime disputes of East Asia, three elements should be noted: territorial disputes over certain islands, seabed resources, and the delimitation principle, which each State supports.

3.2 *Influence of the Territorial Disputes on Maritime Issues*

3.2.1 Japan/ ROK-Territorial Dispute over Takeshima/Dokdo and EEZ Delimitation

As to the continental shelf, Japan and the ROK succeeded in delimiting a part of the Sea of Japan/the East Sea in 1974 (Agreement between Japan and the Republic of Korea concerning establishing a boundary in the northern part of the continental shelf adjacent to the two countries (hereinafter referred to as Japan/ROK Northern CS Agreement.)) It delimits by an equidistance line between the States from the south of Takeshima/Dokdo islands (around it remains undelimited) to the northern end of the East China Sea (for the territorial dispute about Takeshima/Dokdo, see Chapter 7).[37]

However, the two States could not agree on the same area's EEZ. They agreed to delimit the EEZ with the equidistant line but disagreed over the treatment of Takeshima/Dokdo, which both States claim as their EEZ basepoint.[38] Takeshima/Dokdo is a group of inhabited islands located in the center of the Sea of Japan/East Sea. Japan and the ROK have long disputed it for its sovereignty. For the EEZ boundary, Japan has claimed the median line between Takeshima/Dokdo (Japanese side) and Ulleung Island (Korean side). Here, Japan used Takeshima/Dokdo as its EEZ basepoint, considering

Pacific but no severe conflict among States (*see* Chapter 5). *See also* Prescott V. and Schofield C., *The Maritime Political Boundaries of the World* (Brill Nijhoff, 2004), 417, 449. Nishimoto K. and Takeuchi A., "Japan: 6. Maritime Disputes and Overlapping Claims," in Lee S. (ed), *Encyclopedia of Ocean Law and Policy in Asia-Pacific* (Brill Nijhoff, 2022), 110–111.

37 Agreement between Japan and the Republic of Korea concerning establishing a boundary in the northern part of the continental shelf adjacent to the two countries, *signed on* 30 Jan. 1974, *entered into force on* 22 June 1978, 1225 UNTS I–19777.

38 Kim S.K., *Maritime Disputes in Northeast Asia: Regional Challenges and Cooperation* (Brill Nijhoff, 2017), 71–76. Nishimoto and Takeuchi (n 36), 109.

it an "island" that has an EEZ or continental shelf under Art.121 of the 1982 United Nations Convention on the Law of the Sea (hereinafter referred to as UNCLOS).[39]

UNCLOS Art. 121 stipulates that "(1) An island is a naturally formed area of land, surrounded by water, which is above water at high tide" and "(3) Rocks which cannot sustain human habitation or economic life of their own shall have no exclusive economic zone or continental shelf." An "island" can serve as an EEZ and continental shelf basepoint, but a "rock" does not have such a zone. However, UNCLOS does not clearly distinguish between "island" and "rock," and the text "which cannot sustain human habitation or economic life of their own shall" is ambiguous and may be interpreted in a wide variety of means. Thus, state practices and theories are divided on what features qualify as rocks. For example, Japan was positioned to regard small and uninhabited features such as Takeshima/Dokdo and Oki-no-Tori-Shima as "islands" since UNCLOS does not clearly define "rock," and the state practices are not unified.[40] On the contrary, the ROK initially held that it regards Takeshima/Dokdo as a "rock," which cannot be an EEZ basepoint since no permanent residents exist. Thus, it claimed the boundary should be the median line between Oki Islands (Japanese side) and Ulleung Island.[41] However, in 2006, after the Japan-Korea confrontation over the

39 Statement of Shotaro Yachi, the Deputy Assistant Minister of Ministry of Foreign Affairs, at the Sangiin [House of Councillors] Special Committee on the Law of the Sea, 136th Kokkai [National Diet], held on 4 June, 1996 (Japanese). Sangiin, *Dai 136 Kai Kokkai Sangiin Kaiyoho Joyaku tou ni Kansuru Tokubetu Iinkai Kaigiroku* 3 (1996), 30.

40 *Ibid.* This broad interpretation was challenged by *the South China Sea Arbitration* (*The Republic of Philippines v. The People's Republic of China*) (hereinafter The South China Sea Arbitration). The Arbitration Tribunal stated that "the island" must meet the conditions, including a) inhabitation by a stable community of people for whom the feature constitutes a home and b) the life and livelihoods of the human population inhabiting and making its home on the maritime feature. *The South China Sea Arbitration* (*The Republic of Philippines v. The People's Republic of China*) case, [2016] Arbitral Tribunal constituted under Annex VII of the UNCLOS, Award of 12 July, 2016, *RIAA* XXXIII (2020), 227–228, paras. 542–543. However, this judgment has been criticized for ignoring the many state practices of granting EEZs to small offshore features. Kagami Y., "Kokuren Kaiyoho Jouyaku dai 121 Jou 3 Kou wo Meguru Kokka Jikkou to Sono Ruikeika [State Practice under UNCLOS Article 121(3)" (Japanese) in Asada A., Kiriyama T., Tokugawa S., Nishimura T., and Higuchi K. (eds.), *Gendai Kokusaiho No Choryu* I (Toshindo, 2020), 342–359.

41 Lee W., "The Law of the Sea Regime in Northeast Asia; Issues and the Way Forward," *Journal of East Asian Affairs* 32 (2018), 64–65. Kim (n 38), 71–73. Nonaka K., "Kankoku Seifu karamita Takeshima no Houteki Chii-Kokuren Kaiyoho Jouyaku jou no Iwa kara Shima heno Tenkan (1) [The Legal Status of Takeshima, from the Point of View of the

marine survey around it, the ROK changed its position. It has come to use Takeshima/Dokdo as its base point for the EEZ boundary. Since both countries have designated it as the base of their EEZs, boundary delimitation between them has become complex without resolving their territorial dispute (for the discussion about the status of Oki-no-Tori-Shima, see Chapter 5).[42]

3.2.2 Japan and the PRC: Territorial Dispute over Senkaku/Diaoyu Islands and Maritime Dispute

Japan and the PRC have not reached a boundary agreement in the East China Sea. They concluded two provisional agreements for joint development of the seabed resources pending delimitation but failed to calm the tension between the States. The delimitation disputes are tied to the territorial dispute over the Senkaku/Diaoyu Islands. The Senkaku/Diaoyu Islands are about 150 km from Japanese Yonaguni Jima Island, 170 km from Taiwan, and 330 km from the Chinese Mainland. It was incorporated into Japanese territory in 1895, and once, about 200 residents engaged with fish processing industries.[43] Conflicts over the maritime issue, connected with this territorial dispute, have aggravated sharply in the last two decades, partly due to the PRC's maritime expansion. It has attempted to exercise its jurisdiction such as unilateral development of the hydrocarbon resources, intrusion into the territorial water around the Senkaku/Diaoyu Islands by State Oceanic Administration vessels, and drawing a straight baseline around them that could serve as the baseline for EEZ and continental shelf (for the territorial dispute about Senkaku/Diaoyu Islands, see Chapter 7).[44]

South Korean Government: Once a "Rock", Then an "Island" (1)]" (Japanese), *Kaiho Dai Kenkyu Houkoku* 60 (2016), 53–59. Nonaka K., "Kankoku Seifu karamita Takeshima no Houteki Chii-Kokuren Kaiyoho Jouyaku jou no Iwa kara Shima heno Tenkan (2) [The Legal Status of Takeshima, from the Point of View of the South Korean Government: Once a "Rock", Then an "Island" (2)]" (Japanese), *Kaiho Dai Kenkyu Houkoku* 61 (2016), 87–96.

42 Sakamoto S., *Nihon no Kaiyo Seisaku to Kaiyo Ho* [Japanese Ocean Policy and the Law of the Sea] (Japanese) 3rd ed. (Shinzansha, 2023), 443–448.

43 Nakauchi Y., "Senkaku Shoto wo Meguru Mondai [Issues concerning Senkaku Islands]" (Japanese), *Rippo to Chosa* 311 (2010), 22–23. Ministry of Foreign Affairs of Japan, "Japanese Territory Senkaku Islands," https://www.mofa.go.jp/region/asia-paci/senkaku/index.html (accessed 9 Mar. 2023).

44 Ministry of Foreign Affairs of the People's Republic of China, "Statement of the Government of the People's Republic of China on the Baselines of the Territorial Sea of Diaoyu Dao and Its Affiliated Islands" (10 Sept. 2012), https://www.fmprc.gov.cn/mfa_eng/topics_665678/diaodao_665718/201209/t20120912_701814.html (accessed 9 Mar. 2023).

4 Influence of the Resources on Maritime Delimitation Disputes in the East China Sea

4.1 *Background*

The East China Sea is bordered by Japan, the ROK, the PRC, and the Republic of China (Taiwan). It is rich in hydrocarbon resources, which attracted international attention through a 1968 survey by the U.N. Economic Commission for Asia and the Far East (ECAFE). The U.S. Energy Information Administration estimates 200 million barrels of oil resources and 1 and 2 trillion cubic feet of natural gas reserves in this area.[45] The geographic continental shelf extends from mainland China to the Pacific Ocean, dips slightly at the Okinawa Trough on the west side of the Ryukyu Islands, then crosses the Ryukyu Islands and sinks at the Ryukyu Trench. This geological factor is the basis for the Chinese and Korean claims described below.

In the East China Sea, the three States have each endorsed different boundary delimitation principles in favor of their respective interest to gain many resources in the area and failed to delimit. Thus, they concluded joint development agreements pending delimitation. One is Japan/the ROK agreement; the Agreement concerning joint development of the southern part of the continental shelf adjacent to the two countries (hereinafter referred to as Japan/ROK Southern CS Agreement). The others are the Japan/the PRC political agreements, the Understanding of Japan-China Joint Development in the East China Sea, and the Understanding of the development of Shirakaba (Chinese name: Chunxiao) oil and gas field (hereinafter referred to as the 2008 Japan/Japan Consensuses).

4.2 *Positions of the Coastal States*

One of the key obstacles is the disagreement between Japan/ROK and Japan/PRC over the applicable delimitation principles. Japan supports the equidistant line, while the others insist on adopting the equitable principle since, from their view, their legal continental shelf extends to the Okinawa Trough based on the natural prolongation theory.

For critical analysis, *see* Ashley Roach, "China's Straight Baseline Claim: Senkaku (Diaoyu) Islands," ASIL *Insights*, (13 Feb. 2013), https://www.asil.org/insights/volume/17/issue/7/china%E2%80%99s-straight-baseline-claim-senkaku-diaoyu-islands (accessed 9 Mar. 2023).

45 The U.S. Energy Information Administration, "East China Sea" (17 Sept. 2014), https://www.eia.gov/international/analysis/regions-of-interest/East_China_Sea (accessed 9 Mar. 2023).

Since the continental shelf delimitation negotiation with the ROK in the 1970s, Japan has consistently insisted on boundary delimitation based on equidistance lines. Its domestic law defines the limits of its continental shelf in overlapping areas as the median line between Japan and a foreign State unless agreed otherwise (for Japanese EEZ legislation, see Chapter 5).[46] However, it "does not mean that Japan has given up its entitlement beyond the equidistance line in any way; rather, it means that Japan decides to temporally limit its exercise of sovereign rights and jurisdiction to the Japanese side of the equidistance line in a period pending delimitation under international law."[47] This policy is repeated numerous times, such as in the 2015 announcement, "Japan's legal position on the development of natural resources in the East China Sea."[48]

The ROK established the "Submarine Mineral Exploitation Area" outside its territorial waters in 1970. During the continental shelf delimitation negotiation with Japan, it supported the equitable principle and natural prolongation theory. In domestic law, it restrains from exercising jurisdiction within its overlapping EEZ beyond the median line, but no such provision exists for the continental shelf.[49] This text shows that the ROK maintains its delimitation position based on natural prolongation for the continental shelf while supporting the equidistance/relevant circumstances method for EEZ.[50] In

---

46 Haitateki Keizai Suiiki oyobi Tairikudana ni kansuru Houritsu [Law on Exclusive Economic Zone and the Continental Shelf, Act No. 74 of 1996], Art. 1(1) and 2(1).
An English translation is available at https://www.un.org/Depts//los/LEGISLATIONANDTREATIES/STATEFILES/JPN.htm (accessed 9 Mar. 2023).

47 Ministry of Foreign Affairs of Japan, "Japan's Legal Position on the Development of Natural Resources in the East China Sea" (6 Aug. 2015), https://www.mofa.go.jp/a_o/c_m1/page3e_000358.html (accessed 9 Mar. 2023).

48 *Ibid.* In this announcement, Japan restated its East China Sea delimitation policy. First, it believes that boundary delimitation based on the geographical equidistance line is an equitable solution under UNCLOS and international jurisprudence. Second, it also believes there was no room for applying the natural prolongation theory in the area where the distance between two countries' coasts is less than 400 nautical miles. Finally, Japan denied the Chinese view, which regards the Okinawa trough as the geological terminus of the continental shelf of mainland China.

49 Act on the Exclusive Economic Zone and Continental Shelf (Act No. 14605, 21 Mar. 2017) Art. 5(1). An English translation is available at: https://elaw.klri.re.kr/eng_mobile/viewer.do?hseq=42701&type=part&key=44 (accessed 9 Mar. 2023).

50 Lee S. and Yang H.C., "Korea" in Lee S. (ed.), *Encyclopedia of Ocean Law and Policy in Asia-Pacific* (Brill Nijhoff, 2022), 180–181.

2012, it applied to the CLCS for an extended continental shelf up to the Okinawa Trough.[51]

The PRC has been a strong supporter of the equitable principle. Its domestic law states, "Conflicting claims regarding the exclusive economic zone and the continental shelf [...] shall be settled, on the basis of international law and in accordance with the equitable principle, by an agreement delimiting the areas so claimed".[52] As to the delimitation of the East China Sea, the PRC believes it should be done by the equitable principle, stressing that its EEZ and continental shelf extends to the Okinawa Trough.[53]

In 2012, the PRC applied to the CLCS for an extended continental shelf up to the Okinawa Trough.[54]

4.3 *Provisional Arrangements*

Faced with these divergences of view over the boundary, the States tried to enter into provisional arrangements to develop the resources pending delimitation to deter the escalation of conflict. This chapter focuses on the

---

51 The Republic of Korea, "Partial Submission of to the Commission on the Limits of the Continental Shelf Pursuant to Article 76 Paragraph 8 of the United Nations Convention on the Law of the Sea" (26 Dec. 2012), https://www.un.org/depts/los/clcs_new/submissions_files/kor65_12/executive_summary.pdf (accessed 9 Mar. 2023).

52 Exclusive Economic Zone and Continental Shelf Act of 26 June 1998, Art. 2. English translation is available at https://www.un.org/depts/los/LEGISLATIONANDTREATIES/STATEFILES/CHN.htm (accessed 9 Mar. 2023). For an analysis of Chinese policy regarding the Law of the Sea, *see* Zou K., *The International Law of the Sea in the 21st Century* (World Scientific Publishing, 2021), 212–213.

53 Ministry of Foreign Affairs, the People's Republic of China, "China's Oil and Gas Exploration in the East China Sea Is Rightful and Legitimate" (24 July 2015), https://www.fmprc.gov.cn/mfa_eng/wjdt_665385/2649_665393/201507/t20150730_679405.htm (accessed 9 Mar. 2023).

While the PRC sticks to the continental shelf delimitation, it does not say much about EEZ delimitation. In the 2015 statement, the PRC claimed that its EEZ also extends to the Okinawa trough, which seems odd since the title of the continental shelf (natural prolongation) and the EEZ (distance) are different. Japanese researchers analyze that the PRC tries to avoid a single maritime boundary for the Continental Shelf and EEZ since the equidistance principles generally delimit the latter. However, the PRC may accept a single maritime boundary if China's claim that its EEZ prolongs naturally to the Okinawa Trough should be upheld. *See* Sakai H., "Chapter 19 The Quest for a Win-Win Solution in the Delimitation of Continental Shelf in the East China Sea: An Irreconcilable Conflict between China and Japan?" in Kraska J., Long R. and Nordquist M.H. (eds.), *Peaceful Maritime Engagement in East Asia and the Pacific Region* (Brill Nijhoff, 2023), 297.

54 The People's Republic of China, Submission by the People's Republic of China concerning the Outer Limits of the Continental Shelf beyond 200 Nautical Miles in Part of the East China Sea (14 Dec. 2012), https://www.un.org/depts/los/clcs_new/submissions_files/submission_chn_63_2012.htm (accessed 9 Mar. 2023).

non-living resources of the continental shelf (for living resources management, see Chapter 6).

4.3.1 Japan/ROK Southern CS Agreement

In 1974, Japan and the ROK agreed to establish a joint development zone in the East China Sea by shelving the delimitation of overlapping claimed areas. The Japan/ROK Southern CS Agreement is the first application of the idea of joint development, as indicated in the *North Sea Continental* case.[55] It provides a detailed joint development system for the resources in the Joint Development Zone, which is bordered by equidistance lines and natural prolongation.[56] Under this agreement, several explorations were conducted until the early 2000s but failed to discover commercially exploitable deposits.[57] However, it is hasty to conclude that this agreement is a "failure" since it has succeeded in containing the radicalization of conflicts between the two countries for 50 years.

4.3.2 Japan and the PRC 2008 Consensuses

In 2003, the PRC began unilateral natural gas development in the area on the Chinese side of the equidistance line but within 200 miles of the Japanese coast. In response, Japan expressed concern that the deposit may straddle the Japanese side, and in 2008, they reached two political agreements: the 2008 Japan/PRC Consensuses.[58] One establishes a joint development zone around the equidistant line. The other provides for the participation of Japanese companies in the development of Shirakaba/Chunxiao, which the PRC has already developed. These consensuses set forth only main

55 Miyoshi M., "The Joint Development of Offshore Oil and Gas in Relation to Maritime Boundary Delimitation," *Maritime Briefing* 2 (5) (1999), 1.

56 Oda S., "Nikkan Tairikudana Kyotei no Teiketsu [Conclusion of the Japan/ROK Continental Shelf Agreement]" (Japanese), *Jurist* 559 (1974), 98. Miyoshi M., "The Japan-South Korea Agreement on Joint Development of the Continental Shelf," *Energy* 10 (1985), 545.

57 Choi J.H., "Korea-Japan JDZ to End in Deadlock? The Potential for Unilateral Korean Exploration and Exploitation," *Ocean Development & International Law* 51 (2020), 162–163. Kim S.K., "The Uncertain Status of the Korea-Japan Joint Development Agreement of the Continental Shelf and Its Prospects," Asia-*Pacific Journal of Ocean Law and Policy* 7 (2022), 208. Choi and Kim pointed out that the Japanese side is reluctant to continue exploration because of the lack of feasible deposits.

58 Japan-China Joint Press Statement Cooperation between Japan and China in the East China Sea (19 Aug. 2022), https://www.mofa.go.jp/a_o/c_m1/page3e_000356.html (linked as "June 2008 Agreement") (accessed 9 Mar. 2023). For the background and analysis of the consensuses, *see* Miyoshi M., "Japan's Arrangements with South Korea and China for the Development of Oil and Gas in the East China Sea: A Memorandum," *Journal of International Affairs* 134 (2009), 118–119.

frameworks. Thus, it was prescribed that Japan and the PRC shall (i) make every effort for the early conclusion of an agreement that will implement the consensus and (ii) continue consultations for the joint development of deposits outside the agreed area. The 2008 Japan/PRC consensus was initially welcomed. However, several problems soon became apparent. One is the PRC's unilateral development of the Kashi/Tianwaitian field located west of the median line but within 200 nm from the Japanese baseline. The PRC considered that the field is clearly under its jurisdiction. However, Japan believed the field was also under its jurisdiction since it is entitled to the EEZ and continental shelf up to 200 nautical miles in undelimited areas. So, from the Japanese view, such Chinese development infringes on Japanese sovereign rights and the 2008 Japan/PRC consensuses.[59] Due in part to the subsequent deterioration of their relations, only the first round of talks under the 2008 Japan/PRC consensuses took place, and the PRC continued unilateral development.

4.4 *Issue to Be Addressed in the East China Sea*

4.4.1 Applicable Delimitation Principle

In the East China Sea, the three States support different delimitation principles; Japan supports the equidistance/relevant circumstances method and the three-stage approach, the ROK supports both the equidistance/relevant circumstances method (for EEZ) and the equitable principle and natural prolongation theory (for the continental shelf), and the PRC supports the equitable principle and natural prolongation theory (for the EEZ and continental shelf).

Considering the judicial precedent, the equidistance/relevant circumstances method and the three-stage approach, rather than the equitable principle, have become the primary trend for boundary delimitation within 400 nautical miles. Also, as demonstrated in the *Libya/Malta* case, the seabed feature is no longer relevant in such areas. This jurisprudence makes Japan's argument more favorable than that of the PRC and the ROK. In drawing a boundary line, to achieve an equitable result, the boundary will be the equidistance line shifted towards the ROK and PRC, considering the relevant circumstances, such as the length of the coastline. Here, the effect of the uninhabited Senkaku/Diaoyu Islands would be problematic. Neither Japan nor the PRC doubts their status as "islands" that have EEZ and continental

---

59 Public Security Intelligence Agency, "Saikin no Naigai Josei 2009 nen 1 gatsu [Recent Internal and External Situations, Jan. 2009]" (Japanese), (Jan. 2009), https://www.moj.go.jp/psia/kouan_naigai_kako_200901.html (accessed 9 Mar. 2023).

shelf (Art.121(1)). However, in light of *the South China Sea Arbitration* (*The Republic of Philippines v. The People's Republic of China*) (hereinafter referred to as *the South China Sea Arbitration*) criteria, the uninhabited Senkaku/Diaoyu Islands could be regarded as "rocks" that cannot have such maritime area (Art.121(3)).[60] If treated as "rocks," the Senkaku/Diaoyu would not affect boundary delimitation. Even if treated as "islands," they would have only partial effect on the delimitation since if they are allowed full effect, there will be inequity in the area allocated to States.[61]

Another issue to be noted is whether the delimitation should be done by a single or different boundary of the EEZ and the continental shelf. Japan, like many other states, supports a single boundary.[62] On the contrary, the ROK supports the different boundaries: an equidistant line for EEZ and natural prolongation for the continental shelf.[63] The PRC seems to claim a single maritime boundary using natural prolongation since it claims both EEZ and the continental shelf up to Okinawa Trough.[64] Unless the dispute over the boundary delimitation principles of the continental shelf is resolved, it will not be easy to delimit this area with a single boundary line.

Finally, it may be recalled that in the *Nicaragua v. Colombia* case, the Court ruled that the extended continental shelf does not extend into 200 nautical miles from third countries. If this legal principle is applied to the East China Sea, the distance criterion would prevail, and the boundary should be the equidistance line.

4.4.2 Merits and Demerits of the Joint Development Pending Delimitation

The joint development agreements in the East China Sea have yet to produce the anticipated initial results: commercial production under their scheme. However, the Japan/ROK Southern CS Agreement can be classified as a "success" in conflict prevention. In the *Guyana v. Suriname* case, the Tribunal stated that the obligation not to jeopardize or hamper the reaching of the final agreement is "an important aspect of the Convention's objective

60 *The South China Sea Arbitration* case (n 40), 227–228, paras. 542–543.

61 Kaye (n 21), 336. Yiallourides C., *Maritime Disputes and International Law: Disputed Waters and Seabed Resources in Asia and Europe* (Routledge, 2019), 138.

62 Statement of Ichiro Komatsu, the Director-General of International Legal Affairs Bureau, at the Shugiin [House of Commons] Foreign Affairs Committee, 164th Kokkai [National Diet], held on 15 Mar, 2006 (Japanese). Shugiin, *Dai 164 Kai Kokkai Shugiin Gaimu Iinkai Kaigiroku* 5 (2006), 2–3.

63 Kim (n 38), 58–59.

64 Ministry of Foreign Affairs, the People's Republic of China (n 53).

of strengthening peaceful and friendly relations between the nations and of settling disputes peacefully."[65] This Agreement will expire in 2028, and the parties must decide whether to continue or terminate it. Now that the three-stage approach has become mainstream and the ICJ has pronounced that the Extended Continental Shelf would not be entered into other states' 200 nm zones, it might be difficult for Japan to accept the joint development zone based on natural prolongation. However, preventing conflict for 50 years is an outstanding achievement that cannot be ignored. If the agreement is terminated, delimitation disputes will arise and affect bilateral relations.[66]

Contrary to the Japan/ROK Southern CS Agreement, the 2008 Japan/PRC Consensuses would have to be classified as a "failure" at this time since they not only failed to implement joint development but instead increased tensions between the two countries. Joint development in undelimited waters can be described as sharing sovereignty with another country.[67] As mentioned, a joint development agreement only works well with close, friendly relations, shared solid motivation, and a common understanding of its scheme. Unfortunately, the 2008 Japan/PRC Consensuses resulted from political compromise and lacked such elements. Thus, it has led to bilateral confrontations and negative public sentiment.

4.4.3 Unilateral Development and the Obligation Not to Jeopardize or Hamper the Reaching of the Final Agreement

The PRC's unilateral development may violate the UNCLOS obligation not to jeopardize or hamper the reaching of the final agreement (Art. 74(3) and 83(3)). The PRC has been developing resources on the Chinese side of the median line but within 200 nm from the Japanese baseline, and as of October 2022, Japan had identified 18 structures.[68] As stated above, Japan protested China's activities because it believes it has title to the EEZ and continental shelf up to 200 nautical miles beyond the median line. On the

65 *Guyana v. Suriname* case (n 22), 465.

66 Kim (n 57), 212–214. In addition, there has been no official examination of why this agreement does not work. If there is a better way for the agreement to function and commercial development becomes feasible, the decision to terminate or continue will likely change. In considering termination and continuation, it is necessary to review the development system and the conflict prevention outcomes of this agreement.

67 Townsend-Gault and Stormont (n 28), 52–53.

68 Ministry of Foreign Affairs of Japan, "The Current Status of China's Unilateral Development of Natural Resources in the East China Sea" (19 Aug. 2022), https://www.mofa.go.jp/a_o/c_m1/page3e_000358.html (accessed 9 Mar. 2023).

other hand, the PRC believes that the waters and fields on the Chinese side of the median line are clearly under its jurisdiction.

Several Japanese scholars analyzed differences in the two States' views on the "Disputed Area."[69] Japan considers the "Disputed Area" to be an overlapping area of "entitlements" of EEZ and continental shelf under UNCLOS; the "Disputed Area" here is the area between 200 nautical miles from the Japanese and Chinese baselines. The PRC, on the other hand, refers to the "Disputed Area" as the waters in which the two countries have competing "claims"; the "Disputed Area," in its view, is the area between the equidistance line (Japanese claim) and the Okinawa Trough (Chinese claim). From the Chinese view, the development conducted west of the equidistance line would be outside the "Disputed Area" so that no legal issues would arise. However, the importance of considering overlapping "claims" and "entitlements" is emphasized in the judicial precedents.[70] Thus, current Chinese unilateral development activities on the west side of the equidistant line constitute a "violation of obligation not to jeopardize or hamper the reaching of the final agreement," which would undermine the trust between the States and exacerbate the conflict.[71] This analysis seems natural. Behind the differences in the delimitation claims, there is an overlap of title as the factual dispute.[72]

---

69 For example, Sakamoto (n 42), 460–461. Murase S. "Jo ni Kaete-Nichu Tairikudana Kyokai Kakutei Mondai [Introduction Japan/PRC Continental Delimitation Issue]" (Japanese), in Murase S. and Eto J. (eds), *Kaiyo Kyokai Kakutei no Hou* (Toshindo, 2008), v–vi. Sakai (n 53), 298.

70 *Maritime Delimitation in the Area between Greenland and Jan Mayen (Denmark v. Norway)* case, Judgment [1993] *ICJ Report* 1993 para. 59.

71 Sakamoto (n 42), 460–461. Murase (n 69), vi.

72 On the other hand, the Japanese government described the Joint Development Zone in the Japan/ROK SC Agreement as "the area where the two States' claims for rights overlap regarding the continental shelf adjacent to both Japan and the ROK (Statement of the Minister of Foreign Affairs, Iichiro Hatoyama (translated by author))." The emphasis here is on the overlap of rights, not entitlement. However, this Joint Development Zone was established as a practical solution for resource exploitation when the delimitation principle was uncertain during the third United Nations Conference on the Law of the Sea (Statement of the Director-General of Asian Affairs Bureau). Therefore, it is instead a product of political compromise with a tentative nature; it cannot immediately be regarded as a "Disputed Area" between the two States' claims and entitlements. *See* the Statement of Iichiro Hatoyama, the Minister of Foreign Affairs, at the Shugiin [House of Commons] Foreign Affairs Committee, 80th Kokkai [National Diet] held on 6 Apr., 1977 (Japanese). Shugiin, *Dai 80 Kai Kokkai Shugiin Gaimu Iinkai Kaigiroku* 8 (1977), 1. *See also* the Statement of Yosuke Nakae, the Director-General of Asian Affairs Bureau, at the Shugiin [House of Commons] Foreign Affairs Committee,

In addition to the activities with permanent physical changes, there are activities without such changes that raised tension, like the China Coast Guard's harassment of Japanese fishing vessels or the PRC's research activities without prior notification to Japan.[73]

To ease tensions in the East China Sea for implementing 2008 Japan/PRC consensuses, the parties should refrain from acts that "jeopardize or hamper the reaching of the final agreement" and hold talks in the "spirit of understanding and cooperation."[74]

5 Conclusion

This chapter reviews the law on maritime boundary delimitation and then introduces the maritime disputes between Japan/the ROK and Japan/the PRC. The following two points can characterize these maritime disputes.

The first is the presence of resources. The three States insist on different boundary delimitation principles to ensure that the seabed resources are incorporated into their continental shelf. Although in judicial cases, the equidistant line/relevant circumstances method or the three-stage approach has become the primary trend, it is not declared as becoming customary international law. Thus, abandoning the equitable principle will be difficult for the ROK and the PRC.

Second is the existence of territorial disputes. Maritime delimitation in the Sea of Japan/the East Sea and the East China Sea will only be realized by resolving territorial disputes over Takeshima/Dokdo and the Senkaku/Diaoyu Islands. However, territorial disputes are often tied to nationalism, making the States very difficult to resolve.[75]

What options may be available to solve the delimitation dispute? One possible option is the referral to judicial proceedings. UNCLOS provides a

---

80th Kokkai [National Diet] held on 1 Apr. 1977 (Japanese). Shugiin, *Dai 80 Kai Kokkai Shugiin Gaimu Iinkai Kaigiroku* 7 (1977), 2.

73 Japan and the PRC agreed on the "Framework of Mutual Prior Notification for Marine Research Activities," under which each State must give prior notice to other States when conducting research activities in the coastal waters. The Japanese Coast Guard reported 17 harassment incidents and two research activities without prior notice. Kaijo Hoan Cho (Japanese Coast Guard), *The Kaijo Hoan Report 2024* [Japanese Coast Guard Report] (Japanese), https://www.kaiho.mlit.go.jp/info/books/report2024/html/top.html (accessed 8 Nov. 2024).

74 Sakai (n 53), 309–312.

75 Serita K., *Territorial Sea and Exclusive Economic Zone* (Springer, 2023), 165–166.

detailed compulsory dispute settlement procedure, wherein cases can generally be referred without the other party's consent (Part XV). However, as to the boundary delimitation issue in the East China Sea itself, there is little likelihood of being resolved by an international court since both the PRC and the ROK made a declaration to exclude delimitation dispute from the compulsory procedure under Art.298 (1)(a)(i).[76] Judicial resolution may be available for issues not excluded in Art.298, such as the legality of Chinese unilateral activity. However, it is unclear whether such a judicial decision can resolve the dispute since the observations of the judicial decisions depend on the parties' cooperation.[77] The PRC continues to engage in unilateral actions that were found to be illegal in *the South China Sea Arbitration* because it believes the Arbitration itself is null and void.[78]

The second option is to use non-judicial procedures such as voluntary or compulsory conciliation under UNCLOS (for dispute settlement system, see Chapter 15).[79] The non-judicial procedures that seek solutions by considering legal and non-legal elements and dialogues with the States can pave the way for issues that cannot be resolved through bilateral negotiations.[80] The East China Sea issues include legal and non-legal elements, such as delimitation, unilateral activities, the presence of resources, and the joint development scheme. If bilateral negotiations fail, the States can use Conciliation.

76 Kaye (n 21) 339–340. The States can exclude certain disputes, including boundary delimitation, from the compulsory procedure by making declarations under Art. 298 (1).

77 Nishimura Y., "Kaiyō funsō no kaiketsu tetsuzuki to hō no shihai [Maritime Dispute Settlement and the Rule of Law]," *Kokusai Mondai* 666 (2017), 42. Nishimoto (n 32), 11.

78 Statement of the Ministry of Foreign Affairs of the People's Republic of China on the Award of 12 July 2016, of the Arbitral Tribunal in the South China Sea Arbitration, established at the Request of the Republic of the Philippines (12 July 2016) https://www.fmprc.gov.cn/eng/wjdt_665385/2649_665393/201607/t20160712_679470.html (accessed 9 Mar. 2023).

79 Art. 284 (voluntary conciliation) and Art. 298(1)(a) (compulsory conciliation for delimitation). However, it should be noted that the Art. 298 (1)(a) limits the available dispute for compulsory conciliation. In order to submit a dispute to compulsory Arbitration, two conditions must be met: (1) the dispute arises after entry into force of UNCLOS for the States, and (2) the dispute does not include consideration of the sovereignty or other rights over land territory. Since delimitation disputes between Japan/ROK and Japan/PRC arose before the entry into force of UNCLOS and relate to territorial sovereignty, it may be difficult to submit such dispute to compulsory conciliation.

80 The first UNCLOS compulsory conciliation, *the Timor Sea Conciliation*, could successfully resolve the longstanding disputes between Timor-Leste and Australia in the undelimited area and resource development. *Report and Recommendations of the Compulsory Conciliation Commission between Timor-Leste and Australia on the Timor Sea* (Permanent Court of Arbitration, Case No. 2016–10, 9 May 2018).

The third possible option is to activate existing joint development agreements. The Japan/ROK Southern CS Agreement and 2008 Japan/PRC consensuses could serve as a platform for cooperation. Each country should be aware of the value of this platform. In the case of Japan and the ROK, it will be necessary to reconsider the conflict prevention function and the development system of the agreements. As to Japan and the PRC, they should restrain themselves from activities that may jeopardize or hamper the reaching of the final agreement, such as unilateral development, and then proceed with the consultations stipulated in the agreements in the "spirit of understanding and cooperation."

CHAPTER 9

Protection of Vulnerable Individuals and Minority Groups in Japan

Yuko Osakada

1 Introduction

This chapter critically examines the current situations of protection for vulnerable individuals and minority groups in Japan from the perspective of international human rights law, focusing on asylum seekers, refugees, and Indigenous peoples. First, criticisms of the treatment of asylum seekers and refugees by the Immigration Services Agency of Japan will be examined. The history of the enactment and amendment of the Immigration Control and Refugee Recognition Act (the ICRRA), as well as criticisms of the 2021 and 2023 amendment bills, will be examined, clarifying the problems of Japan's immigration administration regarding asylum seekers and refugees. In this chapter, the definition of refugee is the same as in Article 1 of the Refugee Convention, while asylum seekers include those who are not recognized as refugees under the Convention but who seek asylum in other countries for any reason.

Second, the arguments over the Act Promoting Measures to Achieve a Society in which the Pride of Ainu People is Respected (Ainu Policy Promotion Act), which was enacted in 2019, will be examined from the perspective of the United Nations Declaration on the Rights of Indigenous Peoples[1] (the UN Declaration). While this Act legally recognizes the Ainu[2] as an Indigenous people for the first time, it does not stipulate any of the Ainu's rights. This

1 The United Nations Declaration on the Rights of Indigenous Peoples, UNGA Res. 61/295 (September 13, 2007), UN Doc A/RES/61/295.

2 Currently, most Ainu people live in the northern part of Japan, Hokkaido. According to a survey that was conducted by the Hokkaido municipal government in 2017, 13,118 Ainu live in Hokkaido, which is about 0.3 percent of the region's total population (Hokkaido Prefecture, *Hokkaido Ainu Seikatstu Jittai Chōsa Hōkokusho* [Report of the Survey of Socioeconomic Conditions of the Hokkaido Ainu] (Japanese), 2017, 3, https://www.pref.hokkaido.lg.jp/ks/ass/new_jittai.html (accessed June 8, 2023).

 | DOI:10.1163/9789004548824_010

examination will clarify the problems of Japan's Indigenous policy and reveal the challenges that must be overcome to realize the rights of the Ainu.

Finally, this chapter will refer to common difficulties in achieving protection in consistency with international human rights law for asylum seekers, refugees, and Indigenous peoples. It will then indicate what is needed to overcome them.

2 Developments and Challenges of the Immigration Control and Refugee Recognition Act[3]

2.1 *Acceptance of Indochinese Refugees and Establishment of a Refugee Status Determination Procedure*

Japan began sporadically accepting refugees before World War II. However, when the rapid rise of socialism in the three Indochinese countries (Vietnam, Laos, and Cambodia) led people to flee their home countries, their arrival as boat people caused Japan to be confronted with the refugee problem in earnest.[4] The first nine boat people arrived in Japan at the port of Chiba in May 1975. Initially, the Japanese government allowed them to stay temporarily in Japan, but not to settle down. In April 1979, the Cabinet approved a plan to allow up to 500 Vietnamese refugees to settle in Japan for the time being, as well as to allow settlement from the large number of refugees at that time residing in neighbouring countries within Indochina.[5] The quota was gradually expanded, and when the program ended in 2005, a total of 11,319 Indochinese refugees had been allowed to settle in Japan.[6]

The reception of Indochinese refugees triggered calls for Japan to join the Convention relating to the Status of Refugees (the Refugee Convention)[7]. In response, Japan acceded to the Refugee Convention in 1981, and

3 This section is mainly based on my article, "Kokusai Jinkenhō kara Mita Nihon no Nanmingyosei no 40-nen [40 Years of Japan's Refugee Laws and Policies: An Examination Based on International Human Rights]" (Japanese), in *Refugee Studies Journal* 11 (2022) 23–34. The author owes much to books and articles written in Japanese, but limitations on space do not allow for many of them to be cited.

4 Arakaki O., *Refugee Law and Practice in Japan* (Routledge, 2016) 15–18.

5 The Website of Refugee Assistance Headquarters, "Nihon ni Kurasu Nanmin [Refugees Living in Japan]" (Japanese), https://www.rhq.gr.jp/ukeire/ (accessed June 8, 2023).

6 *Ibid.*

7 Convention relating to the Status of Refugees, *adopted on* July 28, 1951, *entered into force on* April 22, 1954, 189 UNTS 137.

the Convention became effective in Japan in early 1982. The Japanese government prepared the ICRRA to ensure the domestic implementation of the Refugee Convention, which came into effect on January 1, 1982.

The definition of refugee in the Immigration Law incorporates Article 1 of the Refugee Convention (and Article 1 of the Refugee Protocol, which eliminates time limits), which states that a person who, "owing to well-founded fear of being persecuted for reasons of race, religion, nationality, membership of a particular social group or political opinion, is outside the country of his nationality" (Article 2, item 3-2 [The numbers in the article are as they were at the time of enactment. The same applies hereinafter]). The requirements for a permanent residence permit for persons who have obtained refugee status have been relaxed (Article 61-2-5), as the livelihood and skills requirements are no longer required. If a person who has been granted refugee status wishes to leave the country, a refugee travel document will be issued upon application (Article 61-2-6). Also, in deportation proceedings, the Minister of Justice may grant special permission to stay in Japan on condition that the refugee status has been granted, even if there is no reason for the objection (Article 61-2-8).

While the acceptance of Indochinese refugees was based on political decisions approved by the Cabinet, the Refugee Status Determination (the RSD) procedure provides a legal basis for granting asylum to refugees who have arrived in Japan, without any restrictions on their country of origin.[8] Since Japan has concluded the Refugee Convention and its Protocol, it is no longer allowed to use its discretion in deciding whether or not to accept refugees, and "recognition of refugee status" (Article 61-2, Paragraph 1) by the Minister of Justice is considered a non-discretionary act. However, Japan has consistently taken a negative stance toward the recognition of refugee status, pursuing its own interpretation of the Refugee Convention, rather than referring to the United Nations High Commissioner for Refugee's "Handbook on Procedures and Criteria for Determining Refugee Status" (the UNHCR Handbook) in interpreting the Convention.[9] As a result, it has been criticized that the perspective of "immigration control", which leaves room for discretion by the Minister of Justice, has continued to prevail in the actual implementation of the Convention, although the recognition of refugee

---

8 Abe K., *Nanmin no Hogo to Heiwa no Kōsō* [Refugee Protection and Peace Initiatives] (Japanese) (Choyokai, 2021) 28.

9 Kitamura Y., "Towards a More Human Rights-Based Refugee Law Reform in Japan." *Yonsei Law Journal* 12 (1 & 2) (2022) 80–83.

status itself should be considered a non-discretionary act.[10] There has also been ongoing criticism that refugee status is not granted by an independent and specialized agency, but by the Minister of Justice and the Immigration Bureau of the Ministry of Justice (now the Immigration Services Agency), whose primary mission is to control and remove undocumented foreigners at border controls.[11]

2.2 *The Partial Amendment of the ICRRA in 2005*

In May 2002, a family of North Korean defectors attempted to flee into the Consulate-General of Japan in Shenyang, China, and were removed by Chinese officials guarding the consulate. This incident led to calls for improvement in Japan's approach to the reception of refugees.[12] Based on the opinions of the Immigration Control Policy Discussion Panel, which received a report from the Sub-Committee on Refugee Issues established in June 2002, the Partial Amendment of the ICRRA came into effect in May 2005, making the first modifications to the RSD system. As a result, first, the limitation of the application period for refugee status (in principle, within 60 days from the date of landing in Japan) was abolished. Second, "permission for provisional stay" was introduced (Article 61-2-4 [the number of the article was the same at the time of the amendment]), and for those who were granted a provisional stay, the deportation procedure was suspended, and the RSD procedure was implemented in advance. Third, those who were granted refugee status and fulfilled certain requirements were uniformly permitted to stay in Japan (Article 61-2-2). Most notably, fourth, a new system of Refugee Adjudication Counsellors (RACs) was introduced at the objection stage (Article 61-2-10).

In the past, a person who was denied refugee status could file an objection with the Minister of Justice, but there was criticism that it was meaningless as the same Minister re-examined the case. Article 61-2-9, paragraph 3 of the revised ICRRA stipulates that "the Minister of Justice is required to hear the opinions of the RACs in making a decision on the objection under

10 Hong S. W., "Nihon Shakai ni okeru Nanmin Ukeire no Ronten [Issues on Refugee Acceptance in Japanese Society]" (Japanese), *Kokusai Kankei Ronsou* 7(2) (2018) 100.

11 Abe (n 8), 28.

12 Fukuoh M., "Nanmin Shinsa Sanyoin Seido ni kansuru Hikakuhouteki Kōsatsu [Some Comparative Legal Observations on the Introduction of "the Refugee Adjudication" to Japan through International Law and Constitutional Law]" (Japanese), *Komazawa Women's University Kenkyu Kiyo* 13 (2006) 211.

paragraph 1, as provided for in the Ordinance of the Ministry of Justice". The lack of independence and transparency had been a serious flaw in Japan's refugee status system, and this has now to a certain extent been rectified.[13]

The United Nations High Commissioner for Refugee (UNHCR) issued its Comments on the Bill to Reform the ICRRA on May 19, 2004.[14] The UNHCR welcomed the introduction of the RACs as "a positive development, which might contribute to improve the quality and the speed of the decisions".[15] However, the UNHCR also pointed out that the RACs would remain within the Ministry of Justice and that decision-making would not be independent from the first instance body, as all asylum decisions would be made by the Minister of Justice.[16] The UNHCR was concerned that, based on the draft provisions, it was unclear whether or not the opinions of the RACs would be binding on the Ministry of Justice.[17]

In 2008, the UN Human Rights Committee (HRC) was also concerned that "the possibility of filing an objection with the Minister for Justice against a negative asylum decision does not constitute an independent review because the refugee examination counsellors advising the Minister upon review are not independently appointed and have no power to issue binding decisions."[18]

When the RACs were first introduced, the Minister of Justice generally respected their opinions. When their opinions differed, the Minister of Justice respected the majority opinion of the three Counsellors.[19] However, in 2013, for the first time since the introduction of the RACs, the Minister of Justice decided not to recognize refugee status in a case in which the Counsellors had stated refugee status should be recognized.[20] It was subsequently revealed that, by the end of 2017, there were 116 cases in which the majority of the Counsellors had decided that refugee status was "appropriate". In 13 of those cases, about 10 percent of the entire cases, the Minister of Justice had

13 Abe (n 8), 30.

14 UNHCR, "UNHCR's Comments on the Bill to Reform the Immigration Control and Refugee Recognition Act of Japan," May 19, 2004, https://www.refworld.org/docid/42b7f4894.html (accessed June 8, 2023).

15 *Ibid.*, para. 20.

16 *Ibid.*, para. 21.

17 *Ibid.*, para. 21.

18 HRC, "Concluding Observations for Japan" (December 18, 2008), UN Doc CCPR/C/JPN/CO/5, para. 25.

19 Fukuoh (n 12), 213; Akiyama M., "Wagakuni no Nanmin Nintei Seido [Refugee Recognition System in Japan]" (Japanese), *The Reference* 69 (5) (2019) 85.

20 Akiyama (n 19), 85.

decided "not to recognize" the refugee status.[21] It is fair to say that the concerns of the UNHCR and the UN Human Rights Committee have been shown to be realistic. The argument that ignoring the opinions of the Counsellors would greatly diminish the significance of the RACs in terms of externality and third-party status is also quite plausible.[22]

2.3 *The Bills for Partial Amendments to the ICRRA in 2021 and 2023*

Foreigners who do not have a residence permit because of an irregular entry or irregular stay are nonetheless supposed to be able to receive permission for a "provisional" stay when applying for refugee status, except in prescribed cases (Article 61-2-4 of the Immigration Control Act). It has been pointed out, however, that in practice the permission for provisional stay hardly works.[23] In fact, in 2019, 733 people were examined for provisional stay but only 25 were granted permission; in 2020, 440 people were examined but only 15 were granted permission.[24] If permission for a provisional stay is not granted, deportation proceedings will be initiated. If the RSD procedure is still ongoing (Article 61-2-6), the effect of repatriation based on a deportation order is suspended (Article 61-2-6), but immigration detention based on a deportation order is still feasible, and it will take place unless provisional release (Article 54) is provided.

Prior to the COVID-19 pandemic, the number of long-term detainees who had been continuously detained for more than six months was an issue: 704 at the end of June 2018, about 2.7 times the 263 who had been detained at the end of December 2013.[25] The maximum duration of detention at the

21 Akasaka M., "Nanminshinseisha no Seizon no Tameni [For the Survival of Refugee Applicants]" (Japanese), *Migrants Network* 198 (2018) 22.

22 Nanba M., ""Nanmin Nintei Seido no Tekiseika no tameno Saranaru Unyō no Minaoshi" no Naiyō to Sono Hikei [Details and Background of the "Further Review of the Operation of the Refugee Status Determination System for the Purpose of Making it More Appropriate"]" (Japanese), *Migrants Network* 198 (2018), 20.

23 Watanabe S., "Nanmin Shinseisha to Shuyō · Sōkan Mondai [Applicants for Refugee Status and Detention/Repatriation Issues]" (Japanese), *Migrants Network* 209 (2020) 18.

24 Immigration Services Agency of Japan, "Reiwa Gannen ni okeru Nanmin Ninteisha Sū Nado ni tsuite" [On the number of refugees approved in 2019] (Japanese), March 2020, 8, https://www.moj.go.jp/isa/content/930005069.pdf (accessed June 8, 2023); Immigration Services Agency of Japan, "Reiwa Ninen ni okeru Nanmin Ninteisha Sū Nado nitsuite [On the number of refugees approved in 2020]" (Japanese), March 2021, https://www.moj.go.jp/isa/content/001345018.pdf (accessed June 8, 2023), 8.

25 Osakada Y., "Nyūkan Shūyō no Genzai: Kikaku Shushi Setsumei mo Kanete [Immigration Detention Now: With Explanation of the Purpose of the Project]" (Japanese), *Houritsu Jihō* 1147 (2020) 59.

Omura Immigration Center at the end of November 2019 was 7 years and 2 months. There were a total of 1,494 detainees at end of June 2018, and approximately 604 (41 percent) were in the process of applying for refugee status.[26] One of the reasons for prolonged immigration detention is the decrease in the number of provisional release permits. In June 2019, a Nigerian man who was on hunger strike died of starvation at the Omura Immigration Center.[27] Against this backdrop, the 16th meeting (September 19, 2019) of the 7th Immigration Control Policy Discussion Panel, a private advisory panel of the Minister of Justice, decided to establish the Subcommittee on Detention and Deportation (SCDD). The SCDD is aimed to solve problems related to the increase in the number of repatriation evaders and prolonged detentions. The SCDD argued that, among the repatriation evaders, more than a few people were abusing or misusing the refugee status application to seek suspension of repatriation since repatriation is uniformly suspended during the RSD process. The SCDD finalized its recommendations in June 2020 and submitted them to the Immigration Control Policy Discussion Panel. Based on these recommendations, a bill for partial amendments to the ICRRA was approved by the Prime Minister's Cabinet in February 2021 and submitted to the National Diet. The 2021 amendment bill was opposed by both ordinary liberal citizens and opposition parties. This opposition, combined with criticism over the government's response to the death of a Sri Lankan woman at a facility of the Nagoya Regional Immigration Services Bureau in March 2021,[28] forced the government to withdraw the proposal, and thus virtually abandon it. However, in March 2023, the amendment bill of the ICRRA, which almost duplicates the 2021 amendment bill, was approved by the Cabinet and submitted to the National Diet.

Regarding the 2021 amendment bill, the Special Rapporteur on the human rights of migrants, Working Group on Arbitrary Detention (WGAD); the Special Rapporteur on freedom of religion or belief; and the Special

26 The Official Website of Mizuho Fukushima (Member of Social Democratic Party, as well as the House of Councillors), https://mizuhoto.org/2091 (accessed June 8, 2023); Osakada (n 25) 58.

27 Osakada (n 25), 59–60; Immigration Services Agency of Japan, "Omura Nyūkoku Kanri Center Hishuyōsha Shibō Jian ni kansuru Chōsa Hōkokusho [Investigation Report on the Death of a Detainee at the Omura Immigration Center]" (Japanese), October 2019, https://www.moj.go.jp/isa/content/930004725.pdf (accessed June 8, 2023).

28 Immigration Services Agency of Japan, "Nagoya Shutsunyukoku Zairyū Kanrikyoku Hishūyōsha Shibō Jian ni kansuru Chōsa Hōkoku ni tsuite [Investigation Report on the Death of a Detainee at the Nagoya Regional Immigration Services Bureau]" (Japanese), August 2021, https://www.moj.go.jp/isa/publications/press/01_00156.html (accessed June 8, 2023).

Rapporteur on torture and other cruel, inhuman or degrading treatment or punishment jointly submitted an expert opinion letter (the 2021 joint letter) on March 31, 2021.[29] The UNHCR also issued comments on the bill (the UNHCR comments) on April 9, 2021.[30] As for the 2023 amendment bill, the Special Rapporteur on the human rights of migrants, the Working Group on Arbitrary Detention, and the Special Rapporteur on freedom of religion or belief submitted an expert opinion letter (the 2023 joint letter) on April 18, 2023.[31] The following is an overview of the discussion regarding what concerns over the bills were expressed in the 2021 and 2023 joint letters and in the UNHCR comments.

The first concern is about the "monitoring measures", which the bill attempted to newly introduce. Under this system, a person who had been issued a detention order or a deportation order was supposed to be placed outside the detention facility under the supervision of a "monitor", *i.e.*, a civilian, if certain conditions were met, such as the payment of a deposit. However, the 2021 joint letter expressed concern that "detention remains mandatory" and that the new monitoring measure would only apply as an exception, at the discretion of a supervising immigration control officer, when it is considered "appropriate" not to detain a person who was subject to deportation until the time that person could be repatriated.[32] The 2023 amendment bill slightly changed the relevant provisions (as reflected in Articles 44-2 and 52-2 of the revised ICRRA) so that a supervising immigration control officer must decide to place a person subject to deportation under the supervision of a monitor if certain conditions are met. This seems to

29 Special Rapporteur on the human rights of migrants, Working Group on Arbitrary Detention; Special Rapporteur on freedom of religion or belief and Special Rapporteur on torture and other cruel, inhuman or degrading treatment or punishment, "Comments on Amendment Bill to the Immigration Control and Refugee Recognition Act of Japan," March 31, 2021, https://www.ohchr.org/Documents/Issues/SRMigrants/Comments/OL-JPN31-03-21.pdf (accessed June 8, 2023).

30 UNHCR "UNHCR Comments on the Bill for Partial Amendments to the Immigration Control and Refugee Recognition Act Submitted to the 204th Diet Session of Year 2021 Based on the Recommendations of the Sub-committee on Detention and Deportation (SCDD), 7th Immigration Control Policy Discussion Panel," April 9, 2021, https://www.refworld.org/docid/607474fc4.html (accessed June 8, 2023).

31 Special Rapporteur on the human rights of migrants, Working Group on Arbitrary Detention, and Special Rapporteur on freedom of religion or belief, "Comments on Amendment Bill to the Immigration Control and Refugee Recognition Act of Japan," April 18, 2023, https://spcommreports.ohchr.org/TMResultsBase/DownLoadPublicCommunicationFile?gId=27995 (accessed June 6, 2023).

32 The 2021 joint letter (n 29), 1–2.

make the "monitoring measure" no longer an exception. Nevertheless, the 2023 joint letter expressed concern again, stating that "detention would still prevail whenever a 'monitoring measure' is not applied."[33] In this regard, the 2023 amendment bill gives the supervising immigration control officers wide discretion in deciding whether to place a person under the supervision of a monitor because it allows them to take into account any matters which are not listed in the condition clause. On this point, the 2021 and 2023 joint letters pointed out that article 9 of the International Covenant on Civil and Political Rights (the ICCPR) "identifies personal liberty as the principle and the detention and restrictions upon that liberty as exceptions which requires States to uphold the principle and only in exceptional cases resort to divergence from it".[34] The 2021 and 2023 joint letters also indicated that immigration detention must be the last resort, which was reaffirmed in objective 13 of the Global Compact for Safe, Orderly and Regular Migration.[35] In addition, the UNHCR expressed its concern that some of those who were being monitored might not be granted a work permit, which would lead to poverty.[36] The UNHCR also asserted that "States are ultimately responsible to ensure people have access to an adequate standard of living, including the means of livelihood for asylum-seekers pending the final decisions on their RSD, and providing State-funded livelihood assistance in the absence of right to work is one of such measures".[37]

The second concern is that the 2021 and 2023 amendment bills would lift the suspension of repatriation. While the repatriation process is automatically suspended under the previous ICRRA until a final decision is made regarding refugee status, including a decision at the appeal stage, the bills would lift the suspension of repatriation for those who have: applied for refugee status for the third time or more; those who have been sentenced to imprisonment in Japan for three years or more; and those who are suspect in a broad sense of being involved in or contributing to terrorism, violence or subversive activities. In this respect, the UNHCR warned that the

33 The 2023 joint letter (n 31), 1–2.

34 The Constitution of Japan also protects the personal liberty in Article 18 as follows: "No person shall be held in bondage of any kind. Involuntary servitude, except as punishment for crime, is prohibited." In Japanese academic studies, personal liberty is considered one of the most important fundamental rights on which all freedoms are based.

35 The 2021 joint letter (n 29), 2; The 2023 joint letter (n 31), 2; The Global Compact for Safe, Orderly and Regular Migration, UN Doc A/RES/73/195 (January 11, 2019).

36 The UNHCR comments (n 30), 43.

37 The UNHCR comments (n 30), 43–44.

"proposal to lift automatic suspension of deportation procedures for certain cases … raises very serious concerns as being undesirable because it increases the risk of refoulement".[38] The UNHCR insisted that "rather than devoting limited resources to legislate and implement any exceptions to the currently-automatic suspensive effect, measures to further improve the RSD quality, including by fully implementing the Recommendations of the 2014 Sub-Committee on RSD System (…) would be crucial".[39] While the 2021 joint letter considered that "it is advisable to accelerate the processing of subsequent [refugee] applications", they were also concerned that "in the absence of any appropriate procedural safeguards that explicitly require individual assessment on the circumstances and protection needs prior to deportation, lifting automatic suspension of deportation procedures for asylum seekers of the above-mentioned categories may entail high risk of refoulement".[40] The 2023 joint letter repeated their concern emphasizing the essential nature of the principle of non-refoulement.[41]

Third, while both the 2021 joint letter and the UNHCR comments welcomed the new references to the term "complementary protection" in the amendment bills, they expressed concern that the criteria proposed under the bill does not reflect wording commonly adopted in international refugee and human rights law.[42] Namely, while the term "special permission for residency on humanitarian grounds' has been used, the introduction of the concept of "complementary protection" in the bill was positively evaluated for clarifying the grant of status as "obligatory rather than discretionary".[43] "Complementary protection" is a legal scheme to protect those who do not meet the definition of refugee set forth in the Refugee Convention but are in need of international protection, and to grant status to such persons. Since Japan is a party to the ICCPR,[44] the Convention against Torture and Other Cruel, Inhuman or Degrading Treatment or Punishment,[45] the Convention on the

38 The UNHCR comments (n 30), 6.

39 *Ibid.*

40 The 2021 joint letter (n 29), 4.

41 The 2023 joint letter (n 31), 5.

42 The 2021 joint letter (n 29), 3–4; The UNHCR comments (n 30), 32–33. *See also* the 2023 joint letter (n 31), 5.

43 The UNHCR comments (n 30), 32.

44 International Covenant on Civil and Political Rights, *adopted on* December 16, 1966, *entered into force on* March 23, 1976, 999 UNTS 171.

45 Convention against Torture and Other Cruel, Inhuman or Degrading Treatment or Punishment, *adopted on* December 10, 1984, *entered into force on* June 26, 1987, 1465 UNTS 85.

Rights of the Child,[46] and the International Convention for the Protection of All Persons from Enforced Disappearance,[47] the obligation to provide supplementary protection arises from the obligations of non-refoulement imposed by these treaties. Although the amendment bills require "fear of being persecuted" for the complementary protection, the monitoring bodies of the above-mentioned human rights treaties do not impose such a requirement for the complementary protection. Therefore, concern was expressed about this restriction of the complementary protection in comparison to international human rights law.

The fourth concern is about the establishment of penalties for not complying with a deportation order or an order to apply for a passport. The UNHCR comments quoted the WGAD as stating that "the criminalization of irregular migration will … always exceed the legitimate interests of States in protecting their territories and regulating irregular migration flows" and argued that "this is particularly so for asylum-seekers and stateless persons".[48]

Fifth, the 2021 and 2023 joint letters and the UNHCR comments also expressed concern that the amendment bills do not provide for maximum period of detention and independent review over the decision to (continue to) detain.[49] Based on the recommendations of UN human rights mechanisms such as the HRC and the WGAD, they considered it necessary for these to be put in place.

Despite criticism from international experts, the 2023 amendment bill was passed without major revisions by the House of Representatives on May 9, 2023, and then by the House of Councillors on June 9, 2023. The revised ICRRA was promulgated on June 16, 2023, with the creation of the new "complementary protection" coming into effect on December 1, 2023, and the rest on June 10, 2024.

2.4 *Towards a More Human Rights-Based Refugee Status Determination System*

In Japan, although certain individual responses have been taken, such as the partial amendment of the ICRRA in 2005, there has been no

46 Convention on the Rights of the Child, *adopted on* November 20, 1989, *entered into force on* September 2, 1990, 1577 UNTS 3.

47 International Convention for the Protection of All Persons from Enforced Disappearance, *adopted on* December 20, 2006, *entered into force on* December 23, 2010, 2716 UNTS 3.

48 The UNHCR comments (n 30), 37. *See also* the 2023 joint letter (n 31), 5.

49 The 2021 joint letter (n 29), 2–3; the 2023 joint letter (n 31), 2–3; the UNHCR comments (n 30), 45–47.

fundamental reform of the RSD procedure to ensure compatibility with international human rights law. Furthermore, the Japanese government has been accused of relying on extremely strict criteria and standards of proof for recognizing refugee status, deviating from the international standards including the UNHCR Handbook, but has done little to address these issues.[50] Instead, in recent years, the Japanese government has insisted on dealing with so-called disguised refugees and repatriation evaders, and has revised the ICRRA, which are highly problematic from the perspective of international human rights law. As has been pointed out since the establishment of the RSD system in 1982, the fact that the Minister of Justice and the Immigration Services Agency, whose primary mission is to control and remove undocumented foreigners at border control, are charged with the task of recognizing refugee status is the main reason for these concerns.[51] As noted above, the significance of the RACs, which were introduced to rectify the lack of independence and transparency in Japan's RSD system, has been called into question in recent years because the Minister of Justice has, in more than a few cases, refused to grant recognition despite the majority opinion of the Counsellors.

In its May 2017 updated version of "Issues Concerning Refugees, Internally Displaced Persons, and Stateless Persons in Japan and the World (Proposals for Japan)", UNHCR called for the enactment of a Refugee Law that clearly defines the rights and obligations of refugees and applicants for refugee status and the establishment of a department that specializes in dealing with refugees. In this regard, the Constitutional Democratic Party of Japan (CPP), the Democratic Party for the People, the Communist Party of Japan (CPJ), the Okinawan Wind, the Reiwa Shinsengumi, and the Social Democratic Party (SDP) jointly submitted a bill to the House of Councillors on the protection of refugees and others (Refugee Protection Bill) and a bill to amend the ICRRA (lawmakers' bill) as a counterproposal to the 2021 amendment bill.[52] The CPP, the CPJ, the SDP, the Okinawan Wind, and the Reiwa Shinsengumi jointly submitted the similar bills to the House of Councillors again as a counterproposal to the 2023 amendment bill.[53] Although we have no room in this chapter to examine this counterproposal in detail, it is

---

50 *See*, for example, Kitamura (n 9), 80–83.

51 Abe (n 8) 36; Watanabe (n 23), 12.

52 The Official Website of the Constitutional Democratic Party of Japan, https://cdp-japan.jp/news/20220422_3554 (accessed June 8, 2023).

53 The Official Website of the Constitutional Democratic Party of Japan, https://cdp-japan.jp/news/20230509_6013 (accessed August 8, 2024).

noteworthy that it seeks to separate the RSD procedure from the Minister of Justice and the Immigration Services Agency by establishing an independent administrative body, namely the Refugee Protection Committee, composed of highly specialized members.

The Japanese government has been so intent on removing those who abuse the RSD system that genuine refugees are not being protected. For the purpose of the human rights treaties and the Refugee Convention, both of which Japan ratified, it is important to initially establish a system in which those who must be protected are definitely protected. From this perspective, it may be worth considering, with reference to the 2021 counterproposal, a fundamental reform which separates the RSD procedure from the Minister of Justice and the Immigration Services Agency and entrusts it to a specialized and independent third-party body.

3 Arguments concerning the Ainu Policy Promotion Act and the UN Declaration on the Rights of Indigenous Peoples[54]

3.1 *The Significance of the UN Declaration on the Rights of Indigenous Peoples*

The Ainu Policy Promotion Act (the Act) came into effect on May 24, 2019. This was the first law to clearly specify the Ainu as an Indigenous people. However, this Act has been criticized by some Ainu people and Ainu rights defenders because it does not recognize any of the Indigenous rights provided for in the UN Declaration. On the other hand, those involved in drafting the Act, including Teruki Tsunemoto, Professor Emeritus of Hokkaido University, have tried to justify this non-reference by relying on the UN Declaration itself.

Although the UN Declaration is not legally binding, its meaning is both politically and legally significant. It is politically significant because representatives of Indigenous peoples actively participated in the Declaration's draft process, allowing many of their voices to be incorporated in the document. Moreover, those who initially voted against the UN Declaration at the GA – Canada, the USA, New Zealand, and Australia – subsequently

54 This section is mainly based on my article, "An Examination of Arguments over the Ainu Policy Promotion Act of Japan Based on the UN Declaration on the Rights of Indigenous Peoples," *The International Journal of Human Rights* 25(6) (2021) 1053–1069. The author owes much to books and articles written in Japanese, but space limits do not allow most of them to be cited.

endorsed it.[55] The UN Declaration is legally significant because it has been incorporated into some domestic laws in countries like Bolivia, and more recently, Canada.[56] It has also been referred to by several domestic courts when ruling in favour of Indigenous peoples.[57] In addition, as the International Law Association indicated, some key provisions in the UN Declaration correspond to existing State obligations under customary international law.[58] Consequently, the UN Declaration should be treated seriously when enacting domestic laws that might affect Indigenous peoples.

Against this backdrop, this section seeks to analyze the arguments over the Ainu Policy Promotion Act from the perspective of the UN Declaration.

3.2 *What Is the Ainu Policy Promotion Act?*

The Act prohibits discrimination and infringement of rights on the grounds of being Ainu and stipulates that national and local governments are responsible for deepening public understanding of the Ainu through education and public relations. The Act also created a subsidy system to promote culture, industry, and tourism, and specified that regional plans prepared by municipalities are to be approved by the Prime Minister based on the basic policy established by the Japanese government. The national government is able to issue subsidies for approved regional plans. When formulating regional plans, it is obligatory to hear the opinions of the people implementing the project, typically local Ainu groups. When specified in regional plans, it is possible to relax regulations on the fishing of salmon and the harvesting of trees in national forests for the purpose of culture tradition, and to reduce or exempt the copyright registration fees and registration fees related to Ainu handicrafts. A characteristic of the Act is that it does not guarantee the rights of Indigenous peoples, but instead adopts regional development measures that enrich the areas inhabited by the Ainu as a whole.

In August 2022, the author conducted field research in Akanko Onsen, Akan-cho, Kushiro City, Japan, to investigate how the subsidy project is

---

55 Gover K., "Settler-State Political Theory, "CANZUS" and the UN Declaration on the Rights of Indigenous Peoples," *The European Journal of International Law* 26(2) (2015) 345–346.

56 Bill 41–2019: Declaration on the Rights of Indigenous Peoples Act.

57 EMRIP, "Ten Years of the Implementation of the United Nations Declaration on the Rights of Indigenous Peoples: Good Practices and Lessons Learned – 2007–2017: Report of the Expert Mechanism on the Rights of Indigenous Peoples" (2017) UN Doc A/HRC/36/56, paras. 57–68.

58 International Law Association (ILA) Committee on the Rights of Indigenous Peoples, "Sofia Conference: Final Report" (2012) 29.

being implemented. The following descriptions are based on that research. As a premise, a total of about 2.4 billion yen (around 17.4 million USD) in subsidies were approved for 34 municipalities in and outside of the Hokkaido in April 2022.[59] In Kushiro City, 15 grant projects were planned for a total of about 465 million yen (around 3.4 million USD) in the fiscal year 2022.[60] Of these subsidy projects, the five projects with which the author had personal experience will be outlined below. The first is an Ainu cultural guide project, called Anytime Ainutime, which is an Ainu culture and nature guide service in Akan.[61] The author participated in this tour and had the valuable experience of learning the Ainu names of plants and the traditional use of those plants. Second, under the Ainu culture-related tourism promotion project, "Lost Kamuy", a program that combines digital art with contemporary and traditional Ainu dance, is being shown at the Lake Akan Ainu Theater "Ikoro".[62] Third, the Akan Ainu Consuln has been working to implement an intellectual property protection project for the branding of Ainu culture in Lake Akan.[63] The Akan Ainu Consuln (1) supervises, produces, and certifies Ainu patterns in light of Ainu culture, (2) supervises the correct use of the Ainu languages, (3) organizes the performance of Ainu dances and Ainu musical instruments at designated locations, and (4) provides Ainu cuisine and its recipes. Particularly noteworthy is the Akan Ainu Consuln's own certification of products using Ainu patterns, as exemplified in the book, *Let's Think: Indigenous Peoples and Laws*, published in December 2022 and edited by the author.[64] We were provided with Ainu patterns

---

59 Cabinet Office of Japan, Reiwa 4 Nendo Ainu Seisaku Suishin Kōhukin Kōhu Kettei Ni Tsuite [Decision on the Subsidy for the Ainu Policy Promotion for Fiscal Year 2022] (Japanese), https://www8.cao.go.jp/ainu/kouhyou/jigyou_keikaku/reiwa4/kouhyou1.pdf (accessed June 8, 2023).

60 Kushiro City, 2022 (Reiwa 4) Nendo Kushiroshi Ainu Seisaku Suishin Kōhukin Jigyō Keikaku Heno Tōsai Yotei Jigyō Ichiran [List of Planned Projects to Be Included in the Ainu Policy Promotion Subsidy Project Plan of Kushiro City for Fiscal Year 2022] (Japanese), https://www.city.kushiro.lg.jp/_res/projects/default_project/_page_/001/007/152/000186460.pdf (accessed June 8, 2023).

61 The English website of Anytime, Ainutime, https://en.anytimeainutime.jp/ (accessed June 8, 2023).

62 The website of Ainu Kotan in Lake Akan (Japanese), https://www.akanainu.jp/lostkamuy/ (accessed June 8, 2023).

63 The website of Akan Ainu Consuln (Japanese), https://a-ainucon.com/ (accessed June 8, 2023).

64 Osakada O., Fukayama N., Maruyama J., and Moriya K. (eds), *Kangaete Miyō Senjū Minzoku to Hō* [Let's Think: Indigenous Peoples and Laws] (Japanese) (Shinzansha, 2022). The picture of the book cover is available at https://www.shinzansha.co.jp/book/b10026214.html (accessed June 8, 2023).

registered in the Akan Ainu Consuln and arranged them for the cover of this book, which was certified by the Consuln. Fourth, as part of the Akan Ainu Kotan revitalization project, a booth was set up for a limited time at the Tancho Kushiro Airport to introduce the activities of the Akan Ainu Consuln and the Ainu culture.[65] The fifth project was designed to strengthen the Ainu culture exhibition corner at the Kushiro City Museum.[66] Through this project, videos of Ainu songs and dances of the Kushiro region were newly filmed and made available for visitors to view. In this way, in Kushiro City, and especially in Lake Akan, city officials and Ainu people work together to proactively plan subsidy projects, which are then implemented for tourism, which is Akan's main source of income.

3.3 *Diverse Evaluations of the Ainu Policy Promotion Act and Emerging Roles/Challenges*

The Ainu's evaluation of the Act is divided, which is significant since they are the affected parties. Some Ainu people criticize the Act's failure to guarantee the rights of Indigenous peoples, such as the right to self-determination and right to the lands, territories and resources as declared in the UN Declaration on the Rights of Indigenous Peoples.[67] Other Ainu people actively praise the Act for how it clearly identifies the Ainu as Indigenous people under the law.[68] However, even among people in the latter group, there are quite a few who see the Act as a starting point rather than an end point.[69] It cannot be said that the adoption of the Act has solved all problems.

Three years have passed since the Act came into effect, and its role and challenges are becoming clearer. First, some local governments, including Kushiro City, have taken advantage of the subsidy project under the Act to move proactively in cooperation with local Ainu groups. In this sense, the Act fulfils a role similar to a trigger which inciting local governments to take

65 The website of Tancho Kushiro Airport (Japanese), http://www.kushiro-airport.co.jp/webtra/c-information/post_485.php (accessed June 8, 2023).

66 The website of Kushiro City Museum (Japanese), https://www.city.kushiro.lg.jp/museum/oshirase/1002239/1002243.html (accessed June 8, 2023).

67 Higashimura T., "No Rights, No Regret: New Ainu Legislation Short on Substance" (April 26, 2019), https://www.nippon.com/en/in-depth/d00479/no-rights-no-regret-new-ainu-legislation-short-on-substance.html (accessed June 8, 2023).

68 "Bill Finally Recognizes Ainu as Indigenous People of Japan," *The Asahi Simbun* (Tokyo, Feburary 6, 2019)

69 *See*, for example, the comments on the Act of Kazushi Abe, the former Vice Director of the Ainu Association of Hokkaido, in Osakada (n 54), 1059–1060.

action. However, since resulting actions depend on the motivation and ability of local governments, regional differences have also become apparent. Second, although some Ainu people now enjoy increased employment and income due to the subsidy project, there are also Ainu people who do not benefit from it, thereby creating a disparity in the impact of the Act. Third, despite the Act's aim of enriching the entire area inhabited by the Ainu people, the effect currently reaches only a few areas with limited results, although this situation may be in part related to the impact of COVID-19.

3.4 *Arguments over the Ainu Policy Promotion Act from the Perspective of the UN Declaration*

As mentioned above, the UN Declaration has been cited as a basis for views not only by opponents but also by advocates of the Act. While this implies that despite its non-binding character, the UN Declaration cannot be ignored completely by the advocates of the Act, the author believes that they misunderstand the Declaration to a certain degree. Therefore, this section will analyze several arguments that attempt to justify the Act from the perspective of the UN Declaration.

3.4.1 Were the Obligations of the UN Declaration Generally Fulfilled by the Act?

First, when considering how clearly designating Indigenous peoples by law forms the basis of policy towards Indigenous peoples and enables various procedural relaxations by alleviating the harmful effects of vertically divided administration, the Act could be evaluated as a form of progress as a transitional law, despite its shortcomings. Nevertheless, the author disagrees with the statement made by Kenichi Ishii, then Minister of Land, Infrastructure, Transport and Tourism, that "the obligations that should be fulfilled per the UN Declaration have been largely satisfied".[70] The core of the UN Declaration is the right to self-determination and collective rights to the lands, territories and resources. In particular, the former is also stipulated in the ICCPR, which was ratified by Japan, and Japan did not make any reservations to the clause on the right to self-determination that is included in said Covenant. Practices of the UN HRC under the State reporting procedure establish that the right to

70 The 8th proceedings of the meeting of the House of Councillors Committee on Land, Infrastructure, Transport and Tourism, the 198th ordinary Diet session (Japanese Only, April 18, 2019), https://kokkai.ndl.go.jp/minutes/api/v1/detailPDF/img/119814319X00820190418 (accessed June 8, 2023), 5.

self-determination applies to Indigenous peoples.[71] As the Act recognizes no collective rights for the Ainu, it can hardly be said that the obligations of the UN Declaration have been generally fulfilled.

3.4.2 Could the Act Be Justified by the Reference to "National and Regional Particularities" in the Preamble to the UN Declaration?

Second, it is important to discuss that Ishii and several researchers justified the Act's failure to guarantee the rights of Indigenous peoples, such as right to self-determination as stipulated in the UN Declaration, by stating that Paragraph 23 of the preamble to the UN Declaration states the need to consider "national and regional particularities", etc.[72] Shortly before the UN General Assembly adopted the UN Declaration, the African Group requested a postponement of the adoption of the Declaration and submitted an amendment consisting of 33 items that would render the Declaration virtually meaningless.[73] In response, negotiations with African countries were led by the Global World Indigenous Peoples' Caucus, which is a body coordinating groups of Indigenous peoples from regions throughout the world. As a result of the negotiations, a compromise was finalized that reduced the amendment to nine items,[74] and the phrase introduced above was included. Judging from the drafting process, it may appear that the claims made by Ishii and several researchers seem correct. However, we must remember that the UN Declaration also contains the following provisions. Paragraph 17 of the preamble to the UN Declaration states that "Nothing in this Declaration may be used to deny any peoples their right to self-determination". Furthermore, Article 45 of the UN Declaration clearly states that "Nothing in this Declaration may be construed as diminishing or extinguishing the rights

---

71 *See*, for example, HRC, "Concluding Observations for Finland" (2013) UN Doc CCPR/C/FIN/CO.6, para. 16; HRC, "Concluding Observations for Chile" (2007), UN Doc CCPR/C/CHL/CO/5, para. 19.

72 The 8th proceedings of the meeting of the House of Councillors Committee on Land, Infrastructure, Transport and Tourism (n 69), 5; Tsunemoto T., "Ainu Shisaku Suishin Hō – Ainu to Nihon ni Tekigō Shita Senjūu Minzoku Seisaku wo Mezashite [The Ainu Policy Promotion Act – Towards Indigenous Peoples Policy Appropriate for the Ainu and Japan]," *Hogaku Kyoshitsu*, Vol. 468 (2019) 65–66.

73 African Group Proposal, May 8, 2007, reprinted in Genugten W., "The African Move towards the Adoption of the 2007 Declaration on the Rights of Indigenous Peoples: The Substantive Arguments behind the Procedures," in Böcker A. G. M. et al. (eds.), *Migration Law and Sociology of Law, Collected Essays in honour of Kees Groenendijk*, (Wolf Legal Publishers, 2008) 409–416.

74 Report of the Global Indigenous Peoples' Caucus Steering Committee, Urgent Information for Indigenous Peoples of All Regions, August 31, 2007.

Indigenous peoples have now or may acquire in the future". In particular, as a provision of the main text, Article 45 carries a stronger meaning than statements made in the preamble. In view of Paragraph 17 of the preamble and Article 45, the UN Declaration does not allow national and regional particularities to be justifications under the Declaration for failure to guarantee the rights of Indigenous peoples. The purpose of Paragraph 23 should be understood as allowing Indigenous peoples of the world to exercise their right to self-determination differently according to their needs and wishes.

3.4.3 Could the Act Be Justified by the Difficulty of Identifying Who Is the Ainu?

The *Jinshin Koseki*, the oldest family register in Japan, referred to the status of residents with categories such as *kyu-dojin* (the former aborigines). It was, thus, possible to identify Ainu individuals through the family register. However, in 1968, when an attempt was made to use the Jinshin Koseki to investigate whether a person was a *Burakumin*, i.e., a member of the low-status social group who had been discriminated against, the head of the Civil Affairs Bureau issued a notice prohibiting access to the *Jinshin Koseki*. Afterwards, it was strictly sealed and stored at either Legal Affairs Bureau or the municipalities.[75] Arguably, the only possible way of identifying Ainu individuals is to trace back their ancestors' names through current family registers which do not refer to the status of residents. This is how the Ainu Association of Hokkaido, the largest Ainu's organization in Hokkaido, determines its membership. Nevertheless, according to Tsunemoto, since family registers were made at different times in several areas in Hokkaido, and since some family registers were also inappropriately stored, thus damaged, it is not possible to identify all the Ainu individuals based on family registers under equal conditions.[76] Therefore, he stated that the Act does not provide for any preferential treatment for Ainu individuals.

However, even in the Nordic countries, which are considered advanced countries in Indigenous peoples' policies, there are disputes over who is a Sami individual. In fact, the UN HRC and the Committee on the Elimination of Racial Discrimination have dealt with disputes between the Finnish

---

75 Ninomiya S., "Kojin Jōhō no Hogo to Koseki Kōkai Gensoku no Kentō [Protection of Personal Information and Principle of Disclosure of Family Register]" (Japanese), *Ritsumeikan Hogaku* 304 (2005) 243–245.

76 Tsunemoto (n 72), 67; FPCJ Press Briefing: What Is the Goal of the Ainu Policy Promotion Act? (November 28, 2019). English translation of report is available at https://fpcj.jp/en/worldnews-en/briefings-en/p=77102/ (accessed December 12, 2024).

government and the Sami Parliament over the treatment of people who were not allowed to register as Sami voters by the Sami Parliament in Finland under the individual communications procedures.[77] Many Indigenous tribes have similar difficulties in determining their membership to a certain degree, but these difficulties are not usually used as an excuse to justify a lack of preferential treatment to Indigenous individuals in general. In any case, according to Article 33(1) of the UN Declaration, it is Indigenous peoples, not a national government, that have the right to determine their own membership.

3.4.4 Could the Act Be Justified by the Lack of a Nationwide Organization Representing the Ainu?

Tsunemoto also defended the Act's failure to provide for the collective rights of the Ainu by pointing out that there is no nationwide organization representing the Ainu.[78] Although the UN Declaration does not clearly stipulate the requirement of a representative organization, the lack of it certainly causes many problems in realizing the Indigenous rights anchored therein. For example, Article 32 of the UN Declaration provides that States shall consult and cooperate with the Indigenous peoples concerned through their own representative institutions in order to obtain their free and informed consent prior to the approval of any project affecting their lands or territories and other resources. The Ainu experience demonstrates that the UN Declaration may not be realizable in practice if the requirement of a representative organization is interpreted too strictly.

However, the argument that the UN Declaration cannot be applied to Indigenous peoples whose communities have been thoroughly dismantled by intense assimilation policies, even in part, is inadmissible because it is contrary to the purpose and objectives of the UN Declaration. Rather, until the Ainu can establish an officially recognized nationwide representative organization, the multiple Ainu organizations in the regions should be treated equally as representative organizations and recognized as the subjects of collective rights. This approach, however, is merely one of the possible ways and any decision about their representative organization should be made by the Ainu themselves, as required by Article 18 of the UN Declaration.

---

77 *See*, for example, *Tiina Sanila-Aikio v. Finland*, Communication No. 2668/2015, UN Doc. CCPR/C/124/D/2668/2015 (2019); *Anne Nuorgam* et al. *v. Finland*, Communication No. 59/2016, UN Doc CERD/C/106/D/59/2016 (2022).

78 Tsunemoto (n 72), 67.

3.4.5 Could the Act Be Justified by a Lack of Public Understanding?

Ishii also stated that it would not be appropriate to take special measures only for the Ainu people, such as granting them land rights, because it might lead to new discrimination due to the lack of public understanding.[79] In this regard, it should be recalled that many of the provisions of the UN Declaration are based on existing human rights treaties or recognized by the practice of treaty bodies, and that international human rights law requires the realization of minority rights, regardless of the level of public understanding. However, we must be vigilant against backlash. A deeper understanding of the majority is therefore required through education and publicity of the history and culture of the Ainu. In this respect, it must be recalled that Article 5(3) of the Ainu Policy Promotion Act requires national and local governments to deepen the public understanding of the Ainu through education, publicity, and other activities. This requirement goes well with Article 15(2) of the UN Declaration, which calls on States "to take effective measures, in consultation and cooperation with indigenous peoples concerned, to combat prejudice and eliminate discrimination and to promote tolerance, understanding and good relations among indigenous peoples and all other segments of society".

3.5 *To Prevent Disparity from Creating Division*

For some time, the Ainu have been known to be diverse in their opinions, with some insisting on the rights approach based on the UN Declaration and other international instruments, while others are reluctant to take the rights approach, fearing that the recognition of their Indigenous rights might encourage discrimination. The author is concerned that what has been perceived as the diversity of Ainu opinions may turn into a dichotomous division due to the disparity in the impact of the Act. In other words, it is true that there are some Ainu people who have increased their income and improved their lives as a result of the subsidy projects under the Act, and that they strongly support the Act and want the subsidies to continue. It is also true, however, that there are certain Ainu individuals who have not benefited from the subsidies. To prevent this disparity from creating a dichotomous division among the Ainu, efforts must be made to eliminate the disparity in the impact of the Act, yet at the same time, given that they will not be able to rely on the subsidies forever, it seems necessary to more seriously consider the rights approach. Of course, the realization of this latter option

---

79 The 8th proceedings of the meeting of the House of Councillors Committee on Land, Infrastructure, Transport and Tourism (n 70) 10.

does not rely on the part of the Ainu alone, but rather of the non-Ainu majority. In this regard, it seems important to conclude by reaffirming that under the Act, the government is responsible for deepening public understanding of the Ainu through educational, public relations, and other activities.

4 Conclusion

The realization of protection consistent with international human rights law for asylum seekers, refugees and Indigenous peoples through democratic procedures is affected by the common difficulty of a lack of public understanding. In 2019, the Cabinet Office of Japan conducted the first public opinion poll on refugee acceptance policies in Japan. Asked, "Do you think we should accept refugees?", 24 percent answered, "We should accept them positively", whereas 56.9 percent responded negatively, saying either "We should accept them 'rather cautiously'" or "we should accept them 'cautiously'".[80] As for the Ainu, in 2015, the Japanese government conducted surveys with regard to discrimination and prejudice against the Ainu. According to the surveys, 72.1 percent of the Ainu survey respondents asserted that discrimination and prejudice are still directed against their race,[81] while 33.6 percent answered that they have actually experienced discrimination.[82] Some of the examples of discrimination that they cited include marriages or relationships meeting opposition from non-Ainu partners' families, and unpleasant experiences at school or in the workplace.[83] Even after the Ainu Policy Promotion Act came into force, some people have repeatedly engaged in hate speech online against the Ainu people, which make some Ainu people unable to openly recognize their Indigenous identity.[84] In this respect, it should be reconfirmed that international human

80 The website of Cabinet Office, Yoron Chōsa [Public Opinion Polls], *Nanmin Nintei Seido no Arikata* [How the RSD system should work] (Japanese), https://survey.gov-online.go.jp/r01/r01-houseido/2-3.html (accessed June 8, 2023); Kitamura (n 9), 85–86.

81 Comprehensive Ainu Policy Office, Cabinet Secretariat, Government of Japan, Kokumin no Ainu ni Taisuru Rikaido nituite no Ishiki Chōsa Hōkokusho [Report of the Awareness Survey on the Ainu] (Japanese), 2016, 5, https://www.kantei.go.jp/jp/singi/ainusuishin/pdf/rikaido_houkoku160322.pdf (accessed June 8, 2023).

82 *Ibid.*, 7.

83 *Ibid.*, 9.

84 *See*, for example, "Discrimination and Inertia Slow Use of Ainu Grants, Two Years after Launch," *The Japan Times* (Tokyo, June 28, 2021), https://www.japantimes.co.jp/news/2021/06/28/national/social-issues/ainu-grants-discrimination/ (accessed June 8, 2023).

rights law requires the realization of rights of asylum seekers, refugees, and Indigenous peoples regardless of the level of public understanding. However, it is also important to be aware of potential backlash, and the majority should be provided with a deeper understanding of the situation through education and publicity based on international human rights.

CHAPTER 10

Impacts of International Human Rights Law on LGBTQ Issues in Japan

Hiroyuki Taniguchi

1 Introduction

In 2011, the United Nations Human Rights Council (UNHRC) adopted a groundbreaking resolution, "Human Rights, Sexual Orientation and Gender Identity."[1] This was the first resolution by the United Nations (UN) dedicated to LGBTQ issues after a long conflict of raising it as an official topic in the international arena.[2] As one of the council members at the time, Japan voted in favor of this resolution. In addition, as discussed below, several UN human rights bodies have repeatedly pointed out that laws and policies on LGBTQ issues are inadequate, as seen in current international human rights standards.

This chapter examines how international human rights laws affect the creation, application, and interpretation of Japanese laws. After an overview of the topic worldwide, the respective sections consist of four sub-sections: the current situation of international human rights laws, that of Japanese law, recommendations from monitoring bodies (*i.e.*, treaty bodies and UN bodies), and the analysis of the impact of international human rights law on the topic in Japan. Three topics will be discussed: legal recognition of same-sex relationships, legal gender alterations, and anti-discrimination legislation.

2 Legal Recognition of Same-Sex Relationships

Marriage has historically been recognized as a union between men and women without a clear legal definition to do so. Under this precondition,

1 UNHRC, 2011, Human Rights, Sexual Orientation and Gender Identity, Resolution of 17 June 2011, UN Doc. A/HRC/RES/17/19.

2 Sanders D., 1996, "Getting Lesbian and Gay Issues on the International Human Rights Agenda," *Human Rights Quarterly* 18 (1996), 67–106.

 | DOI:10.1163/9789004548824_011

same-sex relationships could not be recognized as legitimate couples affordable for State protection or recognition. Some countries even punish their relationships considering them as "unnatural" or "indecent" originating from religious taboos. Legal recognition began in the late 1980s when Denmark passed the registered partnership legislation in 1989. This legal framework is different from marriage but has similar legal effects. In 1999, France created a new legal framework, the PACS, which can use both same-sex and different-sex relationships, in addition to marriage. After this "separate but quasi-equal" protection, the Netherlands opened marriages to same-sex couples for the first time in 2001. As of September 2024, 36 UN member states have abandoned gender restrictions for marriage.[3]

2.1 *International Human Rights Laws and Standards*

The Human Rights Committee (HRC), which monitors the implementation of the International Covenant on Civil and Political Rights (ICCPR), interprets non-discrimination clauses in the ICCPR to include sexual orientation in the case of *Toonen v. Australia*.[4] This interpretation is reflected in individual complaints concerning the different treatments between same-sex and different-sex relationships in criminal codes. In *Young v. Australia*,[5] Mr. Young complains that refusing survivors' pensions is discrimination based on sexual orientation because different-sex couples can apply for it as a de facto relationship without marriage. The HRC admitted his complaint that the different treatment on a pension between different-sex de facto relationships and same-sex relationships amount to sexual orientation discrimination, which is prohibited in Article 26 of the ICCPR. It repeats the same interpretation in *X v. Columbia*[6] and concludes observations in the State reporting system many times.

However, the HRC does not interpret Article 23 of the ICCPR, the marriage and family relationship clause, as including the obligation to open marriage to same-sex relationships. In 2002, two lesbian couples complained that they could not obtain marriage licenses because they were in same-sex relationships.[7] The HRC concluded that it is not a violation of the

3 ILGA, 2024, ILGA World Database, https://database.ilga.org/en.

4 HRC, 1994, *Toonen v. Australia*, Views of 31 March 1994, UN Doc. CCPR/C/50/D/488/1992.

5 HRC, 2003, *Young v. Australia*, Views of 6 August 2003, UN Doc. CCPR/C/78/D/941/2000.

6 HRC, 2007, *X v. Colombia*, Views of 30 March 2007, UN Doc. CCPR/C/89/D/1361/2005.

7 HRC, 2002, *Joslin* et al. *v. New Zealand*, Views of 17 July 2002, UN Doc. CCPR/C/75/D/902/1999.

ICCPR because the clause clearly and intentionally uses the word "men and women" in the context of marriage, and remains a broad margin of discretion for each member State regarding marriage. This interpretation reflects the Yogyakarta Principles, which intentionally exclude "the right to marry" from the proposed list of principles.[8]

Two regional human rights systems have recently been developed. The European Court of Human Rights (ECHR) has interpreted the rights to respect for private and family life in Article 8 of the Convention, containing a positive obligation to create "some special framework" for same-sex relationships to effectively implement the article.[9] This means that it is a violation of the Convention if the Member State has no legal institutions to protect same-sex relationships, as is the case in Japan. Moreover, the Inter-American Court of Human Rights (IACHR) adopted the advisory opinion that each State should abolish the restrictions on marrying same-sex couples under Article 17 of the Inter-American Convention.[10]

2.2 *Legal Situation in Japan*

As many countries have maintained, Japan has historically allowed different-sex couples to marry. This preposition could be seen from the wording of Article 24(1) of the Constitution, which stipulates that marriage can be established only by mutual consent of "both sexes." It is also clear that the legislature imposes a "no-marriage requirement" when people request legal gender alteration, which prevents the situation of legally married same-sex couples after the alteration because the Japanese marriage system is based on different-sex marriage.[11]

Many legal provisions include or interpret to include "de facto marriage [*Jijitsu-kon*]." However, it is unclear whether these provisions apply to same-sex relationships because it uses the word "marriage [*kon*(*in*)]" and does not clearly state same-sex relationships. The court's decisions were divided and unstable. Regarding the alimony case after the dissolution of their de facto relationship, both the Utsunomiya District Court and the following appeal judgment by the Tokyo High Court interpret their relationship included in "de

8 O'Flaherty M. and Fisher J., "Sexual Orientation, Gender Identity and International Human Rights Law: Contextualising the Yogyakarta Principles," *Human Rights Law Review* 8(2) (2008), 207–248.

9 *Case of Oliari and Others v. Italy*, Judgment of 21 July 2015, ECHR, Applications nos. 18766/11 and 36030/11.

10 IACHR, 2017, Gender Identity, and Equality and Non-discrimination of Same-Sex Couples, Advisory Opinion OC-24/15, 24 November 2017.

11 Taniguchi H., "Japan's 2003 Gender Identity Disorder Act," *Asian-Pacific Law & Policy Journal* 14(2) (2013), 108–117.

facto marriage."[12] Conversely, Nagoya District Court rejected the plaintiff's complaint to have victim compensation as a "de facto" partner of the person murdered.[13] In the latter case, the Supreme Court interpreted same-sex relationships as de facto marriages, although one judge dissented.[14]

Under these legally ambiguous circumstances, several local governments have officially recognized same-sex relationships. In 2015, the Shibuya City and Setagaya City created a "Partnership Certification System," which issued certificates to affirm their acceptance of the Partnership Oath by same-sex couples. It has no legal effect since marriage- and family-related legislation is under the State's jurisdiction. The Partnership Certification by the local government is not "legal recognition" but symbolic and not legally binding recognition, which is entirely different from the "Registered Partnership System" or "Civil Union Law" that has legal benefits. As of June 2024, over 450 out of approximately 1800 municipalities have introduced this system, including 28 out of 47 prefectures as a whole, which covers over 85 percent of the Japanese population.

In 2019, simultaneous litigation began questioning the constitutionality of the existing legal framework, excluding same-sex relationships from marriage. This is referred to as the "Marriage for All" Lawsuit. The Sapporo and Nagoya District Courts stated that it breaches Article 14 of the Constitution because same-sex couples have no legal benefits from the current legislation.[15] The Tokyo District Court, in both cases 1 and 2, the Nagoya District Court and Fukuoka District Court, said that it violates Article 24(2) of the Constitution because there is no specific legal framework to protect same-sex relationships.[16] In 2024, the Sapporo High Court ruled that the current laws related to marriage violate Articles 24(1), 24(2) and 14[17]. In contrast, the Osaka District Court finds it constitutional since it is under the discretion of the

12 *Same-Sex Couple Alimony* case, Case no. H30-Wa-30, Judgment of 18 September 2019, Utsunomiya District Court; Case no. R1-Ne-4433, Judgment of 4 March 2020, Tokyo High Court.

13 *Crime Victims* case, Case no. H30- GyoU -76, Judgment of 4 June 2020, Nagoya District Court.

14 *Crime Victims* case, Case no, R4-GyoTsu-318, Judgment of 26 March 2024, Supreme Court of Japan.

15 *Marriage for All Lawsuits*, Case no. H31-Wa-267, Judgment of 17 March 2019, Sapporo District Court; Case no. H31-Wa-597, Judgment of 30 May 2023, Nagoya District Court.

16 *Marriage for All Lawsuits*, Case no. H31-Wa-3465, Judgment of 30 November 2022, Tokyo District Court; Case no. H31-Wa-597, Judgment of 30 May 2023, Nagoya District Court; Case nos. R1-Wa-2827 and R3-Wa-447, Judgment of 8 June 2023, Fukuoka District Court; Case no. R3-Wa-7654, Judgment of 14 March 2024, Tokyo District Court.

17 *Marriage for All Lawsuits*, Case no. R3-Ne-194, Judgment of 14 March 2024, Sapporo High Court.

TABLE 10.1 Comparison of the Judgment of "Marriage for All" Lawsuit

Court	Sapporo DC	Osaka DC	Tokyo DC(1)	Nagoya DC	Fukuoka	Tokyo DC(2)	Sapporo HC
Judgment	17 March 2021	20 June 2022	30 November 2022	30 May 2023	8 June 2023	14 March 2024	14 March 2024
Article 24(1)	Constitutional	Constitutional	Constitutional	Constitutional	Constitutional	Constitutional	Unconstitutional
Article 24(2)	Constitutional	Constitutional	Unconstitutional[a]	Unconstitutional	Unconstitutional[a]	Unconstitutional[a]	Unconstitutional
Article 14(1)	Unconstitutional	Constitutional	Constitutional	Unconstitutional	Constitutional	Constitutional	Unconstitutional
Article 13	Constitutional	Constitutional	(Not discussed)	(Not discussed)	Constitutional	(Not discussed)	Constitutional

a The Tokyo District Court, both cases 1 and 2, and the Fukuoka District Court stated it is an "unconstitutional situation."

legislative branch, and the current situation cannot be considered unreasonable[18] (Table 10.1).

2.3 *Recommendations by Monitoring Bodies*

The first recommendation related to same-sex relationships by UN treaty bodies was the concluding observation of the HRC in 2008.[19] The HRC recommended equal protection for same-sex relationships and de facto marriages of different-sex couples, referring to the Public Housing Act and the Domestic Violence Prevention Act. At that time, Article 23 of the Public Housing Act limited its application to married couples and their relatives, which included de facto different-sex couples as a stable interpretation, excluding same-sex couples who could not marry.

In its subsequent periodic report, the Japanese government informed the HRC of the amendment to Article 23 of the Public Housing Act and explained that there were no obstacles to same-sex relationships in applying for public housing.[20] However, as the shadow report, which is submitted by civil societies as practical information in the review process of state party reports, stated, the amendment was not to abolish the limitation of legally recognized families but to change jurisdiction from the State to the local government. Most new local government ordinances for public housing still exclude same-sex couples under the same conditions as Article 23 of the Public Housing Act. Considering this information, the HRC recommends substantially abolishing the restriction on public housing in its following concluding observation.[21]

Regarding the need for a legal framework for same-sex relationships, Canada and Switzerland recommended introducing same-sex marriages during the third cycle of the Universal Periodic Review.[22] In response to these recommendations, the Japanese government does not accept follow-up, but only notes that it is related to an essential aspect of Japanese society and needs careful consideration.[23] The same recommendation was made by

18 *Marriage for All Lawsuits*, Case no. H31-Wa-1258, Judgment of 8 June 2022, Osaka District Court.

19 HRC, 2008, Concluding Observation: Japan (5th Report), 30 October 2008, UN Doc. CCPR/C/JPN/CO/5.

20 HRC, 2012, Japan: 6th Report, 9 October 2012, UN Doc. CCPR/C/JPN/6.

21 HRC, 2014, Concluding Observation: Japan (6th Report), 20 August 2014, UN Doc. CCPR/C/JPN/CO/6.

22 UNHRC, 2017, UPR (third cycle): Report of the Working Group on the Universal Periodic Review: Japan, 4 January 2018, UN Doc. A/HRC/37/15.

23 UNHRC, 2018, Replies by Japan, 1 March 2018, UN Doc. A/HRC/37/15/Add.1.

eight countries in the fourth cycle.[24] The Japanese government only notes this recommendation for the same reason.[25]

In the third cycle, the Japanese government accepted a recommendation from Timor-Leste concerning the application of the Domestic Violence Prevention Act in same-sex relationships.[26] However, whether same-sex couples are included in the concept of de facto marriage depends on court interpretations, which are not stable within the statutory law system mentioned above.

2.4 *Impact of International Human Rights Discourse*

There are few references in international human rights standards to the legal recognition of same-sex relationships in Japan, including observations by UN treaty bodies. Moreover, the Japanese government clearly expressed a negative attitude toward expanding its legal protections. The judgment of the Nagoya District Court stated that referring to the recommendations in the third cycle of the UPR, it cannot be said that the Japanese government fails to discuss whether marriage is open to same-sex couples. Considering that international human rights law admits broad discretion for each State concerning marriage and family, this seems to be the typical attitude of individual States.

However, this question arises when considering the contradictions between the opinions of the Japanese government in the international arena and in domestic matters. The Japanese government made recommendations during the UPR process for the legal protection of same-sex relationships, stating that it has a significant effect on traditional Japanese family values and needs careful consideration. However, when it comes to the resolutions of the UNHRC, such as the protection of traditional values[27] and protection of the family,[28] both show the same logic as the Japanese government states: Japan votes against these resolutions. It is an apparent contradiction to use the same reasoning in domestic matters that have been voted against

24 UNHRC, 2023, UPR (Fourth Cycle): Report of the Working Group on the Universal Periodic Review: Japan, 21 April 2023, UN Doc. A/HRC/53/15.

25 UNHRC, 2023, Replies by Japan, 8 June 2023, UN Doc. A/HRC/53/15/Add.1.

26 UNHRC, 2017, UPR (third cycle), Report of the Working Group on the Universal Periodic Review: Japan, 4 January 2018, UN Doc. A/HRC/37/15.

27 UNHRC, 2011, Promoting Human Rights and Fundamental Freedoms through a Better Understanding of Traditional Values of Humankind, Resolution of 24 March 2011, UN Doc. A/HRC/RES/16/3.

28 UNHRC, 2014, Protection of the Family, Resolution of 26 June 2014, UN Doc. A/HRC/RES/26/11.

internationally. It is not only criticized as the double tongue of the government but also has crucial problems in good faith.

3 Legal Gender Alteration

The existence of people who live with a gender different from their assigned gender at birth is widely seen in each culture with diverse wording: transgender, *Hijra*, *fa'afafine*, *meti*, and so on. As medical techniques evolved, there was a critical need for legal gender alterations by those who lived in different genders, as they were assigned at birth. Since the late 1970s, many European countries have admitted legal gender alterations with several conditions. Some countries require a certain age, while others require complete sex/gender reassignment surgery such as the removal of breasts, the creation or removal of sexual organs, and the inability to procreate. Recently, this requirement has been loosened from the perspective of human rights. More than 30 countries amended their requirements for medical surgery, age limitations, and court involvement. For instance, legal gender alterations have become an administrative process based on self-determination and identification in Argentina, Malta, and other countries.[29]

3.1 *International Human Rights Laws and Standards*

In 2014, the Office of the High Commissioner for Human Rights (OHCHR) and five other international bodies made a joint statement titled "Eliminating forced, coercive, and otherwise involuntary sterilization: an interagency statement."[30] This statement recommends that each State to abolish sterilization without their own will, including as a condition of legal gender alteration for transgender individuals, as well as the sterilization of persons with disabilities, indigenous populations, ethnic minorities, and other vulnerable groups. The Special Rapporteur on Torture also pointed out that the sterilization requirement for legal gender alterations amounts to inhumane treatment, which is prohibited by international human rights laws.[31]

29 International Lesbian, Gay, Bisexual, Trans and Intersex Association (ILGA), 2023, ILGA World Database, https://database.ilga.org/en.

30 OHCHR et al., 2014, Eliminating Forced, Coercive and Otherwise Involuntary Sterilization: An Interagency Statement, Retrieved from https://apps.who.int/iris/handle/10665/112848.

31 UNHRC, 2016, Report of the Special Rapporteur on torture and other cruel, inhuman or degrading treatment or punishment, UN Doc. A/HRC/31/57, paras. 4850.

More precisely, an Independent Expert on protection against violence and discrimination based on sexual orientation and gender identity (IE-SOGI) submitted an annual report to the UNHRC dedicated to transgender issues.[32] Mr. Victor Madrigal-Borloz, the second appointed IE-SOGI, conducted comprehensive research worldwide on transgender legal situations. He urged the State to ensure "due respect for free and informed choice and bodily autonomy" of trans individuals, with the process based on self-determination by the applicant, through a simple administrative process without requirements such as medical and psychological or other certifications that could be unreasonable or pathologizing.[33]

3.2 *Legal Situation in Japan*

In Japan, the court rejected requests to alter legal gender for a long time. Along with the medical recognition of gender reassignment surgery and the social acceptance of transgender issues, the Act of Special Handling of People with Gender Identity Disorder (GID Act) was passed in 2003. The law was passed unanimously by the full board of parliament after only 10 days. After its enactment, more than 10,000 applications have been accepted for legal gender alterations.

The GID Act includes several conditions that can alter legal gender. According to Article 3 of the Act, the applicant should (1) be over the age of 18 years, (2) not married, (3) have no minor child, (4) remove gonadal organs or have dysfunctional reproductive ability, and (5) have similar external sexual organs. The fourth and fifth conditions require surgical intervention. In addition to these requirements, the applicant should have been diagnosed with a "Gender Identity Disorder" by two or more physicians and request that the Family Court to obtain permission to alter.

Several lawsuits have questioned the constitutionality of the requirements of the GID Act. The Supreme Court of Japan finds it constitutional for the second and third requirements in Article 3:[34] As to the fourth requirement, the Grand Chamber of the Supreme Court of Japan ruled it unconstitutional in 2023, overruling a 2019 judgment that had deemed the

32 IE-SOGI, 2018, Report to the General Assembly, UN Doc. A/73/152, 12 July 2018.

33 IE-SOGI, 2018, Report to the General Assembly, UN Doc. A/73/152, 12 July 2018.

34 *Legal Gender Recognition* cases, Case no. R1-Ku-791, Decision of 11 March 2020, Supreme Court of Japan; Case no. R2-Ku-638, Decision of 30 November 2021, Supreme Court of Japan, respectively.

requirement constitutional "at the present time."[35] In the 2023 judgment, the Supreme Court referred to a joint statement by several international organizations cited above and the Judgment of the European Court of Human Rights.[36] Moreover, the three judges added their individual opinions that the fifth requirement was unconstitutional.

3.3 *Recommendations by Monitoring Bodies*

In the third UPR cycle, New Zealand recommended amendments to the GID Act.[37] Japan has accepted this recommendation, although there has been no discussion of the amendment, and the periodic report does not refer to any progress on this topic.[38] There are several recommendations regarding this point in the fourth cycle.[39]

Although there have been no recommendations from the UN treaty bodies thus far, some dialogue can be found during the review process. In the process of constructive dialogue between the Japanese government and the Committee for the Elimination of All Forms of Discrimination against Women (CEDAW), some experts raised several questions concerning the GID Act.[40]

3.4 *Impact of International Human Rights Discourses*

As mentioned above, the Grand Chamber of the Supreme Court refers to the joint statement and the ECHR Judgment during its review of the constitutionality of the sterilization requirements. However, these references do not seem to be an essential element of the argument but only serve as proof of the trend in international human rights discourse. Japanese courts, particularly the Supreme Court of Japan, are reluctant to refer to international human rights laws. Some recent judgments refer to human rights treaties and the recommendations from treaty bodies; however, they are still rare.

---

35 *Legal Gender Recognition* case, Case no. R2-Ku-993, Decision of 25 October 2023, Supreme Court of Japan; Case no. H30-Ku-269, Decision of 23 January 2019, Supreme Court of Japan, respectively.

36 ECHR, 2017, A.P., *Garçon and Nicot v. France*, Judgment of 6 April 2017, Applications 79885/12, 52471/13 and 52596/13.

37 UNHRC, 2017, UPR (Third Cycle): Japan, 4 January 2018, UN Doc. A/HRC/37/15.

38 UNHRC, 2022, Japan: 4th National Report, 10 November 2022, UN Doc. A/HRC/WG.6/42/JPN/1

39 UNHRC, 2023, UPR (Fourth Cycle): Report of the Working Group on the Universal Periodic Review: Japan, 21 April 2023, UN Doc. A/HRC/53/15.

40 CEDAW, 2017, Summary Record, 7 August 2017, UN Doc. CEDAW/C/SR.1376.

The GID Act is currently under review following a Supreme Court ruling in 2023. As for the wording of the Act, "GID" is no longer used as a technical term in the medical field. The World Health Organization revised the International Classification of Diseases (ICD) to version 11th in 2018, "GID" was diminished from the category within "Mental, Behavioral and Neurodevelopmental Disorders," shifting the concept of "Gender Incongruence" within the category under "Condition related to Sexual Health."

4 Anti-discrimination Legislation

In many countries, "sexual orientation" and "gender identity" are explicit grounds for anti-discrimination legislation. Some countries stipulate this in their constitutions, while others insert it into comprehensive anti-discrimination laws or laws prohibiting discrimination, such as housing, social security, education, and the workplace. Many National Human Rights Institutions (NHRIs) mandates include discrimination based on sexual orientation or gender identity.

According to global research conducted by the ILGA World, the world's most prominent umbrella organization of civil society, more than 10 countries have explicit references to discrimination against LGBTQs in their constitution. Approximately 80 countries legally prohibit discrimination in employment, and approximately 50 in health services, education, and housing. Most of them include "sexual orientation," while an increasing number have included "gender identity," "gender expression," and "sex characteristics" as prohibited grounds of discrimination.[41]

4.1 *International Human Rights Laws and Standards*

There is no specific reference to "sexual orientation" and "gender identity" or other grounds directly related to LGBTQ, such as gender expression or sex characteristics, in major human rights treaties. However, the HRC interprets the ICCPR as prohibiting sexual orientation discrimination in the case of *Toonen v. Australia*.[42] Mr. Nicholas Toonen complained that the so-called sodomy laws in Tasmania, which prohibit same-sex sexual conduct, violated his right to privacy and non-discrimination guaranteed by the ICCPR. The

41 ILGA, 2023, ILGA World Database, https://database.ilga.org/en.

42 HRC, 1994, *Toonen v. Australia*, Views of 31 March 1994, UN Doc. CCPR/C/50/D/488/1992.

HRC finds this a violation of Article 17, Rights to Privacy, and Articles 2 and 26, which are non-discrimination clauses.

Many treaty bodies have followed this interpretation in their general comments and recommendations. For instance, the Committee on Economic, Social, and Cultural Rights (CESCR), which monitors the International Covenant on Economic, Social, and Cultural Rights, adopted the General Comment stating that non-discrimination clauses include sexual orientation and gender identity.[43] The CEDAW adopted General Recommendation No.28, which includes sexual orientation and gender identity in the context of intersectional discrimination prohibited in Article 2 of the Convention on the Elimination of All Forms of Discrimination against Women.[44] Recently adopted General Comments/ Recommendations also include these words such as the Committee against Torture's General Comment No. 2 on the implementation of Article 2 by State parties,[45] and the Committee of the Rights of the Child's General Comment No. 13 on the right of the child to freedom from all forms of violence.[46]

These trends are reflected in the prominent document "Born Free and Equal," published by OHCHR soon after the first LGBTQ specified UN resolution.[47] This document describes five core obligations that each State must follow. One of its obligations is effective legislation for non-discrimination based on sexual orientation and gender identity. The revised version added gender expression and sex characteristics to the list of prohibited grounds for discrimination.[48]

4.2 *Legal Situation in Japan*

Under Japanese law, no law takes "sexual orientation" and "gender identity" as grounds for discrimination for a long time. Some judgments suggest that sexual orientation discrimination is prohibited, despite the lack of specific provisions. A leading example of this is the *Fuchu Youth Hostel* case.[49] A

---

43 CESCR, 2009, General Comment No. 20, 2 July 2009, UN Doc. E/C.12/GC/20

44 CEDAW, 2010, General Recommendation No. 28, 16 December 2010, UN Doc. CEDAW/C/GC/28.

45 CAT, 2008, General Comment No. 2, 24 January 2008, UN Doc. CAT/A/GC/2.

46 CRC, 2011, General Comment No. 13, 18 April 2011, UN Doc. CRC/C/GC/13.

47 OHCHR, 2012, Born Free and Equal: Sexual Orientation and Gender Identity in International Human Rights Law, l, UN Doc. HR/PUB/12/06.

48 OHCHR, 2019, Born Free and Equal: Sexual Orientation, Gender Identity and Sex Characteristics in International Human Rights Law, l, UN Doc. HR/PUB/12/06/Rev.1.

49 *Fuchu Youth Hostel* case, Case no. H3-Wa-1557, Judgment of 30 March 1994, Tokyo District Court; Case no. H6-Ne-1580, Judgment of 16 September 1997, Tokyo High Court.

non-governmental organization named OCCUR booked the Fuchu Youth Hostel, which was managed by the Tokyo Metropolitan Board of Education. They refused their application based on the regulations of sex-segregated accommodations and the facility's purpose of bringing youngsters to a sound uprising. The Tokyo District Court and Tokyo High Court found the rejection to be unlawful and discriminatory based on sexual orientation, contrary to Article 244 of the Local Government Act.

When the human rights protection laws were discussed in the Diet in 2002, the draft bill contained "sexual orientation" as one of the prohibited grounds for discrimination. However, this draft bill did not pass because of anxiety about freedom of the press and the ambiguity of the human rights protection system. Simultaneously, the Human Rights Education and Enlightenment Law, one of the domestic implementations of the UN Decade for Human Rights Education, was passed, and the Ministry of Justice introduced an annual awareness-raising program. Since 2002, "sexual orientation" and "gender identity disorder" have been included in these programs. In addition, the local government began to include sexual orientation and gender identity in its Ordinance or Action Plans on human rights and gender equality.

Discussions on enacting anti-discrimination laws on LGBTQ people emerged alongside the Tokyo Olympics and Paralympics in 2020. The Charter of the International Olympic Committee requires a host State to ensure non-discrimination, including sexual orientation discrimination. This explicit reference was added after the Sochi Olympics when Russia passed the so-called "homosexuality anti-propaganda law," which prohibited the promotion of LGBTQ rights in public spaces (including school education) and invited a boycott of participation in the opening ceremony.

The opposition party proposed the Elimination of the Discrimination Act, which prohibited discrimination and promoted action plans for LGBTQ equality. Conversely, the ruling party planned to submit a draft bill named Understanding Law, which focused on awareness-raising activities without any reference to discrimination or equality. Shortly before the opening of the Tokyo Olympics and Paralympics in 2021, the informal parliamentary group called "LGBT Giren," consisting of every party, agreed to pass the amended Understanding Law to the Diet. However, the draft bill was not sent to the Diet, with strong opposition in the ruling party, the Liberal Democratic Party, concerning the amendment, including the phrase "discrimination must not be tolerated."

Subsequently, the move to pass the bill was fueled by the hosting of the G7 Summit held in Hiroshima, Japan. Despite the opposition and deep regret of human rights activists, significant amendments were made to the proposed Understanding Law. For example, a clause was deleted from the article stating that "discrimination shall not be allowed," and parental consent was recommended concerning school education and new clauses that require giving due consideration to the majority's anxiety about the promotion of human rights related to LGBTQ. The Bill was passed and enacted in June 2023.

4.3 *Recommendations by Monitoring Bodies*

There are several recommendations from treaty bodies concerning the enactment of anti-discrimination laws, including sexual orientation and gender identity. A good example of this is the concluding observations of the 6th report by the HRC.[50] Under the title of "Discrimination based on sexual orientation and gender identity," the HRC recommends Japan to "adopt comprehensive anti-discrimination legislation" and to "provide victims of discrimination with effective and appropriate remedies." In addition to the title, this recommendation could be applied to all grounds of discrimination.

In addition, there are several recommendations during the UPR process on this topic. For example, Canada recommends "take[ing] measures to eliminate discrimination based on sexual orientation and gender identity" in the first cycle.[51] In the second cycle, of the five countries that recommended tackling discrimination based on sexual orientation and gender identity, four of them urged employing legislation.[52] The number of countries increased to 11 in the third cycle[53] and 14 in the fourth cycle.[54] In response, the Japanese government was negative, particularly regarding the enactment of anti-discrimination measures in general.[55] The government of Japan accepted these recommendations regarding awareness-raising treatments.

4.4 *Impact of International Human Rights Law*

Unlike Judeo-Christian or Islamic countries, Japan has no effective sodomy laws derived from religious taboos. In most countries, the human rights

50 HRC, 2014, Concluding Observation: Japan (6th Report), 20 August 2014, UN Doc. CCPR/C/JPN/CO/6.
51 UNHRC, 2008, UPR (first cycle): Japan, 30 May 2008, UN Doc. A/HRC/8/44.
52 UNHRC, 2012, UPR (second cycle): Japan, 14 December 2012, UN Doc. A/HRC/22/14.
53 UNHRC, 2017, UPR (third cycle): Japan, 4 January 2018, UN Doc. A/HRC/37/15.
54 UNHRC, 2023, UPR (fourth cycle): Report of the Working Group on the Universal Periodic Review: Japan, 21 April 2023, UN Doc. A/HRC/53/15.
55 UNHRC, 2018, Replies by Japan, 1 March 2018, UN Doc. A/HRC/37/15/Add.1.

discussion started by questioning sodomy laws as serious interference with one's privacy by criminal laws and as discriminatory treatment based on sexual orientation.[56] In this sense, Japan has no legal clue for starting human rights discussions related to the LGBTQ. Nevertheless, as mentioned above, the courts interpreted sexual orientation discrimination as not allowed under Japanese law in the same year as Views from the HRC in *Toonen v. Australia.*

Despite this pioneering interpretation in the 1990s, Japan failed to effectively protect the human rights of the LGBTQ. Although there are plenty of recommendations from experts in treaty bodies and other countries in the UPR process, Japan has not enacted a legal framework that could explicitly apply to LGBTQ issues until recently. Although Japan's momentum has received attention from the international society, such as hosting the Olympic and Paralympic Games or charting the Group of 7 (G7) summits, which stipulates the discussion of enactment, the legal situation has not changed effectively.

The problem lies in the unique situation of human rights in Japan. The discussion in international human rights law is to include the exact words "sexual orientation" and "gender identity" into comprehensive anti-discrimination laws or each law prohibiting discrimination. In addition to the broad and ambiguous provisions of the Constitution of Japan, there is no comprehensive anti-discrimination law. It is needless to say the provision of the Constitution is insufficient in effectively realizing each human rights and ensuring equal rights for all. In addition, no NHRI complies with the Paris Principles of 1993, which urges each State to establish human rights bodies that are highly independent of the government.[57] The Human Rights Bureau, as stated by the Japanese government in its report to the UN human rights bodies, is not an independent organization, but is under the jurisdiction of the Ministry of Justice and has no remedy process for human rights violations.

In summary, Japan has no framework for human rights protection to which specific words should be added. This situation has also been repeatedly indicated as being improved by all treaty bodies with reference to LGBTQ issues.

---

56 Waaldijk K., "Civil Developments: Patterns of Reform in the Legal Position of Same-Sex Partners in Europe," *Revue Canadienne de Droit Familia* 17 (2000), 62–88.

57 United Nations General Assembly, 1993, Principles Relating to the Status of National Institutions, 20 December 1993, UN Doc. A/RES/48/134.

5 Conclusion

Despite global progress in the human rights protection of LGBTQ, Japan continues to be left behind in this trend. Legal protection for same-sex relationships has not yet been realized, even after 16 years of the first recommendation from the HRC to equalize protection with different-sex de facto marriages to comply with Articles 2 and 26 of the ICCPR. The GID Act, which enables legal gender alteration, has the strictest conditions in the world – those that many countries abolish from the viewpoint of human rights – and the IE-SOGI, appointed by the UNHRC, recommends loosening these conditions. Regarding non-discrimination based on sexual orientation and gender identity, although a kind of basic law was formally passed in 2023, its content was in the lineage of the anti-propaganda law. This law is highly questionable from a human rights perspective.

It cannot be concluded that the legal situation of LGBTQ in Japan is hopeless. Instead, international human rights law has a weak but steady effect on the progress of legal protection for LGBTQ people in Japan. Most recommendations made by monitoring bodies are based on information from civil society. With the recent development in the "Business and Human Rights" field, LGBTQ issues become vital to national action plans and other related concerns. The key will be continuous practical use and monitoring by the private sector to determine whether State power complies with international human rights standards through the available means.

CHAPTER 11

Japanese National Security Policy and International Law

Masatoshi Takeuchi

1 Introduction[1]

The 2014 decision by then-Prime Minister Shinzo Abe's Cabinet to reinterpret Article 9 of the Japanese Constitution[2], and the passing of major security legislation accordingly in September 2015 have been, and continue to be, a source of major controversy in Japanese society and academia.[3] The Legislation for Peace and Security (hereafter: LPS) has been commonly labeled as "War Legislation" by critics.[4] Subsequently, the Kishida administration (Liberal Democratic Party, hereafter: LDP) approved three new key documents, the National Security Strategy (NSS), the National Defense Strategy (NDS), and the Defense Buildup Program, to guide national security policy on December 16 2022.[5] These policy documents come in line with the LPS but with new controversial methods of "countermeasure."[6] Some parties

1 This chapter draws from earlier works of the author: Takeuchi M., "The 2015 Japanese Legislation on Peace and Security and the Japanese Approach to Self Defense Rights", *Bulletin of Toyo Gakuen University* 26 (2018) 61–73.

2 Provisional translation available. http://www.mofa.go.jp/fp/nsp/page23e_000273.html (accessed Mar. 16, 2023).

3 According to Art. 4 of the Cabinet Law, "perform its functions through Cabinet Meetings." Decisions made in these meetings, which are required to be unanimous, are the highest in the executive branch. It is a part of the legislative process but is significant in weight in terms of deciding government policy.

4 Such a label has been consistently used, particularly by the Japanese Communist Party. For example, JCP Chair Kazuo Shii held a press conference on June 9, 2016, to announce its electoral platform. In this conference, Shii explained that "the JCP pledges to work to abolish the war laws, restore constitutionalism, and foil Abe's attempt to revise the Constitution." (emphasis added) "JCP announces election platform focusing on the abolition of unconstitutional war laws" https://www.jcp.or.jp/english/9854/ (accessed June 10, 2025).

5 For general information, see documents provided by the MOD, https://www.mod.go.jp/en/d_policy/index.html (accessed June 10, 2025)

6 The NSS defines countermeasure capabilities to be "capabilities of the SDF to utilize standoff defense capabilities to coordinate effective counter attacks on the other State's

 | DOI:10.1163/9789004548824_012

have criticized this as illegal pre-emptive strikes under the Japanese Constitution and international law.[7]

These developments were considered an example of what LDP administrations have referred to as the doctrine of "Proactive Contribution to Peace."[8] While much of the discussion in the Japanese government has centered around its constitutionality and political ideals (such as the rule of law, democracy, etc.), some key perspectives have been left out, such as that of international law. This chapter shall describe the Japanese government's approach to issues of security, particularly on self-defense rights (hereafter: SDR). This approach shall mainly imply the following two facets: 1. the use of unique concepts and theoretical frameworks emanating from Constitutional theory and domestic cases in discussion of international legal issues, and 2. the relationship between the Ministry of Foreign Affairs (MOFA) and the Cabinet Legislation Bureau (CLB) in determining the boundaries of international legal policy. More specifically, this chapter shall first provide an overview of the background and domestic legal/moral restraints (as represented in Article 9 of the Japanese Constitution), which form the basis of Japan's approach regarding the UN collective security system and security issues in general. Unique legal concepts to be explained include *"senshu-boei"* (placing defense as primary priority), *"ittaika"* (unification), and *"kaketuke-keigo"* (use of weapons for coming to the aid of geographically distant units or personnel under attack) will be explained. The discussion then moves on to several recent security issues (e.g., missile

---

territory, towards an armed attack by use of ballistic missiles, etc., towards Japan [...] ." (translation by Takeuchi), https://www.cas.go.jp/jp/siryou/221216anzenhoshou/nss-j.pdf (accessed June 27, 2023).

7 For example, see the position paper by the Constitutional Democratic Party of Japan. https://cdp-japan.jp/news/20221227_5140 (accessed June 27, 2023). The government takes the existence of "launch of attack" to differentiate countermeasures and pre-emptive strikes.

8 This doctrine has been derived from interpreting the Preamble of the Japanese Constitution, stating the desire "to occupy an honored place in an international society striving for the preservation of peace, and the banishment of tyranny and slavery, oppression and intolerance for all time from the earth. We recognize that all peoples of the world have the right to live in peace, free from fear and want". Academics, as Ito Kenichi coined the term in the early 1990s to address a trend of "negative pacifism," which is described to be serving the interest of only one State and neglecting rest of the States in the international community. Though the wording may be similar, the content of this concept is different from that of "positive peace" by peace theorist Johan Galtung. *See* for example, Ito K., *"Futatsu-no-Shogeki" to Nihon* [Japan's Response to "The Two Shocks"] (Japanese) (PHP Research Institute, 1991)

threats from the DPRK, territorial disputes, cyber-attacks, etc.) that led to the establishment of the 2015 Legislation on Peace and Security. Finally, this chapter shall explore the implications of recent developments to the traditional approach.

2 The Traditional Approach to Security Issues and the Basic Legal Structure of the LPS

2.1 *The Traditional Approach to National Security*

The Post WWII approach (hereafter the traditional approach) towards national security issues can be described in one of the three principles or "pillars" of the Japanese Constitution: pacificism.[9] At its very core of pacifism, the Japanese Constitution borrows strikingly similar language from the Charter of the United Nations (hereafter the UN Charter) and the liberal philosophy that it embodies. This can be particularly found in Article 9 of the Constitution, which utilizes terms like "use of force," "threat of force," and "force," as found in Article 2(4) of the UN Charter. This is no surprise considering the history of drafting the Japanese Constitution.[10] However, after decades of debate framed within internal logic, Japanese Constitutional lawyers seem to have deviated from the interpretation from that of international lawyers and that of the Japanese government in some terms. Most of these issues, particularly regarding the "use of force" and the "right of self-defense" have been dealt with extensively during the deliberation of the 2015 Legislation on Peace and Security.

Article 9 of the Japanese Constitution provides:

1. Aspiring sincerely to an international peace based on justice and order, the Japanese people forever renounce war as a sovereign right

9 It is standard practice among Japanese textbooks of the Constitution to include a section regarding pacificism or Art. 9 of the Japanese Constitution. Other principles include popular sovereignty and respect for fundamental human rights. For a quick understanding of the government's understanding, *see* the 2005 *Handbook on the Research Report on the Constitution of Japan* (English available) by the Research Commission on the Constitution House of Councillors, https://www.sangiin.go.jp/eng/report/ehb/ehb.pdf (accessed Sept. 13, 2024).

10 Yuichi Takano describes the background of drafting Article 9 as "extraordinary" when Japan was under occupation and with the determination to abandon previous doctrines. Takano Y., "Kenpō Kyū Jō [Article 9 of the Constitution]" (Japanese) in Eiichi Fukase (ed.), *Bunken Senshu Nihonkoku Kenpo 3: Sensō no Hōki* [Selected Articles regarding the Japanese Constitution vol. 3: Renouncement of War] (Japanese) (Sanseido, 1977), 130.

of the nation and the threat or use of force as a means of settling international disputes.

2. In order to accomplish the aim of the preceding paragraph, land, sea, and air forces, as well as other war potential, will never be maintained. The right of belligerency of the State will not be recognized.

Most of the restraints placed upon the Japan Self-Defense Forces (hereafter: SDF), which shall be mentioned, can be traced back to this article. Though several interpretations of this article may exist, one common feature is the categorization of wars into "Wars in Self-Defense" and "Wars of Aggression." The prevailing interpretation of Article 9(1) regards "war as a sovereign right of the nation" as "Wars of Aggression" and not "Wars in Self-Defense." Thus, according to the Japanese government, there is room for a force to maintain minimum "self-defense."[11]

Another feature of the traditional approach would be to view war, use of force, and threat of force as part of a continuum to which the Constitution prohibits military force as a whole. As Isao Sato wrote in a *Treatise of the Constitution* in 1991:

> Compared to the constitutions of other states, Article 9 of the Japanese Constitution has been consistent regarding pacifism and the prohibition of war.
>
> Thus, Article 9 first renounces not just wars of invasion but all wars. Second, it renounces not only "wars" but "use of force" and "threats of force." Third, along with this, forces, as well as other war potential, will never be maintained, and the right of belligerency of the state will not be recognized.

Note that the threat of force is at the periphery of this continuum, which is used to emphasize the commitment to pacifism. It should also be mentioned that "use of force" interpreted in mainstream constitutional law is presumed to be "more than combat, but less than war."[12] This interpretation is in agreement with International Law to include *de facto* war (war without

11 Depending on how "In order to accomplish the aim of the preceding paragraph" in Art. 9(2) is interpreted that the constitutionality of war in self-defense is also in question. In 1982, Reijiro Tsunoda (then Director of CLB) differentiated Art. 9 from the Constitutions of other states by stating that Art. 9 permits minimum use of force and minimum weapons, even for wars in self-defense. Reply at 96 session of Diet, Committee on Cabinet (July 8, 1982) vol. 18, 6.

12 On this point, *see* Mizushima A., "Kyu Jōo [Article 9]" (Japanese), *Kihon Hō Kommentar* [Commentaries of the Basic Laws: Constitutional Law] (Nippon Hyoron sha, 1997) 43.

declaration) in the realm, but different in terms of differentiating it from war, whether for defense (*jiei-senso*), aggression (*shinryaku-senso*) or sanction (*seisai-senso*), or combat.

However, another point to be mentioned in understanding the constitutional interpretation is its assertion of connectedness to the UN Charter. For example, in an entry of an encyclopedia of constitutional law, Toshihiro Yamauchi correlates the term in both contexts. "Though they may not amount to the use of force, because such threats may likely endanger the maintenance of international peace and security, the UN Charter prohibits threats of force along with the use of force against the territorial integrity or political independence of any state, or in any other manner inconsistent with the purposes of the United Nations. The Japanese Constitution also prohibits the threat of force along with the use of force to settle international disputes."[13] Thus, it can be roughly stated that Article 9(1) (though the emphasis within the article may differ according to political stances or schools of thought) categorically renounces war, use of force, and threats of force. As it is well documented, such interpretation by the mainstream has caused significant problems for the government, particularly the CLB. Thus, the language found in various legislation is carefully crafted to evade any collision and retain Article 9. Examples include "cooperation" instead of "participation" in Peace Keeping Operations, "inspection" instead of "visitation" in "*jyuyoeikyojitai*" (Situations that Gravely Affect the Peace and Security of Japan), and "*shuhenjitai* (Situations in Areas surrounding Japan)". Some of these terms, such as "*ittaika.*"[14], "*shuhenjitai*", "*kaketsukekeigo*", and "*senshuboei*" (the doctrine of an exclusively defense-oriented posture) are all employed in government documents without proper English translation.

Finally, Article 9 and its language have helped to develop various soft-law based or voluntary restrictions on security issues. A few would include: (1) its defense cost 1 percent frame (GDP)[15] (2) the three non-nuclear

---

13 Yamauchi T., "Buryoku niyoru Kyoi [Threat of Force]" (Japanese), *Kenpo Jiten* [Dictionary of the Constitution] (Sanseido, 2001) 424.

14 The Japanese government has employed this criterion ever since the statement by CLB D-G Hayashi on May 19, 1959.

15 The Miki cabinet introduced this frame in 1976. Ever since, the Japanese government used this GDP 1 percent rule as a rough indicator of an adequate budget for defense. This seems to have changed in an interview with DM Kishi. "Interview with DM Kishi" (Japanese), *Nikkei* (Tokyo, May 20, 2021).

principles[16] and (3) the three principles on arms export (currently the three principles on transfer of defense equipment and technology).[17]

However, as mentioned earlier, this traditional approach has been modified in recent years by the LPS and other factors.

2.2 *The LPS and Its Legal Structure*

The LPS is organized under two key phrases: a "seamless response" to transforming threats and the doctrine of "proactive contribution to peace."[18] The former may perhaps be exemplified where a transition of force is required from police agencies to the SDF, for example, due to the weapons possessed by armed groups, such as the landing of an unidentified foreign force on a remote island disguised as fishermen (described as "grey zone situations").[19] The latter is a doctrine derived from interpreting the Preamble of the Japanese Constitution, stating the desire "to occupy an honored place in an international society striving for the preservation of peace, and the banishment of tyranny and slavery, oppression, and intolerance for all time from the earth. We recognize that all peoples of the world have the right to live in peace, free from fear and want". Academics like Ito Kenichi invented the

16 According to a statement by PM Eisaku Sato at the Budget Committee in the House of Representatives (Dec. 11, 1967), "My responsibility is to achieve and maintain safety in Japan under the Three Non-Nuclear Principles of not possessing, not producing and not permitting the introduction of nuclear weapons, in line with Japan's Peace Constitution." *See,* https://www.mofa.go.jp/mofaj/gaiko/kaku/gensoku/ (accessed June 10, 2025).

17 These principles were declared in the Diet in 1967. According to these principles, "arms" exports to the following countries or regions shall not be permitted: "(1) communist bloc countries, (2) countries subject to "arms" exports embargo under the United Nations Security Council's resolutions, and (3) countries involved in or likely to be involved in international conflicts." https://www.mofa.go.jp/policy/un/disarmament/policy/index.html (accessed June 27, 2023). *See also,* https://www.mofa.go.jp/fp/nsp/page1we_000083.html (accessed June 27, 2023).

18 It should be stressed that such doctrines are neither unique to the Abe Administration nor the LDP. Similar doctrines like "Proactive Pacifism" (*Nōdōteki Heiwa Shugi*) by the Noda Administration (DPJ) have been stated prior.

19 According to the typology of military activity, such situations would be described as an infringement that does not amount to an armed attack. (*Nicaragua* Case, ICJ, 1986, para. 191) Under former interpretations, the SDF would respond with public security operations (*Chian Shutsudō*) and Maritime Security Operation (*Kaijō Keibi Kōdō*). However, these actions would require a lengthy deliberation within the Cabinet. The Cabinet decision of May 14, 2015, enables a swift decision-making procedure by enabling deliberations via telephone.

term in the early 1990s to address a trend he labels "negative pacifism," which is described as serving the interest of only one state and neglecting rest of the states in the international community.[20]

The LPS is composed of partial amendments to ten pre-existing laws[21] and one new legislation,[22] the International Peace Support Act (IPSA). Also, the Cabinet Decisions on July 1, 2014, substantially acted as a precursor of this legislation. It should be described as a group of laws rather than a single legislation. Thus, it can be difficult to discuss or criticize the LPS as a whole. Above this, other elements of the LPS framework can be confusing as well.

First, LPS sets two distinct objectives: national security and contributions to international peace. Most of the amendments regard the use of force or self-defense rights in various situations. However, the IPSL is solemnly focused on the overseas activities of the SDF, such as transport support and logistics support. Also, by relaxing some criteria for PKO operations enshrined in the Act on Cooperation with United Nations Peacekeeping Operations and Other Operations, the SDF may participate in activities to secure

20 Ito K., *"Futatsu no Shōgeki" to Nihon* [Japan's Response to "The Two Shocks"] (Japanese) (PHP Institute, 1991) Though the wording may be similar, the content of these concepts is different from "positive peace" by peace theorist Johan Galtung.

21 Self-Defense Forces Act (Self-Defense Forces Act, Act No. 165 of 1954), Act on Cooperation with United Nations Peacekeeping Operations and Other Operations (Act No. 79 of June 19, 1992), Act Concerning Measures to Ensure Peace and Security of Japan in Situations that gravely affect the Peace and Security of Japan (former Act Concerning Measures to Ensure the Peace and Security of Japan in Situations in Areas Surrounding Japan) (Act No. 60 of 1999, amended as Act 76, 2015), Act on Ship Inspection Operations in Situations that gravely affect the Peace and Security of Japan (Act No. 145, 2018), the Act on the Peace and Independence of Japan and Maintenance of the Nation and the People's Security in Armed Attack Situations, etc. (also known as the Armed Attack Situations Response Act) (Act No. 79, 2003), Act on Measures Conducted by the Government in Line with U.S. Military Actions in Armed Attack Situations, Etc. Act) (Act No. 103, 2004), Act on the Use of Specific Public Facilities, etc. in Armed Attack Situations, etc. (Act No. 114, 2004), Act on the Restriction of Maritime Transportation of Foreign Military Supplies in Armed Attack Situations (Act No. 116, 2004, amended as Act 116, 2006), Act on the Treatment of Prisoners of War and Other Detainees in Armed Attack Situations (Act 117, 2004, amended as Act 5, 2008) Prisoner of Wars, and the National Security Council Establishment Act (Act No. 71, 1986). It should be noted that most of the content has not been changed. Instead, the amended acts merely add situations (such as those which "gravely affect the Peace and Security of Japan") to which it applies.

22 International Peace Support Act (Act 77, 2015).

safety (*anzen-kakuho-katudo*) and so-called *kaketsuke-keigo*.[23] Such activities have been de facto prohibited due to constitutional restraints.

Second, the LPS describes various situations where the SDF may use weapons or force. Distinguished by the intensity of the conflict, they are labeled as (1) Armed Attack Situations (*buryoku-kogeki-jai*), an armed attack against a foreign country resulting in threats to Japan's survival.[24] (2) "Grey Zone" Situations,[25] and (3) Situations that Gravely affect the Peace and Security of Japan.[26] As Figure 11.1 describes, each situation has a different response, legal basis and procedure under both international and domestic law. Of these, perhaps the most controversial situation is situations that gravely affect the peace and security of Japan, where Japan is not yet directly attacked, but in which Japan may take measures including the "use of weapons."[27] Crises in the Korean Peninsula and South China Sea are considered to be examples of this category. In both situations, the probability of Japan initially being engaged is rather low. However, treaties with allies like the United States (ACSA Agreements) shall require the SDF to provide various logistic support and other services.

Based upon several sets of deliberations by Advisory Panels and the ruling parties, the LPS provides additional requirements to be considered in the use of collective SDR. As found in Figure 11.2, such requirements include: 1. The object of attack must be in close relationship with Japan, and 2. The attack must pose a clear danger to fundamentally overturn the people's right to life, liberty, and the pursuit of happiness.

The LPS is designed to enable Japanese forces three areas of activities: logistical support to allies, rescue and evacuation missions, and inspection

23 The concept of *Kaketsuke Keigo* is based upon a hypothetical situation where the SDF is coming to the aid of a geographically distant unit or personnel under attack or the "use of weapons for the purpose of execution of missions."

24 Katsuya Okada (CDP) questioned this term and the use of countermeasure capabilities by asking for specific examples in the Diet. PM Kishida "intentionally refrained" from answering, for it would be "divulging methods in saving the lives of Japanese nationals." "30 *Nichi, Shūin Yosan Iinkai deno Giron* [Discussions in the House of Representatives, Committee on Budget on January 30]" (Japanese), *Yomiuri Shinbun* (Tokyo, Jan. 31, 2023).

25 Grey Zone situations are when an attack (not amounting to the use of force) takes place in which policing power would be insufficient. Examples include when a foreign armed group lands on a remote island, the non-innocent passage of a foreign naval ship, and foreign vessels attacking private vessels with Japanese nationals aboard.

26 As defined in Art. 1 of the Act of Situations that gravely affect the Peace and Security of Japan.

27 Under Japanese terminology, the "use of weapons" and "use of force" are distinguished.

Situation	Action Under IL	Response	Approval of the Diet	Legal Base
Armed Attack Situations	Use of Force	Defense Operations (Individual Rights of Self-Defense)	As a principle, requires approval beforehand. Ex-post facto approval is possible during emergencies.	Armed Attack Situations Response Act
"Grey Zone" Situations	Use of Weapons	Public Security Operations		SDF Act
		Maritime Security Operations	No requirement.	
An armed attack against a foreign country resulting in threatening Japan's survival	Use of Force	Defense Operations (Collective Rights of Self-Defense)	As a principle, requires approval beforehand. Ex-post facto approval is possible during emergencies.	Armed Attack Situations Response Act
Situations that gravely affect the peace and security of Japan.	Use of Weapons	Logistical Support		Act Concerning the Measures for Situations that gravely affect the peace and security of Japan.
		Search Missions		
		Boarding Investigations		Ship Inspection Operations Act

FIGURE 11.1 Based upon Nishihara T. (ed) *Wakaru Heiwa Anzen Hōsei* [Understanding LPS], (Asagumo Shinbun, 2015) 82.

		Requirements Under International law	Requirements of the Advisory Panel Report	Requirements Under the 2014 Cabinet Decsion	2015 Security Legislation
Common Criteria	Substantial Requirements	Existence of an armed attack	an imminent and illegitimate act of aggression against Japan	Existence of an armed attack	Existence of an armed attack, or a clear threat of an armed attack.
	Temporal Requirements	Until the UNSC has taken measures	–	–	–
	Procedural Requirements	Report to the UNSC	–	–	–
	Necessity	○	○	○	Compliance with International Law/Force required within
	Proportionality	○	○	○	
Requirements for rights of collective self-defense	ICJ Nicaragua Case	Declaration by the attacked member State	–	–	–
		Request for Assistance by the attacked State	○		
	Additional elements by the Japanese Gov.	–	The country must be in close relationship with Japan	The country must be in close relationship with Japan	The country must be in close relationship with Japan
			Significant impact on Japan's security	Threat to Japan's survival	Threat to Japan's survival
			Minimum use of force	Pose a clear danger to fundamentally overturn people's right to life, liberty and pursuit of happiness	Pose a clear danger to fundamentally overturn people's right to life, liberty and pursuit of happiness

FIGURE 11.2 Based upon Yamagata H., "Kokusaihō kara mita Shūdan Jieiken Yōnin no Mondaiten [Issues of Accepting Collective Self Defense Rights from International Law]" (Japanese), *Shūdan Jieiken Yōonin wo Hihan suru* [Criticizing the Embracement of the Collective Self Defense Rights] (Nippon Hyoron sha, 2014), 50; Nishiumi M., "Shūdanteki Jieiken [Collective Self Defense Rights]" (Japanese), *Hakumon* 67 (2015) 47.

of vessels. In particular, fueling jetfighters and transporting ammunition are operations which are made possible by the LPS. Also, the geographical concept of "*shuhenjitai* (Situations in Areas Surrounding Japan)" has been retracted. However, SDF operations are restricted to areas "where combat has not occurred."[28]

Third, related to the previous two, the LPS invokes terms that belong only in the terminology of the Japanese legal community. Concepts like "*ittaika*," "*shuhen-jitai*," "*kaketsuke-keigo*," "*senshu-boei*" (the doctrine of an exclusively defense-oriented posture) are all employed in government documents without proper English translation. The difficulty in comprehending these legal terms can be traced back to its origins.

3 Background of the New Approach and the LPS

Several narratives regarding the LPS begin with a symbolic episode during the first Gulf War.[29] Though Japan contributed a substantial amount of financial aid to the US-led multinational coalition, it did not come to the recognition of the Kuwait government in a public ad of gratitude. Accordingly, this left a strong sense of disappointment within the government and the need for further involvement in the international community. The mainstream within MOFA[30] has repeatedly expressed a need for further international involvement along with traditional policy as strengthening ties with the United States. It may be difficult to prove that this experience, along with the subsequent legislation regarding various PKO missions, is the direct origin of the LPS. However, it does portray the LPS as an inter-party (or inter-agency) project by the Japanese government and not a haphazard attempt by the Abe administration.

Another narrative emphasizes the change in the surrounding security environment and the need to adapt. The website of the Cabinet's Office lists

---

28 SDF Act Art. 95(2)

29 Watanabe O., "Abe-seiken no Kaiken, Gunji Taikokukan Kōsō no naka no Shūdan Jieiken [The Amendment of the Constitution by the Abe Administration: Collective Self Defense Rights in the Plot to become a Military Power]," *Shūdan Jieiken Yōnin wo Hihan suru* [Criticizing the Embracement of the Collective Self Defense Rights] (Japanese) (Nippon Hyoron sha, 2014) 3–30.

30 Notable members of this group include Shunji Yanai (Chair of the Advisory Panel for the PM, former-Ambassador to the United States, Judge of the ITLOS), Shotaro Yachi (Director of the NSC), and Nobukatsu Kanehara (Deputy Secretary General of the National Security Secretariat and Assistant Chief Cabinet Secretary in the PM's Office). They are mentioned in Watanabe (n 29), 8.

several cases of the "fundamental transformation of the security environment surrounding Japan." These include missile launches and nuclear experiments by North Korea, activities by Chinese (public) vessels in the vicinity of Senkaku islands, shifts in global power balance, and international terrorism.[31] In addition, incidents such as Chinese vessels in Ogasawara (illegally poaching for red coral) and a leaked video clip of a Chinese vessel ramming into a patrol vessel of the Japanese Coast Guard has had a substantial impact on winning public support. As displayed in the timeline below, from PM Yoshida's statement, which presumably even renounced the right of war of self-defense, discourses regarding national security, international cooperation, and SDR have all converged to reinterpreting Article 9.

In his first term, PM Abe established an advisory panel to discuss four distinct scenarios "about what Japan should do in order to respond [...] effectively under the current security environment surrounding Japan."[32] These four cases, or questions posed were:

(1) Defense of U.S. naval vessels on the high seas

Japanese SDF vessels are permitted to use weapons under SDF Law if they are directly attacked on the high seas (individual SDR). However, under joint operations with allies, the use of weapons may be required to effectively protect U.S. (or other allies) naval vessels.

(2) Interception of a ballistic missile that might be targeting the United States

Putting beside the technical difficulties, Japan would be obliged to intercept a ballistic missile if it had the option of doing so. Theoretically, however, constitutional restraints may prevent such options since Japan has not been the directly targeted.

(3) Use of weapons in international peace operations

From the international legal perspective, issues of PKOs should be distinguished from issues of national security or the use of force in general. However, severe restraints have been placed upon the SDF in PKO operations. The most notable of these is the issue of "*kaketsuke-keigo*." Unlike traditional PKO missions, the modern, robust PKO operations

31 Similar arguments can be found in the cabinet archive. https://warp.ndl.go.jp/info:ndljp/pid/8833367/www.cas.go.jp/jp/siryou/131217anzenhoshou/pamphlet_jp_en.pdf (accessed June 10, 2025).

32 "Report of the Advisory Panel on Reconstruction of the Legal Basis for Security," https://worldjpn.net/documents/texts/JPSC/20140515.O1E.html (accessed June 10, 2025).

TABLE 11.1 Timeline of events up to the 2015 security related legislation

1	June 1946	Statement of PM Yoshida	"By Article 9(2), all armaments and the right of belligerency of the state will not be recognized. Thus, war in self-defense, as the right of belligerency has been renounced"
2	May 1981	Government Statement	From the perspective of international law, a State is presumed to possess the right of collective self-defense, which is the right to use force when a closely related foreign state has encountered an armed attack (and when the home state has not been attacked). Under international law, it is obvious that Japan has the right to collective self-defense. However, Article 9 of the Constitution suggests that the right to collective self-defense is limited to a minimum degree to defend Japan. Using the right to collective self-defense would exceed this minimum degree. Thus, the use of this right would be unconstitutional
3	June 2008	Report of Advisory Panel on Reconstruction of the Legal Basis for Security (first Cabinet of PM Abe)	Deliberated on four situations regarding national security. The report suggested the present legal framework would not yield a proper response to any of the four situations. It concluded with a recommendation to modify (not amend) the interpretation of the Constitution to enable participation in collective self-defense and UN collective security
4	May 2014	Report of Advisory Panel on Reconstruction of the Legal Basis for Security (second Cabinet of PM Abe)	Recognizing the turbulent security environment of the region, the panel deliberated further beyond the previous four situations. The following specific recommendations were made: 1. recognize the right to collective self-defense; 2. reconsider the present stance of absolute

TABLE 11.1 Timeline of events up to the 2015 security related legislation(*cont.*)

		non-participation in UN collective security with military operations; 3. view the issue of so-called "*ittaika* with use of force" as a matter of validity of policy; 4. permit the use of weapons during UN PKO missions, for it is not "the use of force" prohibited in UN Charter Article 2(4); and 5. Permit protection and rescue missions of nationals on foreign soil, and 6. establish a seamless response to interventions that do not constitute an armed attack
5 July 2014	Cabinet Decision on Development of Seamless Security Legislation to Ensure Japan's Survival and Protect its People	Taking consideration of the Advisory Panel Reports, the Cabinet decided to substantially reinterpret Article 9. The right of collective self-defense (although with strict limitations) was recognized
6 Mar. 2015	Common understanding between the ruling parties "The Concrete Policy of Security Legislation"	A common understanding at the congressional level between the main political parties.
7 May 2015	Cabinet Decision regarding Maritime Security Operations, etc.	Enables SDF to respond to threats swiftly by holding deliberations among the NSC and the Cabinet via telephone
8 Sept. 2015	Legislation of Peace and Security (LPS)	Composed of ten amended (pre-existing) laws (Act on Measures to Ensure the Peace and Security of Japan) and one new law (International Peace Support Act)

require the use of weapons for the purpose of executing their mission (or so-called "B-type" in Rules Of Engagement (ROEs) discussions within Japan)[33]. The report strongly suggests that the Constitution permits the SDF personnel's use of weapons "to come to the aid of a geographically distant unit or personnel participating in the same operations who are under attack (so-called "*Kaketsuke Keigo*")", as well as to protect themselves.[34]

(4) Logistics support for the operations of other countries participating in the same UN PKOs and other activities

Logistics support (such as transportation of ammunition and personnel) may be recognized as taking an integral part in the use of force (or "*ittaika*" in Japanese) by participants in the conflict. Thus, the report suggested the abandonment of this impractical concept.

Of the above, cases (1) and (2) are issues regarding the right of collective self-defense, and cases (3) and (4) are issues regarding contributions to the international community.

In his second term, PM Abe established a second panel and furthered the deliberation of other categories of events. Both reports expressed the need for the recognition of the rights of collective self-defense and recommended modifying the interpretation of Article 9. Taking this second report into consideration, the LDP and the Komei Party presented a collection of 15 cases where the LPS may prove to be effective, compared to the previous framework.[35]

4 Definition of Collective Right of Self-Defense by the Japanese Government

This section shall describe a general understanding and possible approaches to the right of self-defense as adopted by the Japanese government. A prominent

33 For example, *see* Yabe A., "Kokusai Heiwa Katsudō niokeru Buki no Ssiyō nitsuite [The use of weapons in International Peace Activities]" (Japanese) *Reference*, No. 692, 2008, http://www.ndl.go.jp/jp/diet/publication/refer/200809_692/069201.pdf (accessed Sept. 10, 2017); Kurosaki M., "'Kaketsuke Keigo' no Hoteki Wakugumi[The Legal Framework of Kaketsuke Keigo]," *Kokusai Mondai* 648 (2016) 6–15.

34 "Report of the Advisory Panel on Reconstruction of the Legal Basis for Security" (n 32) 2.

35 The material (in Japanese) can be found in the following website of an NGO group. https://clearing-house.org/?p=1004 (accessed Mar. 17, 2023).

interpretation of this right can be found in the practice of the ICJ, UN, and other international organizations. The modern concept of self-defense is defined in Article 51 of the UN Charter as an exception to the UN Collective Security system. Within this framework, all "peace-loving states" of the UN are to refrain from utilizing the threat or use of force in international disputes regarding "territorial integrity or political independence of any state, or in any other manner inconsistent with the Purposes of the United Nations."[36] Article 51 provides "the inherent right of individual or collective self-defense if an armed attack occurs against a Member of the UN, until the Security Council has taken measures necessary to maintain international peace and security." Thus, under the UN Charter, SDR (originally a customary or natural right of self-preservation) is restrictively interpreted as only in response to an armed attack. This has been the stance of the ICJ (*Nicaragua* case, *Oil Platform* case) and leading scholars like Ian Brownlie.[37]

An alternative interpretation, as displayed by scholars as Derek Bowett, asserted the possibility of SDR having a wider interpretation when the Collective Security system fails to function.[38] The main point of controversy between these two different strands of interpretation is whether a State may invoke SDR in situations other than an armed attack. Such situations may include protecting nationals overseas, or the preservation of vital economic interests. States like Israel (Entebbe, 1976), the U.K. (Suez, 1956), and the U.S.A. (Grenada, 1983 and Panama, 1989) have exercised the use of force with this wider interpretation of Article 51. Thus, the issue here would be to determine the approach of the Japanese government. Both constitutional lawyers and international lawyers agree that Japan, as a state, retains SDR and may even invoke individual SDR in certain situations.[39] However, what range of interpretations has Japan adopted? The next section shall explore two cases to clarify Japan's approach to this issue. To summarize the conclusion in advance, Japan has adopted a wider interpretation of SDR as a right under international law (under MOFA) with an extremely narrow interpretation under Constitutional theory. Also, additional comments should be added regarding its relevance to the LPS.

36 UN Charter Art. 2(4)

37 Brownlie I., *International Law and the Use of Force by the States* (Oxford Univ. Press, 1963). *See also,* Arend A. and Beck R., *International Law and the Use of Force* (Routledge, 1993).

38 Bowett, D. W., *Self-Defense in International Law* (Praeger, 1958).

39 The prior interpretation would then explain that Japan may not invoke collective SDR due to Constitutional restraints.

5 Government Response to Questions in the National Diet Concerning the Interpretation of Self-Defense Rights

Under Art. 4 of the Act for the establishment of MOFA, MOFA holds the right to authoritative interpretation regarding international treaties and other international promises.[40] In contrast, the CLB holds similar rights *de facto* in terms of domestic law[41]. These two agencies have been the main locus within the Japanese government for deliberating the nature of SDR in specific situations. In this section, two separate discussions within the national Diet regarding SDRs will be considered to sketch the Japanese approach to SDR.

In parliamentary deliberation, the Japanese government has defined collective SDR as the "right to use force when an armed attack occurs not against Japan but against a foreign country."[42] This definition, with an emphasis on "not against Japan but against a foreign country," has been repeated frequently in parliamentary debates. The following cases are records of past deliberations within the Japanese government regarding situations where SDR was considered. In addition, they are listed in the collection of cases the LDP presented to other parties in March 2015.

Both of these deliberations took place during the Gulf War in 1991. The questions were raised in the 120th Session of the House of Representatives, Special Security Committee. The questions raised and the reply by MOFA and CLB follows.

5.1 *Case One: Rescue and Evacuation Missions of Overseas Nationals*

The first case involves emergency rescue and evacuation operations of overseas nationals during times of armed conflict. In such situations, the issue of using force without the consent of the host state emerge.

---

40 International promise (or *Kokusai Yakusoku* in Japanese) is a terminology used within Japanese legal discourse and MOFA to refer to treaties.

41 This may be attributed to the Supreme Court's repressive attitudes to bypass constitutional issues like those related to Article 9. See commentaries on cases such as the *Sunagawa* case (1959) or the *Eniwa* case (1967, Sapporo District Court). Furukawa A., "Jyōyaku no Iken Shinsa: Sunagawa Jiken [Constitutional Review of Treaties: The Sunagawa Case]" (Japanese) in *Kenpō Hanrei Hyakusen II* [Commentary of Constitutional Cases], 5th ed. (Yuhikaku, 2007) 434–5; Ashibe N., "Hōritsu Kaishaku niyoru Kenpō Handan no Kaihi: Eniwa Jiken [Bypassing Constitutional Issues by Legal Interpretation: the Eniwa Case]" in *Kenpō Hanrei Hyakusen II* (Commentary of Constitutional Cases), 5th ed. (Yuhikaku, 2007) 374–5.

42 Replies to the question given by Representative Seiichi Inaba regarding "the Constitution, International Law and Collective Self-Defense Rights," (Question no. 94, House of Representatives, no. 32), May 29, 1981.

1. Question by Tetsuzo Fuyushiba (Komei Party):
"When the life, body, or property of Japanese nationals overseas, and those of Japanese Agencies (as Embassies) are threatened by an act of a foreign State, [...] may rights of self-defense be invoked for the purpose of their protection?"

2. Reply by Ichiro Komatsu (MOFA):
"[...] First, under international law, protecting foreigners within a territory is an obligation of the state of location. However, when the state of location does not have the will nor capacity to remove the infringement, and when the infringement is grave and imminent to the body or life of the foreigner, and when there is no alternative measure, strictly under international law [...] SDR may be invoked." This reply can be evaluated to take a wide interpretation of SDR (as a customary law).

3. Reply by Masasuke Omori (CLB):
"As MOFA answered your question from the perspective of International Law, we would like to answer the same matter from the perspective of Article 9 of the Constitution. [...] Under our constitution, the so-called three conditions must be met to use force. The first is the existence of imminent and unlawful infringement. The second requirement is a lack of alternative measures against this infringement. The third requirement is the use of minimum force. Thus, unless these three requirements are fulfilled, the right of self-defense may not be invoked. Thus, force cannot be used.

Turning to your question [...] when the lives, bodies, or assets of Japanese nationals or Japanese Agencies abroad are under threat, we must consider whether this situation meets the three requirements. Particularly the first requirement, the existence of an imminent and unlawful infringement toward our state must be considered. [...] In general, it seems that this case does not immediately meet the requirements. Thus, as a conclusion, unless these requirements are met, the SDF may not be deployed overseas under our Constitution."

This reply, from the Constitutional perspective, lays out a strict interpretation, much stricter than the ICJ, for the use of force. However, it should be mentioned that such a stance, taking a narrower interpretation than an international organization or legal texts, is not prohibited by international law.

In the current context of the LPS, this situation may be translated to rescue or evacuation missions by SDF in conflict zones. Such transportation operations (and use of weapons in individual self-defense) were also possible under the 1999 SDF Law former-Art.100. The amended 2015 SDF Law (Art. 84.3) recognizes the right to use weapons for the fulfillment of the rescue mission with the consent of the host State. This approach seeks to avoid international responsibility by requiring consent.

5.2 *Case Two: Attack against Japanese Vessels on the High Seas*

The second case involves foreign attacks on the high seas. The issue is the right of self-defense outside the territory of Japan.

1. Question by Tetsuzo Fuyushiba (Komei Party):
"When the life, body, or property of Japanese nationals are threatened by an act of a foreign State on the high seas, [...] may rights of self-defense be invoked?"[43]

2. Reply by Ichiro Komatsu (MOFA):
"As a matter of International Law, when a private or public vessel or aircraft has been attacked on the high seas, as a principle, a State may invoke the individual right of self-defense and remove the threat."[44]

3. Reply by Masasuke Omori (CLB):
"[...] In this case as well, the first of the three requirements must be considered. We believe the same conclusion may be drawn."

In the current context of the LPS, this situation may be translated to situations of piracy or an infringement that does not amount to an armed attack. Responding to such threats would seem to first fall under the jurisdiction of the Japanese Coast Guard as a matter of police authority instead of the SDF as a matter of security. However, if the hostile entity is better equipped in terms of force, the government may decide to conduct an anti-piracy operation or Maritime Security Operation involving the SDF.[45] Though both

---

43 120th Session of the House of Representatives, Special Committee on Security, Committee minutes, no 5, 21 (Mar. 13, 1991), http://kokkai.ndl.go.jp/SENTAKU/syugiin/120/0770/12003130770005.pdf (accessed Nov. 14, 2017).

44 *Ibid.*

45 For a general description of mandates and practices of Maritime Security Operations, *see* Ishii, Y., *Japanese Maritime Security and Law of the Sea* (Brill Nijhoff, 2022), 33–38. Ishii documents three incidents where the Japanese government engaged in Maritime Security Operations: the 2001 Noto Peninsula incident regarding two suspicious

measures could have been taken prior to the LPS, new options like Cabinet meetings via phones (or online meetings) have enabled a swift process.

In each of the above cases, a pattern arises where MOFA (from the perspective of International Law) answers the question with a wide interpretation of SDR, and CLB (from the perspective of the Constitution) answers from a strict interpretation of Art.9. Together, they set the legal framework where policy may be processed. Such an approach has been explained repeatedly by MOFA officials.[46] Thus, one of the features of the Japanese approach to the SDF is its wider interpretation of UN Charter Art. 51. This feature may also be seen as the most controversial situation presented by the government during deliberation, minesweeping activities in the Hormuz strait during a conflict.[47] Explaining minesweeping of the sea lanes as a vital national economic interest, the administration attempted to legitimize collective SDR in this case.

6 Conclusion

In both cases mentioned in the previous section, Article 9 has acted as a severe restraint on the activities of the SDF. It may seem that LPS enables the SDF to play a more flexible role by invoking collective SDRs with broader interpretations based on customary international law. This may be the essence of the concern raised by those opposing the LPS framework. Also, as mentioned in the introduction, the three new key documents published in 2022 have established a new set of policies that retract voluntary restraints, such as the defense cost one percent frame and reviewing the three principles on the transfer of defense equipment and technology.

However, the statutes present several other restraints on invoking these rights. For example, in the case of rescue and evacuation missions on foreign soil, the SDF may use weapons to ensure the mission. However, this

vessels, the 2004 incident where foreign submarines were found in Japanese territorial waters off the coast of Sakishima Islands, and the anti-piracy measures taken off the coast of Somalia.

46 Yanai S., "Nihon Gaikō niokeru Kokusaihō [International Law in Japanese Diplomacy]" (Japanese), *Kokusai Shakai no Hō to Seiji: Nihon to Kokusaihō no 100 Nen* [Law and Politics of International Society: 100 Years of Japan and International Law], vol. 1 (Sanseido, 2001), 163; Komatsu I., *Jissen Kokusaihō* [Praxis of International Law] (Japanese), 3rd ed., (Shinzansha, 2022), 8–10; Yachi S., "Jissen kara Mita Kokusaihō [International Law as Seen from the Viewpoint of a Practitioner]" (Japanese), *Rikkyo Hogaku*, 29 (1987) 162–96.

47 In the face of criticism from other parties, this case scenario was later retracted.

may be taken as a prohibited intervention under international law. Thus, Article 84(3) of the SDF Act requires the consent of the territorial State to conduct such missions in order to preclude the wrongfulness of the act (Art. 20, ILC Draft Articles on State Responsibility). In the case of attacks against Japanese vessels on the high seas, Article 82 of the SDF Law requires the authorization of the PM and Minister of Defense before initiating Maritime Security Operation. From this perspective, though, the severe restraints of Article 9 may not be as evident. Japan is still restrained within the boundaries of domestic law and the Constitution.

CHAPTER 12

Japan and International Criminal Law

Kuniko Ozaki

1 Introduction

This chapter deals with the application of the rules of international criminal law (ICL) in Japan and the specific features of the Japanese perspectives on those rules. The chapter starts with a brief description of the definition and characteristics of ICL. It then proceeds on to the two basic sets of rules of ICL, namely, criminal jurisdiction and international cooperation in criminal matters (extradition and mutual legal assistance (MLA)).

The latter half of this chapter will be devoted to specific international crimes, such as drug offences, transnational organized crime, money laundering, and terrorism, together with related Japanese legislation.

Lastly, responses to the "core crimes" will be discussed. This covers the history of international criminal tribunals, including the Tokyo Tribunal. The International Criminal Court (ICC) and crimes under its jurisdiction will be considered along with the Japanese response.

2 Concept of International Criminal Law[1]

2.1 *ICL and International Crimes*

ICL has been broadly defined as laws dealing with the punishment of individuals who have committed international crimes. There are three categories of international crimes:[2]

1 The following are some of the accessible and comprehensive textbooks on international criminal law written in English. Cryer R., Robinson D. & Vasiliev S., *An Introduction to International Criminal Law and Procedure,* 4th. ed. (Cambridge Univ. Press, 2019), Bantekas I. & Nash S., *International Criminal Law,* 3rd. ed. (Routledge-Cavendish, 2007).

2 This definition and the following categorization are often used in Japanese academic literature. *See* Yamamoto S. *Kokusaikeijihō* [International Criminal Law] (Japanese) (Sanseido, 1991), 12–13.

 | DOI:10.1163/9789004548824_013

a) *Crimes with transnational elements*
These are ordinary crimes under domestic penal codes, such as murder and theft, with certain transnational elements. For example, a murderer may flee to another State, the proceeds of theft may have been sent abroad, or an accomplice may reside in another State. Due to those elements, in order to investigate and prosecute those crimes effectively, the States have to cooperate with each other. Such cooperation can be done either bilaterally or through multilateral agreements.

b) *Transnational crimes of international concern*
These are crimes that inherently involve more than one State and harm the interests of multiple States. While those crimes are punished under domestic penal codes of the relevant States, it is to the benefit of the international community as a whole to cooperate with each other to suppress such crimes. Typical examples are drug offences, international terrorist crimes, and cybercrime. For most of these crimes, multilateral conventions have been adopted to provide legal bases for State-to-State cooperation.

c) *Crimes against the basic values of the international society*
These are "the most serious crimes of concern to the international community as a whole" as expressed in the Preamble of the Statute of the ICC (the Rome Statute)[3]. In other words, these are crimes that violate the basic values or fundamental interests of the international community. Typical examples of these crimes are genocide, crimes against humanity, war crimes, and aggression. These are often called the "core crimes" and are punishable directly under international law, whether or not the conduct constitutes a crime under domestic law, and whether or not the crimes are committed internationally.

It is important to understand the relationship between ICL and other areas of international law. For example, ICL shares common roots with international humanitarian law, the purpose of which is to protect victims of armed conflicts. Serious violations of international humanitarian law constitute war crimes. International human rights law is another area that has much in common with ICL. The criminalization of the slave trade and of human trafficking was an early example of rules of ICL. Conducts constituting genocide and crimes against humanity are tantamount to gross violations of human rights. Moreover, conventions against torture and forced

3 Rome Statute of the International Criminal Court, *adopted on* July 17, 1998, *entered into force on* July 1, 2002, 2187 UNTS 90.

disappearance are human rights conventions adopting the typical format of ICL conventions. Indeed, ICL has been widely recognized recently as an effective measure against serious violations of human rights.

Rules of ICL and State responsibility sometimes overlap with each other. While the former relates to the responsibility of an individual and the latter a State, some international crimes may be committed by individuals as agents of States. Crimes of aggression presuppose the unlawful act of a State. It is to be noted that acts constituting international crimes, especially in the third category, are often backed by States, so that the same conduct may give rise to both individual responsibility and State responsibility.

2.2 *Recent Developments of ICL*

ICL has long been regarded as an exceptional or peripherical area of international law due to the combination of international law and criminal law, which are normally viewed as most contrasting with each other. International law deals with horizontal relationships between sovereign States and its rules are firmly based on the principle of *pacta sunt servanda*. On the other hand, criminal law represents the vertical relationship between a State and an individual under its jurisdiction and presupposes an exercise of enforcement power by the former over the latter. The purpose of criminal law is the protection of the safety and value of the community rather than smooth horizontal relationships among citizens.

In traditional international law, ICL means either,

(a) a part of international law dealing with piracy and treaties on extradition/mutual legal assistance (mainly in common law countries), or
(b) a part of criminal law dealing with the scope of jurisdiction and domestic procedure on extradition and mutual legal assistance (mainly in continental law countries including Japan).

After World War II and especially since the 1960s, the rules of ICL rapidly developed both in quality and quantity.

First, globalization drastically raised the severity of the effects of international crimes. Rapid and easy transborder movement of human beings, commodities, money, and information increased the business opportunities for organized criminal groups, which exploit the potential for illegal trafficking of human beings and goods as well as money laundering. The same goes for international terrorist groups that benefit from the easy movement of terrorists and funding, as well as increased vulnerability of targets. The availability of technology further aggravates the transborder activities of those criminals by enabling them to attack their targets from a safe haven. From the perspective of law enforcement, this means that no single State can meaningfully protect its community without effective international cooperation.

Second, post-WWII international society has experienced a growing notion of common interests (values) across the world. The notions of obligations *erga omnes* and *jus cogens*, hitherto treated as strictly exceptional, have attracted new attention. This has been especially notable in the field of international humanitarian and human rights law. The importance of international cooperation in order to protect such values has been widely recognized, and ICL has been utilized as one of those protection measures. Typical examples are the adoption of the Genocide Convention[4], the four Geneva Conventions (1949 Geneva Conventions)[5] with two Additional Protocols[6], and some human rights conventions.

This tendency was further strengthened during the post-Cold War period. Armed conflicts that became frequent after 1990 were mostly internal or regional, involving non-governmental armed groups. Those conflicts were characterized by attacks on civilians, large-scale violations of human rights, and mass exoduses of refugees. International society reacted through the UN and other international organizations, regional organizations, and NGOs. The Security Council took various measures including imposing sanctions and dispatching PKOs to protect civilians. One of those measures was the establishment of international criminal tribunals to punish those who had committed core crimes during conflicts.

One side-effect of such conflicts was the emergence of so-called failed States. These are States that cannot effectively exercise their jurisdiction

---

4 Convention on the Prevention and Punishment of the Crime of Genocide, *adopted on* December 9, 1948, *entered into force on* January 12, 1951, 78 UNTS 277.

5 Geneva Convention I for the Amelioration of the Condition of the Wounded and Sick in Armed Forces in the Field, *adopted on* August 11, 1949, *entered into force on* October 21, 1950, 75 UNTS 31; Geneva Convention II for the Amelioration of the Condition of the Wounded, Sick and Shipwrecked Members of Armed Forces at Sea, *adopted on* August 11, 1949, *entered into force on* October 21, 1950, 75 UNTS 85; Geneva Convention III Relative to the Treatment of Prisoners of War, *adopted on* August 11, 1949, *entered into force on* October 21, 1950, 75 UNTS 135; Geneva Convention IV Relative to the Protection of Civilian Population in Time of War, *adopted on* August 11, 1949, *entered into force on* October 21, 1950, 75 UNTS 287.

6 Protocol I Additional to the Geneva Conventions of 12 August 1949 and Relating to the Protection of Victims in International Armed Conflict, *adopted on* June 8, 1977, *entered into force on* December 7, 1978, 1125 UNTS 3; Protocol II Additional to the Geneva Conventions of 12 August 1949 and Relating to the Protection of Victims in Non-international Armed Conflicts, *adopted on* June 8, 1977, *entered into force on* December 7, 1978, 1125 UNTS 609.

and therefore may provide criminal/terrorist organizations with safe havens. Together with the rapid development of information technology after 1990 and the increased criminal use of cyberspace, this made close international cooperation even more imperative to fight against international crimes.

The notion of common values of international society has also been reinforced during this period, partly because the end of the Cold War was perceived as a victory for democracy, protection of human rights, and economic freedom. The fight against "crimes that threaten fundamental values of international society" started to have concrete results in international criminal tribunals. International cooperation against terrorism, transnational organized crime, corruption, and cybercrime has also been strengthened through various conventions and relevant international fora.

3 Jurisdiction

3.1 *Structure and Common Features of International Criminal Law*

Sources of ICL are treaties and customary international law. While in traditional international law, bilateral treaties on extradition and mutual legal assistance were the main sources, multilateral conventions in criminal matters are now rapidly becoming predominant. In the field of international humanitarian law, rules of customary international law continue to play important roles, but they have also been replaced by multilateral conventions.

There are two types of rules: obligatory rules make the punishment of relevant crimes a duty of States, and permissive rules allow States to punish such crimes. Many multilateral conventions provide for obligatory rules, while the rules of customary international law are mainly permissive.

A typical permissive rule under customary international law concerns the punishment of piracy. Because piracy is a crime committed on the high seas, customary international law has permitted any State to capture and punish pirates. This rule was later codified in Articles 101 to 107 of the UN Convention on the Law of the Sea[7]. Under those permissive rules, States may also decide not to punish. Indeed, Japan had long taken a cautious position on such punishment. It was not until 2009, after piracy off the coast of Somalia became a serious international issue, that it enacted the Law on

7 United Nations Convention on the Law of the Sea, *adopted on* April 30, 1982, *entered into force on* November 16, 1994, 1833 UNTS 3.

Punishment of and Measures against Acts of Piracy.[8] This law criminalizes acts of piracy and enables Japan's naval vessels to protect any ship from pirates regardless of her flag.

Since most ICL rules have been codified in multilateral conventions, they serve as useful tools to identify the basic elements of ICL. A typical ICL convention contains the following elements:

(a) definition of crime (constituent elements and forms of responsibility)
(b) criminalization and sanction
(c) jurisdiction
(d) international cooperation (extradition and MLA)
(e) preventive and other administrative measures
(f) technical assistance

Of those elements, (a) and (b) are crime-specific elements and will be discussed later in this chapter. Elements (e) and (f) are not of a legal nature. On the other hand, (c) and (d) are basic common rules of ICL that are applicable across various crimes. This and the following two sections will deal with those rules, namely, the rules of criminal jurisdiction and international cooperation, considering the Japanese perspectives and practices.

3.2 *Rules of Criminal Jurisdiction*

Jurisdiction is the authority of a State to make, apply and enforce laws, or the power of a State to regulate affairs pursuant to its laws. Jurisdiction directly arises from the sovereignty of a State.

There are three forms of jurisdiction, namely criminal jurisdiction, administrative jurisdiction, and civil jurisdiction. ICL mainly relates to criminal jurisdiction, but civil jurisdiction may also be relevant, for example, in the context of the right of victims to compensation. There are three categories of criminal jurisdiction:

(a) jurisdiction to prescribe (legislative jurisdiction), which is the authority of a State to make laws applicable to persons, property, or conduct
(b) jurisdiction to adjudicate, which is the authority to apply laws to persons or property through courts and tribunals (to pass judgments on matters brought before domestic courts), and
(c) jurisdiction to enforce, which is the authority to exercise the power of the State to compel compliance with the law, typically through police action.

(a) and (c) are relevant in the context of this chapter.

---

8 Act No. 55 of 2009.

3.2.1 Principles of Legislative Jurisdiction[9]

With regard to legislative jurisdiction, the following principles are generally accepted under the current international law as bases of jurisdiction:
(a) Territoriality principle
(b) "Effects" doctrine
(c) Active personality principle
(d) Passive personality principle
(e) Protective principle
(f) Universal jurisdiction

The existence of more than one basis of legislative jurisdiction means that there are situations in which several of those principles can apply, which results in overlapping jurisdiction. Therefore, international law also provides rules to determine the priority or hierarchy among those principles.

3.2.1.1 *The Territoriality Principle*

The territoriality principle is based on territorial sovereignty. States have the right to exercise jurisdiction over all events on their territory, which includes vessels and airplanes registered in the State. This principle is the most basic and the least controversial. Article 1 of the Japanese Penal Code[10] stipulates that,
(1) This Code applies to anyone who commits a crime within the territory of Japan.
(2) The same applies to anyone who commits a crime on board a Japanese vessel or aircraft outside the territory of Japan.

3.2.1.2 *"Effects" Doctrine*

This is the principle that a State may exercise its jurisdiction over conduct occurring outside its territory that has a substantial effect within its territory. This principle may be interpreted as an extension of the territoriality principle and is now commonly applied in the sphere of economic regulation under anti-trust laws, although this has been controversial in the past.

3.2.1.3 *Active Personality Principle*

This principle is based on the sovereignty of a State over its nationals. States are entitled to legislate with respect to the conduct of their

9 Chapter 4, 2. *See also*, Sato H., Multilayered Structures of International Criminal Law, (Springer, 2021), 133–156.
10 Act No. 45 of 1907.

nationals abroad. This principle is widely accepted, except in cases where legal persons are involved. There have been controversial cases in which the activities of commercial companies established and registered in other States have been regulated by a State, based on their financial or other relationship with their partner companies in that State.

Article 3 of the Japanese Penal Code provides that "[t]his Code applies to any Japanese national who commits one of the following crimes outside the territory of Japan". Unlike Article 1, the list of crimes is limited to certain serious crimes. Article 4 of the Code also stipulates that "[t]his Code applies to any public employees of Japan who commit one of the following crimes outside the territory of Japan". Among the punishable crimes are assistance in escape by a guard, making false official documents, abuse of authority, assault and cruelty by specialized public employees, and bribery.

3.2.1.4 *Passive Personality Principle*

Under the passive personality principle, a State exercises its jurisdiction over crimes committed against its nationals while they are abroad. This principle has not been widely accepted and is regarded as problematic in traditional international law, but recently, increasing numbers of multilateral conventions prescribe this principle, especially in relation to terrorist offences.

The Japanese Penal Code in the past did not recognize this principle either. However, in 2002, a murder was committed by a national of the Philippines on a vessel called "Tajima", which was registered in Panama and operated by a Japanese shipping company. The victim was a Japanese national and the vessel at the time of the commission of the crime was on the High Seas off the coast of Taiwan. At that time, the Penal Code of the Philippines did not apply the active personality principle and the suspects were sent to Panama for investigation and prosecution. Following this case, Japan decided to amend its Criminal Code in 2003 to include the passive personality principle.

Article 3-2 of the Code says, "[t]his Code applies to any non-Japanese national who commits one of the following crimes against a Japanese national outside the territory of Japan".

The list of crimes contains rape, homicide, injury, unlawful capture/confinement, kidnapping, and robbery.

3.2.1.5 *Protective Principle*

Under this principle, a State is entitled to assert jurisdiction over extraterritorial activities by any person that threatens its security. This principle has long been accepted as an exception to territoriality and personality principles, and has been applied to such crimes as espionage, terrorism, murder of government officials, and counterfeiting of currency.

Article 2 of the Japanese Penal Code applies this principle to crimes including insurrection, instigation of foreign aggression, assistance to the enemy, and counterfeiting of currency and official documents.

3.2.1.6 *Universal Jurisdiction*

Universal jurisdiction is jurisdiction over a crime committed abroad by non-nationals. Under this principle, a State enacts a law to punish a crime even when the commission of the crime has a connection neither with its sovereignty nor with its security interests. Universal jurisdiction is the most exceptional jurisdiction and can only be exercised restrictively. A typical example is piracy, as mentioned above. It is now widely accepted that customary international law also allows the core crimes and other serious violations of human rights (such as torture and forced disappearances) to be punished under universal jurisdiction. Because the core crimes are crimes against the common interests of the international community, it follows that any State may punish those who have committed such crimes on behalf of the international community. Indeed, some States have criminal codes that punish the core crimes under universal jurisdiction. However, they often limit their application to cases where the suspects of such crimes are present in their territory or allow wide prosecutorial discretion, in order not to overburden their national criminal justice systems.

Some multilateral conventions impose *aut dedere aut judicare* (extradite or prosecute) obligations on State parties. If a suspect of a certain crime is found in its territory, the State party has a duty to extradite this suspect to the State that has jurisdiction over the crime committed, but if the suspect cannot be extradited for any reason, the host State has to establish its jurisdiction over the crime and bring the case to its authority for investigation and prosecution, even if the crime committed has neither territorial nor personal link to that State. Examples of conventions that impose such obligations include the war crime-related provisions of the 1949 Geneva Conventions, terrorism-related conventions, and some human rights related conventions such as Conventions against Torture[11]

11 Convention against Torture and Other Cruel, Inhuman or Degrading Treatment or Punishment, *adopted on* December 10, 1984, *entered into force on* June 26, 1987, 1465 UNTS, 85.

and Enforced Disappearance[12]. This type of jurisdiction is sometimes called "universal jurisdiction as treaty obligation".

It should be noted that rules on universal jurisdiction in customary international law are permissive, while those in multilateral conventions include obligatory rules. Japanese law is conservative about legislation on universal jurisdiction under customary international law, except for piracy. Its Penal Code has been amended to implement treaty obligations only. Article 4-2 of the Penal Code says that "[b]eyond what is provided in the provisions of Article 2 through the preceding Article, this Code also applies to anyone who commits those crimes outside the territory of Japan prescribed under Part II which are governed by a treaty even if committed outside the territory of Japan".

The following is a typical example of the provisions on criminal jurisdiction in multilateral conventions in Article 5 of the International Convention Against the Taking of Hostages.[13]

> 1. Each State Party shall take such measures as may be necessary to establish its jurisdiction over any of the offences set forth in article 1 which are committed:
> (a) in its territory or on board a ship or aircraft registered in that State;
> (b) by any of its nationals or, if that State considers it appropriate, by those stateless persons who have their habitual residence in its territory;
> (c) in order to compel that State to do or abstain from doing any act; or
> (d) with respect to a hostage who is a national of that State, if that State considers it appropriate.
> 2. Each State Party shall likewise take such measures as may be necessary to establish its jurisdiction over the offences set forth in article 1 in cases where the alleged offender is present in its territory, and it does not extradite him to any of the States mentioned in paragraph 1 of this article.

---

12 International Convention for the Protection of All Persons from Enforced Disappearance, *adopted on* December 20, 2006, *entered into force on* December 23, 2010, 2716 UNTS 3.

13 International Convention against the Taking of Hostages, *adopted on* December 17, 1979, *entered into force on* June 3, 1983, 1316 UNTS 205. *See also*, Ando T., *Kokusai terorizumu nitaisuru houtekikisei no kouzou* [The Structure of Legal Control of International Terrorism] (Japanese) (Kokusaisyoin, 2020).

3. This Convention does not exclude any criminal jurisdiction exercised in accordance with internal law.

3.2.2 Enforcement Jurisdiction

Rules of international law on enforcement jurisdiction are simple. A State cannot exercise enforcement jurisdiction in the territory of another State. Therefore, even if a State exercises legislative jurisdiction by enacting domestic laws that criminalize offences committed outside its territory, it cannot enforce them outside its territory. For example, a State cannot send its police force to the territories of other States to execute an arrest warrant, carry out a search, or seize property, without the consent of the territorial State. In the 1962 *Eichmann* case,[14] Israeli authorities abducted a suspect accused of genocide from the territory of Argentina. The Argentinian government protested against the abduction, but not against the Israeli law that punishes the crime concerned based on universal jurisdiction. Likewise, the Israeli government expressed regret about the abduction but proceeded with the trial of the suspect in Israel.

4 Extradition

4.1 *International Cooperation in Criminal Matters*

Since a State cannot exercise enforcement jurisdiction in the territories of other States without their consent, States must cooperate with each other in order to investigate and prosecute international crimes effectively. The idea behind such cooperation is that criminals should be prosecuted and punished in the most appropriate and effective jurisdiction, and that there should be no "safe haven" for criminals.

The most important forms of such international cooperation are extradition and MLA. Extradition is the surrender, upon request, of a person by one State to another, the person being either accused of a crime in the requesting State or unlawfully at large after conviction. MLA is assistance, upon request, to provide a foreign State with evidence in order for that State to investigate a criminal case. Both extradition and MLA have a long history in traditional international law.

In this section, the rules of extradition will be discussed using Japanese examples.

---

14 *Attorney-General of Israel v. Eichmann* case, Judgment of December 11, 1961, Supreme Court of Israel, 36 ILR 5.

4.2 *Basic Principles of Extradition*

Traditionally, there have been two approaches to extradition. One approach is the continental law approach that regards extradition as an act of comity to the requesting States. In this approach, extradition is executed based on the domestic law of the requested State, and upon request, the requested State extradites on a case-by-case basis. This gives the requested State the utmost flexibility, although it is usually prohibited by domestic law from extraditing its nationals. Another approach is the common law approach to extradite based on extradition treaties. States conclude bilateral extradition treaties with multiple countries and extradite, if requested by the other party to the treaty, as a treaty obligation. The US is an example of States that take this approach. Japan adopts the former approach and its main law on extradition is the 1953 Act of Extradition.[15] Exceptionally, Japan has concluded two bilateral extradition treaties with States, which it has been in close cooperative relationship on crime-related matters, one with the United States in 1980 and another with the Republic of Korea in 2002.

Both approaches share some common principles. First, not all offences are subject to extradition. Extradition requires considerable human and financial resources for both the requesting and requested States. Usually, only serious offences are extraditable offences. Article 2 of the Japanese Act of Extradition provides that "[a] fugitive must not be extradited […] when the requested offence is not punishable by death, life imprisonment with or without work for life or for a long term of three years or more according to the laws and regulations of the requesting country" nor "when the act constituting the requested offence is deemed to have been committed in Japan and would not be punishable under the laws and regulations of Japan by death or imprisonment with or without work for life or for a long term of three years or more". The second principle is called the "dual criminality principle". This principle requires that the underlying act is criminal in both the requesting and the requested States. The Japanese Act of Extradition, in addition to the above-mentioned provision, prohibits extradition in Article 2 "when it is deemed that the act that constitutes the requested offence was committed in Japan or the trial for the offence was held in a Japanese court, but the imposition or the execution of punishment on the fugitive for the requested offence would be barred under the laws and regulations of Japan".

Another principle is the principle of specificity, under which the requesting State can bring proceedings only with respect to crimes for which the

15 Act No. 68 of 1953.

suspect was extradited. The purpose of this principle is to prevent the requesting State from intentionally evading the principles of dual criminality and non-extradition of political offenders (mentioned below).

The principle of reciprocity requires assurances of mutual cooperation. Article 3 of the Act of Extradition provides that the Minister of Foreign Affairs, upon receiving the request, must get a guarantee from the requesting country that it would honor a request of the same kind made by Japan.

4.3 *Restrictions on Extradition*

Since extradition is a strong law enforcement measure directly affecting the basic rights of fugitives, there are several principles that bar extradition, in addition to the normal procedural guarantees during arrest and transfer.

4.3.1 Non-extradition of Nationals

Many civil law jurisdictions prohibit the extradition of nationals. The Japanese Act of extradition in Article 2 prohibits extradition "when the fugitive is a Japanese national", except where bilateral treaties apply. These States have traditionally applied personal jurisdiction extensively and punished their nationals who have committed crimes abroad domestically. By contrast, many common law States are reluctant to apply personal jurisdiction and instead extradite their nationals based on extradition treaties.

4.3.2 Non-extradition of Political Offenders

The principle of non-extradition of political offenders can be traced back to nineteenth-century Europe, based on sympathy for the democratic movements as well as on the practical consideration of not wishing to be involved in the political affairs of other States. This principle has been widely accepted. In the Japanese Act of Extradition, Article 2 prohibits extradition "when the requested offence is a political offence" or "when the extradition request is deemed to have been made with a view to trying or punishing the fugitive for a political offence which the fugitive has committed".

Political offences are divided into absolute political offences and relative political offences. The latter is an ordinary offence with a political purpose and has often been excluded from the non-extradition principle. In the *Zhang Zhenhai* case, the Tokyo High Court acknowledged that while non-extradition is an established international practice for absolute political offences, the application of the principle to relative political offences should be considered on a case-by-case basis. In this case, Zhang hijacked an aircraft that later landed at a Japanese airport. The Chinese

Government requested his extradition, but Zhang claimed that he had committed the hijacking to avoid political punishment by the Chinese Government for being involved in the Tiananmen Incident. The Tokyo High Court concluded that the political nature of the offence did not overwhelm the nature of the crime as an ordinary crime to the extent that the conduct should be regarded as a political offence under the Act on Extradition.[16]

Recently, it has become the practice to deny the application of this principle to terrorist offences. For example, Article 11 of the Terrorist Bombings Convention[17] provides,

> None of the offences set forth in article 2 shall be regarded for the purposes of extradition or mutual legal assistance, as a political offence or as an offence connected with a political offence or as an offence inspired by political motives. Accordingly, a request for extradition or for mutual legal assistance based on such an offence may not be refused on the sole ground that it concerns a political offence or an offence connected with a political offence or an offence inspired by political motives.

4.3.3 Non-extradition and the Protection of Human Rights

There are also rules in international human rights law that prohibit extradition in order to protect the fundamental rights of fugitives.

The classic example is the principle of *non-refoulement* enshrined in Article 33 of the 1951 Refugee Convention,[18] which prohibits any form of return ("refouler") of a refugee to the frontiers of territories where his or her life or freedom would be threatened on account of his or her race, religion, nationality, membership of a particular social group, or political opinion.

Similarly, Article 3 of the Convention against Torture prohibits State parties from extraditing a person to another State where there are substantial grounds for believing that he would be in danger of being subjected to torture. Article 16 of the Convention against Enforced Disappearance has a similar provision. Some terrorism conventions, while denying the application of non-extradition of political offenders, have provisions to protect the rights

---

16 *Zhang Zhenhai* case, Decision of April 20, 1990, Tokyo High Court, *Kotou Saibansho Keiji Hanreishu* [High Courts Reports (Criminal Cases)] 43(1), 27.

17 International Convention for the Suppression of Terrorist Bombings, *adopted on* December 15, 1997, *entered into force on* May 23, 2001, 2149 UNTS 256.

18 Convention relating to the Status of Refugee, *adopted on* July 28, 1951, *entered into force on* April 22, 1954, 189 UNTS 137.

of the offender in extradition. Article 9-1 of the International Convention against the Taking of Hostages provides,

> A request for the extradition of an alleged offender, pursuant to this Convention, shall not be granted if the requested State Party has substantial grounds for believing:
> a. that the request for extradition for an offence set forth in article 1 has been made for the purpose of prosecuting or punishing a person on account of his race, religion, nationality, ethnic origin or political opinion; or
> b. that the person's position may be prejudiced:
>   i. for any of the reasons mentioned in subparagraph (a) of this paragraph, or
>   ii. for the reason that communication with him by the appropriate authorities of the State entitled to exercise rights of protection cannot be effected.

With regard to death penalty, the European Convention on Extradition lists the existence of death penalty in the requesting States as an optional ground for refusal of extradition and depending on the execution method and conditions of detention, extradition may become illegal.[19]

4.4 *Extradition in Multilateral Conventions*

Since the rules of international law on extradition had long been established through bilateral treaties and practices, multilateral conventions dealing with international crimes took advantage of those rules rather than creating new rules. Those provisions, in combination with the provisions on jurisdiction, are intended to deny any safe haven for offenders of international crimes. The following is an example of such a provision in Article 10 of the International Convention against the Taking of Hostages.

> 1. The offences set forth in article 1 shall be deemed to be included as extraditable offences in any extradition treaty existing between States Parties. States Parties undertake to include such offences as extraditable offences in every extradition treaty to be concluded between them.
> 2. If a State Party which makes extradition conditional on the existence of a treaty receives a request for extradition from another State

19 Sato (n 9), 168–169.

> Party with which it has no extradition treaty, the requested State may at its option consider this Convention as the legal basis for extradition in respect of the offences set forth in article 1. Extradition shall be subject to the other conditions provided by the law of the requested State.
> 3. States Parties which do not make extradition conditional on the existence of a treaty shall recognize the offences set forth in article 1 as extraditable offences between themselves subject to the conditions provided by the law of the requested State.
> 4. The offences set forth in article I shall be treated, for the purpose of extradition between States Parties, as if they had been committed not only in the place in which they occurred but also in the territories of the States required to establish their jurisdiction in accordance with paragraph 1 of article 5.

5 Mutual Legal Assistance (MLA)

MLA refers to providing, upon request, another State with evidence in order for that State to investigate a criminal case. Such assistance includes the identification and whereabouts of persons or the location of items, taking testimony under oath, service of documents, execution of search and seizures, and examination of places or sites.

MLA also has a long bilateral tradition, either based on national law or on bilateral treaties. There are some principles and restrictions common to both extradition and MLA, such as requirements of dual criminality, specificity, and reciprocity, as well as political offence exceptions. Those principles and restrictions, however, are applied less strictly in relation to MLA than extradition, because MLA does not involve direct infringement of the physical freedom of individuals.

Japan, in principle, provides legal assistance through domestic legislation. The most important law in this regard is the Act on International Assistance in Investigation and Other Related Matters.[20] Japan has also concluded bilateral MLA treaties with the US, Republic of Korea, China, Hong Kong,[21] the EU, and Russia.

Unlike extradition, provisions on MLA in multilateral conventions vary; some provide for a general duty to cooperate only and others stipulate more

20 Act No. 69 of 1980.

21 Under China's "One Country, Two Systems," Hong Kong is granted the right to conclude criminal mutual assistance agreements by the Chinese government under the Basic Law of the Hong Kong Special Administrative Region.

detailed assistance obligations. Article 18 of the UN Organized Crime Convention[22] provides as follows:

> 1. States Parties shall afford one another the widest measure of mutual legal assistance in investigations, prosecutions and judicial proceedings in relation to the offences covered by this Convention as provided for in article 3 and shall reciprocally extend to one another similar assistance where the requesting State Party has reasonable grounds to suspect that the offence referred to in article 3, paragraph 1 (a) or (b), is transnational in nature, including that victims, witnesses, proceeds, instrumentalities or evidence of such offences are located in the requested State Party and that the offence involves an organized criminal group.
>
> [...]
>
> 3. Mutual legal assistance to be afforded in accordance with this article may be requested for any of the following purposes:
>   (a) Taking evidence or statements from persons;
>   (b) Effecting service of judicial documents;
>   (c) Executing searches and seizures, and freezing;
>   (d) Examining objects and sites;
>   (e) Providing information, evidentiary items and expert evaluations;
>   (f) Providing originals or certified copies of relevant documents and records, including government, bank, financial, corporate or business records;
>   (g) Identifying or tracing proceeds of crime, property, instrumentalities or other things for evidentiary purposes;
>   (h) Facilitating the voluntary appearance of persons in the requesting State Party;
>   (i) Any other type of assistance that is not contrary to the domestic law of the requested State Party.

6 Responses to Transnational Crimes of International Concern

States have been and still are responding to ordinary crimes with transnational elements using traditional measures based on (a) the establishment

---

22 United Nations Convention against Transnational Organized Crime, *adopted on* November 15, 2000, *entered into force on* September 29, 2003, 2225 UNTS 209.

of jurisdiction in accordance with internationally recognized principles, and (b) extradition and MLA based on domestic law, bilateral treaties or both.

6.1 *Drug Crimes, Organized Crime, Corruption*

A number of multilateral conventions have been adopted relating to transnational crimes of international concern. Those conventions are often backed by international organizations that offer fora not only for negotiating and adopting the conventions but for monitoring and assisting the implementation of the conventions by Member States. Within the UN, the United Nations Office on Drugs and Crime (UNODC) serves as secretariat to the Commission on Crime Prevention and Criminal Justice (CCPCJ) and Assemblies of State Parties to several crime-related conventions.

An early significant example of these conventions is the 1988 UN Drug Convention.[23] This Convention consolidates the definition of various drug-related offences, provides rules of jurisdiction, and establishes frameworks for extradition, MLA, and other international cooperation. The Convention also criminalizes money laundering of the proceeds of drug offences. This Convention became a model for the UN Organized Crime Convention.

The Organized Crime Convention applies to serious offences (conduct constituting an offence punishable by a maximum deprivation of liberty of at least four years or a more serious penalty) involving an organized criminal group and of a transnational nature. The Convention also applies to four specific offences (participation in an organized criminal group, money laundering, corruption, and obstruction of justice) that the Convention obligates the member States to criminalize. The Convention then establishes extensive frameworks for jurisdiction, extradition, MLA, and law enforcement cooperation. It also promotes training and technical assistance for building or upgrading the necessary capacity of national authorities. Attached to this Convention are three Protocols, which cover three categories of serious crimes, namely, the Human Trafficking Protocol,[24] the Smuggling of Migrants Protocol,[25] and the Firearms Protocol.[26]

---

23 United Nations Convention against Illicit Traffic in Narcotic Drugs and Psychotropic Substances, *adopted on* December 20, 1988, *entered into force on* November 11, 1990, 1582 UNTS 95.

24 Protocol to Prevent, Suppress and Punish Trafficking in Persons, Especially Women and Children, *adopted on* November 15, 2000, *entered into force on* December 25, 2003, 2237 UNTS 319.

25 Protocol against the Smuggling of Migrants by Land, Sea and Air, *adopted on* November 15, 2000, *entered into force on* January 28, 2004, 2241 UNTS 507.

26 Protocol against the Illicit Manufacturing of and Trafficking in Firearms, Their Parts and Components and Ammunition, *signed on* July 11, 2001, *entered into force on* July 3, 2005, 2326 UNTS 208.

In 2003, the UN Corruption Convention[27] was adopted. This Convention covers various forms of corruption, such as bribery, trading in influence, abuse of functions, and various acts of corruption in the private sector. It follows the examples of the preceding conventions on jurisdiction, extradition, MLA, and other types of international cooperation.

The common characteristics of those UN-sponsored crime conventions are:

(a) criminalization of the target offences by national legislation, and the prosecution and adjudication before national courts,
(b) legislative jurisdiction based on the territoriality principle (active personality and other principles are optional),
(c) *aut dedere aut judicare* obligation when the offender is not extradited on the ground that he or she is a national of that State.

6.2 *Terrorism*

6.2.1 Terrorism Conventions

There is no general convention against terrorist offences, but many conventions have been adopted dealing with criminal conduct typical of terrorism offences. For example, the Convention for the Suppression of Unlawful Seizure of Aircraft,[28] one of the early conventions dealing with hijacking, criminalizes acting "unlawfully, by force or threat thereof, or any other form of intimidation, [to] seize or exercise control of that aircraft" or attempting to do so. There are several other conventions that cover various acts of terrorism in the area of civil aviation. Other areas where terrorism conventions have been adopted are maritime navigation, protection of heads of State and other governmental officials, taking of hostages, use of nuclear or explosive materials, and terrorist bombings.

A slightly different type of convention is the International Convention for the Suppression of the Financing of Terrorism.[29] This Convention requires State Parties to prevent and counteract the direct or indirect financing of terrorists through groups claiming to have charitable, social, or cultural goals or that also engage in illicit activities such as drug trafficking or gun running, and to hold those who finance terrorism criminally, civilly, or administratively liable for such acts. The Convention also provides for the identification, freezing and seizure of funds allocated for terrorist activities.

---

27 United Nations Convention against Corruption, *adopted on* October 31, 2003, *entered into force on* December 14, 2005, 2349 UNTS 41.

28 *Signed on* December 16, 1970, *entered into force on* October 14, 1971, 860 UNTS 105.

29 *Adopted on* December 9, 1999, *entered into force* on April 10, 2002, 2178 UNTS 197.

There are some common characteristics of those terrorism conventions, namely that

(a) they presuppose criminalization by national legislation, and prosecution and adjudication before national courts,
(b) State Parties are required to exercise wider legislative jurisdiction, based on the territoriality and active personality principles, as well as (depending on the nature of the criminal conduct) protective and other principles, and
(c) an *aut dedere aut judicare* obligation applies when the offender is not extradited on any ground.

6.2.2 Terrorism and the UN Security Council

The UN Security Council has played an important role in combating transnational terrorist activities. This is mainly due to the increased transborder attacks by large-scale terrorist organizations, as well as the growing threat of State-sponsored terrorism. Typical examples are the activities of Al-Qaeda and/or Islamic State. In response to those threats, the UN Security Council took various legally binding sanction measures under Article 41 of the UN Charter. These sanctions included criminal law measures such as criminalization of the provision or collection of funds to be used for terrorist acts (Resolution 1373(2001)).

6.3 *Japanese Responses*

Japan has concluded most of the above-mentioned conventions and enacted domestic laws to implement them. In 1991, Japan enacted the Act Concerning Special Provisions for the Narcotics and Psychotropics Control Act, etc. and Other Matters for the Prevention of Activities Encouraging Illicit Conducts and Other Activities Involving Controlled Substances through International Cooperation,[30] by which Japan, for the first time, criminalized money laundering and established a framework for international cooperation that specialized in money laundering. This act not only responds to the 1988 UN Convention, but also to the recommendations adopted by the Financial Action Task Force. The 1999 Act on Punishment of Organized Crimes and Control of Proceeds of Crime[31] further widened the scope of the crime of money laundering.

It took years, however, for Japan to conclude the Organized Crime Convention, mainly because of domestic resistance against the criminalization

30 Act No. 94 of 1991.

31 Act No. 136 of 1999.

of participation in an organized criminal group in Article 5. It was not until 2017 that Japan made the necessary amendments to the 1999 Act and became a party to the Convention.

Japan has enacted several laws to implement the terrorism Conventions and relevant UN Security Council resolutions, including the amendment of the Penal Code mentioned above, and to meet the *aut dedere aut judicare* requirements of those conventions. Among those acts is the Act on Punishment of Financing to Offences of Public Intimidation,[32] which implements the 2002 Financing of Terrorism Convention.

7 Response to the Core Crimes

7.1 *International Criminal Tribunals and Core Crimes*

Rules of international law with regard to the first and second categories of international crimes presuppose national prosecution and adjudication of the crimes. The third category of crimes, the core crimes, has also been prosecuted and adjudicated before national courts in accordance with domestic law. However, the development of the rules on the core crimes is intrinsically linked to the history of international criminal tribunals.

7.1.1 The Nuremberg Military Tribunal[33]

There is an early example of proposal for international criminal tribunals in Article 227 of the Treaty of Versailles,[34] by which the Kaiser was to be arraigned for a supreme offence against international morality and the sanctity of treaties before an international tribunal. However, the first international criminal tribunal that had a decisive impact on the development of the rules on the core crimes was the Nuremberg International Military Tribunal, established by the 1945 London Agreement.[35]

The purpose of the Tribunal was the trial and punishment of major war criminals from the European Axis countries. Those criminals were "[l]eaders, organisers, instigators and accomplices participating in the formulation or execution of a common plan or conspiracy to commit" crimes

32 Act No. 67 of 2002.

33 *See*, for example, Cryer R., et al. (n 1), 115–120.

34 112 BFSP 1 (1919).

35 Agreement for the Prosecution and Punishment of the Major War Criminals of the European Axis Powers and Charter of the International Military Tribunal, *agreed on* August 8, 1945, 82 UNTS 279.

against peace, war crimes and crimes against humanity. The definitions of the crimes are as follows:

> (a) Crimes against peace: namely, planning, preparation, initiation or waging of a war of aggression, or a war in violation of international treaties, agreements or assurances, or participation in a common plan or conspiracy for the accomplishment of any of the foregoing;
> (b) War crimes: namely, violations of the laws or customs of war. Such violations shall include, but not be limited to, murder, ill-treatment or deportation to slave labour or for any other purpose of civilian population of or in occupied territory, murder or ill-treatment of prisoners of war or persons on the seas, killing of hostages, plunder of public or private property, wanton destruction of cities, towns, or villages, or devastation not justified by military necessity;
> (c) Crimes against humanity: namely, murder, extermination, enslavement, deportation, and other inhumane acts committed against any civilian population, before or during the war, or persecution on political, racial or religious grounds in execution of or in connection with any crime within the jurisdiction of the Tribunal, whether or not in violation of the domestic law of the country where perpetrated.

There were twenty-four defendants on four main charges, namely overall conspiracy, crimes against peace, war crimes, and crimes against humanity. Three were acquitted, twelve were sentenced to death, and seven to periods of imprisonment from ten years to life.

With regards to the lower-rank criminals, the allied powers respectively set up separate tribunals in the occupied territory of Germany and prosecuted crimes under the Control Council Law No.10. These trials basically followed the examples of the Nuremberg Tribunal in applicable laws and procedures.

7.1.2 The Tokyo Military Tribunal

On the Pacific front, the International Military Tribunal for the Far East was established in 1946 by a proclamation of the Supreme Commander, for the trial and punishment of major war criminals in the Far East. The establishment of the Tribunal was based on principle 10 of the Potsdam Declaration promising justice for war criminals. The jurisdiction of the Tribunal followed the example of the Nuremberg Tribunal, including definitions of the crimes.

There were 28 defendants, mostly civilian and military leaders of the Japanese government, charged with crimes against peace, war crimes, and murders. Seven defendants were sentenced to death, sixteen received life sentences, one to twenty years' imprisonment, and one to seven years' imprisonment.[36]

Trials of war criminals were also held in various areas of the Pacific by the UK, the US, Australia, China, and the Philippines in accordance with their domestic laws, the most famous of which was the *Yamashita* case. General Yamashita was the commander of the Japanese forces in the Philippines. He was charged with the war crimes committed by the members of the Japanese Army under his command. At the time of the commission of the crimes, Yamashita was in the headquarters far away from the crime scene and communication between him and his forces was not good, but the US Military Commission held him criminally responsible because he failed to control his army. Yamashita petitioned for *habeas corpus*, which was denied by the US Supreme Court.[37] This case is regarded as one of the origins of the doctrine of command responsibility, which is now one of the major grounds of criminal responsibility for the core crimes.

In Article 11 of the San Francisco Peace Treaty,[38] Japan accepted the judgments of the International Military Tribunal for the Far East and of other Allied War Crimes Courts both within and outside Japan and promised to carry out the sentences imposed thereby upon Japanese nationals imprisoned in Japan.

7.1.3 Assessment of the Post-WWII Tribunals

There are positive and negative assessments of those early tribunals.

The tribunals, for the first time in history, established crimes against humanity and crimes against peace as crimes under international law, irrespective of the provisions of domestic law of the States concerned. They also established individual criminal responsibility for those crimes, separately from the responsibility of the States concerned. It was also established that the official position of a person does not relieve him from responsibility under international law, nor does the fact that a person acted pursuant to

---

36 Pritchard R. J., "The International Military Tribunal for the Far East and Its Contemporary Resonance," *Military Law Review* 149 (1995) 25; Boister N. & Cryer R., *The Tokyo International Military Tribunal: A Reappraisal* (Oxford University Press, 2008).

37 In *re* Yamashita case, Decision of February 4, 1946, U.S. Supreme Court, 327 US 1.

38 Treaty of Peace with Japan, *signed on* September 8, 1951, *entered into force on* April 28, 1952.

an order by his government or a superior relieve him from responsibility, provided a moral choice was possible to him. Added to this is the doctrine of command responsibility as mentioned above.

On the other hand, the tribunals have been criticized as being "victor's justice" since all the judges were from victor States and there was no prosecution of victor States' acts. The establishment of crimes against humanity, crimes against peace, and individual responsibility for the acts of the State are also criticized as being an application of *ex post facto* law, and against the principles of *nullum crimen sine lege* and of legality.

It has also been pointed out that the procedure of the tribunals did not satisfy the requirements of due process, especially because of an over-reliance on affidavit evidence and unsworn Statements denying the right to cross-examination, and a disparity of resources between the prosecution and defense, which contravened the "equality of arms" requirement.

7.1.4 Post-Nuremberg Development of the International Law on the Core Crimes

The newly established United Nations played a critical role in confirming those developments in ICL. In 1946, General Assembly Resolution 95 endorsed the Nuremberg principles. In 1948, the Genocide Convention, which criminalizes the most serious forms of crimes against humanity, was adopted. It was followed by the adoption of four Geneva Conventions under the auspices of the Red Cross. Those conventions provide for the duty of the States to punish war crimes and also impose the *aut dedere aut judicare* principle for those crimes. The scope of war crimes was widened under the 1977 First Additional Protocol to the Geneva Conventions. In 1954, the first ILC draft of a "Code of Crimes against the Peace and Security of Mankind" was submitted to the General Assembly.

As mentioned above, the post-Cold War period has experienced intensified internal and regional conflicts, which were accompanied by large-scale violations of human rights and humanitarian law against civilians including ethnic cleansing and genocide. At the same time, this period is characterized by increasing awareness of international protection of human rights and concerted action at the UN Security Council. It was against this background that the International Criminal Tribunal for the former Yugoslavia (ICTY) and the International Criminal Tribunal for Rwanda (ICTR) were established, as the first international criminal tribunals after the Nuremberg and Tokyo Tribunals.

The ICTY was established in 1993 by Security Council Resolution 827 in order to prosecute persons responsible for serious violations of international humanitarian law, namely, genocide, crimes against humanity and war crimes, committed in the territory of the former Yugoslavia after 1 January 1991. The ICTR was established in 1995 by Security Council Resolution 955 in order to prosecute persons responsible for genocide and other serious violations of international humanitarian law committed in the territory of Rwanda and neighboring States, between 1 January 1994 and 31 December 1994. Both Tribunals were established under the Chapter 7 power of the Security Council and have supremacy over the national courts. They were *ex post facto* tribunals and applied customary international law. Their procedural law was in accordance with universally recognized human rights standards, reflecting the lessons learned from Nuremberg and Tokyo Tribunals.

During this period, special national tribunals with international elements were also established in post-conflict situations. For example, a Special Court for Sierra Leone was established based on the 2002 agreement between Sierra Leone and the UN, and the Serious Crimes Panels of the District Court in Dili were created by the United Nations Transitional Administration in East Timor in 2000.

7.1.5 Establishment of the ICC[39]

In the meantime, the creation of a permanent, universal, and multilateral-treaty-based international criminal tribunal was discussed, and in 1998 the Rome Statute was adopted in a diplomatic conference of 160 States. The Statute entered into force in 2002 and the ICC became operational in 2003. The crimes that fall under the jurisdiction of the ICC are (a) genocide, crimes against humanity, and war crimes, when committed after 1 July 2002, (b) offences against the administration of justice, and (c) the crime of aggression, as of 17 July 2018. Each of these crimes is defined in detail in the Rome Statute and other relevant texts. There are also provisions on general principles of criminal law including various modes of criminal responsibility.

In principle, the ICC exercises its jurisdiction over crimes committed in the territories of the State Parties or committed by their nationals. With regard to the crime of aggression, however, the ICC has no jurisdiction when

---

39 There are numerous textbooks and commentaries on ICC. *See*, for example, Schabas W. A., *An Introduction to the International Criminal Court*, 3rd. ed. (Cambridge Univ. Press, 2007), Ambos K. (ed.) *Rome Statute of the International Criminal Court*, 4th.ed. (Beck/Hart/Nomos, 2022). In Japanese, Ozaki K. & Ko K. (eds.) *Kokusai-Keiji-Saibannsho* [International Criminal Court], 3rd. ed. (Toshindo, 2024)

it is committed by a national or in the territory of a State Party that has not ratified or accepted the amendments on the crime of aggression. Investigation starts either when a State Party refers to the Prosecutor a situation in which crimes appear to have been committed, or when the Prosecutor initiates a *proprio motu* investigation subject to authorization by the Pre-trial chamber. Exceptionally, the UN Security Council, acting under Chapter 7 of the UN Charter, may refer any situation including in non-State-Parties to the Court.

The ICC adopts the principle of complementarity, by which the ICC can prosecute and try individuals only if the State concerned does not, cannot, or is unwilling to do so genuinely. This means that a State has primary responsibility for trying the perpetrators of the most serious crimes.

The Rome Statute ensures due process and protects the rights of suspects/accused in accordance with the relevant international human rights standards. The Rome Statue also provides for participation by the victims in criminal proceedings and reparation to the victims.

The ICC does not have its own enforcement power and relies on cooperation by the Member States in this regard. The Rome Statute therefore provides for an obligation of the States Parties to cooperate fully with the ICC with regard to such measures as arrest and surrender, the identification and location of persons or the location of items, the gathering of evidence, including testimony under oath, and the production of evidence, the service of documents, including judicial documents, the execution of searches and seizures, the provision of records and documents, and the protection of victims and witnesses and the preservation of evidence.

7.2 *Rome Statute and the Core Crimes*

While those *ex post facto* tribunals such as Nuremberg/Tokyo tribunals, ICTY and ICTR applied rules of customary international law and occasionally ambiguous statutory definitions of crimes, the Rome Statute clarifies the applicable law in accordance with the principle of *nullum crimen sine lege*, stipulating more detailed definitions of crimes and of general principles of criminal law. Since its adoption, the definition of the core crimes under the Rome Statute has been extensively used in national legislation.

7.2.1 Genocide

Article 6 of the Rome Statute, like the ICTY and ICTR statutes, replicates the definition of genocide under the 1948 Genocide Convention as follows:

> For the purpose of this Statute, "genocide" means any of the following acts committed with intent to destroy, in whole or in part, a national, ethnical, racial or religious group, as such:
> (a) Killing members of the group;
> (b) Causing serious bodily or mental harm to members of the group;
> (c) Deliberately inflicting on the group conditions of life calculated to bring about its physical destruction in whole or in part;
> (d) Imposing measures intended to prevent births within the group;
> (e) Forcibly transferring children of the group to another group.

In addition, the "Elements of Crimes" that were adopted by the Conference of the State Parties to supplement the Rome Statute further clarify the meaning of the elements of genocide. Genocide requires a special intent to destroy a group of a specific nature. The prohibited acts are also specified in the definition. Genocide is therefore regarded as the core of the crimes against humanity under the jurisdiction of Nuremberg/Tokyo tribunals and the most serious of the core crimes.

7.2.2 Crimes against Humanity

Unlike genocide and war crimes, there is no existing authoritative multilateral convention on the crimes against humanity, and definitions have varied in various international tribunals. Article 7 of the Rome Statue is now regarded as a standard definition of the crimes, and the ILC draft on crimes against humanity now before the UN General Assembly follows this definition. Article 7 stipulates that:

> 1. For the purpose of this Statute, "crime against humanity" means any of the following acts when committed as part of a widespread or systematic attack directed against any civilian population, with knowledge of the attack:
> (a) Murder;
> (b) Extermination;
> (c) Enslavement;
> [...]
> (f) Torture;
> (g) Rape, sexual slavery, enforced prostitution, forced pregnancy, enforced sterilization, or any other form of sexual violence of comparable gravity;

(h) Persecution against any identifiable group or collectivity on political, racial, national, ethnic, cultural, religious, gender as defined in paragraph 3, or other grounds that are universally recognized as impermissible under international law, in connection with any act referred to in this paragraph or any crime within the jurisdiction of the Court;
[...]

This definition covers a wide range of large-scale violations of human rights. There is no requirement of nexus to armed conflict nor requirement for discriminatory intention.

7.2.3 War Crimes

Laws and customs regulating warfare can be traced back to ancient times, but the 1949 Geneva Conventions and 1979 Additional Protocols played a crucial role in the development of the rules on war crimes. The concept of war crimes is based on the basic principles of international humanitarian law, namely:

(a) Non-combatants (sick and wounded, prisoners of war and civilians) should be protected
(b) Military objectives and civilian populations should be distinguished (only the former may be attacked)
(c) Collateral civilian damages should be avoided or minimized
(d) Means and methods of war are restricted to reduce unnecessary suffering and to maintain respect for humanitarian principles.

Traditionally, war crimes have been grave breaches of international humanitarian laws on international armed conflict, but the ICTR Statute widened the scope of war crimes to include serious violations of Article 3 of the Geneva Conventions and of the Second Additional Protocol, which are applicable to internal armed conflict. Article 8 of the ICC Statute inherited this concept of war crimes as follows:

> 2. For the purpose of this Statute, "war crimes" means:
> (a) Grave breaches of the Geneva Conventions of 12 August 1949, namely, any of the following acts against persons or property protected under the provisions of the relevant Geneva Convention:
> (i) Wilful killing;
> (ii) Torture or inhuman treatment, including biological experiments;
> [...]

(b) Other serious violations of the laws and customs applicable in international armed conflict, within the established framework of international law, namely, any of the following acts:(i) Intentionally directing attacks against the civilian population as such or against individual civilians not taking direct part in hostilities;(ii) Intentionally directing attacks against civilian objects, that is, objects which are not military objectives;
[...]
(c) In the case of an armed conflict not of an international character, serious violations of article 3 common to the four Geneva Conventions of 12 August 1949, namely, any of the following acts committed against persons taking no active part in the hostilities, including members of armed forces who have laid down their arms and those placed hors de combat by sickness, wounds, detention or any other cause:(i) Violence to life and person, in particular murder of all kinds, mutilation, cruel treatment and torture;(ii) Committing outrages upon personal dignity, in particular humiliating and degrading treatment;
[...]
(e) Other serious violations of the laws and customs applicable in armed conflicts not of an international character, within the established framework of international law, namely, any of the following acts:
(i) Intentionally directing attacks against the civilian population as such or against individual civilians not taking direct part in hostilities;
(ii) Intentionally directing attacks against buildings, material, medical units and transport, and personnel using the distinctive emblems of the Geneva Conventions in conformity with international law;
[...]

7.2.4 Crime of Aggression

This crime has been included for the first in the Rome Statute after the Nuremberg and Tokyo Tribunals. States could not agree on a definition of the crime when the Statute was adopted. It was introduced into the Statute by an amendment adopted in 2010 at the Kampala Review Conference between State Parties and was activated as of 17 July 2018 as follows:

1. For the purpose of this Statute, the “crime of aggression” means the planning, preparation, initiation or execution, by a person in a position

> effectively to exercise control over or to direct the political or military action of a State, of an act of aggression which, by its character, gravity and scale, constitutes a manifest violation of the Charter of the United Nations.
> 2. For the purpose of paragraph 1, "act of aggression" means the use of armed force by a State against the sovereignty, territorial integrity or political independence of another State, or in any other manner inconsistent with the Charter of the United Nations. [...]

7.3 *Japan and the Core Crimes*

Japan concluded the 1907 Convention respecting the Laws and Customs of War on Land and its annex, Regulations concerning the Laws and Customs of War on Land,[40] in 1912.

Before the end of World War II, Japan had separate penal codes applicable to military affairs. There was also a system of Military Tribunals/military commissions to adjudicate members of the armed forces and those who committed war-related crimes. Under the current Constitution adopted after the war, those codes and tribunals have been abolished.

Upon the conclusion of the 1951 San Francisco Peace Treaty, Japan declared that it would conclude the 1949 Geneva Conventions, which it did in 1953. However, Japan did not enact any domestic legislation to implement those treaties, on the assumption that the Penal Code would be sufficient to cover war crimes under these conventions. It was only in 2004 that Japan concluded the 1977 Additional Protocols. This time, Japan enacted the Act on Penal Sanctions against Grave Breaches of the International Humanitarian Law.[41] This Act criminalizes several specific acts that constitute war crimes under the First Protocol but cannot be punished under the Penal Code. The *aut dedere aut judicare* obligation under the Geneva conventions was also implemented at this time.

Notably, Japan has a strong tendency to meet its criminalization obligations in ICL conventions through provisions of existing law rather than through enacting specialized laws.

As for the other core crimes, Japan has not concluded the Genocide Convention. The Japanese Government has most recently explained that since the Convention imposes the obligation to criminalize acts of genocide and related acts on Member States under their domestic laws, it is necessary to

40 *Adopted on* October 17, 1907, *entered into force on* January 26, 1910, 9 UKTS (1910) Cd.5030.

41 Act No. 115 of 2004.

sort out the relationship between the obligations under the Convention and domestic legislation, and that it will strengthen consultation within the Government with a view to consider the future accession.[42]

Japan concluded the Rome Statute in 2007 but has not accepted the amendment on the crime of aggression. The Rome Statute does not provide for a duty of the State Parties to criminalize crimes under the jurisdiction of the ICC domestically. However, due to the nature of the crimes and the principle of complementarity, a number of State Parties have enacted specific legislation criminalizing the core crimes as such and have applied universal jurisdiction. On the other hand, the main provisions of the Japanese Act on Cooperation with the International Criminal Court,[43] to implement the Rome Statue, are those related to the cooperation with the ICC, namely surrender of an offender and provision of evidence.[44] The only criminalizing provision is the creation of offences that obstruct the administration of the ICC. It follows that if the core crimes are committed in Japanese territory or by Japanese nationals, the offender will be punished under the existing Japanese Penal law. Non-Japanese Nationals who commit the core crimes abroad will be extradited or surrendered to the ICC. In the event that a Japanese national commits a crime under the jurisdiction of the ICC that cannot be punished under Japanese law, he or she will also be surrendered to the ICC.

42 Statement of the Foreign Minister Kamikawa, Record of the House of Councillors, Committee on Diplomacy and Defense (Mar. 22, 2024).

43 Act No. 37 of 2007.

44 *See* Meierhenrich J. & Ko K., "How Do States Join the International Criminal Court? The Implementation of the Rome Statute in Japan," *Journal of International Criminal Justice* 7 (2009), 233–256.

CHAPTER 13

Trade, Economic Law and Policy in Japan

Satoshi Kodera

1 Introduction

In order to clarify Japanese approaches to international economic law, this chapter discusses and examines several Japanese practices related to this realm of law. First, to give context, it will analyze the debate in Japan regarding the concept of international economic law. In particular, it will distinguish two approaches to international economic law in Japan and identify the characteristics of each approach.

The next section will clarify the relationship between Japan and the General Agreement on Tariffs and Trade (hereinafter referred to as GATT)[1] and the World Trade Organization (hereinafter referred to as WTO) among the field of international economic law. It will examine how the WTO agreements are implemented within Japan's domestic legal system. To this end, the analysis will focus on the domestic application of the WTO agreements, Japan's implementation of the trade remedy system, and Japan's relationship with the WTO dispute settlement.

Finally, this chapter will address a recent Japanese practice related to international economic security. It will deal with the export control system of Japan and the recent conflict with the Republic of Korea (hereinafter referred to as ROK) with regards to economic security. Then, it will provide an overview of the Economic Security Promotion Act, which was enacted in 2023.

2 Discipline of International Economic Law in Japan

It is necessary to determine what international economic law is in order to discuss its relationship with Japan. This section reviews the debates in Japan on the concept of international economic law and identifies two approaches to the law. Then, it clarifies the recent trends in the discipline of international economic law in Japan.

1 General Agreement on Tariffs and Trade 1947 (GATT 1947), *signed on* October 30, 1947, 55 UNTS 194.

 | DOI:10.1163/9789004548824_014

2.1 *Two Approaches to International Economic Law*

International economic law was not established as an academic discipline in Japan for a very long time. It was not until the Uruguay Round was launched in 1986 that the number of courses on "international economic law" began to increase at universities in Japan. In fact, the Japan Association of International Economic Law was established in 1991 during the period of the Uruguay Round. It must be pointed out that several studies of international economic law existed before the Uruguay Round in Japan[2]. However, it is true that the Uruguay Round and the establishment of the WTO are major milestones in the development of Japanese international economic law.

While there are differing views on how international economic law should be understood in the world, there are two major approaches in Japan:[3] The first is the *Keizai no Kokusai Hō* [the international law of economy] approach, which views international economic law as "international law that regulates economic activities in the international society".[4] This approach focuses on the international source of norms. According to this approach, international economic law is positioned as part of public international law. As a result, private international law and domestic law are not included in international economic law.

The second is the *Kokusai Keizai no Hō* [the law of international economy] approach. This is described as a position that "emphasizes the complex nature of the norms involved in the discipline of the international economy – international law, national law, and the law of merchant custom – and the "functional unity" among the norms".[5] This position differs from the "international law of economy" approach, which focuses on the international scope of norms. Under "the law of international economy" approach, international economic law would include not only public international law, but also private international law, domestic law, customary commercial law, and even soft law.

2 See, for example, Kanazawa Y., *Kokusai Keizai Hō Josetsu* [Introduction to International Economic Law](Japanese) (Yuhikaku, 1979); Sakurai M., *Kokusai Keizai Hō no Kihon Mondai* [Basis Issues of International Economic Law] (Japanese) (Keio Tsushin, 1983).

3 Yoo H.-S., "Kokusai Keizai Hō Josetsu [Introduction to International Economic Law]" (Japanese), in Yoo H.-S. (ed.), *Kōgi Kokusai Keizai Hō* (Toshindo, 2018) (Japanese) 5–7.

4 *Ibid.*, 6.

5 *Ibid.*, 7.

2.2 *Recent Tendency of the Discipline in Japan*

Traditionally, many Japanese scholars have adopted an "international law of economy" approach.[6] One reason for this seems to be that, as noted above, Japanese international economic jurisprudence has developed in relation to the GATT and WTO. In recent years, however, an increasing number of theorists have also adopted "the law of international economy" approach.[7] This tendency reflects upon the current phenomenon of an even closer linkage between international and domestic economies. Furthermore, as noted below with respect to economic security, there has been a phenomenon in recent years of domestic law preceding international legal rules. As a result, it is indispensable to examine the two laws in an integrated manner. In order to understand the whole picture of legal regulation in each area and achieve policy goals, the traditional international/domestic dichotomy needs to be overcome.

In fact, the Japan Association of International Economic Law is now composed of researchers in diverse fields, including public international law, international business law, and domestic economic law such as competition law and intellectual property law.[8] In addition, the society includes not only researchers but also practitioners, aiming to bridge theory and practice. This diversity of research may be one of the characteristics of international economic law in Japan.

3 Japan and the GATT and WTO

As discussed in the previous section, the Japanese approach to international economic law depends on how international economic law is viewed. Even if one were to adopt an "international law of economy" approach, its scope is diverse, including not only trade, but also investment,[9] finance, and development.

6 See, for example, Nakagawa J., Shimizu A., Taira S., and Mamiya I., *Kokusai Keizai Hō* [International Economic Law] 3rd ed. (Japanese) (Yuhikaku, 2019).

7 Kodera S., "Kokusai Keizai Hō Gaku to Shizenjin no Idō [Discipline of International Economic Law and the Movement of Natural Persons]" (Japanese), *Kokusai Keizai Hō Zassi*, 1 (2023).

8 Japan Association of International Economic Law, "Nihon Kokusai Keizai Hō Gakkai Setsuritsu no Keii [The Background of the Establishment of the Japan Association of International Economic Law]" (Japanese), https://www.jaiel.or.jp/about/#01_keii(accessed Jun. 5, 2025).

9 Along with international trade law, international investment law has been studied extensively in Japan. Although this chapter can only deal with a part of trade law, for more

Considering that Japan's international economic law has been formed around the GATT and WTO, this section will focus primarily on Japan's relationship with the GATT and WTO. In particular, the analysis will focus on how Japan has implemented the GATT and the WTO agreements through its own domestic legal system and policies. To this end, three issues will be examined below: the domestic application of the GATT and the WTO agreements, Japan's implementation of the trade remedy system, and Japan's relationship with the WTO dispute settlement.[10]

3.1 *Domestic Application of the GATT and the WTO Agreements*

To date, there are few cases in which the GATT or the WTO agreements have been applied in Japan's domestic courts. In these cases, domestic effects and direct applicability of the GATT and the WTO Agreements were discussed.

3.1.1 GATT

The only case in which the domestic application of the GATT was at issue was the *Nishijin Necktie* case.[11] Japan enacted the Cocoon and Raw Silk Price Stabilization Act (Act No. 310 of 1951, as amended) to promote raw silk exports and stabilize the silk industry. The act was intended to stabilize the market price of raw silk within a certain price range and to secure the income of sericulturalists through the manipulation of supply and demand by the Japan Silk Yarn Cooperation. However, the importation of large quantities of silk yarn and silk fabrics from the People's Republic of China (hereinafter referred as China), ROK, Brazil, and other countries in the 1970s caused turmoil in the Japanese raw silk and silk market. Therefore, in 1976, the Cocoon and Raw Silk Price Stabilization Act was revised and a centralized import

---

information on the relationship between international investment and Japan, see, for example, Ito K., "Perspective on ISDS Reforms", "Regulation on Foreign Investments", in Lee S. (ed.), *Encyclopedia of Public International Law in Asia*, Vol. I, Northeast Asia (Brill, 2021) 220–222.

10 This paper mainly focuses on Japan's policy on the GATT and WTO, although its FTA policy is also important from the perspective of international economic law. For the overview of Japan's FTA policy, *see*, for example, Kodera S., "Trade Policy on Free Trade Agreements in Asia," in Lee (n 9) 213–214.

11 For more information on this case, see, for example, Iwasawa Y., *International Law, Human Rights, and Japanese Law: The Impact of International Law on Japanese Law* (Clarendon Press, 1998) 68–77; Yoo H-S., "GATT 17 Jō no Kokunaiteki Kōka: Nishijin Nekutai Jiken [Domestic Effect of Article 17 of the GATT: Nishijin Necktie Case]" (Japanese), in Yamamoto S., Furukawa T., and Matsui Y. (eds.), *Kokusai Hō Hanrei Hyakusen* (Yuhikaku, 2001) 150–151.

measure was introduced, limiting imports of raw silk to the Japan Silk Yarn Cooperation or those commissioned by it.

Affected by the measure were weavers who had joined the Nishijin Textile Industrial Association in Kyoto and produced silk necktie fabric from raw silk. They claimed that as a result of the centralized import measures, they were unable to purchase inexpensive foreign raw silk and were forced to purchase raw silk at domestic prices that were approximately twice the international price. They filed a claim for state compensation totaling approximately 370 million JPY against the government. They argued that the unilateral import measure violated the provisions of Article 17.1(a) and 2.4 of GATT concerning a state-owned enterprise and was therefore invalid.

In response to this argument, the Kyoto District Court (Judgment of June 29, 1984, Kyoto District Court, 31(2) *Shōmu geppō* 207) held that "the violation of the GATT provision pointed out by the plaintiffs has the effect to have the party correct the said violation by imposing a disadvantage, such as a request for consultations or countermeasures from the party concerned. It is not interpreted as having any further legal effect. The District Court decision was upheld by the Osaka High Court (Judgment of November 25, 1986, Osaka High Court, 33(8) *Shōmu geppō* 2026) and the Supreme Court (Judgment of February 6, 1990, Supreme Court, 36(12) *Shōmu geppō* 2242).

3.1.2 WTO Agreements

The WTO Agreements were at issue in the domestic courts in the *Pork Gate-Price* case.[12] In this case, the defendant company, engaged in the wholesale of meat and other businesses, and its representative director, the defendant, were indicted on charges of violating the Corporation Tax Act (Act No. 34 of 1965, as amended) and the Customs Act (Act No. 61 of 1954, as amended). With regard to violations of the Customs Act, the accused allegedly evaded customs duties totaling about 2.17 billion JPY by filing import declarations based on purchase forms containing false prices for the defendant company's imports of foreign frozen pork from the United States and other countries.

In Japan, the gate-price system is applied to pork imports. Under this system, the government sets a standard import price ("gate price"). When the import price is below the gate price, customs levy a tariff to fill the gap

12 For more information on this case, see, for example, Tanaka S., "Jōyaku no Jidō Shikkōsei: Butaniku Sagaku Kanzei Jiken [Self-Executing Treaty: Pork Gate-Price Case]" (Japanese), in Morikawa K., Kanehara A., Sakai H., and Nishimura Y. (eds.), *Kokusai Hō Hanrei Hyakusen*, 3rd ed. (Yuhikaku, 2021) 24–25.

between these two prices. When the import price exceeds the "gate price," a 4.3 percent ad valorem tariff is applied. The accused allegedly attempted to evade the tariff by declaring a higher price for imported pork than was actually paid.

The accused argued that the price gate system violated the WTO Agreement on Agriculture[13] and was invalid. In response to this argument, the Chiba District Court (Judgment of April 10, 2013, Chiba District Court [Heisei 24 (wa) 496, 896]) denied the direct applicability of the WTO Agreements and held the price gate system to be valid. It stated that "the violation of the WTO Agreements is to be resolved through unified dispute settlement procedures and the WTO Agreement on Agriculture is not directly applicable as a domestic judicial norm". The accused appealed, arguing that the WTO Agreements are directly applicable in light of the intentions of the parties to the treaty and the legislator (subjective criteria) and the clarity of the content of the treaty (objective criteria).

The Tokyo High Court (Judgment of November 27, 2013, Tokyo High Court, 66(4) *Kōsai Hanrei Shū* 1) denied the direct applicability of the WTO Agreements, holding that "although the content of the WTO Agreements has become more detailed and clearer in contrast to the GATT, it has not eliminated the room for flexible dispute settlement through negotiation, and there are still some areas where flexibility in discipline is still possible. Also, the United States and the EC [...] expressly denied the direct applicability of the WTO Agreements in the laws and regulations implementing them domestically and intra-regionally. In the situation where trade is flourishing between Japan and the United States and EU member states, if only Japan were to affirm the direct applicability of the WTO Agreements under these circumstances, a significant imbalance would occur with respect to the fulfillment of obligations under the WTO Agreements in relation to these countries, and Japan could be disadvantaged. This means that the exercise of discretionary power by the legislature and the executive is restricted by judicial review of the WTO Agreements, which is not desirable from the viewpoint of the separation of powers adopted in the Constitution of Japan".[14]

3.2 *Trade Remedies in Japan*

It is possible to understand how Japan has implemented the WTO Agreements through its domestic legal system by examining the trade remedy system. In fact, from a practical point of view, it is of most interest in Japanese practice

---

13 Agreement on Agriculture, *adopted on* April 15, 1994, *entered into force on* January 1, 1995, 1867 UNTS 410.

14 Judgment of November 27, 2013, Tokyo High Court, 66(4) *Kōsai Hanrei Shū* 7.

involving international economic law. There are three types of trade remedy measures authorized by the WTO agreements: safeguard measures, antidumping measures, and countervailing measures. The following sections examine each of the domestic legal systems for implementing these three measures.[15]

3.2.1 Safeguard Measures

Under Article XIX of the GATT and the WTO Agreement on Safeguards,[16] WTO members may take two types of safeguard measures: one is the withdrawal or modification of tariff concessions and the other is quantitative restrictions. Japan has established different legal bases and regulatory authorities for these two types of safeguard measures.[17]

The withdrawal or modification of tariff concessions is based on the Customs Tariff Act (Act No.54 of 1910, as amended). The purpose of the Act is stipulated as follows: "the rates of customs duty, the basis for duty assessment where customs duty is to be levied, the reduction of, or the exemption from customs duty and other system for customs duty" (Article 1 of the Act). Article 9.1 of the Act provides that "in the case where, as a result of a decline in the overseas price of a particular kind of goods or of any other unforeseen development of circumstances [...] there is the fact of an increase in imports of these goods [...] where there is the fact that the imports of these goods cause or threaten to cause serious injury to a Japanese industry involved in the production of goods which are of the same kind as these imported goods or compete directly with these imported goods in their uses [...] if it is found urgently necessary for the National economy [...]," there may be imposed custom duties as a safeguard measure. In addition, the Act is detailed in the Cabinet Order on Emergency Duty (Cabinet Order No. 417 of 1994, as amended). As for the withdrawal or modification of tariff concessions, the Ministry of Finance (hereinafter referred as MOF) is the competent authority.

---

15 This section is mainly based on my article, Kodera S., "Trade Remedies", in Lee (n 9) 216–217.

16 Agreement on Safeguards, *adopted on* April 15, 1994, *entered into force on* January 1, 1995, 1869 UNTS 154.

17 This dual system regarding safeguard measures in Japan has been criticized because it may complicate the procedure for implementation of safeguards and waste precious human resources. See, Araki I., "Japan's Safeguard System Is Unsustainable", *Miyakodayori* 33 (2002), https://www.rieti.go.jp/en/miyakodayori/033.html (accessed Oct. 30, 2024); Kawase T., "Waga Kuni Tsūshō Hō no Genjō oyobi Kadai: WTO Kyōtei Seigōteki na Kokusai Hyōjun Seido eno Hatten ni Mukete [Current Status and Issues of Japan's Trade Remedy Laws: Toward the Development of an International Standards System Consistent with the WTO Agreement] (Japanese), *Hōritsujihō* 77(6) (2005) 54–59.

On the other hand, the imposition of quantitative restrictions is stipulated in the provisions of the Foreign Exchange and Foreign Trade Act (Act No. 228 of 1949, as amended). Article 52 of the Act provides that "for the purpose of achieving the sound development of foreign trade and the national economy, sincerely fulfilling obligations under the treaties and other international agreements Japan has signed, making Japan's contribution to international efforts for achieving international peace, or implementing a cabinet decision set forth in Article 10, paragraph (1), any person who intends to import goods may be obliged to obtain import approval pursuant to the provisions of Cabinet Order." The Cabinet Order referred to in the Act is Article 3.1 of the Import Trade Control Order (Cabinet Order No. 414 of 1949, as amended). It stipulates that "the Minister of Economy, Trade and Industry provides for and publicizes the items of goods subject to import quotas, the places of origin or places of shipment of goods requiring import approval, and other necessary matters concerning import of goods [...]". It is supplemented by Article 2 of the Regulation on Emergency Measures for Increased Imports (Public Notice No. 715 of the Ministry of International Trade and Industry of 1994). The conditions to impose quantitative restrictions are the same as those for the withdrawal or modification of tariff concessions. However, for quantitative restrictions, the Ministry of Economy, Trade and Industry (hereinafter referred as METI) serves as the competent authority.

Japan has only once invoked measures under the WTO Agreement on Safeguards. On December 12, 2000, Japan initiated a safeguard investigation on the imports of Welsh onions, raw shiitake mushrooms, and *tatami omote* (rushes for grass mats) according to the Customs Tariff Act. These products primarily originated from China. On April 23, 2001, following an investigation, Japan took provisional safeguard measures on the import of these products.[18] Japan imposed additional tariffs for 200 days, but no definitive measures were taken. To date, this is the only action taken under the WTO Agreement on Safeguards.[19]

3.2.2 Anti-dumping Measures

Anti-dumping measures in Japan correspond to Article 8 of the Customs Tariff Act. Article 8.1 of the Act provides that "in the case where there is

18 Cabinet Order, "Negi tō ni taishite Zanteiteki ni Kasuru Kinkyū Kanzei ni Kansuru Seirei [Cabinet Order Concerning the Imposition of the Provisional Emergency Duties on Welsh Onion etc]" (Japanese) (Cabinet Order No. 167 of 2001).

19 Multilateral Trade System Department, Trade Policy Bureau, METI, "Sēfugādo [Safeguard]" (Japanese), in *2024 Fukōsei Bōeki Hōkokusho* (2024) 350.

the fact that imports of dumped goods [...] cause or threaten to cause material injury to a Japanese industry [...] or materially retard the establishment of a Japanese industry [...] if it is found necessary for protecting the Japanese industry", there may be imposed an additional custom duty as an anti-dumping measure. It is supplemented by the Cabinet Order on Anti-Dumping Duty (Cabinet Order No.416 of 1994, as amended) and the Guidelines for Procedures Relating to Antidumping Duties.[20]

Article 8.1 of the Act provides for four conditions that need to be met to take anti-dumping measures: (i) the import of dumped goods, (ii) the material injury to a Japanese industry, (iii) the causal relationship between (i) and (ii), and (iv) the necessity to protect the Japanese industry. An anti-dumping investigation is initiated based either on *ex officio* action by the government or on a domestic industry request (Article 8.4 and 8.5 of the Act). The investigating authority is jointly composed of MOF, METI, and other relevant authorities. A final determination of the anti-dumping investigation is generally made within a year from the initiation of the investigation (Article 8.6 of the Act). All of these substantial and procedural provisions follow the WTO Agreement on Implementation of Article VI of the General Agreement on Tariffs and Trade 1994 (hereinafter referred as the Anti-Dumping Agreement).[21]

Historically, Japan has been reluctant to utilize anti-dumping measures. The reasons for Japan's reluctance during the GATT era depend on the particular period. For example, in the 1980s, Japan's Ministry of International Trade and Industry (hereinafter referred as MITI) was said to be reluctant to take anti-dumping measures because the main issue for MITI at the time was the opening up of the Japanese market[22]. Also, Japan suffered from the arbitrary

20 MOF, Ministry of Health, Labour and Welfare, Ministry of Agriculture, Forestry and Fisheries, METI, and Ministry of Land, Infrastructure, Transport and Tourism, *Futō Renbai Kanzei ni Kansuru Tetsuzuki tō ni tsuiteno Gaidorain* [the Guidelines for Procedures Relating to Antidumping Duties] (Japanese), https://www.customs.go.jp/kaisei/sonota/adgl_honbun.pdf (accessed Oct. 30, 2024).

21 Agreement on Implementation of Article VI of the General Agreement on Tariffs and Trade 1994, *adopted on* April 15, 1994, *entered into force on* January 1, 1995, 1868 UNTS 201. For more information, see, Matsushita M. and Kometani K., *Kokusai Keizai Hō* [International Economic Law] (Japanese) (University of Tokyo Press, 2015) 494–496.

22 Shibayama C., "Nihon ga Anti-Dumping Sochi wo Toranakatta 70 Nenkan [70 Years of No Anti-Dumping Measures by Japan]" (Japanese), *Sekai Keizai Hyōron Impact* 2074 (2021), http://www.world-economic-review.jp/impact/article2074.html (accessed Oct. 30, 2024).

application of anti-dumping measures by other countries in the 1980s.[23] This historical background is the reason why anti-dumping measures are less frequently invoked in Japan compared to other countries. This reluctance remained basically unchanged even after the establishment of the WTO. Indeed, as of October 30, 2024, it has taken anti-dumping measures in only eleven cases.[24]

In recent years, however, Japan has tended to utilize these instruments more aggressively. In fact, among these eleven cases, seven were taken after 2015.[25] These seven were on imports from ROK and China. Since the 2000s, Japan has been laying the groundwork for the invocation of anti-dumping measures by developing and revising laws, regulations, and guidelines. Moreover, the Japanese government is making efforts to inform the public about the anti-dumping system[26]. The recent increase in the number of anti-dumping measures is a manifestation of these efforts and is expected to increase steadily in the future.[27]

3.2.3 Countervailing Measures

The basic law for countervailing measures is Article 7 of the Customs Tariff Act and Cabinet Order on Countervailing Duty (Cabinet Order No. 415 of 1994, as amended), and the details are provided in the Guidelines for Procedures Relating to Countervailing Duties.[28] The conditions and procedures to apply countervailing measures are quite similar to those for anti-dumping measures.

---

23 Shibayama C., "Anti-Dumping wo Kiritsuteki ni Sekkyoku Unyō suru Nihon [Japan Operating Anti-dumping in a Disciplined and Proactive Manner]" (Japanese), *Sekai Keizai Hyōron Impact* 2381 (2021), http://www.world-economic-review.jp/impact/article2381.html (accessed Oct. 30, 2024).

24 METI, "Nihon no Chōsa Jirei: Anti-Dumping Sochi [Cases of Investigation: Anti-Dumping Measures]" (Japanese), https://www.meti.go.jp/policy/external_economy/trade_control/boekikanri/trade-remedy/investigation/index.html (accessed Oct. 30, 2024).

25 Anti-dumping Duties on Toluenediisocyanate Originating in China (2015-2020), Potassium Hydroxide Originating in ROK and China (2016–), Polyethylene Terephthalate with a High Degree of Polymerization Originating in China (2017–), Carbon Steel Butt Welding Fittings Originating in ROK and China (2018–), Tris (chloropropyl) phosphate Originating in China (2020–), Dipotassium Carbonate Originating in ROK (2021–), and Hot-dipped Galvanized Steel Wire Originating in ROK and China (2022–).

26 METI, "Bōeki Kyūsai ni Kansuru Yoku Aru Shitsumon [Frequently Asked Questions about Trade Remedies]" (Japanese), https://www.meti.go.jp/policy/external_economy/trade_control/boekikanri/trade-remedy/faq/index.html (accessed Oct. 30, 2024).

27 *Ibid.*

28 MOF, Ministry of Health, Labour and Welfare, Ministry of Agriculture, Forestry and Fisheries, METI, and Ministry of Land, Infrastructure, Transport and Tourism, *Sōsai Kanzei ni Kansuru Tetsuzuki tō ni tsuite no Gaidorain* [the Guidelines for Procedures

Article 7.1 of the Act provides that "when there is the fact that goods the production or exportation of which directly or indirectly subsidized by a foreign country are imported and these imports cause or threaten to cause material injury to a Japanese industry [...] or materially retard the establishment of a Japanese industry [...] if it is found necessary for protecting the Japanese industry," an additional custom duty may be imposed as a countervailing measure.

As of 30 October, 2024, Japan has imposed countervailing measures in only one case, which was against certain dynamic random access memories (DRAM) from ROK. This case was the first time that Japan became a respondent with respect to trade remedies in a WTO dispute settlement.[29] After the imposition of the countervailing measure by Japan on January 27, 2006, ROK requested a consultation with Japan under the WTO dispute settlement on March 14, 2006 (DS336), insisting upon the inconsistency of Japan's measure with respect to the WTO Agreement on Subsidies and Countervailing Measure[30] (hereinafter referred as the SCM Agreement). The Appellate Body found that Japan's measures were found to be inconsistent with the SCM Agreements.[31] After the adoption of the recommendations and rulings by the WTO's Dispute Settlement Body (hereinafter referred as DSB), Japan announced its intention to implement DSB's recommendations and rulings. Subsequently, ROK requested a compliance panel be established under Article 21.5 of the Understanding on Rules and Procedures Governing the Settlement of Disputes (hereinafter referred as DSU),[32] although it eventually requested the panel to suspend its work.[33] Ultimately, the authority for the establishment of the panel lapsed as of 5 March 2010.[34]

Relating to Countervailing Duties] (Japanese), https://www.customs.go.jp/kaisei/sonota/cvdgl_honbun.pdf (accessed Oct. 30, 2024).

29 Kawashima F., "Nihon no Kankokusan DRAM ni Taisuru Sōsai Kanzei [Japan's Countervailing Duties on DRAM from ROK]" (Japanese), *WTO Panel Oyobi Jōkyū Iinkai Hōkokusyo ni Kansuru Chōsa Kenkyū Hōkokusho 2007* (2007) 115.

30 Agreement on Subsidies and Countervailing Measures, *adopted on* April 15, 1994, *entered into force on* January 1, 1995, 1869 UNTS 14.

31 Appellate Body Report, *Japan – Countervailing Duties on Dynamic Random Access Memories from Korea*, WT/DS336/AB/R (November 28, 2007).

32 Understanding on Rules and Procedures Governing the Settlement of Disputes, *adopted on* April 15, 1994, *entered into force on* January 1, 1995, 1869 UNTS 401.

33 Communication of Chairperson of the Panel, WT/DS336/22 (March 5, 2009).

34 Note by the Secretariat, WT/DS336/23 (March 5, 2010).

3.3 *Japan and the WTO Dispute Settlement System*

The most distinctive feature of the WTO is its dispute settlement system, which has *de facto* compulsory jurisdiction. The system also has a two-trial system consisting of a Panel and Appellate Body; a feature that distinguishes it from other international tribunals such as the International Court of Justice.

This section examines Japan's relationship with the WTO dispute settlement system, including the evolution of Japan's participation in this system, and its relationship with recent WTO dispute settlement reforms.

3.3.1 Participation of Japan in the WTO Dispute Settlement System[35]

The WTO Dispute Settlement System is crucial for the trade policy of Japan that is seeking the promotion of the rule of law in the global economy. As of October 30, 2024, after the establishment of the WTO in 1995, Japan participated in twenty-eight cases as the complainant and in sixteen as the respondent. Japan has also actively participated in WTO Dispute Settlement as a third party.[36] To date, three Japanese nationals have served as a member of the WTO Appellate Body.[37]

Japan's participation in the WTO Dispute Settlement System has varied over time. In the early years of the WTO's establishment (1995-2000), Japan participated actively in this system. During this period, Japan was engaged in nine cases as the complainant[38] and in twelve as the respondent.[39] The panel and the Appellate Body admitted Japan's arguments in most cases and rejected them in some cases, such as *Japan – Taxes on Alcoholic Beverage* (DS8, DS10, DS11) and *Japan – Measures Affecting Agricultural Products* (DS76). In both cases, the measures taken by Japan were found to be inconsistent with the

35 This section is mainly based on my article, Kodera S, "Perspective on the WTO Dispute Settlement System", in Lee (n 9) 214–215.

36 For information on the cases in which Japan is currently participating as a third party, *see*, METI, Fukosei Boeki Hokokusho [2024 Report on Compliance by Major Trading Partners with Trade Agreements] (Japanese) 476–477, https://www.meti.go.jp/shingikai/sankoshin/tsusho_boeki/fukosei_boeki/report_2024/pdf/2024_02_17.pdf (accessed Oct. 30, 2024).

37 Mitsuo Matsushita (Terms of office: 1995–1999, 1999–2000), Yasuhei Taniguchi (2000–2003, 2003–2007), and Shotaro Oshima (2008–2012). *See*, the World Trade Organization, "Appellate Body Members," https://www.wto.org/english/tratop_e/dispu_e/ab_members_descrp_e.htm (accessed Oct. 30, 2024).

38 DS6, DS51, DS55, DS64, DS95, DS139, DS162, DS184, and DS217.

39 DS8, DS10, DS11, DS15, DS28, DS42, DS44, DS45, DS66, DS73, DS76, and DS147.

WTO agreements.[40] Following the recommendations and rulings of the DSB, Japan modified the measures in question and made them consistent with the WTO agreements.

After that, Japan used the WTO dispute settlement system infrequently. During the period from 2001 to 2005, Japan was only involved in three cases as the complainant[41] and in three as the respondent.[42] The cases pertaining to Japan during this period were mainly limited as those against the United States regarding trade remedies (DS217, DS244, and DS249).

During the period from 2008 to the present, Japan has started to make active use of the system once again, in particular as the complainant. Japan has filed a suit against different states over various WTO agreements, such as the European Communities (DS376), Canada (DS412), China (DS433, DS454, DS601), Argentina (DS445), Russia (DS463), Ukraine (DS468), ROK (DS495, DS504, DS553, DS571, DS594), Brazil (DS497), and India (DS518, DS584).

Why has Japan begun to actively use the WTO dispute settlement system again? One of the factors is the change in Japan's foreign and trade policy. Japan has shown its willingness to be actively involved in the formation of rules through international economic disputes. To this end, the Japanese government has successively created a department for international economic disputes. In April 2016, Japan set up the International Trade and Investment Dispute Settlement Division under the Economic Affairs Bureau in the Ministry of Foreign Affairs (hereinafter referred as MOFA). Moreover, in April 2017, Japan newly established the General Counsel for International Legal Affairs in METI. Currently, Japan is engaged in international economic dispute resolution, such as the WTO and Investor-State Dispute Settlement (ISDS)[43] based on the cooperation between these relevant departments.

---

40 Appellate Body Report, *Japan – Taxes on Alcoholic Beverages*, WT/DS8/AB/R, WT/DS10/AB/R, WT/DS11/AB/R (Oct. 4, 1996); Appellate Body Report, *Japan – Measures Affecting Agricultural Products*, WT/DS76/AB/R (Feb. 22, 1999).

41 DS217, DS244, and DS249.

42 DS245, DS323, and DS336.

43 To date, Japan appears to have been sued for ISDS in only one case, an investment arbitration related to a renewable energy. Japan introduced a Feed-in Tariff (FIT) system in 2012 with the aim of promoting renewable energy. However, Japan amended the FIT system to adjust supply and demand and to limit the burden on the public and introduced Feed-in Premium (FIP) system in 2022. In 2020, a company from Hong Kong, Shift Energy, filed an investment arbitration with the Government of Japan in relation to the amendment of the FIT system under the Japan-Hong Kong Bilateral Investment Treaty. Although the details have not been published, according to an arbitral award issued in February 2023, the majority opinion of the arbitral tribunal rejected all of the claims of the claimant. *See*, IA Reporter (Lisa Bohmer), "Japan prevails in its first known treaty arbitration" (Feb. 13, 2023), https://www.iareporter.com/articles/japan-prevails-in-its-first-known-treaty-arbitration/ (accessed Oct. 30,

The importance of international economic disputes became even more apparent when the Appellate Body dismissed the panel's finding in *Korea – Import Bans, and Testing and Certification Requirements for Radionuclides* (DS495).[44] In this case, the panel found that the import restriction measures on certain products from Japan, taken by ROK following the accident at the Fukushima Daiichi Nuclear Power Plant in 2011, were inconsistent with the WTO Agreements.[45] However, the Appellate Body reversed some parts of the panel's finding. This case created intense criticism in Japan,[46] and the Japanese government found fault with the Appellate Body's report at the DSB meeting on April 29, 2019.[47] After this case, on August 3, 2020, the Economic Dispute Settlement Division was newly established under the International Legal Affair Bureau of MOFA in order to strengthen its capability to deal with international economic disputes.

3.3.2 The Crisis of the WTO Dispute Settlement System and Japan

The WTO Appellate Body has ceased to function since December 2019. The United States criticized the WTO dispute settlement system, in particular the Appellate Body,[48] and blocked the appointment of Appellate Body members.

The United States, the EU, and several other countries have presented their proposals for the reform of the system. Japan also contributed to the discussion by submitting a proposal for reform with Australia and Chile on April 17, 2019.[49] Japan proposed, for example, that the Appellate Body should consider issues only within the scope provided in the DSU and that an interpretation by

---

2024); UNCTAD Investment Dispute Settlement Navigator, "Shift Energy v. Japan," https://investmentpolicy.unctad.org/investment-dispute-settlement/cases/1194/shift-energy-v-japan (accessed Oct. 30, 2024); MOFA, "Nihon no Tojikoku Anken [Cases to Which Japan was a Party]" (Japanese), https://www.mofa.go.jp/mofaj/gaiko/wto/funso/funsou.html (accessed Oct. 30, 2024).

44 Appellate Body Report, *Korea – Import Bans, and Testing and Certification Requirements for Radionuclides*, WT/DS495/AB/R (April 11, 2019).

45 Panel Report, *Korea – Import Bans, and Testing and Certification Requirements for Radionuclides*, WT/DS495/R (Feb. 22, 2018).

46 For more information on this case, *see*, for example, Fukunaga Y., "Japan's Trade Policy in the Midst of Uncertainty," *Asie. Visions* 112 (2020) 21–22.

47 Statement of Japan at the Meeting of the WTO Dispute Settlement Body on April 26, 2019, https://www.mofa.go.jp/files/000473398.pdf (accessed Oct. 30, 2024).

48 *See*, United States Trade Representative, *Report on the Appellate Body of the World Trade Organization* (2000), https://ustr.gov/sites/default/files/Report_on_the_Appellate_Body_of_the_World_Trade_Organization.pdf (accessed Oct. 30, 2024).

49 Communication from Japan and Australia, *Informal Process on Matter Relating to the Functioning of the Appellate Body*, WT/GC/W/768 (April 18, 2019).

the Appellate Body of any WTO provision should not constitute a precedent for posterior interpretations.[50]

In April 2020, some WTO members launched the multi-party Interim Appeal Arbitration Arrangement (hereinafter referred as MPIA) as a provisional response to the dysfunction of the WTO Appellate Body. The MPIA is an alternative system for resolving WTO disputes that are appealed by a Member under Article 25 of the DSU. As of April 23, 2023, twenty-six WTO members are participants of the MPIA. To date, arbitrators have issued rulings on two cases under the MPIA,[51] and eight cases are ongoing under the MPIA.[52]

Japan initially decided not to participate in the MPIA. However, as the dysfunction of the WTO Appellate Body became more prolonged, calls for Japan's participation in the MPIA increased.[53] In March 10, 2023, the Japanese Government decided to join the MPIA and notified the WTO Dispute Settlement Body of its intent to join the MPIA. On April 11, 2023, Japan and China agreed to use the MPIA in the event of any appeal in the *China – Anti-Dumping Measures on Stainless Steel Products from Japan* (DS601) dispute.[54]

This section examined Japan's implementation of international economic law mainly in relation to the GATT and the WTO. The next section will analyze Japan's current trends in international economic law and policy from the perspective of economic security.

4 Economic Security

In recent years, the link between the economy and security has grown stronger, and this has affected the trade policies of various countries. An important example of this is the invocation of Article XXI of the GATT which provides

50 *See*, Fukunaga (n 46) 27–28.

51 Arbitration under Article 25 of the DSU, *Turkey – Certain Measures concerning the Production, Importation and Marketing of Pharmaceutical Products*, WT/DS583/ARB25 (July 25, 2022); Arbitration under Article 25 of the DSU, *Colombia – Anti-dumping Duties on Frozen Fries from Belgium, Germany and the Netherlands*, WT/DS591/ARB25, (Dec. 21, 2022).

52 DS611, DS610, DS607, DS603, DS602, DS598, DS589, DS601. See, Geneva Trade Platform, "Multi-Party Interim Appeal Arbitration Arrangement (MPIA)," https://wtoplurilaterals.info/plural_initiative/the-mpia/ (accessed Oct. 30, 2024).

53 *See*, for example, Special Task Force on Policy Response to the Non-functioning of the WTO Appellate Body, *Interim Report* (2022), https://www.meti.go.jp/english/report/pdf/0804_InterimReport.pdf (accessed Oct. 30, 2024).

54 Agreed Procedures for Arbitration under Article 25 of the DSU, *China – Anti-dumping Measures on Stainless Steel Products from Japan*, WT/DS601/6 (Apr. 13, 2023).

national security exceptions for WTO members. In *Russia – Measures Concerning Traffic in Transit* (DS512), Russia attempted to justify its measures under Article XXI, and the panel provided its interpretation of Article XXI for the first time within the WTO dispute settlement procedures.[55] Since then, a series of economic and security cases have been referred to the WTO for dispute settlement.[56]

Against the backdrop of this international situation, economic security has been discussed so much in Japan in recent years that it is often referred to as a "buzzword."[57] While the scope of economic security is broad, to identify the link between economic security and Japan's economic policy, this section will examine it from two perspectives. First, it will deal with export controls, which have been an important part of Japan's trade policy. Second, it will analyze a Japanese domestic law regarding economic security that was enacted in 2023.

4.1 *Export Control*

In the context of economic security, export controls have occupied an important position. In the following, this section will review Japan's extremely complex export control system. In addition, it will discuss trade disputes with ROK over export controls, examining the details of the disputes and identifying their most recent development.

4.1.1 The Japanese System of Export Control

In Japan, the relationship between the economy and security has been discussed mainly in relation to export control.[58] After World War II, Japan began to participate in multilateral export control regimes (hereinafter referred as MECRs). The occasion for this was Japan's entry into the Coordinating Committee for Multilateral Export Controls (hereinafter referred as COCOM) in 1952. The participation in COCOM, which aimed to control exports to the Communist bloc, was regarded as an opportunity for Japan to develop

55 Panel Report, *United States – Certain Measures on Steel and Aluminium Products*, WT/DS512/R (Apr. 5, 2019).

56 *See*, for example, Bacchus J., "The Black Hole of National Security: Striking the Right Balance for the National Security Exception in International Trade," *Policy Analysis* 936 (2022), https://www.cato.org/policy-analysis/black-hole-national-security (accessed Oct. 30, 2024).

57 Adler D.E., "Why 'Economic Security' Became Magic Words in Japan," *Foreign Policy* 20 (2023), https://foreignpolicy.com/2023/01/20/japan-china-economic-security-strategic-threat/ (accessed Oct. 30, 2024).

58 For the overview of export control system in Japan, *see*, Kodera S., "Export Control," in Lee (n 9) 217–218.

its security export control policy and system.[59] Subsequently, Japan became a member of other MECRs. Currently, Japan participates in four MECRs: the Nuclear Suppliers Group (NSG), the Australia Group (AG), the Missile Technology Control Regime (MTCR), and the Wassenaar Arrangement (WA).

Japan's export control is mainly conducted by METI based on the Foreign Exchange and Foreign Trade Act.[60] Export controls under the Act can be broadly classified into two categories based on the method of control: list controls and catch-all controls. List controls refer to the permanent restrictions for all regions on the export or provision of specific items (goods and technologies) enumerated in the list. The Export Trade Control Order (Cabinet Order No.378 of 1949, as amended) specifies controlled goods pursuant 48.1 of the Act, while the Foreign Exchange Order (Cabinet Order No.260 of 1980, as amended) regulates controlled technologies pursuant to Article 25.1 of the Act. On the other hand, catch-all controls require exporters to obtain permission from the Minister of METI even for items that are not on the list. Whether an item falls under catch-all controls is determined by two requirements. One is when an exporter "knows" that the items will be used for the development, manufacture, use, or storage of weapons of mass destruction (hereinafter referred as WMD), or the development, manufacture, use of conventional weapons (objective requirement). Another is when METI "informs" an exporter of the risk of items being used as WMD or of military use of items and therefore requires it to obtain a license for a specific transaction (informed requirement).

For the implementation of export control, Japan categorizes import countries into four groups (so-called Group A, Group B, Group C, and Group D).[61] Group A consists of countries and regions that participate in MECRs and enforce strict export control on items. They are listed in the Appended Table III of the Export Trade Control Order.[62] The countries of Group A can enjoy

59 *Ibid.*, 217.

60 For more details of this Act, *see*, Kazeki J., *Syōkai Gaitame Hō: Bōeki Kanri Hen* [Detail Explanation of the Foreign Exchange and Foreign Trade Act: Trade Control] (Japanese) (Shojihomu, 2022).

61 Under the Export Control Order, METI explains that importing countries are categorized into not four, but three categories; Preferred Trade Partner List Countries, UN arms embargo countries, and other countries. METI, "Security Export Control", https://www.meti.go.jp/policy/anpo/englishpage/securityexportcontrolinjapan5.pdf (accessed Oct. 30, 2024). However, in practice, it is understood that "other countries" are distinguished into group B and group C shown in this paper. METI has not clearly published which countries fall into Group B.

62 As of January 1, 2024, twenty-six countries are listed under Group A; Argentina, Australia, Austria, Belgium, Bulgaria, Canada, Czech Republic, Denmark, Finland, France, Germany, Greece, Hungary, Ireland, Italy, Luxembourg, Netherlands, New Zealand, Norway,

preferential treatment such as exemption from catch-all control. Group B consists of countries and regions that participate in international export control regimes and satisfy certain conditions, excluding those in Group A. Group C consists of countries and regions that do not fall within Groups A, B, or D. Finally, Group D consists of countries and regions listed in the Appended Table III-2 or Appended Table IV of the Export Trade Control Order, which are subject to economic sanctions of the United Nations.[63]

4.1.2 Trade Disputes with ROK

Since July 2019, Japan has begun strengthening its export controls for goods to ROK, based on Article 25.1 and Article 48.1 of the Foreign Exchange and Foreign Trade Act.[64] On July 4, 2019, Japan tightened export controls on three semiconductor materials destined for ROK, with the need for individual export licenses now being applied instead of the previous bulk export license.[65] Moreover, on August 2, 2019, Japan's Cabinet decided to exclude ROK from the Group A category of import countries (entered in force on August 28, 2019).

On September 11, 2019, ROK filed a request for consultations with Japan under the WTO dispute settlement procedure on the grounds that Japan's revision of the export license system for three semiconductor materials violates the WTO Agreements, and a panel was established on July 29, 2020 (*Japan – Measures Related to the Exportation of Products and Technology to Korea*, DS590).[66] At the same time, on September 18, 2019, ROK removed Japan from its list of preferential export control countries.

Poland, Portugal, Spain, Sweden, Switzerland, the United Kingdom, and the United States of America.

63 As of January 1, 2024, ten countries are listed under Group D; Afghanistan, Central Africa, Democratic Republic of Congo, Iraq, Lebanon, Libya, North Korea, Somalia, South Sudan, and Sudan.

64 METI, "Update of METI's licensing policies and procedures on in relation to the Republic of Korea," https://www.meti.go.jp/policy/external_economy/export_control_korea/index-en.html (accessed Jun. 9, 2025).

65 In Japan, exporters may obtain either an individual export license or a bulk export license. In the former, exporters are required to obtain an individual export, while in the latter they can make multiple exports under certain conditions. *See*, Center for Information on Security Trade Control (CISTEC), *Overview of Japan's Export Controls*, 4th ed. (CISTEC, 2015) 23–27.

66 Even in Japan, the compatibility of Japan's measures with article XXI of the GATT was widely discussed. See, for example, Kawase T., "Potential Conflict between the WTO System and the Security Trade Control System in the Japan-Korea Dispute", *Research Reports* (the Japan Institute of International Affairs: 2021), https://www.jiia.or.jp/en/column/2021/04/13-research-reports-potential-conflict-between-the-wto-system-and-the-security-trade-control-system-in.html (accessed Oct. 30, 2024).

In recent years, tensions between the two countries have continued in other areas as well,[67] but trade disputes between Japan and ROK have recently shown signs of easing. On March 16, 2023, the Japanese and Korean governments jointly announced that Japan will lift its restrictions on semiconductor material exports to ROK, while ROK will withdraw its complaint to the WTO dispute settlement.[68] After the joint announcement, on March 23, 2023, ROK withdrew its complaint.[69] Finally, on June 27, 2023, Japan reassigned ROK to the Group A category with respect to its export control[70].

However, the outlook for economic issues between the two countries is extremely uncertain and unpredictable. In particular, the economic relationship between Japan and ROK is effectively linked to political issues between the two countries, such as the issue of the wartime labor. Therefore, depending on the political relationship between the two countries, economic disputes between Japan and ROK could flare up.

4.2 *New Legislation on Economic Security*

As identified in the previous section, the link between the economy and security is having an impact on the existing international economic order. In response to these developments, Japan's economic policy and domestic laws are undergoing significant changes. Indeed, economic security has become one of the main pillars of Japan's trade policy. This section analyzes the Economic Security Promotion Act which was enacted in 2023.[71] It will provide an overview of the background of the enactment of the Act and outline its contents.

---

67 Fukunaga (n 46) 18–23.

68 METI, "Japan-Korea Export Control Policy Dialogue Held," https://www.meti.go.jp/english/press/2023/0316_001.html (accessed Oct. 30, 2024).

69 Communication from Korea, *Japan – Measures Related to the Exportation of Products and Technology to Korea*, WT/DS590/5, March 24, 2023.

70 METI, "Cabinet Decision on the Cabinet Order to Partially Amend the Export Trade Control Order," https://www.meti.go.jp/english/press/2023/0627_004.html (accessed Oct. 30, 2024).

71 Regarding economic security, the Act on the Protection and Utilization of Important Economic Security Information (Act No. 27 of 2024), which was passed in 2024, is also important. The Act aims at protecting Critical Economic Security Information (CESI) by establishing a new security clearance system. For an overview of the Act, see, for example, Takai Y., "Jūyō Keizai Anzen Anpo Jōhō no Hogo oyobi Katsuyō ni kansuru Hōritsu ni Tsuite [The Act on the Protection and Utilization of Important Economic Security Information]" (Japanese), *Jurist* 1601 (2024) 15–20.

4.2.1 Enactment of the Economic Security Promotion Act

On 11 May 2022, the Act on the Promotion of Ensuring National Security Through Integrated Implementation of Economic Measures (Act No. 43 of 2022) ("the Economic Security Promotion Act", hereinafter referred as ESPA or the Act) was enacted (promulgated on 18 May 2022).

Economic security emerged as a policy issue for Japan around 2020. In April 2020, an economic division was established in the National Security Secretariat, and in December of the same year, the Strategic Headquarters on the Creation of a New International Order Policy Research Council in Liberal Democratic Party published its recommendations on economic security strategy.[72] Prime Minister at the time, Fumio Kishida, newly established a Minister of Economic Security, and positioned economic security as one of the pillars of his administration in his first policy speech.[73]

In November 2021, the Japanese government held the first meeting of the Council for the Promotion of Economic Security, and on the same day established the Preparatory Office for Economic Security Legislation in the Cabinet Secretariat with the aim of enacting new law on economic security. The Expert Advisory Panel on Economic Security Legislation held several meetings from November 2021 and compiled its recommendations in February 2021.[74]

In response to the recommendations, the Cabinet approved the ESPA on February 25, 2022, which was submitted to the Diet. The Diet passed the ESPA, which was enacted on May 11 and promulgated on May 18, 2022. The EPSA is to be enforced in stages within two years of its promulgation (Article 1 of the Supplementary Provisions of the EPSA), and on August 1, 2022, a portion of the Law went into effect.

---

72 Strategic Headquarters on the Creation of a New International Order Policy Research Council, Liberal Democratic Party of Japan, "Teigen: 'Keizai Anzen Hoshō Senryaku' no Sakutei ni Mukete [Recommendations Toward Developing Japan's "Economic Security Strategy]" (Japanese), Dec. 16, 2020, https://storage.jimin.jp/pdf/news/policy/201021_1.pdf (accessed Oct. 30, 2024).

73 The Government of Japan, "The First Policy Speech by Prime Minister KISHIDA Fumio," https://www.japan.go.jp/kizuna/2021/11/the_first_policy_speech_by_kishida.html (accessed Oct. 30, 2024).

74 The Expert Advisory Panel on Economic Security Legislation, "Proposal on Economic Security Legislation," Feb. 1, 2022, https://www.cas.go.jp/jp/seisaku/keizai_anzen_hosyohousei/dai4/teigen.pdf (accessed Oct. 30, 2024).

4.2.2 Four Systems under the ESPA

The ESPA consists of ninety-nine articles and supplementary provisions and is organized into chapters 1 through 7.[75] Chapter 1 provides the purpose of this act (Article 1), and also stipulates the formulation of a basic policy on the promotion of ensuring security through integrated implementation of economic measures (Article 2).[76]

The ESPA establishes four systems, each corresponding to Chapters 2 through 5 of the Act: the System for Ensuring Stable Supply of Specified Critical Products (Chapter 2), the System for Ensuring the Stable Provision of Specified Essential Infrastructure Services (Chapter 3), the System for Support for Development of Specified Critical Technologies (Chapter 4), and the System for Non-Disclosure of Patent Applications (Chapter 5).

4.2.2.1 *The System for Ensuring Stable Supply of Specified Critical Products*

Chapter 2 stipulates that the government shall establish guiding principles for ensuring stable supply of specified critical products (hereinafter referred to as SCPs) to prevent a situation in which the security of the nation and its citizens is undermined due to actions taken from the outside (Article 6).[77] Based on the said guiding principles, the government may designate SCPs by a cabinet order (Article 7). SCPs are considered to meet all four of the following requirements:[78]

(i) The products must be indispensable for the survival of the people or important products on which the people's lives or economic activities widely depend (gravity).

(ii) The products are or threatened to be excessively dependent upon external parties (externality).

75 For the summary of the ESPA, *see*, Cabinet Office, "Keizai Anzen Hoshō Suishin Hō no Gaiyō [Summary of the ESPA]" (Japanese), https://www.cao.go.jp/keizai_anzen_hosho/suishinhou/doc/gaiyo.pdf (accessed Oct. 30, 2024).

76 The basic policy was decided by the Cabinet on September 30, 2022. Cabinet Decision, "Keizai Shisaku wo Ittaiteki ni Kōzuru Koto ni yoru Anzenhoshō no Kakuho no Suishin ni Kansuru Kihontekina Hōshin [Basic Policy on the Promotion of Ensuring National Security through Integrated Implementation of Economic Measures]" (Japanese), Sept. 30, 2022, https://www.cao.go.jp/keizai_anzen_hosho/suishinhou/doc/kihonhoushin.pdf (accessed Oct. 30, 2024).

77 The Cabinet decided the Guiding Principles on September 30, 2022. Cabinet Decision, "Tokutei Jūyō Busshi no Antei teki na Kyōkyū no Kakuho ni Kansuru Kihon Hōshin [The Guiding Principles for Ensuring Stable Supply of Specified Critical Products]" (Japanese), Sept. 30, 2022, https://www.cao.go.jp/keizai_anzen_hosho/suishinhou/doc/kihonshishin1.pdf (accessed Oct. 30, 2024).

78 *Ibid.*, 9–15.

(iii) There is the need to prevent the situation in which external acts undermine the security of the state and its people (probability).
(iv) It is recognized as particularly necessary to ensure the stable supply of the products (necessity).

In December 2022, eleven products were designated as SCPs in the Order for Enforcement of the Act on the Promotion of Ensuring Security Through Integrated Implementation of Economic Measures (Cabinet Order No. 394 of 2022).[79] In addition, in February 2024, advanced electronic components (capacitors and filtering equipment) were newly designated as SCPs, and uranium was added to the already designated critical minerals (Cabinet Order No. 25 of 2024).

The competent minister over SCPs shall formulate the policies on initiatives for ensuring stable supply of each SCP (Article 8).[80] Business entities are required to submit a plan for initiatives to ensure stable supply of SCPs (Article 9). The government provides support to certified entities, including the procurement of the necessary funds to ensure stable supply of SCPs.

4.2.2.2 *The System for Ensuring Stable Provision of Specified Essential Infrastructure Services*

The purpose of the system is stated in the Guiding Principles on Ensuring the Stable Provision of Specified Essential Infrastructure Services (hereinafter refereed as SEISS) by Preventing the Specified Interference Actions.[81] The guiding principles stipulate that "the system is designed to prevent acts that obstruct the stable provision of SEISS from outside Japan with regard to the

79 Eleven products are as follows; Antimicrobial preparations, fertilizer, permanent magnets, machine tools and industrial robots, aircraft parts, semiconductors, storage battery, cloud program, natural gas, critical minerals, and ship components (Art. 1 of the Order).

80 Cabinet Office, "'Antei Kyōkyū Kakuho wo Hakaru Tame no Torikumi Hōshin' oyobi Nintei Kyōkyū Kakuho Keikaku no Gaiyō ['Policies on Initiatives for Ensuring Stable Supply' and Outline of the Certified Plan for Ensuring a Supply]" (Japanese), https://www.cao.go.jp/keizai_anzen_hosho/suishinhou/supply_chain/sc_houshin.html (accessed Oct. 30, 2024).

81 Cabinet Decision, "Tokutei Bōgai Kōi no Bōshi ni yoru Tokutei Shakai Kiban Ekimu no Anteiteki na Teikyō no Kakuho ni Kansuru Kihon Hōshin [Guiding Principles on Ensuring the Stable Provision of Specified Essential Infrastructure Services by Preventing the Specified Interference Actions]" (Japanese), April 28, 2023, https://www.cao.go.jp/keizai_anzen_hosho/suishinhou/doc/kihonshishin2.pdf (accessed Oct. 30, 2024). For the overview of the system, see, Cabinet Office, "System for Ensuring Stable Provision of Specified Essential Infrastructure Services under the Economic Security Promotion Act", Sept. 4, 2024, https://www.cao.go.jp/keizai_anzen_hosho/suishinhou/infra/doc/infra_gaiyou_eng.pdf (accessed Oct. 30, 2024).

introduction of facilities or the outsourcing of maintenance and management, etc., and to ensure the stable provision of SEISS".[82]

Among fifteen services,[83] those services that form the basis of people's lives and economic activities, and whose stable provision, if disrupted, could undermine the security of the state and its people, may be designated by a cabinet order as "specified essential infrastructure businesses." The competent minister may designate as "a specified essential infrastructure service provider (SEIS provider)", a person who engages in specified essential infrastructure businesses (Article 50.1). As of October 17, 2024, 213 enterprises are designated as SEIS providers.[84]

When specified essential infrastructure service providers introduce specified critical facilities (hereinafter refereed as SCFs) from other enterprises or entrust other enterprises to maintain, manage, or operate SCFs, it must prepare and submit a plan to the competent ministry (Article 52.1). If the minister examines the plan and finds that the SCFs are highly likely to be used as a means for specified interference actions, it may recommend or order the operators to change the contents of the plan or to stop introducing or entrusting the facilities (Articles 52.6 and 52.10).

4.2.2.3 *The System for Support for Development of Specified Critical Technologies*

The purpose of the system is "to work towards the promotion of research and development of specific critical technologies (hereinafter refereed as SCTs) and the utilization of their results through cooperation between the public and private sectors".[85] The Guiding Principles on Research and Development

---

82 Cabinet Decision (n 81)

83 As of October 30, 2024, the following fifteen services are designated; Electricity, gas, oil, water supply, railway, motor truck transportation, international maritime cargo, port and harbor transportation, air transport, airport, telecommunications, broadcasting, postal service, financial services, and credit cards. Of these, port and harbor transportation was added by amending the Promotion of Economic Security Act after the cyber-attack on the Nagoya Port Container Terminal in July 2023.

84 Cabinet Office, "Tokutei Shakai Kiban Jigyōsha toshite Shitei sareta Mono [Persons as specified essential infrastructure services providers]" (Japanese), Oct. 17, 2014, https://www.cao.go.jp/keizai_anzen_hosho/suishinhou/infra/doc/infra_jigyousya.pdf (accessed Nov. 4, 2024).

85 Cabinet Decision, "Tokutei Jūyō Gijutsu no Kenkyū Kaihatsu no Sokushin Oyobi Sono Seika no Tekisetsuna Katsuyō ni Kansuru Kihon Shishin [Guiding Principles on Research and Development of the Specified Critical Technologies and the Appropriate Utilization of their Results]" (Japanese) 4, April 28, 2023, https://www.cao.go.jp/keizai_anzen_hosho/suishinhou/doc/kihonshishin3.pdf (accessed Oct. 30, 2024).

of SCTs and the Appropriate Utilization of their Results describe the background of the system as follows; "In recent years, science, technology, and innovation have been at the core of an intensifying struggle for supremacy among nations, and the research and development of advanced and important technologies and the utilization of their results are not only important for the lives of Japanese citizens and economic activities, but are also essential for Japan to maintain a firm position in the international community over the medium and long term".[86]

SCTs are defined as advanced technology that could become critical to maintaining the future lives of the citizenry and economic activity "for which a situation is likely to arise in which the security of the nation and its citizens is undermined if the relevant technology or the information used in research and development thereof is wrongfully used externally, or if the products or services using such technology are dependent on the outside and the stable use of these products or services is no longer possible due to actions taken from the outside" (Article 61).

However, unlike the above-mentioned SCPs, SCTs are only defined abstractly, and no designation system has been established[87]. In this regard, the Guiding Principles point out that "in identifying the targets of SCTs, given the acceleration of technological development due to digitization, etc. and the possibility of discontinuous technological innovation that suddenly creates new important technologies, it is not appropriate to identify SCTs individually in advance, and it is important to consider a wide range of technological domains that may include SCTs".[88]

The government shall endeavor to provide necessary information, secure funding, develop human resources and improve their quality, and take other measures for the promotion of research and development of SCTs and to appropriately utilize the results thereof (Article 61).

4.2.2.4 *System for Non-disclosure of Patent Applications*

Article 61 of the Patent Act (Act No. 121 of 1959) provides that, in principle, after one year and six months have elapsed from the filing date of a patent application, the application shall be published. Under the Guiding Principles

86 *Ibid.*, 3.

87 Kawashima F., "Keisai Anzen Hoshō Hō no Seitei to Ichibu Shikō [Enactment and Partial Enforcement of the Economic Security Promotion Act]" (Japanese), *Hōgaku Kyōshitsu* 508(2022)46.

88 Cabinet Decision (n 85) 9.

for Non-Disclosure of Patent Applications,[89] a non-disclosure system for patent applications was established to prevent the flowing out of information pertaining to "inventions that, if made known to the public, would be highly likely to create a situation to undermine the security of the nation its citizens through actions taken from the outside" (Article 65.1 of the Act).

The system consists of two procedures: review and security designation. Review is conducted in two stages: the first stage is a screening by the Commissioner of the Japan Patent Office (hereinafter referred to as JPO) from the viewpoint of whether the application includes an invention in certain technology fields that, if made known to the public, would be highly likely to create a situation to undermine the security of the nation and its citizens though actions taken from the outside (primary review) (Article 66.1). These fields are called Specified Technology Fields (STFs).[90] The second stage is the security review by the Prime Minister from the viewpoint of whether it is appropriate to protect information pertaining to the patent application sent from the JPO (secondary review) (Article 67.1). Until the security review is completed, the procedures for publication of the application and assessment are suspended (Article 66.7).

If, as a result of a security review, it is appropriate to protect the information, the Prime Minister shall designate the relevant invention as an invention for security designation (Article 70.1). Once the invention is designated, the following legal effects will be generated: prohibition of abandonment or withdrawal of the patent application (Article 72), permission required to work the inventions (Article 73),[91] prohibition of disclosure of the inventions (Article 74), and obligation to properly manage the inventions (Article 75).

89 Cabinet Decision, "Tokkyo Shutsugan Hikōkai Kihon Shishin [Guiding Principles for Non-Disclosure of Patent Applications]" (Japanese), April 28, 2023, https://www.cao.go.jp/keizai_anzen_hosho/suishinhou/doc/kihonshishin4.pdf (accessed Oct. 30, 2024).

90 As of November 7, 2024, twenty-five fields are designated as STFs (Article 12.1 of the Cabinet Order No 259 of 2023).

91 The meaning of "work (*jisshi*)" is the same as that defined in Article 2.3 of the Patent Act. It means (i) if the invention is a product: the act of producing or using it, transferring or leasing it, exporting or importing it, or offering to transfer or lease it, (ii) if the invention is a process: the act of using it, and (iii) if the invention is a process for producing a product: the act of using, transferring or leasing, exporting or importing, or offering to transfer or lease it, beyond what is provided for in the proceeding item.

5 Conclusion

Since the end of World War II, Japan's international economic law has been shaped and developed around the liberal multilateralism of the GATT and WTO. However, the failure of the Doha Round of the WTO has transformed Japan's international economic law policy. A typical manifestation of this is a series of domestic legislation in terms of economic security. While continuing to maintain and respect the multilateral framework, Japan is trying to contribute to the formation of a new international economic legal order through domestic measures of economic security.

However, it is too early to judge that Japan has abandoned multilateralism and steered towards regionalism, bilateralism, or unilateralism. Rather, like other countries, Japan uses a strategic combination of these in line with its own national interests. What multilateral framework can be established in the face of the transformation of the international economic order as indicated by the US-China confrontaion and the rise of emerging countries? Japan's international economic and legal policy is expected to contribute to the establishment of this new framework.

CHAPTER 14

Japan's Response to International Environmental Law: Between Firm Implementation and Minimalism

Yumiko Kaneto

1 Introduction

Geographically, Japan is separated from the Eurasian continent and consists of a chain of islands stretching from north to south. Here, nature has evolved in isolation, resulting in a diverse ecosystem with many endemic species. Approximately 40 percent of land mammals and vascular plants, 60 percent of reptiles, and 80 percent of amphibians in Japan are considered endemic.[1] On the other hand, Conservation International, a prominent non-profit environmental organization, has designated the whole country as one of the biodiversity hotspots in need of immediate attention.[2] According to the definition of a biodiversity hotspot, nature in Japan is rich but deeply threatened, as more than 70 percent of the pristine nature has disappeared due to various reasons, such as rapid and drastic economic development and land use change, to name a few. The Japanese Red List, published by the Ministry of the Environment in 2020, lists more than 3,500 species as endangered. In addition, Japan is also struggling to cope with the growing number of invasive alien species.

From an industrial and economic perspective, Japan experienced a government-led industrial revolution in the late nineteenth century. Industrial development, especially after the end of World War II, brought severe pollution in the 1960s. Modern Japan has been scarce in primary energy, especially fossil fuels, and relies heavily on imports for about 86.7 percent. In turn, the energy self-sufficiency rate is about 12.6 percent, which is relatively

1 Ministry of the Environment, Environmental White Paper 2013 (Japanese).

2 *See*, Conservation International, Biodiversity Hotspots: Targeted investment in nature's most important places, available at: https://www.conservation.org/priorities/biodiversity-hotspots (accessed Jul. 3, 2023).

 | DOI:10.1163/9789004548824_015

low compared to other countries.[3] Maritime transport is the only way to deliver almost all energy resources. No international power grid connection or pipeline carrying gas or oil to/from neighboring countries exists. This peculiar situation and the level of technological development have implications for Japan's policymaking on global warming as it pursues a just transition and decarbonization.

This chapter aims to examine Japan's response to international environmental law. As a premise for the examination, the geographical, natural, social, and industrial circumstances, as briefly described above, cannot be ignored. It may also be necessary to consider Japanese environmental laws developed under domestic circumstances since many of the obligations under environmental treaties require State parties to adopt and implement specific measures within their jurisdiction. The implementation of international environmental law is, in essence, the incorporation of international environmental law into domestic law. This chapter will first provide a brief overview of the development of Japanese environmental law in the next section, and then focus on examining Japan's response to the Multilateral Environmental Agreements (MEAS).

2 Brief History of the Development of Japanese Environmental Law

The historical development of environmental law in Japan consists of three time periods. The first period began from the Meiji era to the 1960s, during which sporadic environmental problems occurred. The government left them unaddressed, giving priority to industrial development. The second period was from the 1970s to the 1980s when the government began to take specific measures against severe pollution. In the early 1970s, the legislature enacted or revised more than ten pollution control laws, establishing the basic structure of Japanese environmental law. Subsequently, however, some stagnation or regression was seen in this development. The third period was from the 1990s and continues to the present. At the beginning of this period, renewed environmental awareness overcame the regression. Developments in international environmental law in this period introduced novel concepts, such as sustainable development, into Japanese domestic policy. At the same time, emerging global environmental issues, such as ozone depletion and global warming, began to require the country to take

3 Ministry of Economy, Trade and Industry, Agency for Natural Resources and Energy, Energy White Paper 2024 (Japanese).

unprecedented actions. Since the 1980s, Japan has successively concluded numerous MEAs and incorporated their norms into domestic law. As a result, it is no longer possible to envisage a purely domestic environmental policy completely free from international influence. The following subsections provide a more nuanced understanding of each period.

2.1 *Before the 1970s*

Initially, mining was the primary source of pollution in Japan. However, the source shifted to various heavy industries, especially after World War II. Since the 1880s, the Japanese mining industry grew considerably but generated significant air, water, and soil pollution. In particular, the pollution caused by mining at the Ashio Copper Mine in Tochigi Prefecture was so severe that it is considered the origin of industrial pollution in Japan. Mining activities at Ashio severely affected agriculture and fishing. The victims repeatedly protested and clashed with police, who treated the protestors as nothing more than rioters. Shozo Tanaka, a Diet member elected in Tochigi Prefecture, appealed to the Diet to investigate and take action against the problem, but to no avail. During that time, neither the public nor the government had awareness of environmental protection. Therefore, it was entirely up to the mining rights holders to decide whether or not to take preventive measures and compensate for the damage caused by the contamination. It was not until the 1970s that the owner company of the Ashio Copper Mine acknowledged responsibility for the pollution.

After World War II, Japan experienced rapid economic growth from 1955 to 1973 (the annual growth rate was over 10 percent). Nevertheless, this economic development brought about severe pollution. The so-called "four major pollution diseases" also occurred during this period. The Itai-itai disease, for example, was caused by a toxic substance called cadmium, which came from a mining plant in Toyama Prefecture. The pollutant affected people through contaminated water, crops, fish, and shellfish. The cause of the Minamata disease in Kumamoto Prefecture was organic mercury. The wastewater from chemical plants contained this deadly poison, which then accumulated in fish. The local people who ate the fish developed severe neurological illnesses, collectively known as Minamata disease.[4] Nine years

4 As of 2021, fewer than 400 of about 3,000 people certified to have Minamata Disease are still alive. *See*, Minamata Disease Archives, available at: http://nimd.env.go.jp/archives/english/ (accessed Jul. 3, 2023). These numbers come from official patients who have met strict criteria set by the government. The actual number of patients suffering from the disease is unknown. To put an end to this problem, the government enacted the Law Concerning Special Measures for Compensation of Minamata Disease (Act No. 81 of 2009, *in*

after the official discovery of Minamata disease, the same mercury poisoning occurred in Niigata Prefecture, called Niigata Minamata disease or the second Minamata disease. The last one is Yokkaichi asthma, caused by air pollution from sulfuric acid-containing smoke emitted from a petrochemical complex in Mie Prefecture.

Again, any specific legal system to prevent or deal with pollution was still not in place. Thus, the victims had to rely on civil tort law, which is a general law, in order to file several lawsuits against the offending companies to seek compensation. They also sued the public authorities for failing to take prompt action.

The increase in industrial pollution forced the government to enact anti-pollution laws since the late 1950s, such as the Water Quality Control Law[5], the Factory Effluent Control Law,[6] and the Smoke and Soot Regulation Law.[7] However, these legislations were not effective enough to stop or reduce pollution. In particular, the first two water quality control laws had fatal flaws. First, a "harmonization clause" in these laws prevented setting environmental regulations that would hinder industrial activities. Second, they required the designation of areas for their application. In practice, the authorities were reluctant to select areas, preferring to prioritize industrial activities. Delays in area designation exacerbated pollution.

Around this time, concerns about intense urbanization and large-scale degradation of nature led to the enactment of the Public Cleansing Law[8] in 1954 and the Natural Parks Act[9] in 1957. For the same reason, amendments to the Wildlife Protection and Hunting Law[10] in 1963 switched its primary purpose from regulating hunting to protecting wildlife.

2.2 *1970–80s*

Over time, the central government began to treat industrial pollution as a national agenda and to tackle it even more seriously. It also came to believe that the goal should be to prevent pollution through proactive regulation rather than to deal with health hazards after they have occurred.

force on July 15, 2009). Over 60,000 people applied for compensation under the law (Ministry of the Environment, Environmental White Paper 2021) (Japanese). However, the law has not completely resolved the issue. Lawsuits brought by officially uncertified but suffering patients are still ongoing.

5 Act No. 181 of 1958, *in force on* March 1, 1959, *repealed on* June 24, 1971.

6 Act No. 182 of 1958, *in force on* March 1, 1959, *repealed on* June 24, 1971.

7 Act No. 146 of 1962, *in force on* December 1, 1962, *repealed on* December 1, 1968.

8 Act No. 72 of 1954, *in force on* July 1, 1954, *repealed on* September 24, 1971.

9 Act No. 161 of 1957, *in force on* October 1, 1957.

10 Act No. 32 of 1918, *in force on* September 1, 1919, *repealed on* April 16, 2003.

In response to this growing awareness, 14 laws related to pollution control were enacted or amended by the National Diet in 1970 (called the "Pollution Diet"). One of them was the Basic Law for Environmental Pollution Control.[11] This law was initially enacted in 1967 and contained a harmonization clause, as seen in the Water Quality Control Law of the 1950s. The 1970 Diet removed the clause from the Basic Law. The Pollution Diet also amended the Air Pollution Control Act[12] and the Natural Parks Act to improve regulation. New laws have also emerged from the Diet, such as the Water Pollution Control Law,[13] Waste Management and Public Cleaning Law (hereinafter referred to as the Waste Management Law),[14] Act on Prevention of Marine Pollution and Maritime Disaster (hereinafter, the Marine Pollution Prevention Law),[15] and Act on Punishment of Crimes to Cause Pollution Harmful to Human Health.[16] The Pollution Diet strengthened the authority of local governments, allowing them to set, by ordinance, more stringent environmental standards than national laws. Collectively, these laws formed the basic framework of the environmental regulatory system in Japan. The year 1971 saw the establishment of the Environment Agency (it became the Ministry of the Environment in 2001). Subsequently, the improvement of environmental regulations continued. For example, the legislature enacted the Nature Conservation Law[17] and introduced a total quantity control system and no-fault liability to air and water pollution laws.

The Oil Crisis in the 70s hit Japan hard and ended its rapid economic growth. As a result, the country had to focus more on business and industry, and the development of environmental law stalled in the late 1970s. For example, the government stopped setting environmental standards for air, water, and noise pollution after 1975; the Environment Agency significantly relaxed environmental standards for NOx in 1978; industry opposition blocked passage of the Environmental Assessment Law in 1983; and the Agency tightened the conditions for certifying patients with pollution-related diseases. On the other hand, growing environmental awareness led to a diversification of environmental litigation. In addition to ex-post-

11 Act No. 132 of 1967, *in force on* August 3, 1967, *repealed on* November 19, 1993.
12 Act No. 97 of 1968, *in force on* December 1, 1968.
13 Act No. 138 of 1970, *in force on* June 24, 1971.
14 Act No. 137 of 1970, *in force on* September 24, 1971.
15 Act No. 136 of 1970, *in force on* June 24, 1971.
16 Act No. 142 of 1970, *in force on* July 1, 1971.
17 Act No. 85 of 1972, *in force on* April 12, 1973.

damage claims, people began to seek injunctions against hazardous or NIMBY (Not in My Back Yard) facilities to prevent the risk of nuisance and pollution.

2.3 *From the 1990s*

The emergence of global environmental issues, such as ozone layer depletion and global warming, and the United Nations Conference on Environment and Development held in 1992 brought a new turn to Japanese environmental law and increased people's interest in environmental issues. The Basic Act on the Environment,[18] enacted in 1993, has changed the basic structure of environmental law. Until then, individual legislation had existed in parallel, and the relationship between the individual laws was unclear. This parallelism lacked a comprehensive view and overlooked the interrelation among various environmental issues. The Basic Act on the Environment has established underlying principles and policy directions and clarified the roles of each social actor, central and local governments, the private sector, and individuals in environmental matters. It also serves as an umbrella law covering most areas of environmental law. While domestic demands to address severe pollution brought the initial development of environmental law in the 1970s, the strong influence of international environmental law shaped the development of domestic law during this period. The ratification of MEAs led to new legislation and numerous amendments to existing laws. New concepts, such as sustainable development, biodiversity, and the precautionary principle, have also influenced the domestic legal system and stimulated its conceptual transformation.[19]

In 2011, the Great East Japan Earthquake struck the Tohoku region and caused meltdowns at the Fukushima Daiichi Nuclear Power Plant. This disaster had an impact on environmental policy. Before the accident, environmental laws, including the Basic Act on the Environment, had excluded the matters of radiation safety or radioactive contamination from their scope of application because Japan had already begun its nuclear policy in the 1950s, long before the establishment of its environmental policy. All matters related to atomic energy had fallen under the jurisdiction of the Ministry of Economy, Trade and Industry. After the accident, Japan reviewed this situation, reallocated authority among relevant ministries, and decided to remove the exclusion clauses from environmental laws.

18 Act No. 91 of 1993, *in force on* November 19, 1993.

19 For example, on the impact of the biodiversity concept, Oikawa H., *Seibutsutayōsei toiu Logic* [The Logic of Biodiversity] (Japanese) (Keiso Shobo, 2010).

Currently, ensuring and promoting nuclear safety is part of environmental policy.

3 Japan's Response to Multilateral Environmental Agreements

This section primarily examines Japan's response to the MEAs it has concluded, except for treaties regulating fisheries, which are covered in Chapter 6 of this volume. Furthermore, this section will not argue the application of MEAs through national judicial process. This section will focus on how the domestic legal system has reacted to the MEAs.

The section is composed of three parts. The first part will show the general status of Japan's ratification of MEAs (Section 3.1). Rather than listing the MEAs that Japan has ratified, this part will focus on the unratified treaties and amendments to outline Japan's overall position on MEAs. The following two parts will discuss how Japan has domestically implemented the MEAs it has ratified and assess the relationship between MEAs and domestic environmental law. This examination will include an analysis of the forms of domestic acceptance of MEAs (Section 3.2) and an explanation of some trends in Japan's implementation (Section 3.3).

Before entering the subsection, let us briefly discuss Japan's perception of some principles of international environmental law: the precautionary principle/approach and the polluter-pays principle.

How has Japan recognized and applied the precautionary principle? The answer is not crystal clear. Japan's Basic Act on the Environment, influenced by the 1992 Rio Conference, enumerates the fundamental principles of environmental law and policy in Articles 3 to 5 but does not directly incorporate the precautionary principle of the Rio Declaration. Instead, this principle has been mentioned in official planning documents such as the Basic Environment Plan elaborated by the government since 2006 as an overall guiding directive in areas of biodiversity conservation, global warming countermeasures, ozone layer protection, creation of a sound material circle society, and chemical management. At least to a limited extent, it can be said that Japan has recognized and accepted the precautionary principle through the ratification of MEAs that enshrine it or have specific systems that reflect the principle.

It is generally accepted that the polluter-pays principle was first articulated in the 1972 OECD "Council Recommendation on Guiding Principles Concerning the International Economic Aspects of Environmental Policies." This principle, in its original form, called for the internalization of externalities and the prohibition of public subsidies for pollution prevention and control costs. On the other hand, Japan established a unique polluter-pays principle in the 1970s as part of its ex-post response to the devastating pollution damages of the 1950s and 1960s. This Japanese principle has been considered the legal basis for relief provided to victims of pollution-related illnesses. This is why the scope of costs to be borne by polluters is not limited to pollution control measures but also includes environmental restoration costs and damage relief (both health damage and other material damage).

3.1 *Overview of Japan's Status in Ratifying MEAS*

While Japan has been a party to several prominent MEAS, there are few international agreements to which Japan is not a party or from which Japan withdrew. The unconcluded MEAS include the Convention on the Conservation of Migratory Species of Wild Animals (hereinafter, the Bonn Convention),[20] Protocol on Liability and Compensation for Damage Resulting from Transboundary Movements of Hazardous Wastes and Their Disposal,[21] Protocol relating to Intervention on the High Seas in Cases of Pollution by Substances other than Oil,[22] and Convention on the Law of Non-Navigational Uses of International Watercourses(hereinafter, the Watercourses Convention).[23] There are also some regional MEAS whose membership is open to countries outside the relevant region or institution. For example, the Convention on Environmental Impact Assessment in a Transboundary Context (hereinafter, the Espoo Convention)[24] and the Convention on Access to Information, Public Participation in Decision-making and Access to Justice in Environmental Matters (hereinafter, the Aarhus Convention),[25] both adopted by United Nations Economic Commission for Europe (UNECE), provide for procedures for non-UNECE members to become parties to them. If Japan were willing to join, accession to these treaties would be possible. At present, however, Japan has not acceded to any of them.

20 *Signed on* June 23, 1979, *entered into force on* November 1, 1983, 1651 UNTS 333.

21 *Adopted on* December 10, 1999, not yet in force, UNEP/CHW.5/29, Annex III.

22 *Adopted on* November 2, 1973, *entered into force on* March 30, 1983, 1313 UNTS 3.

23 *Adopted on* May 21, 1997, *entered into force on* August 17, 2014, 2999 UNTS 77.

24 *Signed on* February 25, 1991, *entered into force on* September 10, 1997, 1989 UNTS 309. For the membership, *see* Arts. 16-17.

25 *Signed on* June 25, 1998, *entered into force on* October 30, 2001, 2161 UNTS 447. For the membership, *see* Art. 19-3.

An example of an environmental agreement from which Japan withdrew is the International Convention for the Regulation of Whaling,[26] which is discussed in Chapter 6 of this volume. Moreover, the amendments that Japan has not ratified include the Ban Amendment[27] to the Basel Convention on the Control of Transboundary Movements of Hazardous Wastes and their Disposal (hereinafter, the Basel Convention),[28] which aims for a total ban on the export of hazardous waste from Annex VII countries to non-Annex VII countries; the Gaborone Amendment[29] to the Convention on International Trade in Endangered Species of Wild Fauna and Flora (hereinafter, the CITES),[30] which allows international organizations such as the European Union to accede to the Convention. In addition, Japan has reservations about several species listed in Appendices I and II of the CITES.

A close examination of the unratified treaties and amendments reveals that Japan has been reluctant to accept international norms for marine conservation, especially that of living marine resources. This reluctance has underpinned its diplomatic positions not only on fisheries treaties but also on other agreements. For example, while the Bonn Convention requires the parties to prohibit the taking of species listed in Appendix I and to take immediate protective measures for these species, the fact that Japan keeps fishing and bycatching green turtles, seabirds, and cetaceans listed in the Appendix prevents it from acceding to the Convention.[31] In the CITES, all species that Japan currently has reservations are marine creatures.[32] Japan has taken the position of promoting sustainable use of marine resources based on scientific data. Japan makes reservations when it believes that no scientific data proves the degree of endangerment of a given species or that the information itself is insufficient for listing in Appendix I or II. The Government of Japan has opposed the Ban Amendment to the Basel Convention since its adoption. The country is cautious about this amendment, arguing that a total ban on waste exports to non-Annex VII Parties with

26 *Signed on* December 2, 1946, *entered into force on* November 10, 1948, 161 UNTS 72. Japan acceded on April 21, 1951, and withdrew on June 30, 2019.

27 *Adopted on* September 22, 1995, *in force on* December 5, 2019, UNTS A-28911.

28 *Signed on* March 22, 1989, *entered into force on* May 5, 1992, 1673 UNTS 57. Japan acceded on September 17, 1993.

29 *Adopted on* April 30, 1983, *in force on* November 29, 2013, 2993 UNTS 85.

30 *Signed on* March 3, 1973, *entered into force on* July 1, 1975, 993 UNTS 243.

31 Government statement to the House of Representatives Environment Committee, June 6, 2014.

32 10 species of whales in Appendix I and 15 species of sharks and other marine organisms in Appendix II.

adequate processing capacity could impede the effective transboundary use of resources.[33] As for the Watercourses Convention, Japan has not even signed it due to its geographical circumstances. Japan's position on some unratified treaties and amendments is unclear. In the case of UNECE treaties, there are few examples of non-UNECE States subscribing to them.[34] So far, political momentum for ratifying these treaties has not yet developed in Japan.

3.2 *Analysis of the Forms of Domestic Acceptance of MEAS*

How has Japan implemented the MEAS it has ratified?[35] After providing a general discussion of Japan's methods of accepting treaties, including MEAS, this subsection will detail several patterns and trends of domestic implementation of MEAS.

Generally, Japan adopts the doctrine of incorporation for international law (treaties and international customs) to be effective in the domestic legal system. Logically, therefore, it is not necessary to convert the content of the former into the latter to introduce binding international norms into the domestic arena. However, in the case of environmental treaties, national legislation is often considered necessary to apply the treaties in its jurisdictional areas. There are mainly two reasons for this: the first comes from constitutional requirements, and the second derives from the content of the provisions of international environmental law.

The first is that the Constitution of Japan[36] requires legislation to regulate certain matters. The principle of legality of crime and punishment (Article 31) is a typical illustration of such a requirement. Based on this principle,

33 Tsuruta J., "Kokusai Risaikuru wo Meguru Seido Henyō: Asia wo Chūsin ni [Institutional Changes in International Recycle: With Special References to Asia]" (Japanese), *Kenkyū Sōsho* 586 (2010) Institute of Developing Economies, Japan External Trade Organization, 21.

34 The amendment to the Espoo Convention to open the Convention to accession by member States of the United Nations that are not members of the UNECE has been in force since 2014. However, the amendment is not yet operational (Art. 17-3). Concerning the Aarhus Convention, Guinea-Bissau has become the first and so far only country outside the pan-European region to have acceded to the Convention.

35 In recent years, the implementation of MEAS by Japan has been an area of active research in the country: *Shinsedai Hōseisakugaku Kenkyū* [Hokkaido Journal of New Global Law and Policy] (Japanese), Vol. 4–18, 2009–2012; *Ronkyū Jurist* [Quarterly Jurist] (Japanese), No. 7 (2013) and No. 19 (2016); *Kankyō Hōseisaku Gakkai-shi* [Journal of Environmental Law and Policy] (Japanese), especially its No. 23 (2020). This subsection and the following are grounded mainly in these studies.

36 *Promulgated on* November 3, 1946, *in force on* May 3, 1947.

criminal law-related provisions in MEAs (for example, Article 4 of the International Convention for the Prevention of Pollution from Ships of 1973 as modified by the Protocol of 1978 (hereinafter, the MARPOL 73/78)[37] and Article 9.5 of the Basel Convention) necessarily require legislation for their application. Another is the principle of law-based administration, which derives from the doctrine of the separation of powers (Articles 41, 65, and 76 of the Constitution). This principle commands administrative activities to be in accordance with laws. Therefore, when the administration fulfills an international obligation by managing and controlling private actors or imposing certain obligations on them, it needs a basis in legislation.

The second reason for the need for national legislation stems from the content of the MEAs themselves. The addressees of provisions in environmental treaties are primarily the State parties, and many articles tend to be abstract and qualitative. In many cases, they only establish obligations for results and leave the means to achieve the results to the discretion of the State parties. Because of the inadequacy or vagueness of the treaty provisions, national legislation is often indispensable to embody the essence of the treaties and to give them effect.

Due to this dual requirement, it is common in Japan to have domestic legislation in place to implement MEAs. In other words, in practice, very little consideration is given to the direct applicability of treaty articles. When the government finds a possibility to ratify a treaty, the relevant national authorities immediately consider how to prepare internal implementing measures[38].

Japanese policy in treaty implementation is known as the "*kanzen-tanpo-syugi*" [tentative translation: full guarantee approach], which means that once Japan decides to ratify a given treaty, it takes all necessary measures prior to the ratification to ensure full implementation of the treaty. Specifically, there are several approaches to fulfill this policy: (a) the government may reuse existing domestic laws without change, (b) revise existing laws to conform to the conventions, or (c) enact brand new legislation. Cases in which it (d) employs sub-legislative norms or (e) takes no legal action are rare.

---

37 The Convention was signed on November 2, 1973, not in force, 12 ILM 1319; the Protocol, *signed on* February 17, 1978, *in force on* October 2, 1983, 1340 UNTS 61. Japan acceded on June 9, 1983.

38 Matsuda M., "Jitsumu toshite no Jōyaku Teiketsu Tetuduki [Treaty Conclusion Procedures as Practice]" (Japanese), *Shinsedai Hōseisakugaku Kenkyū* [Hokkaido Journal of New Global Law and Policy] 10 (2011) 317–319.

Instances where the approach (a) was taken include the Ramsar Convention on Wetlands of International Importance especially as Waterfowl Habitat (hereinafter, the Ramsar Convention),[39] the Convention Concerning the Protection of the World Cultural and Natural Heritage (hereinafter, the World Heritage Convention),[40] the Convention on Biological Diversity (hereafter, the CBD),[41] and the Convention on Persistent Organic Pollutants (hereinafter, the POPs Convention).[42] A combination of existing laws plays a role in implementing the Ramsar Convention: the Wildlife Protection, Control, and Hunting Management Act (hereinafter, Wildlife Protection Act),[43] the Law for the Protection of Cultural Properties,[44] and the Natural Parks Act. The implementation of the World Heritage Convention also uses existing laws as they are. The Law for the Protection of Cultural Properties with others regulates the protection of cultural heritages. For natural heritage sites, the Nature Conservation Act and the Natural Parks Act, among others, are mobilized. In the case of the CBD, it was judged at the time of ratification that there was no need to amend or abolish existing laws or establish new ones, as Japan already had sufficient legal frameworks for biodiversity conservation. The same was true for the POPs Convention. Related authorities considered it possible to implement the Convention without changing existing legislation: the Act on the Regulation of Manufacture and Evaluation of Chemical Substances (hereinafter, the Chemical Substance Control Act),[45] the Agricultural Chemicals Regulation Act,[46] and the Act on Securing Quality, Efficacy and Safety of Products Including Pharmaceuticals and Medical Devices[47] are used to prohibit and restrict the production and use of targeted substances (Art. 3); the Law for the Control of Export, Import and Others of Specified Hazardous Wastes and Other Wastes (called as the Basel Law)[48] and the Foreign Exchange and

39 *Signed on* February 2, 1971, *in force on* December 21, 1975, 996 UNTS 245, to which Japan acceded on June 17, 1980.

40 *Signed on* November 16, 1972, *in force on* December 17, 1975, 1037 UNTS 151. Japan accepted on June 30, 1992.

41 *Adopted on* June 5, 1992, *in force on* December 29, 1993, 1760 UNTS 79. Japan accepted on May 28, 1993.

42 *Signed on* May 22, 2001, *in force on* May 17, 2004, 2256 UNTS 119. Japan acceded on August 30, 2002.

43 Act No. 88 of 2002, *in force on* April 16, 2003.

44 Act No. 214 of 1950, *in force on* August 29, 1950.

45 Act No. 117 of 1973, *in force on* April 16, 1974.

46 Act No. 82 of 1948, *in force on* August 1, 1948.

47 Act No. 145 of 1960, *in force on* February 1, 1961.

48 Act No. 108 of 1992, *in force on* December 16, 1993.

Foreign Trade Act[49] for regulating imports and exports of the substances; the Act on Special Measures against Dioxins[50] operates for the reduction of releases from unintentionally generated dioxins; the Waste Management Law and the Act on Special Measures Concerning Promotion of Proper Treatment of PCB Wastes[51] and Soil Contamination Countermeasures Act[52] for reducing or eliminating releases from stockpiles and wastes (Art. 6).

Cases of the approach (b) include the Convention on the Prevention of Marine Pollution by Dumping of Wastes and Other Matter (hereinafter, the London Convention)[53] and the 1996 Protocol to the Convention.[54] The implementation of these two led to the amendment of the Marine Pollution Prevention Law and the Waste Management Law. For the Nagoya-Kuala Lumpur Supplementary Protocol on Liability and Redress to the Cartagena Protocol on Biosafety,[55] the Act on the Conservation and Sustainable Use of Biological Diversity through Regulations on the Use of Living Modified Organisms (the 'Cartagena Act'),[56] which is the law governing the enforcement of the Cartagena Protocol, was amended.

In the case of (a) and (b), the relevant laws are given the function not only as a domestic norm but also as a norm undertaking the implementation of the treaty. As a result, the State must maintain these legislations, unable to make amendments that would undermine their nature as laws for treaty implementation.[57]

An example of (c) is the Montreal Protocol on Substances that Deplete the Ozone Layer (hereinafter, the Montreal Protocol)[58]. Since the objective of the Protocol is not to protect national interests but global ones, the government considered existing pollution-related laws ill-suited to regulate CFCs and other substances covered by the Protocol, resulting in new

49 Act No. 228 of 1949, *in force on* June 30, 1950.

50 Act No. 105 of 1999, *in force on* January 15, 2000.

51 Act No. 65 of 2001, *in force on* July 15, 2001.

52 Act No. 53 of 2002, *in force on* February 15, 2003.

53 *Signed on* December 29, 1972, *in force on* August 30, 1975, 1046 UNTS 120. Japan ratified on October 15, 1980.

54 *Signed on* November 7, 1996, *in force on* March 24, 2006. Japan acceded on October 2, 2007.

55 *Signed on* October 15, 2010, *in force on* March 5, 2018, UNTS A-30619. Japan accepted on December 5, 2017.

56 Act No. 97 of 2003, *in force on* February 19, 2004.

57 Matsuda M., *supra* note 38, 305–309.

58 *Signed on* September 16, 1987, *in force on* January 1, 1989, 1522 UNTS 3. Japan accepted on September 30, 1988.

legislation, the Act on the Protection of the Ozone Layer Through the Control of Specified Substances, etc. and Other Measures[59] in 1988. As for the Basel Convention, the existing relevant legislation, the domestic Waste Management Law, could not be used directly to implement the Convention because the definition of waste in the Convention did not match the domestic one. This difference in the basic concept brought about the so-called Basel Law. Concerning the Cartagena Protocol on Biosafety,[60] although relevant national guidelines already existed, they were not enough to cover the entire contents of the Protocol. As a result, the government opted to enact new legislation called the Cartagena Act in 2004.

Moreover, an example of (d) is the Nagoya Protocol on Access to Genetic Resources and the Fair and Equitable Sharing of Benefits Arising from their Utilization to the Convention on Biological Diversity.[61] Without new legislation, only the Guidelines on Access to Genetic Resources and the Fair and Equitable Sharing of Benefits Arising from their Utilization (the ABS Guidelines),[62] a joint notice issued by the six relevant ministries, was prepared to address the Protocol.

Finally, an example of (e) is the United Nations Convention to Combat Desertification in Those Countries Experiencing Serious Drought and/or Desertification, Particularly in Africa.[63] Japan is not in a position to apply the Convention domestically but to assist countries facing desertification (Articles 6, 9.2, and 20). Consequently, Japan has not taken any particular domestic measures to implement the Convention but has contributed to relevant international organizations and provided bilateral assistance through Official Development Assistance (ODA).

The choice of approach among the above five depends on several factors: the contents of the treaty, whether to exist legislation relevant to the treaty, the results of verification of the treaty contents against the existing domestic laws, the distribution of authority among the relevant ministries, to name a few. To take advantage of limited administrative resources and to focus on existing national laws and their structures, in general, Japan first

59 Act No. 53 of 1988, *in force on* May 20, 1988.

60 *Signed on* January 29, 2000, *in force on* September 11, 2003, 2226 UNTS 208. Japan accepted on November 21, 2003.

61 *Signed on* October 29, 2010, *in force on* October 12, 2014, 3008 UNTS 3. Japan accepted on May 22, 2017.

62 *In force on* August 20, 2017.

63 *Signed on* June 17, 1994, *in force on* December 26, 1996, 1954 UNTS 3. Japan acceded on September 11, 1998.

examines the possibility of taking approach (a), then considers (b), and lastly (c).[64] The priority is given to integrate treaty norms without distorting the existing domestic legal system as much as possible. To our knowledge, there is no example of a complete overhaul of legislation to implement a specific treaty.

The approaches (a) through (e) merely enumerate ways to implement a treaty in the domestic legal system. In practice, it does not usually result in one law corresponding to one MEA, as was shown in the national implementation of the POPs Convention. Domestic implementation for a single convention often requires to use several approaches simultaneously. For example, the Basel Convention induced the amendment to the Waste Management Law, the creation of the Basel Law, and the mobilization of the Foreign Exchange and Foreign Trade Act. In the case of the Minamata Convention on Mercury,[65] its implementation needed to enact the Act on Preventing Mercury Pollution of the Environment,[66] amended the Air Pollution Control Act, and used the Water Pollution Control Law without alteration. Thus, all three methods from (a) to (c) were required to make these MEAs applicable.

Putting in place a domestic implementation scheme prior to the ratification is not necessarily the end of the story. Sometimes, additional ex-post measures may supplement the established legal system to address deficiencies or inadequacies in Japan's implementation practices or international amendments to conventions. For example, the Act on Rational Use and Appropriate Management of Fluorocarbons[67] was enacted in 2001, more than ten years after Japan ratified the Montreal Protocol, to achieve the Protocol's objective in a more appropriate manner. Similarly, the Act on Conservation of Endangered Species of Wild Fauna and Flora[68] was established for the CITES in 1992 to combat domestic wildlife smuggling that violates the Convention. The amendment to the Chemical Substance Control Act in 2009 aimed to respond to the amendments to the Annexes to the POPs

64 Koyano M, et al., "Nihon ni okeru Kankyō Jōyaku no Kokunai Jisshi: Panel Discussion [Domestic Implementation of Environmental Treaties in Japan]" (Japanese), *Journal of Environmental Law and Policy*, 23 (2020) 128–131.

65 *Signed on* October 10, 2013, *in force on* August 16, 2017, 3201 UNTS 3. Japan accepted on February 2, 2016.

66 Act No. 42 of 2015, *in force on* August 16, 2017.

67 Act No. 64 of 2001, *in force on* April 1, 2002.

68 Act No. 75 of 1992, *in force on* April 1, 1993.

Convention. An assessment reveals that the amendment to this Chemical Act brought the Act closer to the content of the Convention.[69]

A review of how Japan has incorporated various MEAs into its domestic laws reveals several patterns. One is the way to respond to trade restrictions in MEAs (for example, the Rotterdam Convention on the Prior Informed Consent Procedure for Certain Hazardous Chemicals and Pesticides in International Trade,[70] POPs Convention, Minamata Convention, Montreal Protocol, Basel Convention, CITES, and Cartagena Protocol). Japan has used ordinary trade control systems under the Foreign Exchange and Foreign Trade Act and the Customs Act,[71] and these domestic systems have ensured proper imports and exports at the border following the MEAs, except for the Cartagena Protocol. The Cartagena Law, enacted for the Cartagena Protocol, does not provide for customs inspection of living modified organisms (LMOs) at the time of import and export.[72] The reason is that, in practice, customs officials can't confirm whether the cargo contains LMOs. The case of conventions that include zoning, such as the Ramsar Convention and World Heritage Convention, has also formed a pattern: the use of several existing laws that adopt the same zoning approach without modification. Because some legal schemes for designating and protecting areas were already in place before the ratification of these conventions, and no new legislation was deemed necessary.

Another tendency is the way to implement the many IMO conventions on vessel-source pollution: the Marine Pollution Prevention Law and its amendments have played a central role in undertaking these treaty norms. The predecessor to this law also had served a similar function, allowing Japan to ratify the 1954 International Convention for the Prevention of Pollution of the Sea by Oil (hereinafter, the OILPOL).[73] The current Act, established in 1970, ensures the implementation of various IMO conventions such as the International Convention Relating to Intervention on the High Seas

69 Masuzawa Y., "Stockholm Jōyaku no Kokunai Jisshi: Kokunai Kankyōhō no Shiten kara [Domestic Implementation of the Stockholm Treaty: a Perspective from Domestic Environmental Law]" (Japanese), *Shinsedai Hōseisakugaku Kenkyū* [Hokkaido Journal of New Global Law and Policy] 9 (2010) 239–243.

70 *Signed on* September 11, 1998, *in force on* February 24, 2004, 2244 UNTS 337. Japan ratified on June 15, 2004.

71 Act No. 61 of 1954, *in force on* June 1, 1954.

72 Although, it does provide for obligations such as prior notification for imports, that do not constitute border control enforcement.

73 *Signed on* May 12, 1954, *in force on* July 26, 1958, 327 UNTS 3. Japan ratified on August 21, 1967.

in Cases of Oil Pollution Casualties,[74] MARPOL 73/78, the International Convention on Oil Pollution Preparedness, Response and Co-operation (OPRC Convention),[75] the Protocol to the OPRC Convention on Preparedness, Response and Co-operation to Pollution Incidents by Hazardous and Noxious Substances,[76] the London Convention and its Protocol, and the International Convention for The Control and Management of Ships' Ballast Water and Sediments.[77]

Similarly, there seems to be another common practice when MEAs leave the means, methods, and extent of implementation to the discretion of the contracting parties, including cases where MEAs set only obligations of results. For example, in response to agreements on global warming (the United Nations Framework Convention on Climate Change,[78] Kyoto Protocol,[79] and Paris Agreement[80]) and the CBD, Japan takes the approach of formulating plans based on legislation, which are updated every several years.[81] Regarding treaties on climate change, Japan passed the Act on Promotion of Global Warming Countermeasures[82] in October 1998. While the Act itself does not contain any concrete global warming countermeasures, it does require the government to prepare a planning document outlining the specific measures. The plan for the first commitment period of the Kyoto Protocol was named the Kyoto Protocol Target Achievement Plan. After this first period, its name changed to the Global Warming Action Plan, as Japan decided not to participate in the second commitment period. Since measures to combat global warming cut across various policy

74 *Signed on* November 29, 1969, *in force on* May 6, 1975, 970 UNTS 211. Japan accepted on June 4, 1971.

75 *Adopted on* November 30, 1990, *in force on* May 13, 1995, 1891 UNTS I-32194. Japan acceded on October 17, 1995.

76 *Adopted on* March 15, 2000, *in force on* June 14, 2007, UNTS I-56797. Japan acceded on March 9, 2007.

77 *Adopted on* February 13, 2004, *in force on* September 8, 2017, UNTS I-55544. Japan acceded on October 10, 2014.

78 *Adopted on* May 9, 1992, *in force on* March 24, 1994, 1771 UNTS 107. Japan accepted on May 28, 1993.

79 *Signed on* December 11, 1997, *in force on* February 16, 2005, 2303 UNTS 162. Japan accepted on May 4, 2002.

80 *Signed on* December 12, 2015, *in force on* November 4, 2016, 3156 UNTS 79. Japan accepted on November 18, 2016.

81 The planning approach is a major, but not only, way to implement the global warming treaties and the CBD. Various individual laws are also involved in the implementation of these treaties.

82 Act No. 117 of 1998, *in force on* April 8, 1999.

areas, all relevant ministries and agencies submit medium-term measures under their respective areas of responsibility and compile them in the planning document.[83] The implementation of the CBD also follows the same approach: Article 6 of the Convention obliges States to develop strategic documents, but it is left to each party to decide what measures to take and to what extent is required for biodiversity conservation. In Japan, now based on the Basic Act on Biodiversity,[84] the Ministry of Environment, in collaboration with other relevant authorities, prepares and updates the National Biodiversity Strategy. Such strategies have reflected non-binding international strategic plans adopted periodically under the CBD (2002 Strategic Plan adopted at COP6, 2010 Aichi Targets at COP10, and 2022 Global Biodiversity Framework at COP15).

The treaty implementation through legally mandated planning documents has advantages but also disadvantages.[85] One advantage is that, in contrast to legislation, administrative planning instruments are prompt and flexible to prepare, revise, and enforce. In addition, issues such as global warming and biodiversity conservation require cross-ministerial efforts, and the formulation and implementation of the plans contribute to enhancing cooperation among the relevant ministries. On the other hand, some disadvantages are also evident. Each measure in these plans rests not directly on legislation, and its content and effectiveness depend on the discretion of the responsible ministry. The Global Warming Action Plan leaves measures for the energy conversion and industrial sectors mainly to voluntary efforts by industry associations, even though these sectors are responsible for more than 60 percent of Japan's greenhouse gas emissions. While the government periodically reviews the progress of these efforts, it does not scrutinize the adequacy of the emission reduction targets set by these private actors. In addition, there is no sanction for failing to meet targets. Such a

83 The same approach is in place for climate change adaptation: the Climate Change Adaptation Act (Act No. 50 of 2018, *in force on* December 1, 2018) requires the adoption of national and local adaptation plans.

84 Act No. 58 of 2008, *in force on* June 6, 2008.

85 Fujikura R., "Seibutsu Tayōsei Jōyaku to Cartagena Giteisyo [Convention of Biological Diversity and Cartagena Protocol]" (Ch. 6) (Japanese), in Nishii M. (ed.), *Chikyū Kankyō Jōyaku* [Global Environmental Agreements] (Yuhikaku, 2005) 128–130; Takamura Y., "Kankyō Jōyaku no Kokunai Jisshi: Kokusaihō no Shiten kara" (Japanese), *Ronkyū Jurist* [Quarterly Jurist] 7 (2013) 73–75; Takamura Y. "Kyoto Giteisyo to Paris Kyōtei [Kyoto Protocol and Paris Agreement]" (Japanese), *Ronkyū Jurist* [Quarterly Jurist] 19 (2016) 62–64; Otsuka T., *Kankyō-hō* (Japanese), 4th ed., (Yuhikaku, 2020) 618–621, 783–785.

voluntary bottom-up approach certainly has its advantages in facilitating the transition without placing undue burdens on industries. However, in terms of fairness and consistency, it is not without problems.

3.3 *General Trends in the Implementation of MEAs*

While the previous subsection examined Japan's implementation of MEAs by methodology, this part will discuss more general characteristics. As mentioned earlier, Japan has adopted the so-called full guarantee approach. Therefore, Japan tries to incorporate the contents of the conventions into its domestic laws as carefully and precisely as possible. In practice, ministries examine whether domestic backing measures ensure the full implementation of all treaty provisions. Thus, Japan's enforcement of MEAs is generally precise and faithful to the treaty text, aiming at reliable and firm implementation (Section 3.3.1). However, at the same time, Japan tends to be minimalist in treaty implementation (Section 3.3.2), occasionally lacking a holistic view of realizing the ultimate purposes of the treaty. The following elaborates on these two interrelated aspects.

3.3.1 Firm Implementation

The full guarantee approach taken by Japan is most effective at the time of the conclusion of a treaty. Therefore, this country tends to fall into a "static" legal formalism that relies heavily on legal interpretation at the time of treaty conclusion. However, the norms of environmental treaties are generally 'dynamic' in nature, evolving through decisions and resolutions adopted by the conference of the parties (COP) or other internal institutions, as well as amendments to MEAs. Japan has sometimes responded inadequately or too slowly to this evolving nature of MEAs. For example, the definition of wetlands in the Ramsar Convention (Art. 1) later broadened through documents adopted by the COPs: the Criteria for Identifying Wetlands of International Importance and the Classification System for Wetland Type. However, Japan used only the waterbird-based criteria (Criterion 5–6) in the Criteria document, and for many years only designated waterfowl-related wetlands.[86] It was not until COP7 in 1999 that Japan changed its position.

---

86 Isozaki H., "Kokusai-Kankyōhō to Kokunai Kankyōhō [International Environmental Law and Domestic Environmental Law]" (Japanese), in Otsuka T. and Kitamura Y. (eds.), *Kankyō Hōgaku no Chōsen* [Challenges in Environmental Legal Studies] (Nippon Hyoron sha, 2002) 229–232; Toi A., "Seibutsu Tayōsei Hozen • Shizen Hogo Jōyaku no Kokunai Jisshi: Ramsar Jōyaku no Kokunai Jisshi wo Sozai toshite [Domestic

Systematic and blatant treaty violations are generally unlikely to occur in Japan because of the meticulous preparation for enforcing MEAs. However, this does not mean that Japan's treaty implementation is perfect. Inconsistencies between treaties and corresponding domestic laws may arise for various reasons.

For example, Japan's implementation of CITES in the early years was highly inadequate. Japan was criticized internationally for being insincere and unenthusiastic about implementing the Convention. One of the reasons for the criticism was that Japan had applied the same procedures to species listed in Appendices II and III of the Convention. Subsequent amendments to the relevant administrative regulations corrected this unlawful practice.[87] Even in recent years, Japan has had some issues with the Convention. In 2018, the CITES Standing Committee found Japan in non-compliance with the Convention for the "introduction from the sea" of sei whales listed in Appendix I (CITES, SC70 Sum. 3 (Rev. 1)). Japan subsequently reported corrective measures. In addition, Japan has not taken sufficient action to respond to the recommendation (Conf. 10.10 (Rev. COP17)) to close the domestic market for ivory.

Similarly, the Basel Convention provides for ship-back obligations when a transboundary movement of hazardous waste cannot be completed contractually or in the event of illegal traffic (Arts. 8 and 9). As far as national law is concerned, the Basel Law reflects these obligations in Article 17. However, this article contains an additional requirement for a national authority to issue a ship-back order "when it is found particularly necessary in order to prevent damage to human health or the living environment". There is no such requirement for ship-backs under the Convention. Therefore, the decision of a Japanese authority to issue a ship-back order could differ from the interpretation of the Convention. The additional requirement was seemingly necessary to balance the legal conditions that cause such an order in other environmental laws.[88] There is a separate concern about Japan's implementation

Implementation of Conventions for the Conservation of Biological Diversity and for Protecting Nature: With Special References to the Domestic Implementation of the Ramsar Convention]" (Japanese), *Ronkyū Jurist* [Quarterly Jurist] 7 (2013) 50–52.

87 Kaneko Y., "Washington Jōyaku [Washington Convention]" (Japanese) in Nishii M. (ed.), *supra* note 85, 108–113; Kamigawara K., "Jōyaku Jisshi wo Tūjita Kokunai • Kokusai Sōhōkō no Henka: Washington Jōyaku Seido Jisshi wo Rei toshite" (Japanese), *Shinsedai Hōseisakugaku Kenkyū* [Hokkaido Journal of New Global Law and Policy] 12 (2011) 200–207.

88 Shimamura K., "Kokusai Kankyō Jōyaku no Kokunai Jisshi: Basel Jōyaku no Baai [Domestic Implementation of International Environmental Conventions: The Case of

of the Basel Convention. Annexes XI and VIII of the Convention are helpful tools for determining whether an object is subject to the Convention, and there is no hierarchy between the two. However, in practice, Japan prioritizes Annex XI over the other, which may lead to a discrepancy with the Convention in assessing hazardous waste covered by the Convention.[89]

3.3.2 Minimalism

Incorporating MEAs into domestic law in the least cumbersome way possible can also be described as minimalism. Accordingly, when several options are available, the priority is to use domestic law as it is, without any changes, *i.e.*, approach (a) explained above. However, this approach may pose problems because it is rare for the ultimate objectives of existing laws to coincide entirely with those of conventions. Inconsistencies between the two may lead to misinterpretation or non-compliance with a given MEA. Japan has used this approach in implementing, for example, the Ramsar Convention and World Heritage Convention. In the case of the former, "wise use", a fundamental concept of the Convention, is not explicitly reflected or implied anywhere in the comparable national legislation. This gap could lead to a potential risk of inconsistency between the purpose of the Convention and its national implementation.[90] Regarding the latter, the Law for the Protection of Cultural Properties, one of the implementing laws of the Convention, has subsequently revised its criteria for the designation of historic sites to make it align with the Convention.[91]

Japan's minimalist approach implies fidelity to treaty texts. Accordingly, preparations for treaty implementation are generally limited to the minimum level necessary to fulfill treaty obligations, *i.e.*, no more and no less. In some exceptional cases, however, the laws implementing the MEAs, such as the Cartagena Law for the Cartagena Protocol and the Act on Preventing Mercury Pollution of the Environment adopted for the Minamata Convention on Mercury, impose more stringent obligations than the Conventions.

Basel Convention]" (Japanese) *Shinsedai Hōseisakugaku Kenkyū* [Hokkaido Journal of New Global Law and Policy] 9 (2010) 154–164.

89 Tsuruta J., "Nihon niokeru Basel Jōyaku no Jisshi to sono Kadai [Implementation of Basel Convention in Japan and Its Challenges]" (Japanese) *Shinsedai Hōseisakugaku Kenkyū* [Hokkaido Journal of New Global Law and Policy] 9 (2010) 114–118.

90 Toi (n 86), 52.

91 Shimamura K., "Kankyō Jōyaku no Kokunai Jisshi: Kokunaihō no Shiten kara [Implementation of Environmental Conventions: From the Perspective of Domestic Law]" (Japanese), *Ronkyū Jurist* [Quarterly Jurist] 7 (2013) 86, note 30.

The Cartagena Protocol provides for the Advance Informed Agreement (AIA) procedure for intentional transboundary movements of LMOs (Art. 7-10, 12), which demands risk assessments. However, the Protocol excludes pharmaceuticals for human use from its application (Art. 5), and the AIA procedure does not apply to LMOs for food or feed (Art. 7-2, 3). In contrast to the Protocol, even LMOs for food and feed must undergo risk assessments under the Cartagena Law. In addition, the Ministry of Health, Labour and Welfare has issued notices requiring biodiversity assessments for LMOs in the pharmaceutical sector.[92]

The Act on Preventing Mercury Pollution of the Environment also contains obligations beyond the Minamata Convention. For example, while Article 3 of the Convention does not provide for a ban on primary mercury mining or the identification of mercury sources, the domestic law prohibits such mining (Arts. 4 and 13), as well as imposes a reporting obligation on those who store mercury or mercury compounds over the limit set by administrative order (Art. 22). In addition, the domestic law requires the government, municipalities, and enterprises to endeavor to take the necessary measures for the environmentally sound collection of mercury-using products (Arts. 16-18). However, there is no corresponding provision in the Convention. There is no legal obligation under the Convention for Parties to develop an implementation plan, but Article 3 of the domestic law requires the government to formulate such a plan. The fact that the Convention was adopted in Japan and named after a Japanese place, and the experience of severe mercury poisoning, seem to explain the country's proactivity towards the Minamata Convention.[93]

Because of the minimalist approach, it is rare for Japan to stipulate in domestic legislation something not required by an MEA, even if it contributes to achieving the ultimate treaty objective. One such exception is a measure taken for the Montreal Protocol. The Protocol does not require Parties to safely recover or destroy ozone-depleting substances (ODS) but only recommends it in Decision IV/24. However, Japan enacted in 2001 the Act on Ensuring the Implementation of Recovery and Destruction of

92 Toi A., "Ekkyō Kankyō Songai ni Kansuru Kokusaiteki na Sekinin Seido no Genjō to Kadai [International Liability Regime for Transboundary Environmental Damage]" (Japanese) *Shinsedai Hōseisakugaku Kenkyū* [Hokkaido Journal of New Global Law and Policy] 14 (2012) 295–297.

93 Otsuka T., "Suigin ni Kansuru Minamata Jōyaku no Kokunaihō Taiō to sono Hyōka [Domestic Implementation of the Minamata Convention on Mercury and Its Assessment]" (Japanese) *Kankyō Hōseisaku Gakkai-shi* [Journal of Environmental Law and Policy] 19 (2016) 58–78.

Fluorocarbons Concerning Designated Products (renamed the "Act on Rational Use and Appropriate Management of Fluorocarbons" in 2013), which requires relevant business operators to recover and destroy ODS contained in designated products.[94]

Japan has not necessarily been enthusiastic about the domestic implementation of non-binding instruments, including COP decisions. One such example is its posture towards the Ramsar Convention resolutions on the definition of wetlands, as mentioned above. Another example includes its positions on the IAEA Safety Standards, which are non-binding. Two episodes illustrate this. In 2009, the IAEA Safety Standards Committee adopted the Safety Guide on Severe Accident Management Programs for Nuclear Power Plants (NS-G-2.15) as part of its safety standards. Immediately after its adoption, the Japanese regulator tried unsuccessfully to incorporate it into the domestic regulatory system. The introduction of the Safety Guide could imply that the national safety standards at the time were inadequate, and the regulator feared public criticism. In 2007, Japan accepted the Integrated Regulatory Review Service (IRRS) mission, an IAEA peer review. The IRRS mission made several recommendations and suggestions to Japan on the structure of regulatory bodies and management systems for nuclear facilities. However, Japan did not initiate a follow-up mission to verify progress. This Japanese reluctance changed dramatically after the Fukushima Daiichi nuclear accident in 2011. Japan amended the Atomic Energy Basic Act,[95] emphasizing due compliance with IAEA Safety Standards, and significantly reformed the national nuclear safety regulations.[96]

On the other hand, in some cases, non-binding documents have been actively reflected in domestic law. For example, the 1996 Recommendation of the OECD Council on Establishing and Implementing Pollutant Release and Transfer Registers (PRTR) led to the enactment of the domestic PRTR Law, officially called the Act on the Assessment of Releases of Specified Chemical Substances in the Environment and the Promotion of Management

94 Tsuruta J., "Nihon ni okeru Kokusai Kankyō Jōyaku no Jisshi [Implementaiton of International Environmental Conventions in Japan]" (Japanese), in Nishii M. and Tsuruta J. (eds.) *Kokusai Kankyō Hō Kōgi* [Lectures on International Environmental Law] (Yushindo Kobunsha, 2020) 69–79.

95 Act No. 186 of 1955, *in force on* January 1, 1956.

96 Shiroyama H. and Koyano M., "Genshiryoku no Heiwa Riyō no Anzen ni Kansuru Jōyaku nado no Kokunai Jisshi [Domestic Implementation of Treaties Related to the Safety of Peaceful Use of Nuclear Power]" (Japanese) *Ronkyū Jurist* [Quarterly Jurist], 7 (2013) 57–61, 65; Shiroyama H. "Gyōsei Soshiki ni Kansuru Kokusai Jōyaku nado no Kitei to Kokunai Jisshi" (Japanese) *Ronkyū Jurist* [Quarterly Jurist] 7 (2013) 69–70.

Improvement.[97] Similarly, the Act on the Prevention of Adverse Ecological Impacts Caused by Designated Invasive Alien Species[98] was enacted in response to the Annex to Decision VI/23 adopted at CBD COP6 entitled "Guiding Principles for the Prevention, Introduction and Mitigation of Impacts of Alien Species that Threaten Ecosystems, Habitats or Species".

When, as in the case of the Paris Agreement on climate change and the CBD on biodiversity conservation, the text of a MEA leaves a great deal of discretion to the parties in implementing the treaty, faithful incorporation of international texts is virtually meaningless, and it is impossible to determine whether the treaty implementation remains at a minimum level without excess or deficiency. Regarding climate change, Japan has set a goal of carbon neutrality by 2050 since 2020 but does not have sufficient means or prospects to achieve it. Efforts to conserve biodiversity have been made following the "National Biodiversity Strategy" formulated in response to the non-legally binding Aichi Targets, but little has been accomplished. Japan may be inclined to be passive and minimalist concerning such treaty norms, which allow a great deal of national discretion.

4 Conclusion

The response to severe pollution in the 1970s led to the initial development of Japanese environmental law. The legal framework then established has absorbed many MEAs ratified by Japan, using different approaches. With a few exceptions, such as the OILPOL to which Japan agreed in 1967, it is since the 1980s that Japan has become active in concluding and implementing MEAs. Recent global environmental issues and international norms to tackle them need the involvement of various policy areas, not just environmental policy. Influenced by this global trend, Japan has been striving to integrate environmental perspectives into other policy areas. In other words, greening other policies has been in progress. Moreover since the 1990s, Japan has hosted international conferences related to MEAs (e.g., COP8(1992) of CITES held in Kyoto, COP3 (1997) of UNFCCC in Kyoto, and COP10(2010) of CBD in Aichi).

Japan is generally good at faithful and precise implementation of MEAs once it has decided to ratify them. This attitude has been described as passive

97 Act No. 86 of 1999, *in force on* March 30, 2000.

98 Act No. 78 of 2004, *in force on* June 1, 2005.

from the perspective of the creation of international environmental law.[99] However, as Japan has become more actively involved in MEAs, it has begun to make some contributions. For example, as chair of the host country, it has taken the initiative to adopt important outcome documents, such as the Kyoto Protocol, the Nagoya Protocol, and the Aichi Targets. In addition, the country has traditionally been a major player, particularly in shipping regulation, and has played a leading role in treaty-making. Such examples in recent years include the International Convention on the Control of Harmful Anti-Fouling Systems on Ships[100] and the Hong Kong International Convention for the Safe and Environmentally Sound Recycling of Ships.[101] Regarding the former, Japan had already been regulating organotin tributyltin (harmful anti-fouling paints) under the Chemical Substance Control Act since the 1990s. This situation enabled Japan to take the lead in the treaty negotiations. Concerning the latter, it was gradually recognized that the Basel Convention also applies to the international sale of ships containing hazardous substances for dismantling, being supposed to make such trade more difficult. For Japan, one of the world's leading shipping nations, which relies on other countries for shipbreaking, it became imperative to establish special international regulations suitable for shipbreaking. Japan led the process of drafting and adopting the Convention through the joint efforts of the public and private sectors.

For Japan, the ratification of MEAs and their implementation have been the driving force behind the improvement of domestic law and the strengthening of administrative authority.[102] Today, domestic law and international

99 Ishino K. et al., "Seminar Zadankai: Kankyō Jōyaku to Kankyō Gaikō [Roundtable: Environmental Conventions and Environmental Diplomacy]" (Japanese) *Jurisuto* [Jurist] 1253 (2001) 111–113, 119–121.

100 *Adopted on* October 5, 2001, *in force on* September 17, 2008, UNTS I-56215. Japan ratified on July 8, 2003.

101 *Adopted on* May 15, 2009, *in force on* June 26, 2025. Japan acceded on March 27, 2019.

102 Takamura Y., *supra* note 85, *Ronkyū Jurist* [Quarterly Jurist] 7 (2013) 79. In addition, the Conferences of the Parties held in Japan, for example, the COP5 of the Ramsar Convention in Kushiro in 1993, COP8 of the CITES in Kyoto in 1992, COP3 of the UNFCCC in Kyoto in 1997, and COP10 of the CBD in Aichi in 2010, have also raised public awareness and provided the impetus for legal development.

law in environmental protection are inseparable,[103] and there seem to be no textbooks on domestic environmental law without reference to any MEA.

As long as international environmental agreements are concerned, there is no sign that the Japanese trend of steady but minimalist implementation identified in this chapter will change.

---

103 Okamatsu A., "Chikyū Kankyō Jōyaku no Keisei to Hatten" (Japanese) in Nishii M. (ed.), note 85, 20–21.

CHAPTER 15

Japan and the International Dispute Settlement

Chie Kojima

1 Introduction

As early as the late 19th century, Japan experienced third-party settlement of international disputes in the *María Luz* incident of 1872.[1] It has also become Party to an arbitration in the *Japanese House Tax* case of 1902.[2] After World War II, the peaceful settlement of international disputes became one of the highlighted foreign policies of Japan. Although Japan has not utilized formal means of the settlement of international disputes before international courts and tribunals as an applicant often, recent trends demonstrate

1 *L'affaire du navire péruvien le "María Luz"(Japan/Peru)* (1875). The case concerned the Peruvian ship *María Luz, which* stopped at the bay of Yokohama in 1832, and carried two hundred and thirty-one Chinese coolies. Immigrants who signed labor contracts for very little pay. The Japanese authorities were requested by the British chargé d'affaires to investigate the situation on board the *María Luz*. The governor of Kanagawa prefecture removed all the coolies from the ship. Subsequently the court of Kanagawa prefecture pronounced the captain of the *María Luz* guilty of abusing the Chinese coolies and forcibly detaining them onboard. The Peruvian government protested these actions and contended that Japan illegally exercised jurisdiction over internal matters of the ship. Japan replied that a ship engaging in slave trade should not be protected, and that it exercised jurisdiction properly as the mistreatment of coolies occurred in the harbor of Yokohama. For the entire domestic and international proceedings, *see* Colombo, G.F., *Justice and International Law in Meiji Japan: The María Luz Incident and the Dawn of Modernity* (Routledge, 2023). *See also*, Ishimoto Y., International Arbitration in the Meiji Era, *Japanese Annual of International Law*, 7, 1963, 30–37.

2 *Japanese House Tax* (*Germany, France, and Great Britain v. Japan*), PCA Case No. 1902-02, Award of the Tribunal, May 21, 1905. The dispute concerned perpetual leases entered into by Japan with foreigners, aimed at giving them access to real property for the establishment of foreign neighborhoods. These foreign settlements were to remain outside the Japanese municipal system, and the foreign occupants of the land were therefore not obliged to pay taxes. In 1894 and 1896, the Japanese government wished to abolish the system of foreign concessions, and for this purpose entered into treaties with the governments of Great Britain, Germany, and France. These treaties provided for the leases to be held in perpetuity and granted exemptions from taxes and other charges. A dispute arose between the Parties when Japan asserted that only the land itself, but not the buildings constructed on it, enjoyed exemption from the payment of taxes (a summary cited from the PCA, available at https://pca-cpa.org/en/cases/69/ (accessed Dec. 27, 2023)).

 | DOI:10.1163/9789004548824_016

Japan's increasing experience in international dispute settlement and willingness to engage in the proceedings even as a respondent.

As Churchill, Lowe, and Sander write, "[t]he fact is that not all disputes are, or need to be, settled. Some can be left unresolved, even indefinitely, as long as the dispute can be contained and any costs - economic, political, or other – arising from the dispute can be kept within acceptable limits."[3] Maritime boundary disputes, which are discussed in Chapter 8 of this volume, are such examples. Japan and its neighboring countries such as the Republic of Korea (ROK), the People's Republic of China (PRC), and the Russian Federation, concluded fishery agreements to accommodate fishing activities by their nationals in disputed maritime areas. Making efforts to enter into such provisional arrangements pending delimitation is also a duty under the United Nations Convention on the Law of the Sea (UNCLOS).[4] While the relationships between Japan and these States are maintained without successful maritime delimitations, the only reason these areas should be delimited is to protect and conserve their ecology and biological diversity, as fishery agreements do not cover these issues.

On the other hand, territorial disputes with neighboring countries, which are discussed in Chapter 7, are the disputes that cause high economic and political costs to Japan. Japan unsuccessfully proposed to the ROK to settle the dispute over Takeshima (referred to by the ROK as "Dokdo") before the International Court of Justice (ICJ) in 1954, 1962, and 2012. As to the Senkaku Islands (referred to by the PRC as "Diaoyu" Islands), the Japanese government maintains there is no sovereignty question because it controls the territory effectively.[5] These territorial disputes cannot be resolved easily by third-party international dispute settlement, and negotiations remain as viable means to avoid escalation.

In light of these backgrounds, this chapter discusses, firstly, various peaceful means of dispute settlement in international law post-World War II, secondly, cases before the international courts and tribunals in which

---

3 Churchill R., Lowe V. and Sander A., *The Law of the Sea*, 4th ed. (Manchester University Press, 2022), 851.

4 Arts. 74(3) and 83(3) of the United Nations Convention on the Law of the Sea, *opened for signature on* December 10, 1982, 1833 UNTS 3 (*entered into force on* November 16, 1994) [UNCLOS].

5 Article 2(4) of the United Nations Charter reads: All Members shall refrain in their international relations from the threat or use of force against the territorial integrity or political independence of any state, or in any other manner inconsistent with the Purposes of the United Nations.

Japan appeared as a Party, and finally concludes with some observations as to Japan's attitude towards international dispute settlement.[6]

2 The Peaceful Settlement of International Disputes under the Charter of the United Nations

States have an obligation, under international law, to settle disputes by peaceful means. Article 33 of the Charter of the United Nations stipulates this obligation as follows:

> 1. The Parties to any dispute, the continuance of which is likely to endanger the maintenance of international peace and security, shall, first of all, seek a solution by negotiation, enquiry, mediation, conciliation, arbitration, judicial settlement, resort to regional agencies or arrangements, or other peaceful means of their own choice.
> 2. The Security Council shall, when it deems necessary, call upon the Parties to settle their dispute by such means.

This provision lists the most popular means of international dispute settlement, but some of them are not utilized as often as other means. The list is described as a "toolbox, from which States can choose the dispute settlement procedure most suited to the dispute in question, and States may use different means at different stages of the dispute."[7] However, when a treaty designates specific means of international dispute settlement, the Parties must use the specific procedure they agreed to. The procedure for the settlement of disputes under UNCLOS, as described below, is one of such examples.

Negotiation is often the first choice of settling an international dispute. Negotiation is characterized as a flexible means of settling an international dispute due to the fact that the Parties can decide the procedure and take into account not only law, but also political elements. It is, however, often observed that the power balance between the Parties may influence the

---

6 The cases before the dispute settlement mechanism at the WTO, in which Japan became a Party, are excluded in this chapter. The WTO cases are discussed in Chapter 13.

7 Churchill, Lowe and Sander (n 3), 856.

outcome of the negotiations.[8] Negotiation becomes mandatory when a treaty provides its Parties to enter into exchange of views, consultation, or negotiation, prior to bringing the dispute before a third-party settlement mechanism. An example is Article 4(3) of the Dispute Settlement Understanding of the World Trade Organization (WTO), which contains an obligation for a Party of an international trade dispute to enter into consultations in good faith upon the request of the other Party, before the establishment of a panel as the next step of settlement. Negotiation, either of voluntary or mandatory nature, must be based on the principle of good faith in international law.

Good offices, mediation, and conciliation are means of settling an international dispute with the involvement of a third party at different degrees. These means do not entail decisions with a binding effect. Conciliation involves the establishment of a conciliation commission to investigate the dispute from every perspective and give recommendations to the Parties. A dispute between Norway and Iceland over the continental shelf boundary around Jan Mayen island was resolved by conciliation in 1981, in which both Parties accepted the recommendations given by the commission and integrated them into the bilateral treaty in 1981.[9] Conciliation is provided as a means of settling international disputes in several treaties such as the 1969 Vienna Convention on the Law of Treaties (Article 66 and Annex) and UNCLOS (Article 284, 297, 298 and Annex V). The *Timor Sea Conciliation* (*Timor-Leste v. Australia*)[10] was the first time that the compulsory conciliation proceedings under Article 298 was utilized by a contracting Party to UNCLOS. Since the success of the *Timor Sea Conciliation*, the use of conciliation proceedings is discussed as potential means of resolving maritime boundary disputes in East Asia including the Japan-ROK maritime boundary dispute.[11]

The following sections focus on third-party judicial settlements with binding decisions and Japan's involvement in them. With a particular focus

8 Iwasawa Y., *Kokusaihō* [International Law] (Japanese) 2nd ed. (University of Tokyo Press, 2023), 604.

9 Conciliation Commission on the Continental Shelf Area between Iceland and Norway: Report and Recommendations to the Governments of Iceland and Norway (1981), RIAA XXVII (2006), 1.

10 Report and Recommendations of the Compulsory Conciliation Commission between Timor-Leste and Australia in the Timor Sea (2018), PCA Case No. 2016–10.

11 *See*, Klein N., "The Timor Sea Conciliation and Lessons for East Asia in Resolving Maritime Boundary Disputes," 6 *Journal of Territorial and Maritime Studies* 30 (2019).

on standing judicial institutions such as the ICJ and the International Tribunal for the Law of the Sea (ITLOS).

2.1 *Japanese Judges*

Japanese judges are regularly appointed to the international courts and tribunals permanently established under the League of Nations, the United Nations, and international conventions of a universal nature such as UNCLOS and the Rome Statute of the International Criminal Court.[12] Japanese judges elected to the Permanent Court of International Justice (PCIJ) include Judge Yorozu Oda (1922–1930), Judge Mineichiro Adachi (1931–1934), and Judge Harukazu Nagaoka (1935–1942). Japanese judges elected to the ICJ include Judge Kotaro Tanaka (1961–1970), Judge Shigeru Oda (1976–2003), Judge Hisashi Owada (2003–2018), and Judge Yuji Iwasawa (2018–present). Japanese judges elected to the ITLOS include Judge Soji Yamamoto (1996–2005), Judge Shunji Yanai (2005–2023), and Judge Hidehisa Horinouchi (2023–present). As of 2023, Japan has nominated two conciliators under Article 2 of Annex V of UNCLOS and four arbitrators, under Article 2 of Annex VII of UNCLOS. Japanese judges elected to the International Criminal Court (ICC) include Judge Fumiko Saiga (2008–2009), Judge Kuniko Ozaki (2010–2018), and Judge Tomoko Akane (2018–present).

2.2 *International Court of Justice*

The ICJ is the judicial body of the United Nations, a successor of the PCIJ under the League of Nations. Its 15 judges represent the world's major legal systems. The ICJ has jurisdiction over any issues on international law, including matters provided in the Charter of the United Nations and existing treaties.[13] Japan became Party to the Statute of the International Court of Justice in 1954 and later a member of the United Nations in 1956. Cases cannot be submitted unless all Parties agree. Nevertheless, Article 36(2) of the Statute of the ICJ provides that States can make optional clause declarations accepting the jurisdiction of the ICJ in advance so that, among States making declarations, a case can unilaterally be brought before the ICJ. The *Whaling in the Antarctic* case[14] was initiated based on both Parties' declarations under Article 36(2) of the Statute of the ICJ.

---

12 Rome Statute of the International Criminal Court, *adopted on* July 17, 1998, *entered into force on* July 1, 2002, 2187 UNTS 90.

13 Statute of the International Court of Justice, Art. 36(1).

14 *Whaling in the Antarctic* (*Australia v. Japan, New Zealand intervening*), [2014] ICJ Rep. 226.

Regarding this optional clause declaration, Japan maintains the position that "Japan places importance on the peaceful settlement of international disputes and the rule of law in the international community. From this perspective, it has maintained its declaration recognizing the jurisdiction of the ICJ as compulsory and has called on other States to make a declaration for the same effect."[15] Japan made its first optional clause declaration to recognize the compulsory jurisdiction of the ICJ pursuant to Article 36(2) of the ICJ Statute in 1958. The 1958 declaration stated that Japan accepted the compulsory jurisdiction of the ICJ except for two types of disputes: firstly, "disputes which arise on and after the date of the declaration with regard to situations or facts subsequent to the same date and which are not settled by other means of peaceful settlement", and secondly, "disputes which the Parties thereto have agreed or shall agree to refer for final and binding decision to arbitration or judicial settlement". Around this time, Japan intended to submit cases to the ICJ, including the dispute with Australia over pearl fishery in the Arafura Sea, the dispute with the ROK over Takeshima, and the dispute with Russia over the Northern Territories (referred to by Russia as "South Kuril Islands").

The 1958 declaration was terminated on July 9, 2007, and a new declaration was submitted. Under the 2007 declaration, Japan aimed to avoid a sudden submission of a case by a foreign State before the ICJ by making a reservation that the declaration does not apply to "disputes in respect of which any other Party to the dispute has accepted the compulsory jurisdiction of the International Court of Justice only in relation to or for the purpose of the dispute; or where the acceptance of the Court's compulsory jurisdiction on behalf of any other Party to the dispute was deposited or ratified less than twelve months prior to the filing of the application bringing the dispute before the Court."[16]

The 2015 declaration gathered much attention from the international community because it was made after the judgment in the *Whaling in the Antarctic* (Australia v. Japan, New Zealand intervening) case of 2014. The declaration states that Japan "recognizes as compulsory ipso facto and

15 Ministry of Foreign Affairs of Japan, ICJ and Japan, available at: https://www.mofa.go.jp/files/100028922.pdf (accessed Dec. 27, 2023).

16 The policy to avoid a sudden submission of a case by a foreign State before the ICJ was influenced by the statement of Peru that it intended to submit a case against Japan regarding the extradition of former President of Peru, Mr. Alberto Fujimori, who was staying in Japan. Tamada D., "International Dispute Settlement," *Encyclopedia of Public International Law in Asia* (Brill Nijhoff, 2021).

without special agreement, in relation to any other State accepting the same obligation and on condition of reciprocity, the jurisdiction of the International Court of Justice, over all disputes arising on and after September 15, 1958 with regard to situations or facts subsequent to the same date and being not settled by other means of peaceful settlement".[17] It also made a reservation that the declaration does not apply to:

> (1) any dispute which the Parties thereto have agreed or shall agree to refer for final and binding decision to arbitration or judicial settlement;
> (2) any dispute in respect of which any other Party to the dispute has accepted the compulsory jurisdiction of the International Court of Justice only in relation to or for the purpose of the dispute; or where the acceptance of the Court's compulsory jurisdiction on behalf of any other Party to the dispute was deposited or notified less than twelve months prior to the filing of the application bringing the dispute before the Court;
> (3) any dispute arising out of, concerning, or relating to research on, or conservation, management or exploitation of, living resources of the sea.

Upon making this declaration, the Japanese government expressed its view that disputes relating to research on, or conservation, management or exploitation of, living resources of the sea are rather suitable for the dispute settlement procedures under UNCLOS. This is because the Convention has provisions regarding such resources and dispute settlement procedures allowing the involvement of experts from the scientific or technical perspective.[18] This explanation may be critically viewed as only disputes between States Parties to UNCLOS concerning the interpretation and application of UNCLOS may be brought before the dispute settlement procedures under Part XV of UNCLOS. In fact, in the *Whaling in the Antarctic*, Australia and New Zealand argued that Japan breached its obligations under the International Convention on the Regulation of Whales and not its obligations under UNCLOS. However, it is important to note that recent developments in international jurisprudence indicate that the fundamental obligations under UNCLOS can be interpreted and applied by taking into consideration relevant rules of international law outside UNCLOS as observed in the 2016

17 Japan's optional clause declaration is available at the website of the ICJ. *See*, https://www.icj-cij.org/declarations/jp (accessed Dec. 27, 2023).

18 Ministry of Foreign Affairs of Japan (n 15).

South China Sea Arbitration[19] and the 2024 *Advisory Opinion on Climate Change and International Law*.[20] There is a future possibility that the obligation to protect and preserve the marine environment, including the due diligence obligations arising from Articles 192 and 194 of UNCLOS, may be interpreted and applied broadly by the international courts and tribunals having jurisdiction under Part XV of UNCLOS through the systematic integration of external rules.

2.3 *International Tribunal for the Law of the Sea*

As described in Chapters 5 and 6, Japan is an active participant in the making and development of the law of the sea. It is at the same time a strong supporter of the legal regime based on UNCLOS, including the dispute settlement procedure under Part XV of UNCLOS.[21] The Fourth Basic Plan on Ocean Policy, issued on April 28, 2023, under the framework of the 2007 Basic Act on Ocean Policy,[22] promotes the rule of law in the ocean and the use of third-party dispute settlement bodies, including the ITLOS.

Any dispute concerning the interpretation and application of UNCLOS must be settled under Part XV of UNCLOS. Part XV is divided into two: Section 1 (General Provisions) provides the fundamental principles of

19 *South China Sea Arbitration* (*The Republic of The Philippines v. The People's Republic of China*), Award, July 12, 2016, PCA Case No. 2013–19. The Arbitral Tribunal in the *South China Sea Arbitration* referred to the Convention on Biological Diversity (CBD) and the Convention on International Trade in Endangered Species of Wild Fauna and Flora (CITES) in applying and interpreting Article 194(5) of UNCLOS. The Tribunal noted that the CBD provided an internationally accepted definition of an ecosystem and that CITES formed part of the general corpus of international law with universal adherence (paras. 945, 956).

20 *Request for Advisory Opinion submitted by the Commission of Small Island States on Climate Change and International Law*, Advisory Opinion, May 21, 2024. The ITLOS interpreted Part XII of UNCLOS evolutionarily and stated that States must apply the precautionary approach in exercising due diligence to prevent, reduce and control marine pollution from anthropogenic greenhouse gas emissions (para. 242). Paragraph 388 of the Advisory Opinion reads: [...] Article 192 does not specify how the marine environment must be protected and preserved against present and future harms. Other provisions of the Convention and external rules inform the content of article 192 and shape the types of measures that may be implemented to protect and preserve the marine environment. In this regard, the Tribunal has addressed the relevance of international instruments on climate change, including the UNFCCC and the Paris Agreement [...]. Other agreements, such as [...] "the Fish Stocks Agreement" [...], and the CBD, may also provide relevant guidance [...].

21 Nishimoto K., "Contribution to the Development of the Law of the Sea," in Lee S. (ed.), *Encyclopedia of Ocean Law and Policy in Asia-Pacific* (Brill Njihoff, 2023), 145.

22 Act No. 33 of 2007.

international dispute settlement. Article 279 of UNCLOS stipulates an obligation to settle disputes by peaceful means by referring to Articles 2(3) and 33(1) of the UN Charter; Section 2 stipulates the compulsory procedures entailing binding decisions. When the Parties to a dispute cannot solve the dispute by the peaceful means of their choice under section 1, they must use the compulsory procedures under section 2. Since the Parties to UNCLOS agree on the compulsory procedures in advance when entering into UNCLOS, a Party to a case can unilaterally submit it to the procedures listed under Article 287. States can choose, when signing, ratifying, or acceding to UNCLOS, one or more of the preferred means of settling international disputes from (a) the International Tribunal for the Law of the Sea established in accordance with Annex VI; (b) the International Court of Justice; (c) an arbitral tribunal constituted in accordance with Annex VII; and (d) a special arbitral tribunal constituted in accordance with Annex VIII for one or more of the categories of disputes specified therein. Japan has not made any choice under Article 287 of UNCLOS. If a dispute concerning the application and interpretation of UNCLOS rises with another State, it is likely that the case goes to an arbitral tribunal constituted under Annex VII.[23]

Certain types of international disputes are excluded from section 2 of Part XV of UNCLOS. Article 297(1) provides that disputes concerning the exercise by a coastal State of its sovereign rights or jurisdiction are subject to the compulsory procedures under section 2 of Part XV of UNCLOS if it is alleged that (a) a coastal State has acted in contravention of the provisions of UNCLOS in regard to the freedoms and rights of navigation, overflight or the laying of submarine cables and pipelines, or in regard to other internationally lawful uses of the sea specified in article 58; (b) a State in exercising the aforementioned freedoms, rights or uses has acted in contravention of UNCLOS or of laws or regulations adopted by the coastal State in conformity with UNCLOS and other rules of international law not incompatible with UNCLOS; or (c) a coastal State has acted in contravention of specified international rules and standards for the protection and preservation of the marine environment which are applicable to the coastal State and which have been established by UNCLOS or through a competent international organization or diplomatic conference in accordance with UNCLOS. Article 297(2) further provides that a coastal State is not obliged to submit a dispute to the compulsory procedures if that dispute arose out of the exercise by the coastal State of a right or discretion in accordance with

23 UNCLOS, Art. 287(5).

Article 246 (marine scientific research in the exclusive economic zone and on the continental shelf) or a decision by the coastal State to order suspension or cessation of a research project in accordance with article 253. Such a dispute must be submitted to the compulsory conciliation procedure under section 2 of Annex V of UNCLOS. Article 297(3) uses similar wording and stipulates that certain fishery disputes, including disputes arising from coastal States' failure to determine total allowable catches and their harvesting capacities, the allocation of surpluses to other States, and the terms of conservation and management measures, must be resolved by compulsory conciliation.

Under Article 298(1) of UNCLOS, States may opt out of the compulsory dispute settlement procedures under section 2 of Part XV of UNCLOS by making declarations excluding the following three categories of disputes: (1) disputes concerning the interpretation or application of Articles 15, 74 and 83 relating to sea boundary delimitations, or those involving historic bays or titles, (2) disputes concerning military activities, including military activities by government vessels and aircraft engaged in non-commercial service, and disputes concerning law enforcement activities in regard to the exercise of sovereign rights or jurisdiction excluded from the jurisdiction of a court or tribunal under Article 297, paragraph 2 or 3; and (3) disputes in respect of which the Security Council of the United Nations is exercising the functions assigned to it by the Charter of the United Nations, unless the Security Council decides to remove the matter from its agenda or calls upon the Parties to settle it by the means provided for in UNCLOS.

Although Japan has not made any declaration with regard to the optional exceptions under Article 298(1), it is unable to bring its maritime boundary cases or potential overlapping claims with PRC, ROK, Palau, the Russian Federation, and the United States to adjudication under section 2 of Part XV of UNCLOS because PRC, ROK, Palau, and the Russian Federation made optional declarations excluding maritime boundary delimitation from compulsory dispute settlement procedures under said article,[24] and because the

24 *See* Chapter 8 for these maritime boundary disputes. The PRC declared: "The Government of the People's Republic of China does not accept any of the procedures provided for in Section 2 of Part XV of the Convention with respect to all the categories of disputes referred to in paragraph 1 (a) (b) and (c) of Article 298 of the Convention." The ROK declared: "In accordance with paragraph 1 of Article 298 of the Convention, the Republic of Korea does not accept any of the procedures provided for in section 2 of Part XV of the Convention with respect to all the categories of disputes referred to in paragraph 1 (a), (b) and (c) of Article 298 of the Convention." Palau declared: "The Government of the Republic of Palau declares under paragraph 1 (a) of Article 298 of

United States is not a party to UNCLOS. The overlapping claims with PRC, ROK, Palau, and the Russian Federation are still governed by the general obligation to settle disputes by peaceful means under Section 1 of Part XV of UNCLOS and the possible overlapping claims with the United States to be governed by the peaceful settlement of dispute under the Charter of the United Nations. It has to be noted however, that under Article 298(1)(a)(i), a State having made a declaration must, when such a dispute arises subsequent to the entry into force of UNCLOS and where no agreement within a reasonable period of time is reached in negotiations between the Parties, at the request of any Party to the dispute, accept submission of the matter to conciliation under Annex V, Section 2.[25]

3 Japan's Participation in the Adjudication before the International Courts and Tribunals

Japan's interests in the exploitation of living marine resources beyond its EEZ resulted in several international disputes, which led to Japan's attempt to utilize international adjudication. As early as Japan becoming a Member State of the United Nations, it had sought to resolve its dispute with Australia over pearl fisheries before the ICJ, but successful bilateral negotiations interrupted this attempt.

Since the 1990s, Japan has defended itself for the sustainable use of marine living resources in actual cases as a Party. Japan was Party to the

---

the 1982 United Nations Convention on the Law of the Sea that it does not accept compulsory procedures entailing binding decisions relating to the delimitation and/or interpretation of maritime boundaries." The Russian Federation declared: The Russian Federation declares that, in accordance with article 298 of the United Nations Convention on the Law of the Sea, it does not accept the procedures, provided for in section 2 of Part XV of the Convention, entailing binding decisions with respect to disputes concerning the interpretation or application of articles 15, 74 and 83 of the Convention, relating to sea boundary delimitations, or those involving historic bays or titles (...).

25 UNCLOS provides certain requirements to be satisfied for the parties to seek compulsory conciliation under Article 298(1)(a). The requirements include that the dispute does not involve the concurrent consideration of unsettled territorial disputes (Art. 298(1)(a)(i)). Furthermore, Article 298(1)(a)(iii) states that compulsory conciliation is not available for "any sea boundary dispute finally settled by an arrangement between the parties, or to any such dispute which is to be settled in accordance with a bilateral or multilateral agreement binding upon those parties". Accordingly, it is said that most cases of the delimitation of the EEZ and continental shelf with Japan's neighboring States are excluded from the compulsory conciliation procedure.

following cases: (1) *Southern Bluefin Tuna Cases* (*New Zealand v. Japan, Australia v. Japan*), Provisional Measures, ITLOS, 1999;[26] (2) *Southern Bluefin Tuna Case between Australia and Japan and between New Zealand and Japan*, Award on Jurisdiction and Admissibility, Arbitral Tribunal constituted under Annex VII of UNCLOS, Decision of 4 August 2000;[27] (3) *The Hoshinmaru Case* (*Japan v. Russian Federation*), Prompt Release, ITLOS, 2007;[28] (4) *The Tomimaru Case* (*Japan v. Russian Federation*), Prompt Release, ITLOS, 2007;[29] and (5) *Whaling in the Antarctic* (*Australia v. Japan, New Zealand intervening*), Merits, ICJ, 2014.

3.1 *Southern Bluefin Tuna Cases*

In 1999, Australia and New Zealand instituted proceedings under Annex VII of UNCLOS on a dispute concerning the conservation and management of southern bluefin tuna.[30] The ITLOS was at the same time requested to prescribe provisional measures while pending the constitution of an arbitral tribunal under Annex VII of UNCLOS. The dispute arose because the Parties failed to agree on an increase of TAC in the Commission established under the Convention for the Conservation of the Southern Bluefin Tuna, concluded between Australia, Japan and New Zealand in 1993, and was followed by Japan's unilateral experimental fishing in 1998 and 1999. Consultations were held under Article 16(1) of the Convention without success, which led Japan to initiate its unilateral action. New Zealand and Australia argued that Japan failed to comply with its duty to cooperate in the conservation of southern bluefin tuna by undertaking the programme unilaterally and against the

26 *Southern Bluefin Tuna Cases* (*New Zealand v. Japan; Australia v. Japan*), Provisional Measures, Order of 27 August 1999 [1999] ITLOS Rep. 280.

27 *Southern Bluefin Tuna Cases* (*Australia v. Japan; New Zealand v. Japan*), Jurisdiction and Admissibility (2000), RIAA XXIII (2006), 1.

28 *The "Hoshinmaru" Case* (*Japan v. Russian Federation*), Prompt Release [2005–7] ITLOS Rep. 18.

29 *The "Tomimaru" Case* (*Japan v. Russian Federation*), Prompt Release [2002] ITLOS Rep. 10.

30 Southern Bluefin Tuna is explained in the Award of the Arbitral Tribunal as "a migratory species of pelagic fish that is included in the list of highly migratory species set out in Annex I of the United Nations Convention on the Law of the Sea. Southern Bluefin Tuna range widely through the oceans of the Southern Hemisphere, principally the high seas, but they also traverse the exclusive economic zones and territorial waters of some States, notably Australia, New Zealand and South Africa. They spawn in the waters south of Indonesia. The main market for the sale of Southern Bluefin Tuna is in Japan, where the fish is prized as a delicacy for sashimi" (Award of August 4, 2000, para. 21).

precautionary principle. On August 27, 1999, the ITLOS ordered the three Parties to refrain from conducting experimental fishing programmes involving the catching of southern bluefin tuna, and to resume negotiations to reach an agreement on measures for the conservation and management of the fish stock. Although the ITLOS did not directly mention the precautionary principle, it stated that "the Parties should in the circumstances act with prudence and caution to ensure that effective conservation measures are taken to prevent serious harm to the stock of southern bluefin tuna".[31] The Tribunal further stated that while it could not "conclusively assess the scientific evidence presented by the Parties", it found that "measures should be taken as a matter of urgency to preserve the rights of the Parties and to avert further deterioration of the southern bluefin tuna stock."[32]

In 2000, the Arbitral Tribunal constituted under Annex VII of UNCLOS examined Japan's objections to the jurisdiction of the Tribunal. Japan argued that the dispute concerned the interpretation and implementation of the 1993 Convention for the Conservation of the Southern Bluefin Tuna. On this point, Australia maintained its position that the dispute did not relate solely to Japan's obligations under the 1993 Convention, but also involved its obligations under UNCLOS and customary international law. Japan further argued that the dispute should have been resolved by mediation or arbitration under the provisions of the 1993 Convention.[33]

The Arbitral Tribunal constituted under Annex VII of UNCLOS reflected on the procedural aspect of the case, namely whether the dispute falls under the 1993 Convention or under both the 1993 Convention and UNCLOS.

---

31 *Southern Bluefin Tuna Cases* (*New Zealand v. Japan; Australia v. Japan*) (n 26), para. 77.

32 *Ibid.*, para. 80.

33 Article 16 of the 1993 Convention provides:

1. If any dispute arises between two or more of the Parties concerning the interpretation or implementation of this Convention, those Parties shall consult among themselves with the goal of resolving the dispute by negotiation, inquiry, mediation, conciliation, arbitration, judicial settlement or other peaceful means of their own choice.

2. Any dispute of this character not so resolved shall, with the consent in each case of all Parties to the dispute, be referred, for settlement, to the International Court of Justice or to arbitration; failure to reach agreement on reference to the International Court of Justice or to arbitration shall not absolve Parties to the dispute from the responsibility of continuing to seek resolution by any of the various peaceful means referred to in paragraph 1 above.

3. In cases where the dispute is referred to arbitration, the arbitral tribunal shall be constituted as provided in the Annex to this Convention. The Annex forms an integral part of this Convention.

The Tribunal examined the two conditions set by Article 281(1) of UNCLOS: (1) whether no settlement has been reached by recourse to a peaceful means of the Parties' own choice; (2) the agreement between the Parties does not exclude any further procedure. In the view of the Tribunal, the first condition is met since the Parties negotiated under Article 16 of the 1993 Convention and no settlement had been reached. However, as to the second condition, the Tribunal concluded that Article 16 of the 1993 Convention excluded the applicability of Section 2 of Part XV of UNCLOS because the ordinary meaning of Article 16 suggests that the consent of all Parties to the dispute is necessary for recourse to any means of dispute settlement; this differs from Article 286 of UNCLOS which allows a dispute to be submitted to a court or tribunal "at the request of any Party to the dispute."[34] The Tribunal therefore concluded that Article 16 of the 1993 Convention "exclude[s] any further procedure" within the contemplation of Article 281(1) of UNCLOS.

3.2 *Hoshinmaru and Tomimaru Cases*

In 2007, Japan brought two prompt release cases against the Russian Federation before the ITLOS. The *Hoshinmaru* Case concerned the release of the 88th *Hoshinmaru* and its 17 crew members and the *Tomimaru* Case concerned the release of the 53rd *Tomimaru*. In the *Hoshinmaru* Case, Japan claimed that the Russian Federation did not comply with Article 292 of UNCLOS concerning the prompt release of the vessel and its crew upon the posting of a bond and that the amount requested in said bond by the Russian Federation was excessively high. The master of the *Hoshinmaru* carried a valid fishing permit when operating in the Russian EEZ but violated the Russian fisheries legislation by falsely reporting the catches. Although the Tribunal noted the importance of accurate monitoring of catches in the management of marine living resources, it found that the amount of the bond set by the Russian Federation was not reasonable and that the vessel's value should not be included in the bond. The decision was complied with by the Parties and the *Hoshinmaru* and its crew were released upon posting of a bond set by the ITLOS.[35] In the *Tomimaru* Case,

34 *Southern Bluefin Tuna Cases (New Zealand v. Japan; Australia v. Japan)* (n 27), para. 57.

35 After the judgment, the owner of the *Hoshinmaru* transferred the deposit of 10 million roubles (approximately 46 million yen) to the bank account specified by the Russian Federation. Originally, the Russian Federation requested 25 million roubles (approximately 120 million yen) for the release. *See*, Ministry of Foreign Affairs of Japan, Press Release of August 16, 2007 (in Japanese).

the Tribunal concluded that the object of Japan's application ceased to exist since the domestic proceedings in the Russian Federation for the confiscation of the vessel had been concluded and the crew returned to Japan while pending its decision.[36]

3.3 *Whaling in the Antarctic Case*

Japan became Party to a case submitted to the ICJ for the first time in the *Whaling in the Antarctic* case. The case concerned the legality of Japan's scientific whaling programme, JARPA II, under the International Convention for the Regulation of Whaling (ICRW). The dispute was submitted by Australia in 2010 by invoking both Parties' optional clause declarations made under Article 36(2) of the ICJ Statute. Australia was admitted to appoint a Judge *ad hoc*, Judge Charlesworth, whereas Japan had its own national Judge on the bench, Judge Owada. The intervening non-party, New Zealand, had its national Judge, Judge Keith.

Australia argued that JARPA II was not a programme with purposes of scientific research as defined by Article VIII of the ICRW and that Japan breached its obligations under the Schedule to the ICRW, including (1) the obligation to respect the moratorium setting zero catch limits for the killing of whales from all stocks for commercial purposes (para. 10(e)); (2) the obligation not to undertake commercial whaling of fin whales in the Southern Ocean Sanctuary (para. 7(b)); and (3) the obligation to observe the moratorium on the taking, killing, or treating of whales, except minke whales, by factory ships or whale catchers attached to factory ships (para. 10(d)).[37] Japan maintained its view that JARPA II was undertaken for purposes of scientific research under Article VIII, paragraph 1, of the ICRW and contested all alleged breaches.

The Court determined, firstly, whether JARPA II involved scientific research and, secondly, if the killing, taking, and treating of whales is "for purposes of" scientific research by examining whether, in the use of lethal methods, the programme's design and implementation are reasonable in relation to achieving its stated objectives. In the Court's view, relevant elements of a programme's design and implementation included: decisions

---

36 The domestic proceedings consisted of an administrative case against the shipowner and the criminal case against the captain. In the administrative case, the Russian court decided the confiscation of the vessel and imposed monetary fines. In the criminal case, the Russian court decided monetary fines against the captain. *See*, Ministry of Foreign Affairs of Japan, Press Release of 6 July 2007.

37 *Whaling in the Antarctic* (n 14), para. 48.

regarding the use of lethal methods, the scale of the programme's use of lethal sampling, the methodology used to select sample sizes, a comparison of the target sample sizes and the actual take, the time frame associated with a programme, the programme's scientific output, and the degree to which a programme co-ordinates its activities with related research projects.[38]

For the first question, the Court rejected the four criteria advanced by Australia in order to constitute "scientific research" in the context of Article VIII[39] by stating that they "appear largely to reflect what one of the experts that it called regards as well-conceived scientific research, rather than serving as an interpretation of the term as used in the Convention."[40] The Court held that it did not consider it necessary to devise alternative criteria or to offer a general definition of "scientific research". For the second question, the Court examined the evidence submitted by Japan in detail and concluded that JARPA II involved activities that can broadly be characterized as scientific research, but the evidence did not establish that the programme's design and implementation are reasonable in relation to achieving its stated objectives.[41] It therefore concluded that the special permits granted by Japan for killing, taking, and treating of whales under JARPA II were not "for purposes of scientific research" under Article VIII(1) of ICRW. The Court thus ordered Japan to revoke permits previously granted and refrain from granting further permits under JARPA II.

In the *Whaling in the Antarctic case*, the claims submitted by Australia and New Zealand did not involve any violation of UNCLOS by Japan. However, a question was raised regarding Japan's breach of the duty of cooperation under paragraph 30 of the Schedule to the International Convention for the Regulation of Whaling. Although the International Convention for the Regulation of Whaling is a special treaty in relation to UNCLOS, a general treaty, the duty of cooperation is also stipulated under Articles 65 and 120 of UNCLOS concerning the conservation of marine mammals in the EEZ and in the high seas respectively. On this question, the ICJ found that Japan

38 *Ibid.*, para. 88.

39 Australia's scientific experts presented four criteria as essential characteristics of scientific research in the context of the ICRW: (1) defined and achievable objectives (questions or hypotheses) that aim to contribute to knowledge important to the conservation and management of stocks, (2) "appropriate methods", including the use of lethal methods only where the objectives of the research cannot be achieved by any other means, (3) peer review, and (4) the avoidance of adverse effects on stock. *Ibid.*, para. 74.

40 *Ibid.*, para. 86.

41 *Ibid.*, para. 227.

has complied with its obligations under paragraph 30 of the Schedule to the International Convention for the Regulation of Whaling with regard to JARPA II.[42]

Japan complied with the decision of the ICJ by emphasizing the importance of the international legal order and the rule of law. In 2019 Japan withdrew from ICRW and resumed commercial whaling. In 2024, the Fisheries Agency of Japan decided to include North Pacific fin whales in the total allowable catch for its commercial whaling.[43]

4 Conclusion

Japan's participation in international adjudication as a Party and its compliance with the decisions indicate its commitment to peaceful settlement of international disputes under the Charter of the United Nations, and its accumulating experience with formal means of settlement of international disputes, which were previously considered as Western mechanisms of dispute settlement. Furthermore, Japan not only engaged in the judicial proceedings of the international courts and tribunals, but also participated in the advisory proceedings. Japan submitted a written statement and gave an oral statement in the *Legality of the Threat or Use of Nuclear Weapons* in 1995.[44] It also submitted a written statement in the *Request for an Advisory Opinion Submitted by the Sub-Regional Fisheries Commission* (*SRFC*) in support of the advisory jurisdiction of the ITLOS and to present its views on the substantive part of the request.[45]

Japan promotes the maintenance of "the free and international order based on the rule of law" as its policy.[46] In light of the situation where the

42 Judges Sebutinde and Bhandari as well as Judge ad hoc Charlesworth voted against the finding of the Court.

43 Fisheries Agency, *Catch Limits for Western North Pacific Fin Whales Calculated in Line with the IWC's Revised Management Procedure* (*RMP*), Doc. RW/S23/02, available at: https://www.jfa.maff.go.jp/e/whale/attach/pdf/index-42.pdf (accessed Jun. 17, 2025).

44 *Legality of the Threat or Use of Nuclear Weapons*, Advisory Opinion [1996] ICJ Rep. 226.

45 *Request for an Advisory Opinion Submitted by the Sub-regional Fisheries Commission* (*SRFC*), Advisory Opinion [2015] ITLOS Rep 4.

46 Statement by Foreign Minister Hayashi Yoshimasa, Seven years since the issuance of the Arbitral Tribunal's award as to the disputes between the Republic of the Philippines and the People's Republic of China regarding the South China Sea, July 12, 2023, available at https://www.mofa.go.jp/press/release/press1e_000448.html (accessed Dec. 27, 2023).

award of the *South China Sea Arbitration* was not complied by the PRC, the then-Foreign Minister Hayashi reiterated Japan's "strong opposition to unilateral attempts to change the status quo by force or coercion" in his statement in 2023.[47] He further emphasized that "the Tribunal's award is final and legally binding on the Parties to the dispute" and "[t]he claim by China that it will not accept the award is against the principle of peaceful settlement of disputes in accordance with international law, in particular UNCLOS, and undermines the rule of law as a fundamental value of the international community".[48]

47 *Ibid.*
48 *Ibid.*

Bibliography

Abe K., *Nanmin no Hogo to Heiwa no Kōsō* [Refugee Protection and Peace Initiatives] (Choyokai, Saitama, 2021)

Adler D. E., "Why 'Economic Security' Became Magic Words in Japan", *Foreign Policy* 20 (2023)

Akasaka M., "Nanminshinseisha no Seizon no Tameni [For the Survival of Refugee Applicants]", *Migrants Network* 198 (2018)

Akashi K., "Nihon no Kokusaihōgaku Taigaihassin no 100-nen [One Hundred Years of External Communication of Japanese International Law]", *Kokusaishakai no Hō to Seiji* [Law and Politics in International Society] (Sanseido, Tokyo, 2001)

Akiyama M., "Wagakuni no Nanmin Nintei Seido [Refugee Recognition System in Japan]", *The Reference* 69 (5) (2019)

Ambos K. (ed.), *Rome Statute of the International Criminal Court*, 4th ed. (Beck/Hart/Nomos, Baden Baden, 2022)

Ando T., *Kokusai Terorizumu ni taisuru Hōtekikisei no Kōzō* [The Structure of Legal Control of International Terrorism] (Kokusaisyoin, Tokyo, 2020)

Anghie A., "Finding the Peripheries: Sovereignty and Colonialism in 19th Century International Law", *Harvard International Law Journal* 40 (1999)

Anzilotti D., *Corso di diritto internazionale*, 3rd ed. (Cedam, Padova, 1928)

Arend A. and Beck R., *International Law and the Use of Force: Beyond the U. N. Charter Paradigm* (Routledge, London, 1993)

Asada A., Kiriyama T., Tokugawa S., Nishimura T., and Higuchi K. (eds.), *Gendai Kokusaihō no Chōryū* [Tide of Modern International Law] 1 (Toshindo, Tokyo, 2020)

Ashibe N., "Hōritsu Kaishaku niyoru Kenpō Handan no Kaihi [Bypassing Constitutional Issues by Legal Interpretation: the Eniwa Case]", in *Kenpō Hanrei Hyakusen II* [Commentary of Constitutional Cases vol. 2] 5th ed. (Yuhikaku, Tokyo, 2007)

Bantekas I. and Nash S., *International Criminal Law*, 3rd ed. (Routledge-Cavendish, Abingdon, 2007)

Beckman R., Townsend G., Schofield C., Davenport T., and Bernard L. (eds.), *Beyond Territorial Disputes in the South China Sea: Legal Frameworks for the Joint Development of Hydrocarbon Resources* (Edward Elgar Publishing, Cheltenham, 2013)

Bergbohm C., *Jurisprudenz und Rechtsphilosophie* (Duncker & Humblot, Leipzig, 1882)

Blake G. H., Hildesley W. J., Pratt M. A., Ridley R. J., and Schofield C. H. (eds.), *The Peaceful Management of Trans-boundary Resources* (Graham & Trotman/Martinus Nijhoff, London/Boston, 1995)

Boister N. and Cryer R., *The Tokyo International Military Tribunal: A Reappraisal* (Oxford University Press, Oxford, 2008)

Bowett D. W., *Self-Defense in International Law* (Praeger, Manchester, 1958)

Brownlie I., *International Law and the Use of Force by the States* (Oxford Univ. Press, Oxford, 1963)

Center for Information on Security Trade Control (CISTEC), *Overview of Japan's Export Controls*, 4th ed. (CISTEC, Tokyo, 2015)

Chimni B. S., Miyoshi M., and Surya P., "State Practice of Asian Countries in the Field of International Law", *Asian Yearbook of International Law* 11 (2003–2004)

Choi J. H., "Korea–Japan JDZ to End in Deadlock? The Potential for Unilateral Korean Exploration and Exploitation", *Ocean Development & International Law* 51 (2020)

Churchill R. R., "Joint Development Zones; International Legal Issues", in Fox H. (ed.), *Joint Development of Offshore Oil and Gas*, vol. II (British Institute of International & Comparative Law, London, 1990)

Churchill R., Lowe V., and Sander A., *The Law of the Sea*, 4th ed. (Manchester University Press, Manchester, 2022)

Colombo G. F., *Justice and International Law in Meiji Japan: The María Luz Incident and the Dawn of Modernity* (Routledge, London, 2023)

Cosenza E. M. (ed.), *The Complete Journal of Townsend Harris: First American Consul and Minister to Japan* (C.E. Tuttle Company, Rutland, 1959) (translated into Japanese by Seiichi S., *Harris Nihon Taizaiki* [Harris in Japan] (1)(2)(3) (Iwanami Shoten, Tokyo, 1953))

Cryer R., Robinson D., and Vasiliev S., *An Introduction to International Criminal Law and Procedure, 4th ed.* (Cambridge Univ. Press, Cambridge, 2019)

Ejima A., "A Gap between the Apparent and Hidden Attitudes of the Supreme Court of Japan towards Foreign Precedents", in Groppi T. and Ponthoreau M. C. (eds.), *The Use of Foreign Precedents by Constitutional Judges* (Hart Publishing, Oxford, 2013)

Evans M., "Maritime Boundary Delimitation", in Rothwell D. R., Elferink A. G. O., Scott K. N., and Stephens T. (eds.), *The Oxford Handbook of the Law of the Sea* (Oxford University Press, Oxford, 2016)

Fitzmaurice G., "The General Principles of International Law Considered from the Standpoint of the Rule of Law", *Recueil des Cours* 92 (1957)

Fox H. (ed.), *Joint Development of Offshore Oil and Gas*, vol. II (British Institute of International & Comparative Law, London, 1990)

Fox H. and Philippa W., *The Law of State Immunity*, 3rd ed. (Oxford Univ. Press, Oxford, 2015)

Fujikura R., "Seibutsu Tayōsei Jōyaku to Cartagena Giteisyo 6 [Convention on the Biological Diversity and Cartagena Protocol (Chap. 6)]", in Nishii M.

(ed.), *Chikyū Kankyō Jōyaku* [Global Environmental Agreements] (Yuhikaku, Tokyo, 2005)

Fukamachi T., "Kokusai Saiban ni okeru 'Zen-Kindai / Hi-Oushū no Ryōiki Shihai' no Enyō to Hyōka [Employing 'pre-Modern' and 'non-Europe' concept in International Tribunals and its Evaluation]", in Yanagihara M. and Kanehara A. (eds.), *Kokusaihō kara mita Ryōdo to Nihon* [Territory and Japan from the Perspective of International Law] (University of Tokyo Press, Tokyo, 2022)

Fukunaga Y., "Japan's Trade Policy in the Midst of Uncertainty", *Asie.Visions* 112 (2020)

Fukuoh M., "Nanmin Shinsa Sanyoin Seido ni kansuru Hikakuhōteki Kōsatsu [Some Comparative Legal Observations on the Introduction of 'the Refugee Adjudication' to Japan through International Law and Constitutional Law]", *Komazawa Women's University Kenkyū Kiyō* [The Faculty Journal of Komazawa Women's University] 13 (2006)

Fukuzawa Y., "Tsūzoku Kokken Ron [Popular Theory of National Constitution]", *Fukuzawa Yukichi Zenshū* [Collected Edition of Fukuzawa Yukichi] 4 (Iwanami Shoten, Tokyo, 1959)

Furukawa A., "Jyōyaku no Iken Shinsa [Constitutional Review of Treaties: The Sunagawa Case]", in *Kenpō Hanrei Hyakusen II* [Commentary of Constitutional Cases vol.2] 5th ed. (Yuhikaku, Tokyo, 2007)

Genugten W., "The African Move towards the Adoption of the 2007 Declaration on the Rights of Indigenous Peoples: The Substantive Arguments behind the Procedures", in Hart B., Böcker A. G. M., Havinga T., Minderhoud P. E., Put H., Leeuwen L. E., Jettingoff A., and Zwaan K.M. (eds.), *Migration Law and Sociology of Law, Collected Essays in honour of Kees Groenendijk* (Wolf Legal Publishers, Nijmegen, 2008)

Gover K., "Settler-State Political Theory, 'CANZUS' and the UN Declaration on the Rights of Indigenous Peoples", *The European Journal of International Law* 26 (2) (2015)

Hall E. W., *A Treatise on International Law* (Clarendon Press, Oxford, 1880)

Hamamoto S., "International Law, Regional Developments: East Asia" (updated September 2017), in *Max Planck Encyclopedia of Public International Law* (online edition)

Hamamoto Y., "The Incident of a Submarine Navigating Underwater in Japan's Territorial Sea", *The Japanese Annual of International Law* 48 (2005)

Harada N., *Senkakushotō—Sakuhō Ryūkyū Shiroku wo Yomu* [The Senkaku Islands: From the Reading of Sakuhō Ryūkyū Shiroku] (Yojyu Shorin, Okinawa, 2006)

Hatano A., "The Internalization of International Human Rights Law: The Case of Hate Speech in Japan", *New York University Journal of International Law and Politics* 50 (2) (2018)

Hayashi M., "Japan: New Law of the Sea Legislation", *International Journal of Marine and Coastal Law* 12 (1997)

Hirobe K., "The Japanese Practice Concerning International Treaties", *Archiv des Völkerrechts* 25 (1) (1987)

Hong S. W., "Nihon Shakai ni okeru Nanmin Ukeire no Ronten [Issues on Refugee Acceptance in Japanese Society]", *Kokusai Kankei Ronsō* [Internationmal Relation Studies] 7 (2) (2018)

Inoue K., *Senkakurettō – Uotsurishotō no Shitekikaimei* [The Senkaku Islands: Historical Clarification of Uotsuri Islands] (Gendai Hyoronsha, Tokyo, 1972)

Ishii Y., *Ekkyōhannzai no Kokusaitekikisei* [International Regulation on the Transboundary Crimes] (Yuhikaku, Tokyo, 2017)

Ishii Y., *Japanese Maritime Security and Law of the Sea* (Brill Nijhoff, Leiden, 2022)

Ishii Y., "M/V Guanabara: Japan's First Trial on Piracy under the Anti-piracy Act", *Maritime Safety and Security Law Journal* 1(2015)

Ishimoto Y., "International Arbitration in the Meiji Era", *Japanese Annual of International Law*, 7 (1963)

Ishimoto Y., "Meijiki ni okeru Chūsai Saiban no Senrei [Arbitrages internationaux in Meiji période]", *Hōgaku Zasshi* [Journal of Law and Politics of Osaka City University] 9 (3/4) (1962)

Ishino K. et al., "Seminar Zadankai: Kankyō Jōyaku to Kankyō Gaikō [Roundtable: Environmental Conventions and Environmental Diplomacy]" (Japanese) *Jurisuto* [Jurist] 1253 (2001)

Ito F., "International Law [Kokusaihō]", in Aomi J. (ed.), *Kindai Nihonshi Taikei* [System of Modern Japanese History] (Yuhikaku, Tokyo, 1979)

Ito K., *"Futatsu no Shōgeki" to Nihon* [Japan's Response to the "Two Shocks"] (PHP Research Institute, Tokyo, 1991)

Iwasawa Y., *International Law, Human Rights, and Japanese Law: The Impact of International Law on Japanese Law* (Clarendon Press, Oxford, 1998)

Iwasawa Y., *Jōyaku no Kokunai Tekiyō Kanōsei: Iwayuru "Self-Executing" na Jōyaku ni Kansuru Ichi Kōsatsu* [Domestic Applicability of Treaties: A Study on So-Called "Self-Executing" Treaties] (Yuhikaku, Tokyo, 1985)

Iwasawa Y., *Kokusaihō* [International Law], 2nd ed. (University of Tokyo Press, Tokyo, 2023)

Japan Association for Environmental Law and Policy. (ed.), *Kankyō Hōseisaku Gakkai-shi* [Journal of Environmental Law and Policy] 23 (2020)

Japan Association of Modern East Asian History, *Higashi Ajia Kindaishi 3* (*Ajia ni okeru Kindai Kokusaihō*) [Modern History of East Asia vol.3 (Modern International Law in Asia)] (Yumani Shobou, Tokyo, 2000)

Jouannet E., "Structure intellectuelle de la pensée internationaliste classique et colonialisme européen", Report at the inaugural ESIL Conference in Florence, 2004, published as: Emmanuel L., "Colonialisme européen et néo-colonialisme contemporain (Notes de lecture des manuels européens du droit des gens entre 1850 et 1914)", *Baltic Yearbook of International Law* 6 (2006)

Kagami Y., "Kokuren Kaiyōhō Jōyaku dai 121 Jō 3 Kō wo Meguru Kokka Jikkou to Sono Ruikeika [State Practice under UNCLOS Article 121(3)", in Asada A., Kiriyama T., Tokugawa S., Nishimura T., and Higuchi K. (eds.), *Gendai Kokusaihō no Chōryū* [Tide of Modern International Law] 1 (Toshindo, Tokyo, 2020)

Kamigawara K., "Jōyaku Jisshi wo Tūjita Kokunai-Kokusai Sōhōkō no Henka: Washington Jōyaku Seido Jisshi wo Rei to shite [National and International Shift through the Implementation of the International Agreements: In the Reference to the Implementation of Washington Convention System]", *Shinsedai Hōseisakugaku Kenkyū* [Hokkaidō Journal of New Global Law and Policy] 12 (2011)

Kanazawa Y., *Kokusai Keizai Hō Josetsu* [Introduction to International Economic Law] (Yuhikaku, Tokyo, 1979)

Kanehara A., "'Pandemic- Kokusaihō' niokeru-Kaiyohō: Diamond Princess-gō nikakaru Kikōchisochi ['Pandemic International Law' and the Law of the Sea: the Diamond Princess and Port State Measures]", *Kokusai Mondai* [International Affairs] 699 (2021)

Kanehara A., "The Japanese Legal System concerning Innocent Passage of Foreign Vessels", *Japanese Annual of International Law* 42 (1999)

Kaneko Y., "Washington Jōyaku [Washington Convention]" (Japanese) in Nishii M. (ed.), *Chikyū Kankyō Jōyaku* [Global Environmental Agreements] (Yuhikaku, Tokyo, 2005)

Kato M., "Nihon no kokka syōnin jitsumu [Japan's Practice on Recognition of States]", *Kokusaihō Kenkyū* [Tokyo Review of Iinternational Law] 5 (2017)

Kawajiri E. and Nishiwaki E., "Hōrei Kaisetsu Tai Gaikoku Minji Saibankenhō (Shuken Menjyohō) no Seitei [The enactment of the Act on Civil Jurisdiction over Foreign States]", *Toki no Hōrei* [Legislative Hours] 1847 (2009)

Kawase T., "Waga Kuni Tsūshō Hō no Genjō oyobi Kadai: WTO Kyōtei Seigōteki na Kokusai Hyōjun Seido eno Hatten ni Mukete [Current Status and Issues of Japan's Trade Remedy Laws: Toward the Development of an International Standards System Consistent with the WTO Agreement]", *Hōritsu Jihō* [Legal Hours] 77 (6) (2005)

Kawashima F., "Keizai Anzen Hoshō Hō no Seitei to Ichibu Shikō [Enactment and Partial Enforcement of the Economic Security Promotion Act]", *Hōgaku Kyōshitsu* [Magazine for Law Students] 508 (2022)

Kawashima F., "Nihon no Kankokusan DRAM ni Taisuru Sōsai Kanzei [Japan's Countervailing Duties on DRAM from Korea]", *WTO Panel Oyobi Jōkyū Iinkai Hōkokusyo ni Kansuru Chōsa Kenkyū Hōkokusho 2007* [Research Report of WTO DSB 2007] (2007)

Kaye S., "Chapter 20 State Practice as a Factor Impacting Potential East China Sea Boundaries", in Kraska J., Long R., and Nordquist M. H. (eds.), *Peaceful Maritime Engagement in East Asia and the Pacific Region* (Brill Nijhoff, Leiden, 2023)

Kazeki J., *Syōkai Gaitame Hō: Bōeki Kanri Hen* [Detail Explanation of the Foreign Exchange and Foreign Trade Act: Trade Control] (Shojihomu, Tokyo, 2022)

Kelsen H., *Das Problem der Souveränität und die Theorie des Völkerrechts* (Mohr, Tübingen, 1920)

Kim S. K., "The Uncertain Status of the Korea-Japan Joint Development Agreement of the Continental Shelf and Its Prospects", *Asia-Pacific Journal of Ocean Law and Policy* 7 (2022)

Kim S. K., *Maritime Disputes in Northeast Asia: Regional Challenges and Cooperation* (Brill Nijhoff, Leiden, 2017)

Kitamura Y., "Towards a More Human Rights-Based Refugee Law Reform in Japan", *Yonsei Law Journal* 12 (1 & 2) (2022)

Klein N., "The Timor Sea Conciliation and Lessons for East Asia in Resolving Maritime Boundary Disputes", *Journal of Territorial and Maritime Studies* 6 (1) (2019)

Kobashi M., "Ryōkai Tō ni okeru Gaikoku Senpaku no Kōkō ni Kansuru Hōritsu ni tsuite [On the Law concerning the Navigation of Foreign Vessels in the Territorial Sea etc.]", *Unyu Seisaku Kenkyū* [Transport Policy Research] 11 (3) (2008)

Kodera S., "Kokusai Keizai Hō Gaku to Shizenjin no Idō [Discipline of International Economic Law and the Movement of Natural Persons]", *Kokusai Keizai Hō Zassi* [International Economic Law Review] 1 (2023)

Kodera S., "Trade Policy on Free Trade Agreements in Asia," in Lee S. (ed.), *Encyclopedia of Public International Law in Asia, Vol. I, Northeast Asia* (Brill, Leiden, 2021)

Kojima C., "2019 Amendment to the Nature Conservation Act", *Asia-Pacific Journal of Ocean Law and Policy* 4 (2019)

Kojima C., "Fisheries, Sedentary", in Wolfrum R. (ed.), *Max Planck Encyclopedia of Public International Law IV* (Oxford Univ. Press, Oxford, 2012)

Kojima C., "Implementation of the United Nations Law of the Sea Convention in Japan", in Lee S., and Gullett W. (eds.), *Asia-Pacific and the Implementation of the Law of the Sea: Regional Legislative and Policy Approaches to the Law of the Sea Convention* (Brill Nijhoff, Leiden, 2016)

Kojima C., "Integration of General Principles of International Environmental Law into the Law of the Sea: Assessment and Challenges", *Marine Policy* 149 (2023)

Kojima C., "Japan: Settlement of Maritime Disputes", in Lee S. (ed.), *Encyclopedia of Ocean Law and Policy in Asia-Pacific* (Brill Nijhoff, Leiden, 2022)

Kojima C., "Japan's Decision to Withdraw from the International Convention for the Regulation of Whaling", *Asia-Pacific Journal of Ocean Law and Policy* 4 (1) (2019)

Kojima C., "Japan's Legal Regime for Preventing and Controlling Accidental Discharges of Oil and Hazardous and Noxious Substances from Ships and Offshore Facilities", in Telesetsky A., Gullett W., and Lee S. (eds.), *Marine Pollution Contingency Planning: State Practice in Asia-Pacific States* (Brill Nijhoff, Leiden, 2017)

Kojima C., "Japan's New Law to Introduce Traceability in the Fisheries Sector", *Asia-Pacific Journal of Ocean Law and Policy* 6 (2021)

Kojima C., "Japan's Practice regarding the Regulation on Navigation of Foreign Vessels", in McDorman T. L., Zou K., and Lee S. (eds.), *Regulation on Navigation of Foreign Vessels: Asia-Pacific State Practice* (Brill Nijhoff, Leiden, 2019)

Kojima C., "Legal Structures of Marine Protected Areas in Japan", *Asia-Pacific Journal of Ocean Law and Policy* 5(1) (2020)

Kojima C., "State Report Overview," Japan volume, in Lee S. (ed.), *Encyclopedia of Ocean Law and Policy in Asia-Pacific* (Brill Nijhoff, Leiden, 2022)

Kokusaiho Jirei Kenkyukai (ed.), *Kokka Shōnin* [Recognition of States] (Nihon Kokusai Mondai Kenkyujo, Tokyo, 1983); *Ryōdo* [Territory] (Keio Tsushin, 1990)

Komatsu I., *Jissen Kokusaihō* [Praxis of International Law], 3rd ed. (Shinzansha, Tokyo, 2022)

Koskenniemi M., *The Gentle Civilizer of Nations: The Rise and Fall of International Law 1870–1960* (Cambridge University Press, Cambridge, 2002)

Koyano M., Tsuruta J., Shimamura K., Seike H., Takayura Y., Toi A., and Masuzawa Y., "Nihon ni okeru Kankyō Jōyaku no Kokunai Jisshi: Panel Discussion [The Implementation of International Environmental Law in Japan: Panel Discussion]", *Kankyō Hō Seisaku Gakkaishi* [Journal of Environmental Law and Policy] 23 (2020)

Kurosaki M., "'Kaketsuke Keigo' no Hōteki Wakugumi [The Legal System of so-called 'Kaketsuke-Keigo']", *Kokusai Mondai* [International Affairs] 648 (2016)

Lee S. and Lee H. E., *The Making of International Law in Korea: From Colony to Asian Power*, (Martinus Nijhoff, Leiden, 2016)

Lee S. and Yang H. C., "Korea", in Lee S. (ed.), *Encyclopedia of Ocean Law and Policy in Asia-Pacific* (Brill Nijhoff, Leiden, 2022)

Lee W., "The Law of the Sea Regime in Northeast Asia; Issues and the Way Forward", *Journal of East Asian Affairs* 32 (2018)

Lissitzin J. O., *International Law Today and Tomorrow* (Oceana Publications, Inc., New York, 1965)

Lorimer J, *The Institutes of Law of Nations* 1 (William Blackwood & Sons, Edinburgh and London, 1883)

Maclaren G. and James R., "Negotiating Joint Development Agreements", in Beckman R., Townsend-Gault I., and Schofield C. (eds.), *Beyond Territorial Disputes in the South China Sea: Legal Frameworks for the Joint Development of Hydrocarbon Resources* (Edward Elgar Publishing, Cheltenham, 2013)

Maehara M., *Kokusaihō Kōgi (Jō)* [Lecture on International Law (vol. 1)] (Rikkosha, Tokyo, 1936)

Mälksoo L., *Russian Approaches to International Law* (Oxford University Press, Oxford, 2015)

Masuzawa Y., "Stockholm Jōyaku no Kokunai Jisshi: Kokunai Kankyōhō no Shiten kara [The Implementation of Stockholm Convention: From the Perspective of the National Environmental Law]", *Shinsedai Hōseisakugaku Kenkyū* [Hokkaidō Journal of New Global Law and Policy] 9 (2010)

Matsuda H., *Kokusaihō to Kempō Chitujo: Kokusai Kihan no Jisshi Kengen* [International Law and Constitutional Legal System: The Competence to Implement International Norms] (University of Tokyo Press, Tokyo, 2020)

Matsuda M., "Jitsumu toshite no Jōyaku Teiketsu Tetuduki [Treaty Conclusion Procedures as Practice]", *Shinsedai Hōseisakugaku Kenkyū* [Hokkaidō Journal of New Global Law and Policy] 10 (2011)

Matsui Y., "Gurōbaruka Suru Sekai ni okeru Fuhen to Chiiki – Daitōwa Kyōeikenron ni okeru Fuhenshugi Hihan no Hihanteki Kentō [The Universal and the Regional in the Globalized World – Critical Consideration of the Critique of Universalism in Daitowa Kyoeiken Theory]", *Kokusaihō Gaikō Zassi* [The Journal of International Law and Diplomacy] 102 (4) (2004)

Matsui Y., "Kindai Nihon to Kokusaihō (1) (2) [Japan and Modern International Law vol. 1, 2]", *Kagaku to Shisō* [Science and Thought] 13 and 14 (Shinnihon Shuppannsha, Tokyo, 1974)

Matsui Y., *Kokusaihō Gakusha ga Yomu Senkaku Mondai* [The Senkaku Issue as Read by International Law Scholars] (Nippon Hyoronsha, Tokyo, 2014)

Matsushita M. and Kometani K., *Kokusai Keizai Hō* [International Economic Law] (University of Tokyo Press, Tokyo, 2015)

Matsushita M., *Daitōwa Kokusaihō no Shomondai* [Problems of Daitōwa International Law] (Nihon Hori Kenkyukai, Tokyo, 1942)

Meierhenrich J. and Ko K., "How Do States Join the International Criminal Court? The Implementation of the Rome Statute in Japan", *Journal of International Criminal Justice* 7 (2009)

Messineo F., "Is There an Italian Conception of International Law," *Cambridge Journal of International & Comparative Law*, 2(4) (2013)

Miyoshi M., "Japan's Arrangements with South Korea and China for the Development of Oil and Gas in the East China Sea: A Memorandum", *Journal of International Affairs* 134 (2009)

Miyoshi M., "The Japan-South Korea agreement on joint development of the continental shelf", *Energy* 10 (1985)

Miyoshi M., "The Joint Development of Offshore Oil and Gas in Relation to Maritime Boundary Delimitation", *Maritime Briefing* 2 (5) (1999)

Mizushima A., "Kyu Jōo[Article 9]", in Kobayashi T. and Serizawa H. (eds.), *Kihon Hō Komentāru* [The Commentary of Basic Law], 4th ed. (Nippon Hyoron sha, Tokyo, 1997)

Mizushima T., "Shuken Menjo [Sovereign Immunity]", *Juristo* [*Jurist*] 1321 (2006)

Mizushima T., *Syuken Menjyo no Kokusai Hō* [Public International Law Aspects of Foreign State Immunity] (University of Nagoya Press, Nagoya, 2012)

Morikawa K., Kanehara A., Sakai H., and Nishimura Y. (eds.), *Kokusai Hō Hanrei Hyakusen* [Leading Cases of International Law], 3rd ed. (Yuhikaku, Tokyo, 2021)

Murase S. "Jo ni Kaete-Nichu Tairikudana Kyōkai Kakutei Mondai [Introduction Japan/PRC Continental Delimitation Issue]", in Murase S. and Eto J. (eds.), *Kaiyō Kyōkai Kakutei no Hō* [Law on the Maritime Delimitation] (Toshindo, Tokyo, 2008)

Murase S. and Eto J. (eds.), *Kaiyō Kyōkai Kakutei no Hō* [Law on the Maritime Delimitation] (Toshindo, Tokyo, 2008)

Murase S. and Okuwaki N., *Kokka Kankatuken* [State Jurisdiction] (Keiso Shobo, Tokyo, 1998)

Mutsu M., *Kenkenroku* (1895) English translation available (translated by Gordon Mark Berker, *Kenkenroku: A Diplomatic Record of the Sino-Japanese War, 1894–95* (University of Tokyo Press, Tokyo, Reprint 1995)).

Nakagawa J., Shimizu A., Taira S., and Mamiya I., *Kokusai Keizai Hō* [International Economic Law] 3rd ed. (Yuhikaku, Tokyo, 2019)

Nakamura K., "The Passage through the Territorial Sea of Foreign Warships Carrying Nuclear Weapons: An Interpretation of the Convention on the Territorial Sea and the Contiguous Zone and Its Application to the Broken Soviet Nuclear-Powered Submarine", *The Japanese Annual of International Law* 25 (1982)

Nakauchi Y., "Kokkai no Shōnin wo Yōsuru 'Jōyaku' no Han-i: Genzai no Un-yō to Kokkai de Giron to Natta Jirei no Kōsatsu [The Scope of 'Treaties' Requiring the Diet's Approval: An Analysis on the Operation Today and Examples of Discussions at the Diet]", *Rippō to Chōsa* [Legislative and Research] 429 (2020)

Nakauchi Y., "Senkaku Shotō wo Meguru Mondai [Issues concerning Senkaku Islands]", *Rippō to Chōsa* [Regislative and Research] 311 (2010)

Nanba M., "'Nanmin Nintei Seido no Tekiseika no tameno Saranaru Unyō no Minaoshi' no Naiyō to Sono Hikei [Details and Background of the 'Further Review of the Operation of the Refugee Status Determination System for the Purpose of Making It More Appropriate']", *Migrants Network* 198 (2018)

Negishi Y., *Conventionality Control of Domestic Law: Constitutionalised International Adjudication and Internationalised Constitutional Adjudication* (Nomos, Baden-Baden, 2022)

Ninomiya S., "Kojin Jōhō no Hogo to Koseki Kōkai Gensoku no Kentō [Protection of Personal Information and Principle of Disclosure of Family Register]", *Ritusmeikan Hōgaku* [Ritsumeikan Law Review] 304 (2005)

Nishihara T. (ed.), *Wakaru Heiwa Anzen Hōsei* [Understanding LPS] (Asagumo Shinbun, Tokyo, 2015)

Nishimoto K. and Takeuchi A., "Japan: 6. Maritime Disputes and Overlapping Claims", in Lee S. (ed.), *Encyclopedia of Ocean Law and Policy in Asia-Pacific* (Brill Nijhoff, Leiden, 2022)

Nishimoto K., "Contribution to the Development of the Law of the Sea", in Lee S. (ed.), *Encyclopedia of Ocean Law and Policy in Asia-Pacific* (Brill Nijhoff, Leiden, 2023)

Nishimoto K., "Enchō Tairiku Dana no Kyōkai Kakutei [Delimitation of the Extended Continental Shelf]", *Tōhoku Law Review* 5 (2018)

Nishimoto K., "Fukushima Daiichi Gensiryoku Hatudensho kara no Syorisui no Haisyutu to Kokusaihō [Discharge of Treated Water from Fukushima Daiichi Nuclear Power Plants and International Law]", *Hōgaku Kyōshitsu* [Magazine for Law Students] 496 (2022)

Nishimoto K., "Nihon no Tairikudana no Genkai Settei to Kyōkai Kakutei [Demarcation and Delimitation of the Japanese Continental Shelf]", in Sakamoto S., Ueki T., and Nishimoto K. (eds.), *Nihon no Kaiyōhō Seido no Tenbō* [The Prospects of the Japanese Legal System on the Law of the Sea] (Yushindo, Tokyo, 2024)

Nishimoto K., "The Obligation of Self-Restraint in Undelimited Maritime Areas", *Japan Review* 3 (1) (2019)

Nishimura Y., "Kaiyō Funsō no Kaiketsu Tetsuzuki to Hō no Shihai", *Kokusai Mondai* [International Affairs] 666 (2017)

Nishiumi M., "Shūdanteki Jieiken [Collective Self Defense Rights]" (Japanese), *Hakumon* 67 (2015)

Nonaka K., "Kankoku Seifu karamita Takeshima no Hōteki Chii-Kokuren Kaiyōhō Jōyaku jō no Iwa kara Shima heno Tenkan (2) [The Legal Status of Takeshima, from the Point of View of the South Korean Government: Once a 'Rock', Then an 'Island' (2)]", *Kaiho Dai Kenkyū Hōkoku [Report of Japan Maritime Safety Academy]* 61 (2016)

O'Flaherty M. and Fisher J., "Sexual Orientation, Gender Identity and International Human Rights Law: Contextualizing the Yogyakarta Principles", *Human Rights Law Review* 8 (2) (2008)

Oda S., "Nikkan Tairikudana Kyōtei no Teiketsu [Conclusion of the Japan/ROK Continental Shelf Agreement]", *Juristo* [Jurist] 559 (1974)

Ohata T., "Higashi Ajia ni okeru Bankoku Kōhō no Juyō to Tekiyō [Reception and Application of the Law of Nations in East Asia]", in Japan Association of Modern

East Asian History (ed.), *Higashi Ajia Kindaishi 2* [Modern History of East Asia vol. 2] (Yumani Shobou, Tokyo, 1999)

Oikawa H., *Seibutsu Tayōsei toiu Logic* [The Logic of Biodiversity] (Keiso Shobo, Tokyo, 2010)

Okamatsu A., "Chikyū Kankyō Jōyaku no Keisei to Hatten [The Formation and Development of the Earth Environmental Agreements]", in Nishii M. (ed.), *Chikyū Kankyō Jōyaku* [Agreements on the Environment of the Earth] (Yushindo Kobunsha, Tokyo, 2005)

Okuzono J., "Kaijyōhoanchō: Kaijyō Jieitai Kankei no Henka to Kaizoku Taishohō [The Japan Coast Guard: Changes of the Relationship with Maritime Self-Defense Force and the Counter-Piracy Act]", in *Kaizokutaishohō no kenkyu* [Studies on the Japanese Act on Punishment of and Measures against Piracy] (Yushindo, Tokyo, 2016)

Onuma Y., "When Was the Law of International Society Born?", *Journal of the History of International Law* 2 (2000)

Oppenheim L. F. L. (H. Lauterpacht ed.), *International Law* 1, 8th ed. (Longmans, Green & Co., New York, 1955)

Osakada O., Fukayama N., Maruyama J., and Moriya K. (eds.), *Kangaete Miyō Senjū Minzoku to Hō* [Let's Think: Indigenous Peoples and Laws] (Shinzansha, Tokyo, 2022)

Osakada Y., "Kokusai Jinkenhō kara Mita Nihon no Nanmingyosei no 40-nen [40 Years of Japan's Refugee Laws and Policies: An Examination Based on International Human Rights]", *Nanmin Kenkyū Journal* [Refugee Studies Journal] 11 (2022)

Osakada Y., "Nyūkan Shūyō no Genzai: Kikaku Shushi Setsumei mo Kanete [Immigration Detention Now: With Explanation of the Purpose of the Project]", *Hōritsu Jihō* [Legal Hours]1147 (2020)

Osawa A., *Kokusaihō Chitsujo Ron: Tōitsuteki Chitsujo no Naka ni Okeru Kokusaihō Chitsujo no Hōritsuteki Chii ni Tsuite* [On International Legal Order: The Legal Status of International Legal Order in the Unified Order] (Iwanami Shoten, Tokyo, 1931)

Otsuka T., "Suigin ni Kansuru Minamata Jōyaku no Kokunaihō Taiō to sono Hyōka [National Legal Responses to the Minamata Convention on Mercury and its Evaluation]", *Kankyō Hōseisaku Gakkai-shi* [Journal of Environmental Law and Policy] 19 (2016)

Otsuka T., *Kankyō-hō* [Environmental Law], 4th ed. (Yuhikaku, Tokyo, 2020)

Oya M., *Keihō Kōgi Sōron* [General Lecture of the Penal Code], New ed. (Seibundo, Tokyo, 2000)

Ozaki K. and Ko K. (eds.), *Kokusai-Keiji-Saibannsho* [International Criminal Court], 3rd ed. (Toshindo, Tokyo, 2024)

Ozaki K., "The International Criminal Court and the International Military Tribunal for the Far East: Lessons Learnt or Not?", in Dittrich V., Lingen K., and Osten P. (eds.), *The Tokyo Tribunal: Perspectives on Law, History and Memory* (Torkel Opsahl Academic EPublisher, Brussels, 2020)

Ozaki K., *Kokusai Keiji Saibannsho* [International Criminal Court] (Toshindo, Tokyo, 2022)

Prescott V. and Schofield C., *The Maritime Political Boundaries of the World* (Brill Nijhoff, Leiden, 2004)

Pritchard R. J., "The International Military Tribunal for the Far East and Its Contemporary Resonance," *Military Law Review* 149 (1995)

Roberts A., Stephan P., Verdier P-H., and Versteeg M. (eds.), *Comparative International Law*, (Oxford University Press, Oxford, 2018)

Röling B. V. A., *International Law in an Expanded World* (Djambatan, Amsterdam, 1960)

Rothwell D. R., Elferink A. G. O., Scott K. N., and Stephens T. (eds.), *The Oxford Handbook of the Law of the Sea* (Oxford University Press, Oxford, 2016)

Saburi H. and Sakai H., "Chūka Minkoku ni taisuru Yakusoku Tegatakin Seikyū Kawase Soshō Jiken [Promissory Notes Invoice Case against the Republic of China]", in Yakushiji K., Sakamoto S., Asada M. and Sakai H. (eds.), *Hanrei Kokusaihō* [Cases of International Law], 3rd ed. (Toshindo, Tokyo, 2019)

Sakai H., "Chapter 19 The Quest for a Win-Win Solution in the Delimitation of Continental Shelf in the East China Sea: An Irreconcilable Conflict between China and Japan?", in Kraska J., Long R., and Nordquist M. H. (eds.), *Peaceful Maritime Engagement in East Asia and the Pacific Region* (Brill Nijhoff, Leiden, 2023)

Sakamoto S., *Nihon no Kaiyō Seisaku to Kaiyō Hō* [Japanese Ocean Policy and the Law of the Sea], 3rd ed. (Shinzansha, Tokyo, 2023)

Sakamoto Y., *Rekishi kara himotoku Takeshima/Dokdo mondai* [Taleshima/Dokdo Issues from a Historical Perspective] (Shimizu Shoin,Tokyo, 2021)

Sakota A., "Ryōkai ni okeru Gunkan, Hi-Shōgyō-teki Seifusenpaku no Kōdō ni taisuru Engankoku no Sochi [Coastal States Measures against Acts of Warships and Ships Operated for Non-commercial Purposes]", in Sakamoto S., Ueki T., and Nishimoto K. (eds.), *Nihon no Kaiyōhō Seido no Tenbō* [The Prospects of the Japanese Legal System on the Law of the Sea] (Yushindo, Tokyo, 2024)

Sakurai M., *Kokusai Keizai Hō no Kihon Mondai* [Basis Issues of International Economic Law] (Keio Tsushin, Tokyo, 1983)

Sanders D., 1996, "Getting Lesbian and Gay Issues on the International Human Rights Agenda", *Human Rights Quarterly* 18 (1996)

Sato C., "Wagakuni no 'Kaiyō Hōgoku' Seido no Tokuchō to Kadai [Features and Challenges in Japan's System on Marine Protected Areas]", in Sakamoto S., Ueki T. and Nishimoto K. (eds.), *Nihon no Kaiyōhō Seido no Tenbō* [The Prospects of the Japanese Legal System on the Law of the Sea] (Yushindo, Tokyo, 2024)

Sato H., *Multilayered Structures of International Criminal Law* (Springer, Cham, 2021)

Schabas W. A., *An Introduction to the International Criminal Court*, 3rd ed. (Cambridge Univ. Press, Cambridge, 2007)

Schachter O., "Invisible College of International Lawyers" *Northwestern University Law Review*, 72(2)(1977)

Schmitt C., *Völkerrechtliche Großraumordnung mit Interventionsverbot für raumfremde Mächte: Ein Beitrag zum Reichsbegriff im Völkerrrecht* (Duncker & Humblot, Berlin, 1939) (translated by Okada Izumi, "Ikigai Rekkyo no Kansho Kinshi wo Tomonau Kokusaihōteki Kōkuiki Chitsujo – Kokusaihōjō no reich gainen heno kiyo [International Legal Broad Order with Prohibition of Interference by Extraterritorial Powers – Contribution to the Reich Concept in International Law]", *Nazis to Schmitt* (Bokutakusha, Tokyo, 1976))

Schultz S., "The Buffet Doesn't Stop until COVID-19 Walks In: How the Hands-Off Approach of Flag States Exposed Legal Nightmares Onboard Cruise Ships during a Global Pandemic and Why Changes Must Be Made", *George Mason International Law Journal* 13 (2022)

Serita K., *Nihon no Ryōdo* [Japan's Territory] (Chuokoron Shinsha, Tokyo, 2002)

Serita K., *Territorial Sea and Exclusive Economic Zone* (Springer, Singapore, 2023)

Seta M., "Kansenshō -hasseiji-niokeru-gaikokuseki-Cruise-sen-nitaisuru-nauiseuien-gannkoku-no-taiō [Coastal State Responses against Foreign Cruise Vessels in Internal Waters during the Pandemic: towards a New System]", *Kokusaihō Gaikō Zassi* [The Journal of International Law and Diplomacy] 120 (2021)

Shimamura K., "Kokusai Kankyō Jōyaku no Kokunai Jisshi: Basel Jōyaku no Baai [The Implementation of International Environmental Law: In the Case of Basel Convention]", *Shinsedai Hōseisakugaku Kenkyū* [Hokkaidō Journal of New Global Law and Policy] 9 (2010)

Shimoyama K., "Keisō Suiiki deno Kaiyō Chōsa ni kansuru Ichi Kōsatsu [Marine Research in the Disputed Area]", *Tōsho Kenkyū Journal* [The Journal of Islands Studies] 13 (2023)

Shin H., "Jinken Jōyaku no Chokusetsu Tekiyō Kanōsei: Kokunai Saibansho no Shihōken to Jōyaku Kihan [Direct Applicability of Human Rights Treaties: Judicial Power of National Courts and Treaty Norms]", in Shin H., *Jinken Jōyaku no Gendaiteki Tenkai* [Contemporary Development of Human Rights Treaties] (Shinzansha, Tokyo, 2009)

Shiroyama H., "Gyōsei Soshiki ni Kansuru Kokusai Jōyaku nado no Kitei to Kokunai Jisshi [The Provision and the Implementation of Convention regarding the Administrative Office]", *Ronkyū Jurist* [Quarterly Jurist] 7 (2013)

Shiroyama H. and Koyano M., "Genshiryoku no Heiwa Riyō no Anzen ni Kansuru Jōyaku nado no Kokunai Jisshi [The Implementation of Convention regarding the Safety of Peaceful Use of Nuclear Energy]", *Ronkyū Jurist* [Quarterly Jurist] 7 (2013)

Sobashima H., Nakatani K., Ishino K., Otsuka T., Kitamura Y., and Nishii M., "Seminar Zadankai: Kankyō Jōyaku to Kankyō Gaikō [Seminar Discussion: Environmental Agreements and Environmental Diplomacy]", *Juristo* [Jurist] 1253 (2003)

Sugihara T., *Kokusaihōgaku Kōgi* [Lectures on International Law], 2nd ed. (Yuhikaku, Tokyo, 2013)

Sugihara T., Mizukami T., Usuki T., Yoshii A., Kato N., and Takada A., *Gendai Kokusaihō Kōgi* [Lectures on Modern International Law], 5th ed. (Yuhikaku, Tokyo, 2012)

Tabata S., "Kindai Kokusaihō ni okeru Kokka Byōdō no Gensoku ni tsuite [On the Principle of Equality of States in Modern International Law]", *Hōgakuronsō* [Kyoto Law Review] (1944)

Tabata S., "Kokusaihō Chitsujo no Tagenteki Kōsei [Pluralist Composition of International Legal Orders]", *Hōgakuronsō* [Kyoto Law Review] (1942/1943)

Tachi S., *Heiji Kokusaihō Ron* [Outline of International Law in Peacetime], 3rd ed. (Nippon Hyoronsha, Tokyo, 1933)

Taijudo K. and Yakushiji K., "Shuken Menjo [Sovereign Immunity]", in Japanese Society of International Law (ed.), *Kokusai Kankeihō Jiten* [Dictionary of International Relations Law], 2nd ed. (Sanseido, Tokyo, 2005)

Taijudo K., "Kokka no Saibanken Menjo [The Jurisdictional Immunity of States]", in Terasawa H. and Uchida H. (eds.), *Kokusaihō no Kihonteki Mondai* [Basic Issues of International Law] (Yuhikaku, Tokyo, 1986)

Taijudo K., *Ryōdo-Kizoku no Kokusai Hō* [International Law of Territorial Attribution] (Toshindo, Tokyo, 1998)

Takahashi S., *Äusserungen über völkerrechtlich Bedeutsame Vorkommnisse aus dem chinesisch-japanischen Seekrieg und das darauf bezügliche Werk* (Verlag von E. Reinhardt, München, 1900)

Takahashi S., *Cases on International Law during the Sino-Japanese War* (Cambridge University Press, Cambridge, 1899)

Takai Y., "Jūyō Keizai Anzen Anpo Jōhō no Hogo oyobi Katsuyō ni kansuru Hōritsu ni Tsuite [The Act on the Protection and Utilization of Important Economic Security Information]", *Juristo* [Jurist] 1601 (2024)

Takamura Y., "Kankyō Jōyaku no Kokunai Jisshi: Kokusaihō no Shiten kara [The Implementation of International Environmental Law: From the Perspective of National Law]", *Ronkyū Jurist* [Quarterly Jurist] 7 (2013)

Takamura Y., "Kyōto Giteisyo to Paris Kyōtei [From the Kyoto Protocol to the Paris Agreement]", *Ronkyū Jurist* [Quarterly Jurist] 19 (2016)

Takamura, Y., "Release of Radioactive Substances into the Sea and International Law: The Japanese Experience in the Course of Nuclear Disaster", in Caron D.D., Kelly M.J., and Telesetsky A. (eds.), *The International Law of Disaster Relief* (Cambridge University Press, Cambridge, 2014)

Takano Y., "Kenpō Kyū Jō [Article 9 of the Constitution]", in Fukase E. (ed.), *Bunken Senshū Nihonkoku Kenpō 3: Sensō no Hōki* [Selected Articles regarding the Japanese Constitution vol. 3: Renouncement of War] (Sanseido, Tokyo, 1977)

Takata T., "The Conclusion by Japan of the United Nations Convention on the Law of the Sea (UNCLOS) and the Adjustment of Maritime Legal Regime", *Japanese Annual of International Law* 39 (1996)

Takeuchi A., "Shima wo Meguru Keisō Suiiki no Kyōdō Kaihatu ni kansuru Itikōsatsu [Joint Development Agreements in the Disputed Area concerning Islands]", *Tōsho Kenkyū Journal* [The Journal of Islands Studies] 11 (2021)

Takeuchi M., "The 2015 Japanese Legislation on Peace and Security and the Japanese Approach to Self Defense Rights", *Bulletin of Toyo Gakuen University* 26 (2018)

Talmon S., "The Constitutive versus the Declaratory Theory of Recognition: Tertium Non Datur?", *British Yearbook of International Law* 75–1 (2004)

Tamada D., "International Dispute Settlement", in Lee S. (ed.), *Encyclopedia of Public International Law in Asia* (Brill Nijhoff, Leiden, 2021)

Tanaka S., "Jōyaku no Jidō Shikkōsei: Butaniku Sagaku Kanzei Jiken [Self-Executing Treaty: Pork Gate-Price Case]", in Morikawa K., Kanehara A., Sakai H., and Nishimura Y. (eds.), *Kokusai Hō Hanrei Hyakusen* [Leading Cases of International Law], 3rd ed. (Yuhikaku, Tokyo, 2021)

Tanaka T., "Kokusaihō to Kokunaihō no Kankei wo Meguru Shogakusetsu to Sono Rironteki Kiso [Doctrines and their Theoretical Foundations regarding the Relationship between International and Domestic Law]", in Hirobe K. and Tanaka T. (eds.), *Kokusaihō to Kokunaihō: Kokusai Kōeki no Tenkai* (*Yamamoto Sōji Sensei Kanreki Kinen*) [International Law and Domestic Law: The Development of International Public Interest (Festschrift for Prof. Sōji Yamamoto for his 60th Anniversary)] (Keiso Shobo, Tokyo, 1991)

Tanaka Y. "Recent Developments in the Jurisprudence Concerning the Delimitation of the Continental Shelf Beyond 200 Nautical Miles: Analysis of the Mauritius/Maldives and Nicaragua v. Colombia Cases," *International Law Studies* 103 (2024)

Tanaka Y., *Predictability and Flexibility in the Law of Maritime Delimitation*, 2nd ed. (Hart Publishing, Oxford, 2019)

Taniguchi H., "Japan's 2003 Gender Identity Disorder Act", *Asian-Pacific Law & Policy Journal* 14 (2) (2013)

Tatematsu S., "Kaizoku Taishohō no Seitei [The Enactment of the Piracy Act]", *Toki no Hōrei* [Legislative Hours]1847 (2009)

Tobisawa T., *Chikujo-Kaisetu Taigaikokuminjisaibanhō* [Commentary of the Act on the Civil Jurisdiction of Japan with respect to a Foreign State] (Shoji Homu, Tokyo, 2009)

Toi A., "Ekkyō Kankyō Songai ni Kansuru Kokusaiteki na Sekinin Seido no Genjō to Kadai [Current Situation and Problems of International Responsibility System regarding the Transboundary Environmental Harm]", *Shinsedai Hōseisakugaku Kenkyū* [Hokkaidō Journal of New Global Law and Policy] 14 (2012)

Toi A., "Seibutsu Tayōsei Hozen Shizen Hogo Jōyaku no Kokunai Jisshi: Ramsar Jōyaku no Kokunai Jisshi wo Sozai toshite [The Implementation of the Convention regarding the Conservation of Biological Diversity and the Protection Nature: In the Reference to the Implementation of the Ramsar Convention]", *Ronkyū Jurist* [Quarterly Jurist] 7 (2013)

Townsend G. and Stormont W., "Offshore Petroleum Joint Development Arrangements: Functional Instrument? Compromise? Obligation?", in Blake G., Hildesley W., Pratt M., Ridley R., and Schofield C. (eds.), *The Peaceful Management of Trans-boundary Resources* (Graham & Trotman/Martinus Nijhoff, London & Boston, 1995)

Triepel H., Völkerrecht und Landesrecht (C.L. Hirschfeld, Leipzig, 1899)

Tsuruta J., "Kokusai Risaikuru wo Meguru Seido Henyō: Asia wo Chūsin ni [The Institutional Transformation of International Recycle System: Focus on Asia]", in, Institute of Developing Economies, Japan External Trade Organization. (ed.), IDE-JETRO *Kenkyū Sōsho* [IDE-JETRO Study Report] 586 (2010)

Tsuruta J., "Nihon niokeru Basel Jōyaku no Jisshi to sono Kadai [The Implimentation and Issue of Basel Convention in Japan and Issue]", *Shinsedai Hōseisakugaku Kenkyū* [Hokkaidō Journal of New Global Law and Policy] 9 (2010)

Tsuruta J., "Nihon niokeru Kokusai Kankyō Jōyaku no Jisshi [The Implementation of International Environmental Law in Japan]", in Nishii M. and Tsuruta J. (eds.), *Kokusai Kankyō Hō Kōgi* [Lectures on International Environmental Law] (Yushindo, Tokyo, 2020)

Urano K., *Senkakushōtō, Ryūkyū, Chūgoku* [The Senkaku Islands, Ryukyu, China] (Sanwa Shoseki, Tokyo, 2002)

van Logchem Y., *The Rights and Obligations of States in Disputed Maritime Areas* (Cambridge University Press, Cambridge, 2021)

Verdross A., *Die Einheit des rechtlichen Weltbildes auf Grundlage der Völkerrechtsverfassung* (Mohr, Tübingen, 1923)

Waaldijk K., "Civil Developments: Patterns of Reform in the Legal Position of Same-Sex Partners in Europe", *Revue Canadienne de Droit Familia* 17 (2000)

Wada H., *Hoppō Ryōdo Mondai: Rekishi to Mirai* [The Northern Territories Issue: History and Future] (Asahi Shimbun, Tokyo, 1999)

Watanabe O., "Abeseiken no Kaiken: Gunji Taikokukan Kōsō no naka no Shūdan Jieiken [The Amendment of the Constitution by the Abe Administration: Collective Self Defense Rights in the Plot to become a Military Power]", in Watanabe O., Yamagata H., Urata I., Kimijima A., and Ozawa R., *Shūdan Jieiken Yōnin wo Hihan suru* [Criticizing the Embracement of the Collective Self Defense Rights] (Nippon Hyoron sha, Tokyo, 2014)

Watanabe S., "Nanmin Shinseisha to Shuyō Sōkan Mondai [Applicants for Refugee Status and Detention/Repatriation Issues]", *Migrants Network* 209 (2020)

Wenzel M., *Juristische Grundprobleme* (Dümmler, Berlin, 1920)

Woker H. and Bernard L., "A New Constraint to the Entitlement of a Continental Shelf beyond 200 Nautical Miles? – Implications of the Recent Case Law," *The International Journal of Marine and Coastal Law* 40(1) (2025)

Xue H., *Chinese Contemporary Perspectives on International Law: History, Culture and International Law* (Martinus Nijhoff, Leiden, 2012)

Xue S., "Why Joint Development Agreements Fail", *Contemporary Southeast Asia* 41 (2019)

Yabe A., "Kokusai Heiwa Katsudō niokeru Buki no Siyō ni tsuite [The Use of Weapons in International Peace Activities]", *Reference* 692 (2008)

Yachi S., "Jissen kara Mita Kokusaihō [International Law as Seen from the Viewpoint of a Practitioner]", *Rikkyō Hōgaku* [St. Paul's Review of Law and Politics] 29 (1987)

Yakushiji K., "Legislation of the Act on Civil Jurisdiction over Foreign States, Acceptance of the U.N. Convention on Jurisdictional Immunity of States and Their Property, and Their Possible Effects upon the Jurisprudence of Japanese Domestic Courts on State Immunity", *Japanese Yearbook of International Law* 53 (2010)

Yamada S., "Kokunai-hō no Kokusai-hō Tekiōteki Kaishaku to Kenryoku Bunritsu: Beikoku ni okeru Charming Betsy Canon no Shōkai o Chūshin ni [Consistent Interpretation of Domestic Law to International Law and Divison of Powers: How Charming Is the Charming Betsy Canon?]", *Okayama Daigaku Hōgakkai Zasshi* [Okayama Law Review] 65 (3–4) (2016)

Yamada C., "UN Convention on Jurisdictional Immunities of States and Their Property", *Japanese Yearbook of International Law* 53 (2010)

Yamagata H., "Kokusaihō kara Mita -Shūdan Jieiken Yōnin no Mondaiten [Issues of accepting Collective Self Defense Rights from International Law]", in Watanabe O., Yamagata H., Urata I., Kimijima A., and Ozawa R., *Shūdan Jieiken Yōonin wohihan suru* [Criticizing the Embracement of the Collective Self Defense Rights] (Nippon Hyoron sha, Tokyo, 2014)

Yamamoto H., "Foreign Precedents in Constitutional Litigation in Japan", in Okada N., Sasada E., and Hasebe Y. (eds.), *Kempō no Kitei to Kempōron: Shisō, Seido, Unyō (Takami Katsutoshi Sensei Koki Kinen)* [Fundamentals of the Constitution and Constitutional Theory: Thoughts, Institutions and Practice (Festschrift for Prof. Katsutoshi Takami for his 70th Anniversary)] (Shinzansha, Tokyo, 2015)

Yamamoto H., "Kokken teki Shii' vs 'Transnational Jinken Hōgen-ron' ['Thoughts of National Constitution' vs 'Theory of Transnational Source of Human Rights Law']", in Yamamoto H., Yokoyama M., and Takayama K. (eds.), *Global-ka to Hō no Hen-yō* [Globalization and Transformation of Law] (Nippon Hyoron sha, Tokyo, 2018)

Yamamoto S., Furukawa T., and Matsui Y. (eds.), *Kokusai Hō Hanrei Hyakusen* [Leading Cases of International Law] (Yuhikaku, Tokyo, 2001)

Yamamoto S., *Kokusaihō* [International Law], New ed. (Yuhikaku, Tokyo, 1994)

Yamamoto S., *Kokusaikeijihō* [International Criminal Law] (Sanseido, Tokyo, 1991)

Yamauchi S., "Meiji Kokka niokeru Bunmei to Kokusaihō [Civilization and International Law in the Meiji State]", *Hitotsubashi Ronsō* [The Hitotsubashi Review] 115 (1) (1996)

Yamauchi T., "Buryoku niyoru Kyōi [Threat of Force]", in Osuka A., Kuriki H., Higuchi Y. and Yoshida Y. (eds.), *Kenpō Jiten* [Dictionary of the Constitution] (Sanseido, Tokyo, 2001)

Yanai S. and Asomura K., "Japan and the Emerging Order of the Sea: Two Maritime Laws of Japan", *Japanese Annual of International Law* 21 (1977)

Yanai S., "Nihon Gaikō ni okeru Kokusaihō [International Law in Japanese Diplomacy]", in Japanese Society of International Law. (ed.), *Kokusai Shakai no Hō to Seiji: Nihon to Kokusaihō no 100 Nen [Law and Politics of International Society: 100 years of Japan and International Law]* 1 (Sanseido, Tokyo, 2001)

Yasui K., *Oshū Kōiki Kokusaihō no Kiso Rinen* [Fundamental Ideas of International Law of Great Area] (Yuhikaku, Tokyo, 1942)

Yiallourides C., *Maritime Disputes and International Law: Disputed Waters and Seabed Resources in Asia and Europe* (Routledge, London, 2019)

Yokokawa S., "Mokuji no Kokka Shōnin to Nihon no Kokka Jikkō [Implied Diploimatic Recognition and Japan's Implementation]", in Kokusaiho Jirei Kenkyukai. (ed.), *Kokusaihō Jirei Kenkyū (Kokka Shōnin)* [Digest of Japanese Practice in International Law (1) Recognition of States] (Nihon Kokusai Mondai Kenkyujo, Tokyo, 1983)

Yokota K., *Kokusaihō no Kiso Riron* [Fundamental Theory of International Law] (Yuhikaku, Tokyo, 1949)

Yokota Y., "Kokka Shōnin ni kansuru Wagakuni no Kokunai Tetsuzuki [National Procedures in the Framework on State Recognition]", in Kokusaiho Jirei Kenkyu-kai (ed.), *Kokusaihō Jirei Kenkyū* (*Kokka Shōnin*) [Digest of Japanese Practice in International Law (1) Recognition of States] (Nihon Kokusai Mondai Kenkyujo, Tokyo, 1983)

Yokota Y., "Kokusaihō to Kokunaihō no Kankei ni Kansuru Shin Nigen Ron no Kanōsei: ILO 88gō Jōyaku no Nihon heno Tekiyō no Jirei no Kentō [The Validity of Neo-dualism regarding the Relationship between International Law and Municipal Law: In case of Application of ILO Convention No. 88 in Japan]", *Chuo Law Journal* 13 (4) (2017)

Yoo H. S., "Kokusai Keizai Hō Josetsu [Introduction to International Economic Law]", in Yoo H. S. (ed.), *Kōgi Kokusai Keizai Hō* [Lecture of International Law] (Toshindo, Tokyo, 2018)

Zou K., *The International Law of the Sea in the 21st Century* (World Scientific Publishing, Singapore, 2021)

Index

www.ingramcontent.com/pod-product-compliance
Lightning Source LLC
LaVergne TN
LVHW012051011026
849162LV00017B/141